Praise for *The Sound of Freedom*

"A notable addition to the historical record . . . Arsenault's book is a timely reminder of the worm of history turning once more. We have only just witnessed another triumphant procession on the Washington Mall, where another exemplary African-American, himself the product of another David and Delia, was sworn in as the 44th president of the United States—something Anderson would likely have been hard-pressed to imagine taking place." **—Boston Globe**

"You won't find a richer examination of this event . . . *The Sound of Freedom* is a book to sing about."
—Terri Schlichenmeyer, *Houston Style Magazine*

"Outstanding . . . provides critical perspective on [Anderson's] most significant achievement." **—Ron Wynn, *BookPage***

"This vivid tribute to her work and times does [Anderson's] memory a great service." **—Publishers Weekly**

"Arsenault excels at contextualizing the concert, probing the ways in which Jim Crow laws and racial prejudices permeated all aspects of African-American life." **—Kirkus**

"In this moment of change and hope, Raymond Arsenault has given us the perfect book for contemplation and activism. Deeply researched, vividly written, sparkling and dramatic, *The Sound of Freedom* is more than a biography of Marian Anderson, her struggles and triumphs over time. It is a call to reconsider the enduring legacies of our segregated heritage, our culture of disrespect. From Marian Anderson's Lincoln Memorial concert that awakened the country to the cruelties and deprivations of apartheid America, every stunning detail of this bold and heartening book calls upon us to continue the still incomplete fight for liberty and justice for all."
—Blanche Wiesen Cook, author of *Eleanor Roosevelt*, volumes I & II

The Sound of Freedom

MARIAN ANDERSON, THE LINCOLN MEMORIAL, AND THE CONCERT THAT AWAKENED AMERICA

Raymond Arsenault

BLOOMSBURY PRESS
New York   Berlin   London

Published by Bloomsbury Press, New York

All papers used by Bloomsbury Press are natural, recyclable products made
from wood grown in well-managed forests. The manufacturing processes
conform to the environmental regulations of the country of origin.

LIBRARY OF CONGRESS CATALOGING-IN-PUBLICATION DATA

Arsenault, Raymond.
The sound of freedom : Marian Anderson, the Lincoln Memorial, and the concert that awakened
America / Raymond Arsenault.—1st U.S. ed.
p. cm.
Includes bibliographical references and index.
ISBN 978-1-59691-578-7 (alk. paper hardcover)
1. Anderson, Marian, 1897–1993.   2. Concerts—Washington (D.C.)—History—20th
century.   3. United States—Race relations—History—20th century.   4. African Americans—
Civil rights.   I. Title.   II. Title: Marian Anderson, the Lincoln Memorial, and the concert that
awakened America.

ML420.A6A77 2009
782.1092—dc22
[B]
2008053563

First published by Bloomsbury Press in 2009
This paperback edition published in 2010

Paperback ISBN: 978-1-60819-056-0

1 3 5 7 9 10 8 6 4 2

Designed by Sara Stemen
Typeset by Westchester Book Group
Printed in the United States of America by Quebecor World Fairfield

In memory of my father
Oscar Wilfred Arsenault
(1921–2007)

Contents

October 1964

T H E date was October 24, 1964. President Lyndon Baines Johnson, the wily Texan who had overseen the recent passage of a landmark civil rights act, was in the White House. With the president's declaration that the United States would soon overcome the seemingly intractable problems of racism and poverty, an ideal that he would later characterize as the "Great Society," there was an air of expectation in Washington. But on that night there was also a reminder of how far the nation had come since the Great Depression of the 1930s, when Johnson had first entered the political arena. Five hundred yards southwest of the White House, a large auditorium known as Constitution Hall was jammed with concertgoers, and on the stage a solitary figure held forth.

The woman standing in the spotlight, dressed in a floor-length satin gown, was the world-famous contralto Marian Anderson. The occasion was the opening concert of her long-awaited farewell tour. At the age of sixty-seven, after a half century of almost constant touring, Anderson had announced her retirement from the concert stage. The people seated in the front rows could see that she was no longer young, that her brown face was lined with wrinkles, her hair tinged with strands of gray. Her voice, though still beautiful, was no longer what it once was. Nearly sixty years of singing had taken their toll, and at the upper and lower ends of her three-octave range she now strained to deliver the perfect note. Yet no one seemed to care. Just seeing and hearing her perform onstage one more time was enough to send chills down the spine of almost everyone in the hall.[1]

No one in the audience had to be told who she was or that this was a special occasion, a moment of sweet irony. They had come to bear witness to the perseverance of a living legend. Year after year, polls had revealed that Marian Anderson was one of the most admired women in the world. Respected and beloved, she had no rival among black women as an icon of racial pride and accomplishment. Part of her mystique was a magical voice, an assortment of sounds so haunting and ethereal that more than one maestro had judged her to be the greatest singer of the twentieth century. But Anderson was more than a superbly gifted artist. She was also a symbol of resolute courage and human dignity.[2]

Twenty-five years earlier, the proprietors of Constitution Hall—the Daughters of the American Revolution—had banned her from the hall, not because of anything she had done, but simply because she was black. Thousands of Americans rushed to her defense, pleading with the Daughters to relax the hall's "white artists only" policy, but to no avail. When no other auditorium large enough to accommodate her many fans could be found, she had no choice but to sing in the open air. The concert, held at the Lincoln Memorial on Easter Sunday 1939, attracted no fewer than seventy-five thousand people. Black and white, they came to hear the sound of freedom, and she did not disappoint them. Broadcast over a national radio network and memorialized in newsreels, her bravura performance represented an iconic moment in the history of American democracy. The Lincoln Memorial would be the scene of other such moments—most notably in August 1963, when Dr. Martin Luther King Jr. delivered his "I Have a Dream" speech at the March on Washington—but Anderson's 1939 recital was the first time that the modern civil rights struggle invoked the symbol of the Great Emancipator in a direct and compelling way.

As she stood on the stage of Constitution Hall twenty-five years later, Anderson represented a triumph of the human spirit. Yet one suspects that few members of the audience appreciated how difficult it had been for her to assume the mantle of leadership in a cause that transcended music. Originating in the impoverished black community of South Philadelphia, her story is one of struggle against self-doubt, racial prejudice, and numerous other obstacles that would have vanquished a person of lesser resolve. During the 1930s, as the rising force of fascism promoted rank bigotry and racial oppression, her unprecedented conquest of the music world stood as a testament to the illegitimacy of racial prejudice. But this was only the beginning of a career that ultimately broke all barriers large and small, from the color bar at Constitution Hall to the all-white casting tradition at the famed Metropolitan Opera. How this modest, unassuming woman, born into poverty and burdened with the social stigma of a dark skin, became one of the most extraordinary and influential figures of the twentieth century is the subject of this book.

CHAPTER 1

Freedom's Child

. . . we here highly resolve that these dead shall not have died in vain—
that this nation, under God, shall have a new birth of freedom—
and that government of the people, by the people,
for the people, shall not perish from the earth.
—ABRAHAM LINCOLN[1]

MARIAN Anderson was born in the shadow of freedom. Less than a mile from her birthplace on Webster Street in South Philadelphia stood two enduring icons of American democracy: the Liberty Bell, a cracked but enduring piece of bronze that symbolized the resiliency of an emerging nation; and Independence Hall, the redbrick building where delegates to the Continental Congress signed the Declaration of Independence in 1776, and where eleven years later the Founding Fathers crafted the Constitution itself. Nearby two other historic sites testified both to the promise and the unrealized ideal of racial justice. At the junction of Sixth Street and Lombard, a sign marked the spot where, in 1787, the Reverend Richard Allen had founded the Free African Society, which later evolved into the African Methodist Episcopal Church; and a few blocks away, black Philadelphians could still visit the meeting hall where Quakers had formed America's first antislavery society in 1775. In 1847, seven decades after the society's founding, Pennsylvania achieved the total abolition of slavery, and with the passage of the Thirteenth Amendment in 1865 the rest of the nation followed suit. Yet at the time of Anderson's birth, on February 27, 1897, the transition from slavery to freedom was unfinished business. In Philadelphia, as in other communities across the nation, Americans were still trying to define the meaning of democracy in a multiracial society.[2]

The Civil War generation initiated the process of emancipation in 1862, but thirty-five years later Americans were still grappling with the implications of granting citizenship to millions of former slaves. The civil rights acts and constitutional amendments of the Reconstruction era had promoted a model of full participation in American life. But during the last quarter of the nineteenth century the U.S. Supreme Court issued a series of decisions that relegated African Americans to second-class citizenship. Beginning with the *Slaughterhouse* case of 1873, which all but nullified the equal protection clause of the Fourteenth Amendment; and continuing through the *Civil Rights Cases* of 1883, which gutted the Civil Rights Act of 1876; and *Plessy v. Ferguson*, the 1896 decision that established the "separate but equal" doctrine, the Court encouraged and validated a national culture of racial discrimination.

The heightened racism of the post–Reconstruction era was most obvious in the South, where a de jure system of codified segregation known as Jim Crow was in full force by the first decade of the twentieth century. But Northern blacks living in places such as Philadelphia also experienced increased segregation and discrimination and a general lowering of expectations during these years. In the mid-1880s, in the wake of the *Civil Rights Cases,* state legislatures in thirteen Northern states, including Pennsylvania, passed laws that afforded blacks a measure of protection against the worst excesses of white supremacist institutions. But as Marian Anderson entered the world in 1897, a mere seven months after the *Plessy* decision, legislative protection did little to alter the harsh realities of black life in the City of Brotherly Love.[3]

Anderson's parents and paternal grandparents were recent migrants to Philadelphia. All four of her grandparents had been born into slavery in Virginia. Benjamin Anderson, her paternal grandfather, was born and raised on a plantation in King William County, in the lowlands of the Virginia tidewater. His wife, Mary Holmes Anderson, whom he married in 1869, was a native of nearby King and Queen County. During the first two decades of their marriage, the Andersons lived and worked on a small, hardscrabble farm in King William, bearing eight children. Five children—four sons and a daughter—survived into adulthood. The oldest son, John Berkley Anderson, born in 1875, would become Marian's father.

Benjamin and Mary (also known as Isabella) Anderson moved to Philadelphia sometime in the early 1890s, settling into a large, ramshackle house on Fitzwater Street. The surrounding neighborhood, part of South Philadelphia's Thirtieth Ward, was both predominantly black and ethnically diverse. There, among a tumultuous mix of inner-city African, Italian, Irish, and Jewish Americans, John Anderson courted and married Anna Delilah Rucker in 1895. A schoolteacher in the Appalachian hill town of Lynchburg, Virginia,

Anna Rucker met John in Philadelphia while visiting her older sister, Alice Ward. Grant Ward, Alice's husband, introduced the couple, who decided to marry after a whirlwind courtship, despite denominational differences. John was a devout Baptist who "neither drank, smoked nor chewed," and Anna was a lifelong Methodist. Anna's parents, Robert and Ellen Rucker, were both natives of Boonsboro, a small town nestled in the foothills of Bedford County just west of Lynchburg.

During Anna's childhood, her father was an up-and-coming business-man who eventually became the co-owner of a livery stable in downtown Lynchburg. A leading figure in the local black community, he could often be seen transporting passengers to and from the train depot. Although the family achieved only a modicum of financial success, all four of the Rucker children harbored strong ambitions and respect for education, including Anna, who attended the all-black Virginia Seminary and College. While she did not remain long enough to acquire full teaching credentials, under Virginia law Annie was certified to teach in the state's black schools. This was not the case, however, in Philadelphia, which required full credentials for all teachers.[4]

Had Anna Anderson been allowed to teach in Philadelphia, Marian's childhood and the family's circumstances might have been substantially dif-ferent. But, as it was, her mother had little choice but to find employment wherever she could. Prior to Marian's birth, she provided day care for a num-ber of small children, but she eventually supplemented her husband's income by taking in laundry, working in a tobacco factory, and scrubbing floors at Wanamaker's department store. John Anderson was, by all accounts, a hard worker, but like most black men of his day he had little formal education. One of the few steady jobs open to a black man with his limited skills was as a laborer at the Reading Railroad Terminal in central Philadelphia. Work-ing long hours for low pay, he shoveled coal, sold ice, and performed a variety of odd jobs, some of which were dangerous. While he also moonlighted as a small-time liquor dealer, his total income did not amount to much.

During the first four years of their marriage, the Andersons lived in a tiny rented room on Webster Street, but when Anna became pregnant for a second time they were forced to move in with John's parents. Both of Marian's younger sisters were born in her grandparents' house—Alyse in 1900 and Ethel May in 1902. Only after the addition of Ethel May did the family of five find the resources to rent a house of their own on Colorado Street, just a few blocks from Benjamin and Isabella Anderson's residence. "It was a small house," Marian recalled years later, "but big enough for our purposes. The living room contained a minimum of furniture. Behind it was a little dining room, and behind that a shed kitchen . . . This house did not have a real bathroom, but Mother was undaunted. We were lathered and rinsed at least once a day, and on Saturday a huge wooden tub was set in the center of the kitchen floor. After sufficiently warm water was poured in, we were lifted inside. Mother would kneel and give us a good scrubbing with Ivory soap. Then we were put to bed."

The modest amenities of the Colorado Street house were hardly shocking when judged by the standards of the rural South. Indeed, many black families in the Deep South, or for that matter many families in Philadelphia, would have leaped at the opportunity to live in a two-story house with three bedrooms and an indoor kitchen. It was also clear, however, that the Andersons' standard of living fell far short of middle-class respectability, and that their prospects of moving up into the middle class were dim. As long as John and Annie Anderson remained healthy enough—or lucky enough—to earn a steady income, they could maintain a measure of working-class solvency. But, like most black Philadelphians, they lived in a racially circumscribed world that fostered more insecurity than opportunity.[5]

The absence of upward mobility and the inability to achieve long-term security are among the central themes of W. E. B. Du Bois's *The Philadelphia Negro: A Social Study*. Published in 1899, two years after Marian Anderson's birth, Du Bois's classic survey of black life in a Northern city provides a detailed and revealing profile of black Philadelphians at the end of the nineteenth century. With nearly sixty thousand inhabitants, Philadelphia's black community was the fourth largest in the nation in the late 1890s. Only New Orleans, Washington, and Baltimore harbored a larger number of blacks. In its entirety, black Philadelphia represented an unmanageable subject for a lone researcher, even for one as talented as Du Bois, a highly trained sociologist and the first African American to earn a Ph.D. at Harvard. Accordingly, he decided to draw most of his conclusions from a case study of a single ward. For more than a year, from September 1896 to January 1898, he lived in the Seventh Ward "in the midst of dirt, drunkenness, poverty and crime," as he later put it. The Andersons lived a few hundred yards to the south, just beyond the border separating the Seventh and Thirtieth Wards, but Du Bois's findings would probably not have been appreciably different had he concentrated on the neighborhoods surrounding Webster Street.[6]

After conducting a house-to-house canvass and distributing numerous questionnaires, Du Bois concluded that the black inhabitants of the Seventh Ward lived in a tangle of pathology, though not necessarily one of their own making. Contrary to the conventional wisdom of the day, the primary barriers to racial progress were environmental and not hereditary. The root of the "race problem," he determined, was an almost unbroken pattern of racial prejudice that stifled educational and occupational opportunities, driving black Philadelphians into "listless despair." More often than not, the avenues of upward mobility were closed to black workers, including those with college degrees. As a case in point, he related the story of a recent "graduate of the University of Pennsylvania in mechanical engineering . . . Well recommended," the young man "obtained work in the city, through an advertisement, on account of his excellent record. He worked a few hours and then was discharged because he was found to be colored. He is now a waiter at the University Club, where his white fellow graduates dine."[7]

Du Bois did not identify racism as the sole cause of social and economic inertia among black Philadelphians. He also had strong words for those in the black community who failed to display a sense of personal responsibility, who were either unwilling or unable to help themselves. Yet he kept coming back to the harsh realities of life imposed by a white supremacist culture that missed few opportunities to denigrate and marginalize a despised racial minority. "No matter how well trained a Negro may be, or how fitted for work of any kind," Du Bois concluded, "he cannot in the ordinary course of competition hope to be much more than a menial servant." While he conceded that many blacks were in dire need of uplift, subjecting them to the crippling effects of white contempt benefited no one. "Without doubt social differences are facts not fancies and cannot lightly be swept aside," he declared, "but they hardly need to be looked upon as excuses for downright meanness and incivility."[8]

Du Bois documented the impact of racism on all elements of the black community, but he expressed special concern for the natural leaders of the race, the group he later identified as the "Talented Tenth." In his view, the key to black progress was the unshackling of the most talented and industrious members of the race. "Above all, the better classes of the Negroes should recognize their duty toward the masses," he insisted. "They should not forget that the spirit of the twentieth century is to be the turning of the high toward the lowly, the bending of Humanity to all that is human; the recognition that in the slums of modern society lie the answers to most of our puzzling problems of organization and life, that only as we solve those problems is our culture assured and our progress certain."[9]

Du Bois looked to the Talented Tenth for long-term solutions to the race problem. But he also turned to the black church as the only functioning institution capable of mitigating at least some of the social pathology burdening black Philadelphians. "The Negro church has become a centre of social intercourse to a degree unknown in white churches . . . ," he reported, adding a historical and contemporary note: "The Negro churches were the birthplaces of Negro schools and of all agencies which seek to promote the intelligence of the masses; and even today no agency serves to disseminate news or information so quickly and effectively among Negroes as the church . . . Night schools and kindergartens are still held in connection with churches, and all Negro celebrities, from a bishop to a poet like Dunbar, are introduced to Negro audiences from the pulpit. Consequently all movements for social betterment are apt to centre in the churches. Beneficial societies in endless number are formed here . . . the minister often acts as an employment agent; considerable charitable and relief work is done . . . The race problem in all its phases is continually being discussed, and, indeed, from this forum many a youth goes forth inspired to work. Such are some of the functions of the Negro church, and a study of them indicates how largely this organization has come to be an expression of the organized life of Negroes in a great city."[10]

WHEN Du Bois wrote these words, he had no knowledge of the extended Anderson clan living just south of the Seventh Ward. Yet it is difficult to imagine a more apt example of a church-centered black family. From grandparents to parents to children of all ages, their lives were wrapped around the religious and social activities of three distinctively different black churches. Marian's grandfather, Benjamin Anderson, was a religious dissenter who called himself a "Black Jew." His church, a storefront on Rosewood Street, was the creation of a charismatic preacher named William Saunders Crowdy. Drawing upon Old Testament themes, especially the Jewish Exodus from Egypt, Crowdy attracted a small but enthusiastic congregation of "Israelites" who celebrated the Sabbath on Saturday. Observing Passover and other Jewish holidays, they donned traditional Jewish garb, skullcaps for the men and long white gowns with head scarfs for the women. Benjamin's attachment to Crowdy drew considerable criticism from the rest of the family, with the exception of Marian, who was unusually close to her soft-spoken and gentle grandfather. Marian's mother and grandmother attended the Bainbridge Street Methodist Church, later renamed the Tindley Temple. Well-known for its talented choir, the church became one of Philadelphia's largest congregations after the arrival of Charles Albert Tindley in 1902. A Maryland-born minister and composer, Tindley was one of the founders of the modern gospel-music tradition. In 1903, he wrote the words and music to "I Shall Overcome," the hymn that was later transformed into the 1960s freedom song "We Shall Overcome."[11]

The rest of the Andersons, including Marian, were faithful members of Union Baptist Church. Founded in 1832, Union Baptist, with more than a thousand members, was one of the largest and most influential black churches in the city at the turn of the century. Only Bethel AME had a larger congregation, and no church in the city boasted a more celebrated music program. Although John Anderson played no role in the musical life of the church, he was a church officer who often acted as an usher during Sunday services. His sister Mary, blessed with a beautiful voice, was a stalwart member of the choir, and she, more than anyone else, nurtured her young niece's talent.[12]

From an early age, Marian displayed an affinity for music. Before she turned two, she was already singing made-up songs while banging on a toy piano, and by the age of four everyone in the family recognized that she had a gift for singing. In 1903, just after her sixth birthday, she joined Union Baptist's junior choir, and later in the year her aunt Mary bought her a cheap violin, which she played until the strings broke. But with no money for lessons, her interest waned. Several years later she resumed her rudimentary instrumental training after her father purchased a piano from his brother Walter. But once again she was hampered by a lack of formal instruction. Almost by default, she began to concentrate on her singing.

Alexander Robinson, the director of Union Baptist's junior choir, was, as Anderson's biographer has noted, "the first professional musician to recognize her extraordinary voice, with its well-developed lower range that extended upward nearly three octaves, unusual in a young child." Anderson herself later credited Robinson with stimulating her love of singing. "It gave him pleasure to work with those young voices," she recalled, "and since he loved music and understood enough to communicate his feeling to us, he was able to do something with us. It was not long before the group was singing so well that it was invited to appear before the older children's Sunday school, which convened in the afternoon." The group was good, but Marian's voice was the main attraction. Before long she was singing duets and solos in the choir and filling the alto role in an all-girl quartet. On occasion she also sang duets with her aunt Mary, who began taking her to nearby churches, sometimes to sing and sometimes just to listen to some of the beautiful choral voices that could be heard all over Philadelphia.[13]

Over time these visits became a source of income for the struggling Anderson family. At first Marian sang for a quarter or two, often at YMCA, YWCA, or charity gatherings. But, by the time she was eight, it was not unusual for her to bring home several dollars after making the rounds on a Sunday afternoon or evening. Despite her young age, there is no indication that she felt exploited in any way. Indeed, in her autobiography, she describes the joy of encountering a makeshift handbill advertising one of her appearances: "One day when I was on my way to the grocery to buy something for my mother, my eyes caught sight of a small handbill lying across the street. Even from a distance it looked vaguely familiar. I picked it up, and there in the corner was my picture with my name under it. 'Come and hear the baby contralto, ten years old,' it said. I was actually eight. What excitement! Clutching the paper in my hand, I hurried to the grocer's. When I got home I discovered that I had bought potatoes instead of the bread Mother had sent me for. Before I could explain what possessed me, Mother turned me around and hurried me back to the store. I trotted away again, still holding fast to the handbill that proclaimed my fame. I have a far more vivid memory of the handbill than of the actual singing at the concert."[14]

By the time she was ten, the "baby contralto" was beginning to attract attention from some of black Philadelphia's most prominent choral directors. Emma Azalia Hackley, a locally renowned singer and voice teacher, was not only the director of the choir at the Church of the Crucifixion but also the founding director of the People's Chorus, a choir of one hundred voices recruited from black churches across the city. Organized in 1904, the People's Chorus included many of the city's finest singers, so it was no small honor for Marian Anderson to be selected as the youngest member of Hackley's all-star choir. Despite her age, she was soon singing solos, as audiences marveled at hearing such a big voice pouring out of such a small body. Realizing that people sitting far from the stage might have trouble seeing her young prodigy, Hackley proudly placed Anderson on an elevated riser so that "no one in the back of the hall" would "have the slightest difficulty in seeing her."[15]

Anderson's musical accomplishments gave her a special status among her peers and a range of experience well beyond the normal expectations for a young black girl growing up amid the poverty of the Eighth Ward. The People's Chorus, in particular, took her to other parts of the city, including some predominantly white neighborhoods. Contact with whites was not entirely foreign to her even before she joined the People's Chorus. White families dotted the Thirtieth Ward, and a handful even lived on Colorado Street. Moreover, from 1906 on Anderson attended an integrated school, the Stanton Grammar School, where roughly half of the students and all of the teachers were white. Yet seeing a bit of the white city outside her neighborhood was somehow different. Although the young singer continued to live in a black-majority community, she caught an early and tantalizing glimpse of a wider world.

Anderson's childhood was marked by poverty and material deprivation. But in most senses she was not an impoverished child. As a member of a close and loving family, with strong ties to Union Baptist, she enjoyed the benefits of emotional, cultural, and spiritual security. "Life with Mother and Father, while he lived, was a thing of great joy," she recalled years later, adding, "It is easy to look back self-indulgently, feeling pleasantly sorry for oneself and saying I didn't have this and I didn't have that. But that is only the grown woman regretting the hardships of a little girl who never thought they were hardships at all. Certainly there were a lot of things she did not have, but she never missed them, because she didn't really need them. She had the things that really mattered."[16]

As she entered adolescence, Anderson was, by all accounts, a happy, well-adjusted child. But, unfortunately, the coming years would not be so kind to her and her family. Like many working-class families, the Andersons lived on the margins of subsistence, leaving them vulnerable to downward mobility and real hardship. One major setback could plunge them into an economic and social free fall. In the Andersons' case, the setback occurred in early December 1909, when John Anderson suffered a serious accident at the Reading Terminal. Struck on the head by a heavy object, he lay in bed for nearly a month before succumbing to heart failure. His unexpected death at the age of thirty-four traumatized the family. Approaching her thirteenth birthday, Marian was old enough to understand the probable consequences of losing her father. But neither she nor her younger sisters had much time to adjust to the family's altered circumstances. A few hours after the funeral, in the middle of the night, the grieving family moved out of the rented house on Colorado Street and into a spare room in the Fitzwater Street house occupied by Benjamin and Isabella Anderson. Marian's grandparents were already providing shelter for two grown children and two small grandchildren, plus a couple of boarders. So the addition of four new residents created less than ideal living conditions for an extended family that had little but love to share. Marian's mother had considered returning to her family's home in Virginia, but her late husband's parents insisted that she bring the girls to live in their home.

Life on Fitzwater Street—and later on Christian Street, where the Andersons moved into a large house in 1910—proved difficult for all concerned. Isabella Anderson was a strong-willed, sometimes overbearing woman who ruled with an iron hand. Her soft-spoken husband tried to counter her stern presence, but he could do little to protect his daughter-in-law and grand-daughters from Isabella's dictatorial ways. Marian and her sisters gravitated toward their gentle and sympathetic grandfather during the year following their father's death, but they suffered a second shock when Benjamin Anderson died in late 1910. Thereafter, Marian's mother found it increasingly difficult to raise her daughters without interference from her mother-in-law, who appeared to look down on Anna. The older woman was lighter skinned and never missed an opportunity "to remind people that she was part Indian." The most significant point of conflict occurred during the summer of 1912 when Marian graduated from the Stanton School. Anna Anderson made plans for her daughter to attend high school in the fall, but was overruled by a mother-in-law who had come to depend on the supplemental income derived from her granddaughter's singing and domestic work. Since Marian's two cousins, one of whom was seventeen, were working full-time and contributing to the household income, it seemed reasonable to ask Marian to do the same.

Marian herself had mixed feelings about dropping out of school. She had never been a conscientious student, and the music program at Stanton, though modest, had always been her favorite school activity. While she was disappointed that she would not be able to participate in the normal round of high school social events, choosing work over school allowed her to concentrate on her music. Despite the obvious tensions in the household, she also felt a deep responsibility toward her family and was eager to contribute her fair share of income. Delivering laundry part of the day was a small sacrifice to pay for the opportunity to sing whenever and wherever she could find an engagement.[17]

Sometimes she sang with her sisters, both of whom also had rich and lustrous voices, but most of the time she sang solo. After joining the senior choir at Union Baptist in 1910, she became a featured performer and the pride of the church. Poised beyond her years, with a growing confidence and sophistication, she began to think about a professional career. Wherever she went, she received plaudits and encouragement, though not enough money to pay for voice lessons or enrollment in high school. At one point, Union Baptist's pastor, the Reverend Wesley Parks, interrupted a service to take up a special collection for the church's favorite singer, but the money collected was too meager to underwrite Anderson's education. Fortunately, Parks found a more profound and lasting way of influencing Anderson's career. As a young man, he had befriended the mother of Roland Hayes, the greatest black tenor of the day. Parks later became a great admirer of Hayes's music and in 1911 established a tradition of inviting Hayes to headline Union Baptist's annual gala concert. Hayes returned year after year, and "his appearance was the highlight of the Philadelphia concert season," though not everyone approved of his choice of songs. "Mr. Hayes sang old Italian airs, German lieder, and French songs exquisitely," Anderson recalled. "Even people with little understanding of music knew it was beautiful singing and they were proud that Mr. Hayes was one of their own and world-famous. But after a time a few grumbled that they did not understand what he was singing. And there were some who said, 'If our Marian were on the program, we would understand what *she* was singing about.' So eventually I was permitted to appear on his program and sing two or three numbers."[18]

Meeting Roland Hayes changed Marian Anderson's life. From the first time that she heard him sing in 1911 until his death in 1977, he served as her primary role model and mentor. Born in Curryville, Georgia, in 1887, Hayes moved to Tennessee at the age of eleven and later attended Fisk University, where he sang with the Jubilee Singers. When Anderson first met him, he was only twenty-four. But he was already a rising star among black concert artists. One of the few singers of his day to attempt a mix of European folk songs and traditional "Negro music," he established a musical style that Anderson embraced as her own. She was also drawn to his quiet dignity and seriousness of purpose. He was a professional's professional, and she sought to emulate his dedication to "the only real freedom, the freedom to produce and to create," as Hayes's close friend and biographer MacKinley Helm once characterized his philosophy.[19]

The bond between them was based on mutual respect, and Hayes took an immediate interest in Union Baptist's golden-voiced contralto. He, along with others who recognized her promise, urged her to study with a professional voice teacher, preferably a white teacher who could help launch her career. In March 1914, she participated in a People's Chorus concert that drew favorable attention from the music critic of the *Philadelphia Tribune*, a local black newspaper. Noting Anderson's "singularly rare contralto voice," the critic provided her with enough encouragement to prompt a series of inquiries about studying with a professional teacher. Most of the city's white voice teachers held classes in the Presser Building, on Chestnut Street, but none of the Presser teachers that she approached was willing to accept her as a student. Whether because of racism or the suspicion that she did not have the necessary funds to pay for a teacher's services, they turned her away.[20]

Later in the year, with the help of the Union Baptist congregation, she tried again. After several members of the church assured her that they would pay her tuition, Anderson steeled her courage and walked a dozen city blocks to the Philadelphia Music Academy on Spruce Street. Hoping to complete an application, she instead received a bitter lesson in the realities of racial prejudice. "I went there one day at a time when enrollments were beginning, and I took my place in line," she recounted. "There was a young girl behind a cage who answered questions and gave out application blanks to be filled out. When my turn came she looked past me and called on the person standing behind me. This went on until there was no one else in line. Then she spoke to me, and her voice was not friendly. 'What do *you* want?' I tried to ignore her manner and replied that I had come to make inquiries regarding an application for entry to the school. She looked at me coldly and said, 'We don't take colored.' I don't think I said a word. I just looked at this girl and was shocked that such words could come from one so young . . . I did not argue with her or ask to see her superior. It was as if a cold, horrifying hand had been laid on me. I turned and walked out."

Anderson later remembered this incident as one of the formative experiences of her life. As she told a *Ladies' Home Journal* reporter in 1960, the rejection provided a "painful realization of what it meant to be a Negro." In the short term, it forestalled all thought of studying with a white voice teacher. "I tried to put the thought of a music school out of my mind," she remembered, "for I could not help thinking of other music schools and wondering whether this would be their attitude too. I would not risk rejection again, and for some years the idea was not mentioned."

Anderson puzzled over why this episode was so dispiriting. Reflecting upon her early years, she conceded that she was no stranger to subtle forms of racial prejudice, even at the tender age of seventeen. "There were times when we heard our relatives and friends talking," she recalled, "and we knew we might come in contact with this, that, or the other thing. In some stores we might have to stand around longer than other people until we were waited on. There were times when we stood on a street corner, waiting for a trolley car, and the motorman would pass us by. There were places in town where all people could go, and there were others where some of us could not go. There were girls we played with and others we didn't. There were parties we went to, and some we didn't."[21]

WHAT Anderson did not acknowledge—and perhaps did not even recognize consciously—was the significant hardening of race relations in cities like Philadelphia during the first two decades of the twentieth century. Several factors contributed to this trend: the example set by the Jim Crow South, the spread of imperialist condescension toward the "little brown brothers" of the world, the lingering popularity of Social Darwinism, the rising tensions related to interracial economic competition, and the use of blacks as strikebreakers. But the most obvious stimulus for the new protocol was a sudden shift in racial demography. Between 1890 and 1920, the black population of Philadelphia more than tripled, from 39,371 to 134,229, while during the same years the white population increased by a modest 60 percent. For the first time in the city's history, the white majority felt threatened by a seemingly unending influx of black migrants.

Following the advent of the Great War in 1914, some of these newcomers found work in the city's burgeoning industrial plants, and by 1917 one estimate put the number of black factory workers at over thirty thousand. But the widespread perception that these economic gains would lead to social disruption led many whites to call for heightened vigilance in racial control. Writing in 1921, Sadie Tanner Mosell, the future chairperson of the Philadelphia Commission on Human Relations and the future wife of Judge Raymond Pace Alexander, documented the recent "ghettoization" of black Philadelphians. "Such social privileges as the service of eating houses and the attending of white churches and theaters by Negroes," she observed, "were practically withdrawn after the influx of Negro migrants into Philadelphia."

Years later the historian E. Digby Baltzell concluded that "the steady migration of Negroes into the city . . . also contributed to the segregation of Negro children in the schools and the closing of most of the city's commercial and entertainment centers to Negroes." According to Baltzell, by the early 1920s, "one rarely saw a Negro in the major downtown department and clothing stores, in banks, moving-picture houses, theaters, or other public places. No major department store or bank had Negroes in white-collar positions dealing with the public. No Negro lawyer could obtain office space in the center city business district." On the rare occasions when blacks did venture out of their neighborhoods, they "sat in the balconies of the big movie palaces" or ate dinner at one of the few restaurants that welcomed their business.[22]

Philadelphia did not follow the Southern pattern of maintaining segregation through a codified system of discriminatory ordinances. But, on any given day, black Philadelphians faced an unpleasant array of segregationist customs that paralleled the legalized bigotry of Jim Crow. Indeed, on the city's worst days these customs shaded into a violent vigilantism that rivaled the lynch-law culture of the Deep South. In August 1911, a group of white citizens living in Coatesville, Pennsylvania, a small town located less than twenty-five miles from downtown Philadelphia, seized a black man named Zach Walker from the town jail and burned him to death on the front lawn of a local church. The gruesome lynching drew the attention of Du Bois, who wrote a bitterly sarcastic account of Walker's death in *Crisis* magazine: "Once more a howling mob of the best citizens in a foremost state of the Union has vindicated the self-evident superiority of the white race . . . It must warm the hearts of every true son of the republic to read how the brawn and sinew of Coatesville rallied to the great and glorious deed . . . Ah, the splendor of the Sunday night dance. The flames beat and curled against the moonlit sky. The church bells chimed. The scorched and crooked thing, self-wounded and chained to his cot, crawled to the edge of the ash with a stifled groan, but the brave and sturdy farmers pricked him back with the bloody pitchforks until the deed was done." For Du Bois, who thought he had seen it all, the Coatesville lynching signaled the end of black forbearance. "Some foolish people think of punishing the heroic mob, and the governor of Pennsylvania seems to be real provoked," he wrote. "We hasten to assure our readers that nothing will be done . . . But let every black American gird up his loins. The great day is coming. We have crawled and pleaded for justice and we have been cheerfully spit upon and murdered and burned. We will not endure it forever. If we are to die, in God's name let us perish like men and not like bales of hay."[23]

Such stern words of warning were unusual, even in the most militant circles of the black intelligentsia. But as the decade progressed, talk of race war became increasingly common. With the stresses and strains of mass migration and world war, the threat, and sometimes the reality, of interracial violence became a fact of life in many Northern cities, including Philadelphia. In July 1918, the city witnessed its first major race riot since the 1870s. The riot began on Ellsworth Street, less than a mile from the Andersons' residence, when a mob began throwing rocks at Adelia Bond, a black woman who worked as a city court probation officer. Sitting on the front steps of the house that she had recently purchased, Bond became the target of local whites who resented her move into the neighborhood. Frightened but determined to stand her ground, she grabbed a pistol and fired it into the air. Four days of intermittent rioting ensued, resulting in two deaths and widespread property damage in several black neighborhoods.[24]

Whether these episodes of racial conflict had any appreciable impact on Marian Anderson's life is unclear. But she must have had some sense of the deteriorating state of race relations in her native city. In this setting, her reluctance to approach the white voice teachers who could help launch her career was entirely reasonable. For the time being, her only option was to find the best black voice teacher available, which she did in late 1914. Mary Saunders Patterson, black Philadelphia's most prominent voice teacher, lived on Fitzwater Street just a few blocks from the Andersons. But she apparently did not meet Marian until John Thomas Butler, an elocutionist who often performed dramatic readings in local churches, arranged an interview. Patterson and Anderson had several friends in common—including Roland Hayes, who sometimes stayed in Patterson's home when visiting Philadelphia—and the pairing of teacher and student seemed natural from the start. Butler offered to pay for the tuition, but Patterson generously agreed to waive her fees until Anderson herself had the necessary funds.

Patterson's lessons had an immediate impact on Anderson's singing and vocal repertoire. In addition to refining her pupil's voice control and projection, she introduced Anderson to the classical tradition of Italian, French, and German folk songs. Anderson had heard Roland Hayes sing such songs but had never tried to sing them herself. Intrigued from the outset, she soon came to love them as much as Hayes. During the year that she studied with Patterson, Anderson developed a new style that raised expectations of future glory. She was now eighteen and ready to expand her horizons beyond the limited world of South Philadelphia's black churches.

She had already made one foray into New York, where she sang for National Baptist Convention delegates attending a conference at the massive Abyssinian Baptist Church in Harlem. But many of her friends, particularly

her colleagues in the People's Chorus, worried that a lack of formal education would hinder her chances of excelling as a professional singer. To remedy the situation, the People's Chorus, with the help of G. Grant Williams,
the editor of the *Philadelphia Tribune*, staged a benefit concert in June 1915.
The goal, Williams informed his readers, was to raise funds for the musical
education of a young woman who "without a doubt, possesses one of the best
contralto voices ever heard in this city for one of her years."

The concert raised $250, enough to pay for voice lessons with Agnes
Reifsnyder, a talented white contralto who often performed in the concert
halls of southeastern Pennsylvania, and to facilitate Anderson's enrollment at
William Penn High School, an integrated school specializing in business
education. In the fall of 1915, after a summer of working with Reifsnyder on
"medium and low tones" and controlled breathing, Anderson entered William Penn as an eighteen-year-old freshman. She looked years younger than
her actual age, and no one seemed to regard her as anything out of the ordinary. But the three-year gap in her education fueled her determination to
make up for lost time. She was also conscious of her family's continuing
struggle to make ends meet. "I knew deep in my heart by this time that what
I wanted most was to study music," she later recalled, "but I also knew that I
had to prepare myself to get a job as soon as possible—both to help Mother
and to have some money for music studies." A family friend had promised
her an office job if she "learned to type and take dictation," but her business
studies at William Penn did not go well. As she later confessed, her "heart
was not in these studies," and the only thing that kept her going was a weekly
music class that gave her the opportunity to sing.[25]

After three years of frustration, she transferred to South Philadelphia
High School for Girls in 1918. By that time singing had become her life. In
April 1916, she had experienced a taste of success when she sang the contralto
solo in the People's Chorus's Easter production of Handel's *Messiah*. The lead
singer was Roland Hayes, and the concert drew widespread praise from the
city's music critics. After nearly a year of study with Reifsnyder, Anderson
was in fine form and attracted attention as far away as New York. Writing in
the NAACP magazine, the *Crisis*, an admiring critic insisted that Anderson's
performance was the highlight of the concert. Hayes and the chorus deserved
praise, "but most exquisite was the dark, sweet full-blossomed contralto—
Marian Anderson, who felt with her soft strong voice the sorrows of God.
Few voices have ever sung 'He was despised and rejected of men' with so deep
feeling and significance. It brought a sob to the throat of two thousand."

No one was more impressed than Hayes, who promptly arranged for Anderson to sing at an "autumn musicale" sponsored by an Episcopal church in Rosemount, Pennsylvania. He also invited her to come to Boston the following Easter to join him, Harry Burleigh, and a large chorus of black singers in a performance of Felix Mendelssohn's *Elijah*. Anderson leaped at both opportunities to sing with her idol, but the Boston concert brought unexpected consequences. Following a masterful night of singing, Hayes and Anderson visited the studio of Arthur Hubbard, a prominent voice teacher who had been instructing Hayes for several years. As soon as Hubbard heard Anderson's voice, he urged her to move to Boston to become his student. At Hayes's suggestion, Hubbard offered to let her live and work in his house as a means of covering the cost of tuition. Anderson was thrilled at the prospect of studying with Hubbard, but the return to Philadelphia brought her back to the constricting realities of family dynamics. "Grandmother told Mr. Hayes that we had no money to pay for lessons," she recalled, with some regret, "and Mr. Hayes replied that Mr. Hubbard was willing to let me earn my way by working in his home. Grandmother was not impressed. So far as she was concerned, I could sing and what was the need of lessons? There were discussions pro and con. Mother would not oppose Grandmother, and Grandmother decided that a young girl should not be sent away from home. To Boston I did not go."[26]

Disappointed but resigned to her fate, Anderson did not leave Philadelphia in 1917. Many others, however, did. The same month that brought her disappointment also brought an American declaration of war against Germany and Austria-Hungary. The United States had finally decided to enter the Great War, and nothing would ever be quite the same again. By October, a number of Anderson's neighbors, black and white, had shipped out as part of the American Expeditionary Force, and some would soon be fighting and dying in the trenches of France and Belgium. Over the next thirteen months, until the war ended in Allied victory and an uncertain peace, more than a million Americans would discover a part of the wider world that they had never expected to see. For many soldiers, the war would serve as a testing ground for self-worth, manhood, and the responsibilities of citizenship. This was especially true for African Americans, who were grudgingly accepted into the armed forces and generally assigned menial tasks far away from the front lines. But even for those who never made it to the front, the war was an eye-opening experience that expanded the realm of the possible.[27]

Marian Anderson experienced the war vicariously from afar. But she, too, had the sense that a new era was dawning. Approaching adulthood at the age of twenty, she began to look beyond the boundaries of Philadelphia. For her, the first theater of exploration was not Europe but a strange region known as the Deep South. In December 1917, she received a last-minute invitation to participate in a Christmas concert in Savannah, Georgia. Cosponsored by two black institutions, the Cuyler Street School chorus and the Georgia State Industrial College for Colored Youth glee club, the December 28 concert was held in the city's sprawling Municipal Auditorium. With only four days to reach Savannah, Anderson had little time to plan the first major journey of her life. But no amount of planning would have prepared her for what she later termed the "shocks to come."

As she and her mother boarded a Washington-bound train and headed south, she thought she was ready for whatever Dixie might offer. She was wrong. Even the worst slights she had experienced in Philadelphia had not prepared her for the institutionalized racism of the South. "Mother had grown up in Virginia," she later explained, "and we had friends who had come from farther south, so I had heard about Jim Crow, but meeting it bit deeply into the soul." The first shock came at Union Station in the nation's capital: "At Washington we changed trains, and this time our bags were taken to the first coach—the Jim Crow car! The windows were badly in need of washing; inside and outside the car was not clean, and the ventilation and lighting were poor. When the air became much too stuffy and windows were raised . . . you would get, along with your fresh air, smoke and soot from the train's engine . . . The night seemed interminably long as we sat through it." As the train hurtled southward into the dark, she found herself fantasizing about marauding whites breaking into the Jim Crow car. Fearful of every sound and jolt, she hardly slept a wink and only calmed down when the train pulled into the Savannah station.[28]

After such a journey, the warm welcome in Savannah was a pleasant surprise. A small group of black school administrators met Marian and her mother at the station and escorted them to the president's house at Georgia State Industrial College. There, as Marian later put it, they "became acquainted first-hand with genuine Southern hospitality." Their host, President Richard R. Wright Sr., was one of the leading black educators in the South. Born into slavery in Dalton, Georgia, in 1855, he went on to become the valedictorian of Atlanta University's first graduating class in 1876 and later served as an army officer during the Spanish-American War. He was also the father of nine children, one of whom, Richard R. Wright Jr., was the first black to earn a Ph.D. in sociology at the University of Pennsylvania. Through his son, President Wright had close ties to Philadelphia, which is how he learned about the promising young contralto from Union Baptist.[29]

Anderson had no contact with white Savannah until she arrived at the Municipal Auditorium, where nearly a thousand people had gathered to hear the Christmas concert. Roughly a third of the audience was white, all sitting near the stage either in box seats or in the dress circle. All of the blacks in the hall, including Anderson's mother, sat in a specially designated section farther back. This was the first time that Anderson had ever sung before a strictly segregated audience, but she did not let this seemingly strange arrangement affect her performance. She sang six songs, including two spirituals, "Deep River" and "Go Down, Moses," arranged by her fellow Pennsylvanian Harry T. Burleigh, a noted tenor and composer who would later become one of her closest friends. The crowd responded to each song with thunderous applause, and the reviews that appeared in the city's white newspapers the next day were no less enthusiastic. "Her voice is exquisitely rich and full and mellow," the *Savannah Press* reported. "Her control is marvelous, the music just seeming to come without any effort from the singer." The music critic for the *Savannah Morning News* agreed, declaring that Anderson possessed "one of the most remarkable voices ever heard in Savannah. A contralto, its range is amazing and the upper notes as perfect and full as the lower, with a lovely middle register. Something unusual in its quality, difficult to analyze, made it sound more like an exquisite wind instrument than like the human voice, the tones ringing out like a clarinet." This would not be the last time that a critic had difficulty describing the unique sounds coming out of Anderson's mouth.[30]

Anderson regarded the Savannah concert as an important milestone in her musical career. But its importance transcended music. Perhaps for the first time in her life, she fixed her attention on race as an inescapable issue. "Throughout our stay in Savannah," she remembered, "my thoughts went often to that first coach. We returned to Washington under the same conditions, a bit wiser but sadder and so ashamed. I had looked closely at my people on that train. Some seemed to be embarrassed to the core. Others appeared to accept the situation as if it were beyond repair. Of course some fitted neither of these classes. Habit, I thought, can be good if it has an elevated aim; it can be devastating if it means taking bad things for granted; and I wondered how long it would take people on both sides to see a change."[31]

OVER the next five years, Anderson and other African Americans witnessed both change and resistance, as actions and reactions pushed the nation slowly but surely toward an eventual reconsideration of its racial mores. Personally, she experienced a series of successes that both elevated her stature in the music world and reminded her of how far she had to climb. In April 1918, she sang at the Academy of Music, Philadelphia's most prestigious concert venue, for the first time. Appearing as a soloist with the popular New York Clef Club Syncopated Orchestra, she performed brilliantly. Dressed in a white satin gown adorned with rosebuds, she charmed the crowd and most of the critics. Nevertheless, one admiring white reviewer, writing in the *New York Age*, warned her that she was "now at the critical stage of her career. Her future will largely depend on her decision to continue to study; for if she enters the professional field at this time she will never rise above the level of mediocrity." Anderson took these stinging words to heart, but it would be more than a year before she found a means of remedying the situation.[32]

In the meantime, she enrolled at South Philadelphia High School for Girls, performed a second recital at the Academy of Music in the spring of 1919, and made a second trip to the South two months later. This time the journey took her to Tennessee, where she sang at Fisk University and several other black schools and churches. Once again she did not go alone. Her companion throughout the weeklong tour was Billy King, a talented young black pianist who was her accompanist. Both Anderson and King were thrilled to perform at Fisk, Roland Hayes's alma mater and the home of the famed Jubilee Singers. Once they were in Nashville they reveled in the reflected glory of one of black America's most cherished institutions. But getting there was a trial.[33]

Even something as simple as getting a meal on the train required a measure of negotiation. As Anderson recalled, "Billy spoke to a porter who happened to be passing through our car, and inquired about the chances of getting some hot food in the dining car. The porter was kind enough to go to the dining room to make inquiries for us, and he returned with the message that if we appeared at a given time we would be served. At the fixed time, Billy King and I started from our coach to the dining car. We passed through a coach occupied by white people, and we noticed immediately that the accommodations, though not first class, were much better than in our car. The dining car was empty when we reached it. Nevertheless we were seated at one end of it, where curtains could be drawn. Our seats were those occupied by the waiters when they ate, and the curtains no doubt were there to be drawn if a waiter should happen to be finishing his meal when the guests began to arrive." The meal offered a lesson in racial solidarity. "We had fine hot meals, and the service was excellent," recounted Anderson. "The chef and the waiters, it seemed to me, put themselves out to make us comfortable; there were extra things at our table, and even extra-large portions. This was their way of saying that they were glad we had the courage to come back and be served."[34]

Anderson had less success in the segregated rail terminals along the route from Washington to Nashville. "I knew about the separate waiting rooms," she wrote years later, "but no matter how much you are prepared and steeled for them they have their effect on you. I noticed the facilities in the Negro waiting rooms were indifferent. Some might have places where you could purchase a magazine or newspaper; some might not. Probably the Negro trade in some stations was meager, for those who could afford other modes of travel used them to avoid the humiliation." This was the state of travel four decades before the Freedom Riders successfully challenged racially segregated train and bus depots. But when Anderson wrote her autobiography in the 1950s, a few short years before the Freedom Rides, she was still trying to fathom a seemingly gratuitous system of discrimination: "I suppose it was naive of me to think then, as I think now . . . that if one only searched one's heart one would know that none of us is responsible for the complexion of his skin, and that we could not change it if we wished to, and many of us don't wish to, and that this fact of nature offers no clue to the character or quality of the person underneath."[35]

The second trip to the South advanced Anderson's continuing education in the ways of white folks. But later in the summer she learned that the hard lessons of racial injustice were not limited to the region below the Mason-Dixon Line. In late June 1919, she traveled to Chicago to take part in a six-week operatic course taught by Oscar Saenger, a noted New York voice teacher. A partial scholarship allowed her to join dozens of other aspiring singers at the Chicago Conservatory of Music for intense rounds of private and group lessons. Most of the students had considerably more experience than Anderson, especially when it came to singing in Italian and other foreign languages. But she did her best to take advantage of the situation, which included unexpected exposure to some of the nation's finest black musicians. In late July, as the course was winding down, Chicago welcomed the founding conference of the National Association of Negro Musicians (NANM). Dedicated to the support and encouragement of black musicians and composers, including young artists in need of training and financial aid, the NANM urged its members to interact with the students in Saenger's course.

The interaction took place, but not before a major disturbance threatened the NANM's plans. On Sunday, July 27, the worst race riot in Chicago's history broke out on the city's south side. The riot began at a Lake Michigan beach, where white bathers and a white policeman had harassed a seventeen-year-old black student named Eric Williams. After Williams was struck by a rock and knocked off his raft, the policeman reportedly prevented lifeguards and other potential rescuers from reaching the distressed swimmer as he flailed in the water. Williams drowned. Enraged onlookers attacked the policeman, ultimately igniting an interracial brawl that spilled over into adjoining neighborhoods. Over the next four days rampaging whites wreaked vengeance on any black who dared to appear on the city's streets. By the time the violence subsided, forty people were dead and close to five hundred were wounded. The vast majority of the casualties were black, and many were recent migrants to a city that was unaccustomed to a significant black presence.

All of this happened as Anderson and others were preparing for a joint recital with members of the NANM at the Grace Presbyterian Church. Hampered by the riot and an unexpected transit strike, organizers postponed the recital for two days and moved the location to a local YMCA gymnasium. In this setting, surrounded by the chaos of racial and class struggle, many leading black musicians heard Marian Anderson's voice for the first time. In what amounted to a national debut, she elicited "a wave of intense enthusiasm," as Nora Douglas Holt, the music critic for the *Chicago Defender*, put it. All of the young singers performed creditably, but, according to Holt, "the greatest height was reached when Marian Anderson, a high school girl, exhibited a voice equal to that of Rosa Raisa, the wonderful contralto of the Chicago Grand Opera Company, and everyone stood and acclaimed her with cries of bravo and bis, while tears of joy were in the eyes of many of the musicians who felt that a new era in music has arisen for our people."

In the aftermath of the recital, discussions of Anderson's seemingly unlimited potential ensued, and nearly two hundred dollars was raised to establish a scholarship fund that would underwrite her future training. Some even talked about sending her to the Yale School of Music, but she had to remind them that she still had two years of high school to complete.[36]

Anderson returned from Chicago full of conflicting images, from burning buildings and rioting in the streets to standing ovations and dreams of celebrity. At twenty-two, she was still learning about the world, especially the ups and downs of being a talented and ambitious black person in a society sharply divided by race and class. During her first year at South Philadelphia High School, she was preoccupied with meeting the challenges of her classes and fitting in with classmates who were three or more years her junior. But she could not help but notice the general malaise and mood of disillusionment that had gripped the country. In Philadelphia, as in other American cities, a Red Scare raised the specter of political subversion and class warfare; and returning veterans suffering economic and social dislocation wondered aloud what had happened to the nation that had gone to war to make the world safe for democracy. Black veterans who had survived the vagaries of war in Europe found themselves out of work and out of favor with a white majority that refused to recognize their past sacrifices and their present claims to full citizenship. If a black soldier who had risked his life for his country could not break through the wall of prejudice, what hope was there for a young girl who had only her untrained voice to give?[37]

The conventional answer to this question might have quashed the dreams of an ordinary person. But within Anderson's heart and soul, hidden beneath a quiet demeanor, was a fierce determination to succeed. She was fortunate to have a cast of friends and admirers who believed in her, but most of all she believed in herself. As her manager Sol Hurok noted many years later, she was always "strong in her inner integrity. And by being herself she . . . won citadels that never have been breached by doughtier warriors." Through a combination of emotional maturity, natural intelligence, religious faith, and raw talent, she kept her focus on an art form that magnified her energy. When others might have given up, she kept going, all the while improving on what nature had given her. The year 1920 was such a time. Early in the year she was fortunate to find a teacher who cared nothing about race, a man who had both the imagination and fortitude to take her to the next level.

Giuseppe Boghetti was as eccentric as he was talented. Born into a Russian-Jewish family in Philadelphia in 1896, he changed his name from Joe Bogash to Giuseppe Boghetti when he thought it would help his flagging singing career in Europe. Still in his early twenties, he returned to the United States after the First World War to work as a voice teacher in New York and

Philadelphia. By 1920, he had a rising reputation but fewer students than more established teachers. Lucy Wilson, the principal at South Philadelphia High, and Lisa Roma, a young white musician and close friend of Wilson's, thought that Boghetti would be both affordable and helpful to Anderson. The audition, as described by Anderson, provided some of the most anxious moments of her young life: "I remember that Dr. Wilson and Miss Roma accompanied me to Mr. Boghetti's studio. Mr. Boghetti was short, stocky, and dynamic. He could be pleasant, but there were times when he could be stern and forbidding. At that first meeting he was severe, even gruff. He began by declaring that he had no time, that he wanted no additional pupils, and that he was giving his precious time to listen to this young person only as a favor to Miss Roma. Dr. Wilson did not look happy. I was amazed. My song was 'Deep River.' I did not look at Mr. Boghetti as I sang, and my eyes were averted from him when I had finished. He came to the point quickly. 'I will make room for you right away,' he said firmly, 'and I will need only two years with you. After that, you will be able to go anywhere and sing for anybody.' Then he began to talk about his fees as if the lessons would begin at once."

In actuality, the lessons did not begin at once, primarily because Anderson did not have enough money to pay for them. The shortfall was soon remedied, however, by a benefit concert sponsored by Union Baptist Church and several of Anderson's neighbors. Held in the Union Baptist sanctuary, the concert featured Anderson and three other soloists singing an exotic collection of songs entitled "In a Persian Garden." Virtually the entire surrounding community turned out, not only to hear the music but also to support a young artist who was fast becoming a local legend. After expenses, the concert netted nearly six hundred dollars, more than enough to cover the cost of at least a year of lessons.

Boghetti proved to be an extraordinary teacher and a powerful influence on Anderson's career. A consummate professional, he introduced her to a wide range of operatic pieces and composers, including Schubert, Verdi, and Brahms. He also coached her in Italian and saw to it that she received tutoring in French. Realizing that he had the equivalent of a diamond in the rough, he worked long hours with the young singer, far beyond the normal routine of voice lessons. Indeed, in the first few weeks of her training with Boghetti she never seemed to have enough time for all that he wanted to accomplish. At that point, she was still in high school and had other demands on her time. Only after her graduation from South Philadelphia High School for Girls in late June 1921 did she have the luxury of devoting virtually all of her time and energy to music. Becoming a high school graduate at the age of twenty-four was a belated but important milestone in her life. Although she was not enough of a scholar to earn the right to become one of the designated student speakers at the graduation ceremony, she experienced the joy of hearing one of her classmates deliver an address entitled "We Have Music and Marian Anderson." It would take another decade before the rest of the world could say the same, but against all odds the "dark contralto" was on her way.[38]

CHAPTER 2

Singing in the Dark

Abide with me, fast falls the eventide;
The darkness deepens; Lord, with me abide.
When other helpers fail and comforts flee,
Help of the helpless, oh, abide with me.
—FROM THE HYMN "ABIDE WITH ME"[1]

MARIAN Anderson's emergence from the limited world of black church music actually began a few weeks before her high school graduation, when she made her first appearance at Carnegie Hall in New York. The occasion was the annual concert of the Martin-Smith Music School, which hired Anderson as an assisting artist. Her role was not large enough to draw a review, but singing in America's greatest concert hall was a thrill nonetheless. The following winter she sang there for a second time, participating in a farewell concert for the noted black tenor Sidney Woodward. These two appearances, however, turned out to be more of a tease than anything else. Under Boghetti's guidance, Anderson was developing the skills and poise that would eventually take her to the top of her profession. But during the early 1920s she had neither the experience nor the professional backing to enter the world of mainstream concert artistry. She also had the wrong skin color. Although the Jazz Age would ultimately spawn a number of black musical celebrities, the prospects for black artists at the beginning of the era did not look promising. Some, such as Josephine Baker, found greener pastures in Europe. But racial stereotypes and restrictions sometimes dogged them even there. When Roland Hayes presumed to sing the lieder songs of Schubert and Beethoven in Berlin in 1924, incensed Germans nearly rioted.

Despite the Berlin incident, Hayes and a few other black artists developed a loyal following on the Continent and in England. But during these years few had the financial resources to follow their lead. For most the only option was to remain in the United States, living and working on the dark side of the color line. Among jazz, blues, and popular artists, this meant a life of recording "race records" and traveling the circuit of black vaudeville houses, jazz clubs, and juke joints. Classical black artists such as Anderson had even fewer options. For them, musical opportunities were confined to churches, semiprofessional choral societies, and black schools and colleges. Making a living wage in this world was difficult, but with a bit of luck and pluck, and a lot of stamina, a black classical artist could move toward middle-class respectability.[2]

This was the world that Anderson and her accompanist Billy King embraced in February 1922, when they made their second tour. Three years earlier, in the summer of 1919, they had completed a brief trial run in Tennessee. But this time they went in the winter, adding stops in West Virginia and Indiana. Once again they received a warm and enthusiastic welcome at all of the black institutions on the tour. Yet there was still the nagging problem of uncertain and often unpleasant traveling conditions. Anderson and King learned that Jim Crow travel offered few amenities and little peace of mind. Without a manager to smooth the way, they discovered the mysteries of "Berth 13." As Anderson later explained, "I tried to make my own travel arrangements, but I found that often if I presented myself at a railroad ticket window, sometimes even in Philadelphia, there would be no reservations available. At other times the agent would sell me what was called 'Berth 13.' I discovered that Berth 13 was a euphemism in the trade. It meant the drawing room. Of course if the drawing room had been sold I could not even get Berth 13. In most cases, however, Berth 13 was accepted as a valid reservation by the Pullman conductor . . . If we were lucky—and these things seemed to depend a lot on what ticket seller was behind a window—we got ordinary berths, as other people did, instead of Berth 13. But this might lead to other unpleasantnesses. You would naturally have to use the washroom in the morning, and you never knew what you would encounter when you entered. One woman might say 'good morning' pleasantly; another might stare at you; and a third might look you up and down and flounce out."[3]

Despite such problems, Anderson and King repeated and expanded the tour in 1923, and for four years thereafter they spent much of the winter and early spring on the road. They made money, but never enough to make a real difference in their lives. When Anderson was home in Philadelphia, she augmented her income by giving occasional voice lessons to young students. But her most important source of supplemental income grew out of a friendship with Charles Hirsch, a white Philadelphia doctor and music aficionado. Anderson and other aspiring artists often sang informally at Hirsch's home, sometimes with Joseph Pasternack, the conductor of the Philharmonic Society of Philadelphia, in attendance. Pasternack doubled as a representative of the Victor Recording Company, and after hearing Anderson sing several spirituals in Hirsch's parlor, he persuaded her to sign a recording contract. In 1923, spirituals were still a novelty among American music lovers; Harry T. Burleigh had published his first collection of spiritual arrangements as recently as 1917, and prior to Anderson the only artist to attempt to put spirituals on a vinyl record was Hayes, who, according to the musicologist Allan Keiler, "had made a few private recordings of spirituals for a small company." So when Anderson went into a studio in December 1923 to record "Deep River" and "My Way's Cloudy," she was making musical history. Fifteen more sessions over the next twelve months produced six finished recordings.⁴

In the meantime, both Hayes and Anderson reached other milestones. In early December 1923, Hayes, with the help of several influential white musicians, breached a long-standing color bar when he appeared as a soloist with the Boston Symphony Orchestra. Prior to Hayes, no black artist had ever sung with one of the nation's leading orchestras. But Hayes proved that he belonged on the highest rung of the classical ladder, not only by singing gloriously at the breakthrough concert, but also by securing a long-term management contract with the Boston Symphony Orchestra Concert Company. A month later he sang with the highly regarded Detroit Symphony Orchestra, even though several of the Motor City's downtown hotels turned him away. Anderson's triumph was less spectacular, musically speaking. But it nonetheless represented a major turning point in her career. Just before Christmas, three weeks after Hayes's Boston Symphony debut, she became the first black artist to perform as a soloist with the Philharmonic Society of Philadelphia. Held at the Academy of Music, where Anderson had first sung in 1918, the concert drew a crowd of three thousand, the largest audience in the five-year history of the society. She sang both operatic pieces and spirituals, but at that point in her career she displayed the most command and feeling singing Burleigh's arrangements of "My Lord, What a Mornin'" and "Heav'n, Heav'n." The spirituals brought down the house and prompted one critic to proclaim, "She has one of the most superb contralto voices that has been heard in Philadelphia for a very long time."⁵

Anderson's performance with the Philharmonic Society demonstrated her potential as a concert artist and widened her reputation. But it also underscored the problem of obtaining professional management. If she was so good, why was she depending on her musically talented but personally erratic accompanist as her manager? Billy King did his best, within the limits of his training and the racial barriers that any black man would face in the 1920s. But nearly everyone close to the situation knew that Anderson was in desperate need of a professional manager, if only to help with travel arrangements. In Boghetti, she had found a gifted voice teacher who believed in her, and who cared nothing about race. But for her career to blossom she also needed a manager or promoter who knew the ins and outs of the concert stage, someone who could negotiate for her from a position of strength while avoiding the pitfalls of racial prejudice. It would take her more than a decade to find such a person.

In the interim she relied on a series of well-meaning but less-than-ideal managers. The first, aside from herself and Billy King, was G. Grant Williams, the enterprising editor of the *Philadelphia Tribune*. As the city's leading black editor, Williams was in a position to boost Anderson's local career. But he had little experience and few contacts outside of the Philadelphia area. To Anderson's dismay, he also suffered from a series of maladies that forced him to retire in early 1924. Anderson then turned to a Harlem agent affiliated with the Donald Music Bureau. Specializing in New York venues, the agent arranged for her to sing at a popular Harlem dance hall known as the Renaissance Casino. Her recital there on February 24, 1924, drew a large and enthusiastic crowd, which led to a second booking at Town Hall, a more prestigious venue in midtown Manhattan, on April 10.[6]

Realizing that the Town Hall recital could catapult her career to a new level, Anderson and Boghetti worked on the program for several weeks. "Mr. Boghetti gave me four new songs, including Brahms's 'Von ewiger Liebe,'" Anderson later recalled, "and he assured me that I was doing fine with them. I had a great desire to sing lieder in such a hall because Roland Hayes had done them so movingly." Before walking out onstage, she "felt for all the world like a prima donna," but the assurances of a packed house proved false: "My heart sank. There was only a scattering of people in the hall. I had been misled, and the enthusiasm drained out of me." Despite all of her preparation, the opening number, Handel's "Ombra mai fu," did not go well. "Billy King went to the organ at the side of the stage," she remembered. "I stood quite remote from him and felt miserably alone. I had had a lot of experience and had been foolish enough to think that I was prepared for anything, but I was only twenty [she was actually twenty-seven], and I had a great deal to learn." She made it through the Handel stanzas with some difficulty, but from there things went from bad to worse: "I got to the Brahms songs. The first three were not easy, but 'Von ewiger Liebe' was especially difficult. I sang the German as best I could, having learned it phonetically. I did not feel that it was bad; on the other hand, it was not like Roland Hayes's singing of lieder. Somehow the program came to an end, though I felt it had dragged on endlessly. And the next morning the newspaper comments were not complimentary. One writer said that the voice was good. Another said, 'Marian Anderson sang her Brahms as if by rote.'"

The Town Hall fiasco traumatized Anderson and nearly ended her musical career. "I was embarrassed that I had tried to sing in one of New York's concert halls without being fully ready," she later confessed, "and I went back to Philadelphia deeply disturbed. I did not want to see any music. I did not want to hear any. I did not want to make a career of it . . . I felt lost and defeated. The dream was over." For two months Anderson withdrew into a deep depression, constantly rehashing the concert in her mind and making only occasional visits to Boghetti's studio. She was also disconsolate over the recent death of her aunt Mary, who had succumbed to a cerebral hemorrhage at the age of forty-seven, and the impending marriage of her on-again, off-again boyfriend, Orpheus "King" Fisher, an architect whom she herself would marry nineteen years later. The only thing that seemed to save her from complete despair was a preoccupation with a new house on South Martin Street, just across the street from Union Baptist. For the first time since her father's death fifteen years earlier, she would share a house with her mother and sisters but not with her meddling grandmother. The new house was small but large enough to accommodate a small studio—if she ever decided to sing again.[7]

THE man who brought her back to music—the same man who would later play a pivotal role in the 1939 Lincoln Memorial concert—was Walter White, an energetic, light-skinned NAACP leader who had followed Anderson's career for nearly a decade. The son of a mixed-race Atlanta postal worker and the great-grandson of President William Henry Harrison, White was a protégé of James Weldon Johnson, the NAACP's executive secretary, who had become a major figure in the ongoing cultural explosion known as the Harlem Renaissance. An aspiring novelist, White also fancied himself as something of a cultural maven, involving himself with a string of intellectuals, entertainers, and celebrities, black and white, including Paul Robeson, Roland Hayes, and George Gershwin. In the spring of 1924, he was busily promoting the careers of Hayes and a black tenor from Texas named Jules Bledsoe as part of a general campaign to raise the profile of African-American entertainers. After helping to boost press coverage of Hayes's recent American tour, White pressured Bledsoe's new agent, Sol Hurok, to expand the singer's upcoming tour beyond the traditional venues of black churches, colleges, and YMCAs. When the Russian-born promoter ignored White's entreaties, Bledsoe tried to get out of his contract, albeit unsuccessfully.

A former medical student at Columbia, Bledsoe had decided to forgo a career as a doctor after a stirring performance at New York City's Aeolian Hall, where George Gershwin's "Rhapsody in Blue" had premiered in February 1924. Bledsoe's concert took place in April, the same month as Anderson's disappointing appearance at Town Hall, and White was on hand for both concerts. "I had watched Miss Anderson's struggle against poverty and prejudice with more than ordinary interest," White recalled in 1948. But he agreed with the critics who suggested that she was not quite ready for the bright lights of Town Hall. "That evening Marian sang badly," he wrote in his autobiography, "though those who have listened to her in later years will find difficulty in believing that anyone with so great a voice could ever sing other than perfectly. Perhaps her performance that evening was due to stage fright. Some believe that the fault was due to the voice teacher with whom she was studying. He was a devotee of the bel canto school, and had attempted to raise Marian's voice a full octave. The New York critics that next day were harsh, even bitter. Most of them recognized the existence of a great voice, but some of them pontifically declared that it had been ruined."

White's criticism was more gentle, but in a letter to Hayes he remarked that, even though he considered her voice to be "marvelous . . . she sings too mechanically and without any great depth of feeling." Convinced that she had unlimited potential, he conspired with Hayes to get her back on track. The NAACP had recently decided to honor Hayes with the Spingarn Medal, the organization's most prestigious annual award, and the site of the upcoming conference at which the medal would be presented was Anderson's home city of Philadelphia. By the time the conference convened in July, Hayes would be back in Europe and unable to accept the medal in person, but Harry Burleigh agreed to accept it on his behalf. Thus, it seemed only natural to invite their dear friend to sing at the ceremony. The only hang-up was Anderson's recent "retirement" from singing, which proved to be a serious obstacle. "We invited Marian to sing," White explained, "but received a flat refusal. It took long persuasion to change her mind." After she finally came around, she did her best to honor the man who had inspired and mentored her for more than a decade. "On Spingarn Medal night in crowded Witherspoon Hall," White remembered, with obvious pride, "she sang superbly and was forced to give encore after encore and then to take curtain call after curtain call. When at last the applause had subsided, Marian burst into tears and exclaimed, 'Thank God! I've got my faith again!'"[8]

As dramatic as this moment was, it was not the only episode that brought Anderson's career back to life. Boghetti, though maligned by some New York critics as an advocate of the controversial bel canto technique, also had a hand in reviving her spirit, and her prospects. His uplifting intervention would take nearly a year to bear fruit, however, and during the fall and winter of 1924, Anderson continued to struggle as she and King resumed their Southern and Midwestern touring. Even though Anderson had regained her form, it was not a good time for a black artist to be traveling and performing in the heartland. The Ku Klux Klan, with several million members, was at the height of its influence, and demagogic politicians were on the prowl, vigilantly policing any perceived breach of racial etiquette. No longer just a Southern phenomenon, the Klan's political power stretched from Maine to Oregon and was particularly strong in urban areas, where rural migrants were looking for a sense of belonging.

One of the few cities to escape the Klan's surging brand of "100 percent Americanism" and Anglo-Saxon purity was New York City, which had it own traditions of ethnic and racial conflict, but which, despite the Town Hall setback, proved to be a good place for Anderson to regenerate her career. New Yorkers, as much as any group of Americans, prided themselves on being discerning judges of music. Accordingly, various New York institutions sponsored musical competitions at all levels. One of the best known was a wide-open annual contest cosponsored by the National Music League and Lewisohn Stadium, an outdoor amphitheater that had opened on the Upper West Side of Manhattan in 1915. Formally affiliated with the City College of New York, the stadium hosted a variety of events from athletic contests to orchestral concerts and was a popular venue for a wide spectrum of New York music enthusiasts. The annual Lewisohn musical competition, open to both vocal and instrumental artists, was a grueling and complicated affair involving multiple rounds of auditions and performances. The prize was an invitation to perform as a soloist with the New York Philharmonic during one of its summer concerts. It was not a competition for the faint of heart, and Anderson would never have thought of entering it on her own.

Boghetti, however, believed that it was just what she needed to restore her confidence. Unbeknownst to Anderson, he submitted her name as a participant in the 1925 vocal competition, where she would face more than three hundred other hopefuls. Though more than a little hesitant, she agreed to go through with it and spent the late spring preparing three numbers, including the challenging aria "O mio Fernando" from Gaetano Donizetti's opera *La Favorita*. In late June she and approximately sixty others made it through the first round, which was held at Aeolian Hall, the same hall where Jules Bledsoe had debuted the previous year. A week later she returned for the semifinal competition, which normally reduced the field to seven finalists. But in an unprecedented show of consensus the judges canceled the final round and awarded the vocal prize to Anderson. Suddenly, the seemingly overmatched young woman who had faltered at Town Hall was the toast of the town. On August 26, as promised, she performed under the stars at Lewisohn Stadium with the New York Philharmonic. Singing "O mio Fernando," three spirituals, and "Song of the Heart," a black art song written by James Weldon Johnson's brother, J. Rosamond Johnson, she delighted a near-capacity crowd of seventy-five hundred. The reviews were uniformly positive, with one critic retracting his criticisms of the previous spring in the face of "the astonishing vocal power displayed by the young singer last night." Upon her return to Philadelphia, local music enthusiasts marked the New York triumph with a special reception held in a thousand-seat hall at John Wanamaker's department store, where Marian's mother had scrubbed floors for several years and where her sister Alyse had recently found work. The irony of the situation went unrecorded, but this was as good as life got for black Philadelphians in 1925.[9]

Even so, life was different for Marian Anderson in the wake of the Lewisohn Stadium competition. She was still black, and Jim Crow was still very much in evidence. But somehow she began to edge her way into the American mainstream as the first quarter of the twentieth century drew to a close. "That fall, when Billy King and I resumed our concerts," she later recalled, "the effects of the contest and the stadium appearance were noticeable. Almost without my realizing it, I was at a point where I had to compete with singers who were well established. It was possible to increase fees and to obtain more engagements, and the range and character of these engagements began to change. We had invitations from Canada and the West Coast. Morning musical clubs here and there asked for dates, and so did several regular concert series. Even in the South the nature of audiences changed a little. When there was a concert in a Negro school auditorium, there would be white people in the audience."[10]

Anderson's new stature brought added income and a measure of professional satisfaction. But it also brought her face-to-face with the continuing dilemma of racially segregated concert halls. Later in her career, from the early 1940s on, she refused to sing in front of all-white audiences, and she drew the line at what was sometimes called horizontal segregation. In other words, she would not sing when black patrons were forced to sit in the balcony or in the back of the hall. Until the NAACP advised otherwise in the early 1950s, she would allow so-called vertical segregation, in which an imaginary line perpendicular to the stage divided the hall into black and white sections. As long as the seats were "separate but equal," following the *Plessy* mandate of 1896, she agreed to perform.

At this early stage of her career, however, she was in no position to dictate seating policy. Setting limits of any kind was simply out of the question and would effectively have closed the opportunity to tour in most areas of the nation. If she wanted access to the nation's concert halls, she had no choice but to adapt to whatever arrangements local officials and theater managers required. As Anderson soon learned, systems of segregation varied from community to community and from theater to theater. The most extreme arrangements, which she sometimes encountered in the Deep South, forced her to deliver two separate concerts, one for whites and a second for blacks. More often whites and blacks shared the hall at the same time, invariably under separate and unequal conditions in which blacks entered and exited the hall through a Jim Crow door, had no access to restrooms, and sat in inferior seats. Whites received preferential treatment, and even prominent black institutions such as Fisk and the Hampton and Tuskegee Institutes subscribed to a paternalistic ethos that accommodated white patrons, often in a spirit of racial deference.[11]

Though Anderson found segregation demeaning and distasteful, she could not do much about it in the 1920s and 1930s. One way of avoiding complicity with the worst abuses of segregation was to sign a contract with a booking agency powerful and knowledgeable enough to pick and choose her engagements. Finding such an agency was no easy task for a black artist, as Anderson discovered in 1925. Following a Carnegie Hall performance with the famed Hall Johnson Negro Choir, she received a surprise visit from Arthur

Judson, the owner of the nation's most influential theatrical management agency. "Mr. Judson came back to see me," she recalled. "He was kind enough to say that he had not been aware that I could give that sort of performance. He thought that his office would be able to do something for me, and he spoke casually of being in a position to launch me at a fee of seven hundred and fifty dollars a performance. He had offices in New York and Philadelphia and suggested that I come to see him in either place." Two days later she and Boghetti visited Judson's Philadelphia office to discuss terms. Judson had ten years of experience as a theatrical and musical manager, but he had never represented a black singer. Though intrigued by Anderson's potential as a concert performer, he began to have second thoughts as soon as the conversation turned to the inevitable complications of booking a black artist in Southern venues. To Anderson's disappointment, the meeting produced no contract and no sense of where she should go next.[12]

During the next two years, she and Billy King devoted considerable time and energy to annual tours of the Southeast during the winter months and the Midwest during the weeks surrounding Easter. The Southern tour of approximately a dozen concerts took them as far west as Tennessee and as far south as Florida, while the Midwestern tour centered on Ohio and Indiana. All told, they performed in scores of venues, including municipal halls, black churches, colleges, and schools; and more often than not they drew capacity crowds. Most of the concertgoers were black, but a growing number were white. Personal contact with white fans was relatively rare, since both Anderson and King generally stayed in private homes or black-college dormitories while on tour. Nevertheless, she built up a network of admirers that transcended race, a highly unusual occurrence in the "tribal twenties."[13]

By most standards, especially by the standards of black America, Anderson had a good life by 1927, the year she turned thirty. But it was not enough for someone who aspired to greatness. The experiences of the past three years had revealed both her potential and her current limitations. If she was ever going to approach the top rank of concert artists, she had to do something dramatic to alter her circumstances. "I was going stale," she wrote years later. "I had to get away from my old haunts for a while; progress was at a standstill; repeating the same engagements each year, even if programs varied a little, was becoming routine; my career needed a fresh impetus." The burden of dealing with racial segregation and discrimination compounded her dissatisfaction, but her primary concern was musical inertia. In addition to the problems of the tour, her studies with Boghetti had reached an impasse, sparking the realization that she would never master the singing of German lieder under his direction. Consequently, she began to look to Europe for her professional salvation.[14]

FOLLOWING the prevailing conventional wisdom among classical musicians, Anderson became convinced that she had to go abroad for proper training and validation. New World music lovers of a classical persuasion still depended on the Old World for cultural cues, and no American artist could expect to be taken seriously or ascend to the highest level without first proving himself in Europe. All of the great maestros—from Arturo Toscanini to Leopold Stokowski to Serge Koussevitzky—had European roots, and virtually all of America's leading concert artists had studied in Europe at one time or another. Black performers had the added incentive of gaining some relief from the strictures of American racism, and it was no accident that the first person to urge Anderson to emigrate was Lawrence Brown, Roland Hayes's accompanist.[15]

Brown and Hayes had close contacts in England, where they had lived off and on for nearly a decade, and Anderson decided to study there. Gathering $1,500 in savings, she informed her family and a stunned Boghetti that she had booked passage on the *Île de France* in late October. Anderson, along with millions of other Americans, had just experienced the euphoria following Charles Lindbergh's solo flight across the Atlantic, and now she, too, was headed east, a lone adventurer in search of fulfillment. While she had no clear plan as to what she would do after she arrived in London, she did have several letters of introduction, and Brown and others had already notified British friends of her impending arrival. At the outset, she hoped to stay with the noted composer Roger Quilter, but his illness prompted a shift to the home of John Payne, a prominent black baritone who had lived in England since 1919. Anderson had met Payne in Philadelphia several years earlier, when he had urged her to call him if she found herself in London. Their reunion in 1927 proved to be mutually beneficial and the beginning of a long and close friendship.

Payne's home, a palatial three-story house near Regent's Park owned by Lady Mary Cook, served as a focal point for a small community of black musicians who had migrated to England since the end of the First World War. Anderson, like others before her, took full advantage of Lady Mary's generosity and Payne's many contacts. One of the most important contacts was Amanda Aldrich, a renowned black contralto and voice teacher who had studied with Jenny Lind. The daughter of Ira Aldrich, a distinguished actor who had made Shakespeare's Othello his own during a long career on the English stage, she lived in the Kensington section of London with her sister Irene, once a popular contralto on the continental concert circuit. Both Roland Hayes and John Payne had studied with Amanda Aldrich and recommended her to Anderson.

Anderson eventually spent many hours in Aldrich's studio, but during her first two months in England she studied German lieder under one of the grand masters of the genre, Raimund von Zur-Mühlen. An aged German living at Wiston Old Rectory in Sussex, Zur-Mühlen agreed to take Anderson on as a student as long as his health held out. Unfortunately, Zur-Mühlen's condition was such that Anderson only had two sessions with him. Nevertheless, she remained in Sussex until mid-December, when it became clear that he was not going to recover. Only then did she return to London, where she soon became involved in a whirl of activities. In late January, a benefit concert organized by the famous black bandleader Noble Sissle brought a number of black artists to London, including Josephine Baker and Alberta Hunter, both of whom were enjoying considerable success in Paris and the French Riviera. Just prior to the concert, Hunter moved into a room adjoining Anderson's room at the Payne house, and the two women soon became friends. Over the next few months the outgoing Hunter introduced Anderson to a wide circle of friends, including Paul Robeson, who, along with his wife, Essie, was in London rehearsing a new production of the musical *Show Boat*.

Anderson also developed a friendship with Roger Quilter, who led her to Mark Raphael, a noted baritone who specialized in the music of Franz Schubert. The year 1928 marked the centennial of Schubert's death, and Raphael was busy preparing several concerts honoring his favorite composer. Anderson, an aspiring Schubert aficionado, spent many enjoyable and profitable hours with Raphael, who deepened her understanding of the composer's musical subtleties. She also benefited from the tutelage of Louis Drysdale, a Jamaican émigré who had opened a voice studio in London's West End in 1926. By the time Anderson arrived, Drysdale had already attracted several high-profile students, including Florence Mills, the star of the popular musical review *Blackbirds of 1926*, Ethel Waters, and Nell Hunter. Anderson's work with Drysdale refined her approach to Italian masters such as Donizetti and Verdi, leaving her with a thirst for more.[16]

Anderson's time in London was the most frenetic period of her young life. When she wasn't studying voice, she was busy taking language lessons at the Hugo Institute or attending recitals and stage plays. During her eleven-month stay, she was privileged to hear some of the greatest singers of the day, include Lily Pons, Elisabeth Schumann, and Elena Gerhardt, the incomparable mistress of German lieder. During a concert at Queen's Hall, Gerhardt's performance of Schubert's *Winterreise* brought Anderson to tears, confirming her belief that singing lieder was among the highest forms of vocal art. Soon thereafter, with encouragement from Raphael and Quilter, Anderson agreed to deliver a concert of her own. All throughout the winter and spring she had given brief, impromptu recitals at the Payne house or in Quilter's parlor, but the June 15 recital at Wigmore Hall was her public debut. With the Robesons in attendance, she sang a mixed program of spirituals and songs by European composers ranging from Schubert and Schumann to Debussy and Purcell. The challenging program drew little response from London's notoriously harsh music critics, but Anderson was pleased with her first European performance. Two months later she offered a second recital at a summer Promenade concert, known locally as the Proms, and this time the reviews were universally enthusiastic.

The August concert at the Proms prompted a flurry of interest, including inquiries from record companies and the BBC. She accepted an offer from the Gramophone Company and devoted her final weeks in England to recording several operatic arias and spirituals. After delivering a farewell concert on the BBC radio network and enjoying a raucous bon voyage party at the Payne house, she boarded the *Aquitania* on September 22 and headed for home. She was sad to leave her new coterie of friends and teachers, but there had never been any question about her return to the United States. Racially and socially, England had provided her with a breath of fresh air and an independent experience unavailable in Philadelphia. But the contrast between the racial atmosphere in the United States and that in England was as not great as she had hoped. While England had no Jim Crow, there was considerable resentment of black performers in native musical and theatrical circles. From the early 1920s on, chronic unemployment among white actors and singers had fostered a backlash against the practice of providing visiting black performers with work permits. Opposition to black artists sometimes shaded into outright racism, as in 1923 when some Londoners became irate over the collaboration between Paul Whiteman's white jazz orchestra and several black musicians appearing at the Hippodrome. Later incidents periodically refueled the racial tension surrounding black artists, and British officials responded by making it increasingly difficult for foreign nationals with dark skin to obtain work permits.[17]

Anderson returned home with a new perspective on the musical world. While her savings were all but gone, she now knew what she had to do. In the rarefied world of classical music, there was no substitute for European training and achievement. Sooner or later she would have to return to Europe to make her mark. But first, for her own sake and for the good of her family, she needed to restore her financial situation. At the time of her return, in late September 1928, the American economy was in the midst of headlong expansion, and the Big Bull market was in full swing. The American entertainment industry was flourishing as never before, and Anderson had high hopes that her skills might be more marketable in the wake of her English sojourn. The concert stage faced increasing competition from radio and films, but she seemed poised to rise to the next level of popularity and exposure. Before she could do so, however, she needed to secure professional management, an inescapable reality that brought her back to Arthur Judson's office.

Anderson and Billy King already had several black colleges and churches under contract for the 1929 tour, but she hoped that with Judson's influence she could add other concert venues to the schedule. After a frank discussion of mutual interests and concerns, he offered her a one-year contract, assigning her to the second tier of the Judson empire. Under this arrangement, her booking agent was not Judson himself, who managed the agency's top fifty attractions, but rather George Leyden Colledge, who ran the "recital" division. Accustomed to receiving up to $350 per concert, she would now receive $500, minus a 20 percent commission to the agency. She also had to pay all of the traveling and publicity expenses for her and King, as was then common for virtually all touring performers. This did not leave much for her at the end of the day, which is why she had hoped that Judson could follow through with his original estimate of $750 per concert. A smaller than expected fee was only the first of many disappointments in her association with the Judson agency. Colledge did his best to expand the tour, but his unfamiliarity with the Southern circuit hampered his efforts. Anderson and King had compiled a large card file of personal and institutional contacts, mostly in the South, and Colledge relied on the file. But he added little else.[18]

Anderson was determined to sing more lieder and to perform in front of a variety of audiences, not just the black concertgoers already familiar with her music. Two weeks after her return from England, she gave a homecoming recital at Philadelphia's Academy of Music. Singing before a packed house, she sang a varied program, but with a large offering of German lieder. For the first time, she treated an American audience to three songs by Schubert and one by Schumann. Many in the audience were unfamiliar with these songs and unable to judge the quality of her German. But several professional critics, though generally enthusiastic about her performance, could not resist a few jabs at her clumsy elocution. She had learned a great deal in England, but not enough to disguise her lack of language training. Undaunted, she continued to experiment with lieder in later concerts, including a November recital at Savannah's Municipal Auditorium, the site of her first Southern concert in 1917. In her final concert of the year, held at Carnegie Hall on December 30, she returned to the New York stage for the first time in three years. Once again the crowd was more enthusiastic than the critics, who praised her beautiful rendition of spirituals but had nothing positive to say about her awkward rendition of Schubert.[19]

During the winter and spring of 1929, she delivered a half dozen major recitals before returning to Philadelphia for a quiet summer. The off-season gave her a chance to return to Boghetti's studio for some polishing and to dabble in piano and vocal theory with a local white composer named Harvey Hebron. But, in her most reflective moments, she thought about little else but returning to Europe. The next visit, she hoped, would be to Germany itself, where she could immerse herself in the study and practice of lieder. As a first step, she wrote to Elena Gerhardt, the woman who had dazzled her in London in 1928, to see if she might accept her as a student. Gerhardt responded graciously, inviting Anderson to join her at a retreat in upstate New York in August. For a variety of reasons, Anderson could not accept Gerhardt's invitation to New York. Nor was she able to follow Gerhardt's later suggestion that she come to Poland in September to study at the Leipzig Conservatory, where Gerhardt was an instructor. As modest as Anderson's earnings were with Judson, she could not afford to go off to Europe without some reasonable expectation of singing for money.

While she was mulling over Gerhardt's offer, an alternative route to the Continent emerged through a chance meeting with Eric Simon, a German music promoter living in New York. Simon proposed a series of concerts in Berlin and several other European cities. A few days later, however, a third alternative presented itself. An enticing, last-minute invitation to appear at a summer music festival at the University of Washington drew her to the West.

Never having seen the Pacific, she headed for Seattle in June. Her recital, delivered outdoors in the university football stadium, received rave reviews and led to a second invitation to return to Seattle in August.[20]

The West Coast adventures revived her spirits, but as the fall 1929 season approached, she was still uncertain about her future with the Judson agency. The first season under Colledge's direction had been a severe disappointment. The length of her tour had actually fallen from thirty-plus concerts in 1927, the year before she went to England, to sixteen in 1929. Moreover, the prospects for the immediate future were not much better, with twenty-one concerts scheduled for the coming season. With nowhere else to turn, Anderson reluctantly renewed her contract with Judson. But she was increasingly restive as the decade came to a close.[21]

STILL looking for some means of returning to Europe, Anderson soon found it in an unlikely place. In mid-November, just after the stock market crash that would help send the nation and much of the world into the Great Depression, Anderson delivered a bravura performance at Chicago's Orchestra Hall. Among the concertgoers that night were George Arthur and Ray Field, representatives of Julius Rosenwald, the philanthropic Chicago millionaire who had established the Rosenwald Fund in 1917. Designated for the "well-being of mankind," the Rosenwald Fund often underwrote black institutions, especially schools, and sometimes offered fellowships to black artists and intellectuals. Enthralled by Anderson's recital, Arthur and Field sought her out after the final curtain and urged her to apply for a Rosenwald fellowship. Within a week, she had submitted an application for a fellowship that would support several months of study in Germany, and three months later she received word that she had been awarded a $1,500 fellowship. In accepting the fellowship, her response to Arthur was both gracious and telling. "It is my true ambition to become a great artist and a credit to my race in every way possible," she wrote on March 6, 1930. "I do not feel that the voice is my personal property, it belongs to everybody. I do feel that I should make every effort to present it to the public in the best form possible. It is also my sincere wish to, in the future, help some talented Negro boy or girl who has ambitions to become a great singer. It is my earnest prayer that some day my financial position will permit me to do this."[22]

Anderson eventually developed a plan to split the fellowship in two, using the first half to fund a six-month stint in Berlin beginning in June 1930, and the second half for a similar visit in 1931. With little planning and no fanfare, she left New York on June 12 and arrived in Germany a week later. Following a long train ride and several linguistic misadventures, she made contact with Max Walter, a concert-bureau manager whom Colledge had contacted prior to Anderson's departure. Walter found lodging for Anderson at the elegant Berlin home of Matthias and Gertrud von Erdberg, a semiretired theatrical couple who embraced the task of tutoring their new boarder in German. Berlin reminded Anderson of London, which she visited for several weeks in August and September. After giving two recitals at the Proms, she returned to Berlin just in time to meet Billy King, who had insisted on joining her for a series of concerts arranged by Walter. Two of the concerts were in Prague, Czechoslovakia, where they enjoyed a brief interlude before King returned to the United States and Anderson began a serious regimen of leider training. With Walter's help, she hired Kurt Johnen and Walter Raucheisen, two of Berlin's finest musicians, as her teachers.

The city's most celebrated accompanist, Raucheisen joined Anderson onstage for her first German recital, held at the famed Bachsaal Hall in October. Though somewhat startled both by her appearance and her willingness to sing the most challenging European songs, several German critics lavished her with praise. One wrote, "Marian Anderson, Negro contralto, tall, slim, elegant in appearance, obviously used to appearing on the stage, enjoyed a tremendous success yesterday at the Bachsaal. Her complexion is not altogether black, but she has a dark, blue-black dark voice, which she handles with accomplishment and taste . . . In sound her voice sounds somewhat unusual to our ears, exotic; but we readily take a fancy to its appeal . . . Interesting women concert singers are few and far between. Here we have one who will continue to engage our attention."[23]

Walter had been less than enthusiastic when Anderson approached him with the idea of performing a full-scale recital in a major Berlin concert hall, and she had been forced to put up $500 of her own money as backing for the concert. But the performance at the Bachsaal ended whatever doubts he had harbored about her ability to perform under pressure. Even when employed in highly imperfect German, her voice was a wonder to behold. In the days and weeks following the concert, Walter saw to it that Anderson made the rounds of the city's music lovers, performing brief recitals at several fashionable salons. Most important, he contacted several leading musical figures in Scandinavia, including the Norwegian concert manager Rule Rasmussen and the Finnish pianist Kosti Vehanen. Rasmussen responded almost immediately with an open invitation for a series of Anderson recitals in the capital cities of Oslo, Stockholm, and Helsinki, plus concerts in smaller cities if there was enough popular interest. The proposal offered two noted accompanists, Sverre Jordan in Norway and Vehanen in Sweden and Finland.

Anderson wasted no time in accepting Rasmussen's proposal. Despite her recent success and the kindnesses of Walter and the von Erdbergs, she couldn't wait to get out of Germany. Buffeted by hyperinflation and political intrigue on both the right and the left, the Weimar regime was coming apart at the seams. Street violence was on the rise, especially in areas where the rising Nazi Party had enlisted hordes of unemployed youths, some of whom were nothing more than thugs. Living in a comfortable suburb with the von Erdbergs shielded Anderson from some of the civil unrest. But the emerging danger and disorder were palpable realities for all Berliners, especially those belonging to non-Aryan ethnic and racial groups. While Anderson encountered nothing beyond curiosity, she was relieved to head northward to the relative calm of Scandinavia.[24]

Once there, she discovered an enthusiastic public that couldn't decide which was more alluring, her dazzling voice or her exotic skin color. Singing in Stavanger and Bergen before going on to Oslo, she created a sensation that left her both exhilarated and puzzled. "The reaction in Norway, I think, was a mixture of open-minded and curiosity," she recalled years later. "These audiences were not accustomed to Negroes. One of the newspapers described the singer as being 'dressed in electric-blue satin and looking very much like a chocolate bar.' Another paper made the comparison with *café au lait*. And so it went. The comments had nothing to do with any prejudice; they expressed a kind of wonder." She found the Swedes less demonstrative, despite the best efforts of Helmer Enwall, a Stockholm promoter who collaborated with Rasmussen. But, following a disappointing first concert in Helsinki, the reaction of the Finns proved equal to that of the Norwegians.

In Finland, Anderson was fortunate to team up with Kosti Vehanen, with whom she forged a strong personal and musical bond. From the outset, the courtly Finn guided and protected her in a way that no previous accompanist had done. "He was a well-trained musician, had studied in Germany, and spoke German fluently, and he could help me with lieder," she explained. "He also knew some French and Italian . . . A man of culture and a gentleman, Kosti Vehanen was an invaluable aid to me. It is not too much to say that he helped me a great deal in guiding me onto the path that led to my becoming an accepted international singer." Vehanen remained with Ander-

son for the rest of an exhausting tour, through Finland, on to Denmark, back
to Oslo and Stockholm, and finally to Denmark again, where she sang a farewell recital in Copenhagen on December 8.[25]

Despite a disappointing fee schedule, it was all breathless and enchant-
ing, a whirlwind of more than a dozen concerts in three weeks. It changed her
life. "The first trip to the Scandinavian countries was an encouragement and
an incentive," she later reflected. "It made me realize that the time and energy
invested in seeking to become an artist were worth while, and that what I had
dared to aspire to was not impossible. The acceptance by these audiences may
have done something for me in another way. It may be that they made me feel
that I need not be cautious with such things as Lieder, and it is possible that I
sang with a freedom I had not had before. I know I felt that this acceptance
provided the basis for daring to pour out reserves of feeling I had not called
upon . . . If these people believed in me as an artist, then I could venture to be
a better one. I could face the challenge of bigger things."[26]

Soliciting the approval of white folks could be a challenging or, at worst,
harrowing experience for an African-American artist in the pre–World War
II era. But Anderson found Scandinavian audiences to be among the most
enthusiastic of her career. Removed from the tensions of a biracial society,
she felt liberated, personally and even musically. When she left Copenhagen
in mid-December, she was eager to return for more. Back in the United States
before the end of the year, she honored the commitments of her third season
with the Judson agency, during which she displayed a new confidence and
improved skills in German. The 1931 tour was the most ambitious to date,
with more than thirty concerts from coast to coast. But the effects of a deepening economic depression could be seen in disappointing ticket sales and
sparse audiences. Anderson found little charm in any of this, and within a
week of the tour's end she was on a boat to Germany.[27]

In late May 1931, she resumed her Rosenwald-backed studies in Berlin,
working once again with Kurt Johnen. Remaining in Berlin through the
summer, she performed a recital in August that demonstrated how far she had
come. Her stage presence and command of German drew high praise from
several critics, including Max Friedlander, a distinguished professor emeritus
at the University of Berlin and Schubert scholar, who judged her interpretation of Brahms's *Vier ernste Gesänge* to be "the very greatest miracle which I
ever heard in the long years of my life." She did not sing again in Berlin in
1931, but a contract with Germany's highly acclaimed concert bureau Wolff
and Sachs led to a string of engagements in Czechoslovakia. By mid-October,

she was back in Scandinavia for a grueling schedule of twenty-two concerts arranged by Helmer Enwall. Throughout the tour the audiences were larger and, if anything, more enthusiastic than they had been the previous year.

During one recital in Finland, Anderson's rendition of a beloved Finnish folk song nearly led to a joyous riot. "She rendered the song admirably," Kosti Vehanen recalled a decade after the incident, "only in the last phrase her breath became short, and she took a breath in the middle of the sentence. The song had never been done this way before, but it happened that the pause came at just the right place; it gave to the meaning of the words a greater degree of beauty. I felt big tears rolling down my cheeks and could scarcely see the music. The last tone vanished; no one moved; and after a stillness as of a closing prayer of gratitude, the applause broke out—applause so powerful that I am sure that we have never before or since heard such an expression of deep and sincere appreciation." Following the concert, the appreciation approached the level of hysteria. "As we left the hall," Vehanen continued, "the people were waiting again to greet her. It was impossible to get to our car. Only one policeman was on hand. He tried to clear a way for us, but he was utterly helpless. The people stormed around Marian in an effort to catch a last glimpse of her or to touch her dress. She was almost in danger of her life as we made a second attempt to get into the car. Her black lace gown was badly torn by people who wanted to have a souvenir. Finally, as we managed to get into the car, my foot was caught between the side of the car and the door. Just then a few strong men who were standing nearby came to our rescue. But our chauffeur could not drive away until other policemen came. At last we were able to drive on, with the cries of joy ringing in our ears."[28]

As Anderson well knew, black Americans sometimes faced unruly mobs, but in America the members of the mob seldom let out cries of joy. While she never commented publicly on the irony of the situation, the contrast between her growing fame in Scandinavia and her difficulties in breaching the color line in the United States could hardly have been more obvious. Her second tour had many memorable moments, but the highlight of the season was a visit with the distinguished Finnish composer Jean Sibelius. Arranged by Vehanen, who had known the composer for several years, the meeting took place at Sibelius's beautiful country house in Jarvenpaa. Anderson sang four songs that evening, all Sibelius compositions sung in Finnish. Despite a few linguistic missteps, Sibelius and his guests were utterly charmed by her unaffected warmth and dignity, not to mention her voice. Years later Anderson recalled the thrill of Sibelius's reaction to her singing: "When I was finished he arose, strode to my side, and threw his arms around me in a hearty embrace. 'My roof is too low for you,' he said, and then called out in a loud voice to his wife, 'Not coffee, but champagne.' "²⁹

IN December 1931, Anderson reluctantly returned to the United States, where she remained for nearly two years. While she was pleased to see her mother and sisters again regularly, these were not the happiest two years of her life. By the time she began her fourth Judson tour in January 1932, the hard times that had enveloped the nation were more obvious than ever. This was especially true among black Americans, whose only solace was that they didn't have far to fall. Anderson herself felt the pinch of economic depression in a reduced number of concerts and lower fees. In the South, Hampton Institute was one of the few venues that could still support her annual visit, and new venues were almost out of the question. Maintaining a coherent tour week by week was impossible, and some months, including the normally busy months of March and May, saw her singing a single recital after traveling a thousand miles to get there. When she sang at Boston's Symphony Hall in April 1932, the hall was half-empty. The only encouraging developments were the opportunity to sing spirituals with the Hall Johnson Negro Choir in the spring of 1932 and to study with Frank La Forge the following summer.

Unfortunately, studying with La Forge, one of New York's leading voice teachers, turned out to be a mixed blessing. Concerned about the trajectory of Anderson's career, Arthur Judson strongly encouraged her to become a soprano, and he introduced her to La Forge in the hope of facilitating her transition to the higher range. Neither Anderson nor La Forge took Judson's suggestion seriously, but their collaboration advanced her study of German lieder and led to several recordings. During the summer of 1932, Anderson, like many other Americans, was essentially unemployed, so working with La Forge at least gave her something to do. It also gave her time to follow politics for the first time in her life. Her younger sister Alyse had become deeply involved in the politics of the resurgent Democratic Party, and the entire Anderson household became energized by the presidential candidacy of Franklin D. Roosevelt. At the time, Marian had no inkling that her life would later become entwined with the Roosevelts'. But at least she knew who they were and shared some of Alyse's enthusiasm for the politics of reform.

The fall of 1932 brought the election of Roosevelt and the promise of better times. Yet no relief was in sight for a woman who had dared to aspire to the heights of the musical world. The fall season under Judson was virtually nonexistent, and the situation did not get much better during the winter and spring of 1933. As Roosevelt took the oath of office and launched the legislation of his "First Hundred Days," Anderson sang a total of four recitals and one radio broadcast during the first five months of the year. Desperate for funds, she began to think about alternatives to the concert stage, such as opening a vocal studio or starting a career in radio broadcasting. She also felt that she had reached the end of the line with Judson, but she could never quite bring herself to cut the ties with the agency that still represented her only chance for advancement. Or so it seemed until July 1933, when she received a cable from Helmer Enwall offering her a contract for twenty Scandinavian recitals to be given in October and November. Soon thereafter she received two more cables, one upping the offer to forty concerts and another to sixty. But Anderson needed little coaxing. Without saying a word to Judson, she agreed to go to Scandinavia for a twenty-concert tour, with the possibility of other tours to follow.[30]

When she arrived in Finland in mid-September, she was overcome with emotion, feeling that she had returned to an adopted home. After a tearful reunion with Kosti Vehanen, whom she had not seen in nearly two years, the preparation for the tour began. Two weeks later she gave two stirring concerts in Helsinki, before embarking on the most arduous schedule of her career. Performing three and sometimes four concerts a week, she swept over Scandinavia like a wave. Virtually every performance was a sellout, and even the Swedish king was on hand when she sang in Stockholm on October 20. The schedule had few breaks, and during her first two months on tour she gave thirty-four concerts. The contrast with her recent experiences in the United States could hardly have been more stark, prompting her to cancel the coming season with Judson. She would take her chances in a part of the world that respected and honored her work, that paid her well enough to support herself and her family, and that did not subject her to demeaning racial restrictions.

The only problem was the likelihood of exhaustion. Not wanting to disappoint Enwall, she somehow maintained a breakneck pace for an entire year. "Before I was through I had done more than a hundred concerts—I think the exact number was one hundred and eight—within a twelve month period," she later recalled with a mixture of satisfaction and wonder. "I sang nearly everywhere in Sweden, Norway, Finland, and Denmark. I sang in the remote north of Sweden and Finland in churches of small communities. In some towns there were two or three concerts; in Stockholm there were more." Virtually every concert, it seems, added to her expanding mystique, not only as the first black singer to tour the Nordic region but also as a supremely talented adopted daughter. As Anderson herself acknowledged with uncharacteristic pride, "The newspapers ran caricatures, photographs, all sorts of articles about me. One piece went so far as to term the whole thing 'Marian Fever.'"

Anderson benefited from her conquest of Scandinavia in countless ways, from enhanced confidence and social ease to personal satisfaction and financial security. "It was a wonderful time for me, the period of this extended Scandinavian tour," she later insisted. "My total earnings were the highest of my career. I sent money home to my family. I bought new evening dresses and clothes for street wear. I purchased a great deal of music, and for the first time I could indulge in the luxury of having it bound in leather. I bought luggage, and gifts for friends." For the first time in her life, she became conscious of high fashion and the role that it could play in her public image. Under Kosti's influence, she began to wear longer, full-length gowns, the first of which she bought at "N. K., an exclusive and beautiful store in Stockholm where the latest Paris models were to be found."[31]

By the spring of 1934, she was ready for Paris itself. Beginning in February, Enwall had begun negotiating concert dates in London and several of continental Europe's grandest cities, including Paris, Vienna, and Milan. As great as her fame was north and west of the Baltic Sea, Anderson was still virtually unknown in the major music capitals to the south. Enwall was determined to change this, though he had some concern about how much energy his client would have in the wake of the prolonged Scandinavian tour. He also worried about her propensity for homesickness or, more accurately, the longing for her family. Fortunately for Enwall, the latter problem all but disappeared when Anderson invited her mother to join her in Europe. Accompanied by Billy King, Mrs. Anderson arrived in early May, a few days after her daughter's Paris debut.

The turnout at the famous Salle Gaveau on May 2 was disappointing, just a few hundred people scattered throughout the hall. But the critical reaction was uniformly positive. "MARIAN ANDERSON. Don't forget this name, it will be famous before very long in Paris," the journal *Le Jour* proclaimed, before describing her "beautiful contralto" and trying to "define the indefinable, that is, the strange charm and . . . succession of fascinations radiated by her extraordinary personality." The recital also impressed Fritz Horowitz, the French concert promoter who had handled the local arrangements for Enwall. He prevailed upon Anderson to give a second Parisian concert a few weeks later and a third in June.[32]

The second concert, with Anderson's mother in attendance, was one of the milestones of her career. Not only was the concert a near sellout and a musical triumph, but it also brought Sol Hurok, the famed Ukrainian-born promoter of Anna Pavlova and Isadora Duncan, into Anderson's life. When it came to choosing clients, the man known as "the impresario" preferred dancers to singers, and the only black singer signed by his agency, Jules Bledsoe, had not worked out well. Indeed, Anderson and King had made a futile effort to talk with Hurok at his New York office earlier in the decade. By contrast, the man who accompanied Horowitz into Anderson's dressing room at intermission couldn't have been more gracious, or more eager. Before Anderson went out for the second half of the recital, she agreed to meet Hurok the following day. Years later Anderson recounted the meeting in her autobiography: "With Kosti I went to Mr. Horowitz's office the next day. I still have a vivid picture of the scene in my mind. Mr. Horowitz sat at one side of his big desk, while Mr. Hurok occupied the chair behind it. Kosti and I took seats in front of it. In those days Mr. Hurok was built along generous lines. In recent years he has slimmed himself down so he looks like the dapper man about town, but in June 1934 he had the impressive bulk befitting the grand impresario. I cannot tell you how big and important he seemed to me; Kosti and I felt inadequate in his presence. As Mr. Hurok slowly lifted his cane, which he held at his side, and placed it before him on the desk, his shoulders seemed to broaden. I think I would have run away if I had dared."

Hurok asked Anderson a series of questions about her past, especially her experiences with the Judson agency, and minutes later he said the words that the nervous young woman had been waiting to hear: "I might be able to do something for you." While the initial offer was somewhat disappointing, a guarantee of fifteen concerts and a fee of $500 per concert, Anderson left the meeting with the feeling that her career had just turned a corner. A beaming Kosti suggested that a celebratory schnapps was warranted, as they both began to contemplate life under the management of the most famous impresario in the world. Before anything official could happen, she would have to sever her ties with Judson. She handled that problem in short order. Two weeks after the meeting with Hurok, she sent Judson a vague list of demands, arguing that it was "impossible" for her to "continue working under our former conditions." As expected, Judson flatly rejected her demands, effectively releasing her from her contract. None of this sat well with Billy King, who had romantic feelings for Anderson and already felt threatened by Kosti and her European success. He thought that she was making the biggest mistake of her life and told her so in an impassioned letter sent just after he and her mother returned to Philadelphia. "A wrong step at this time will spoil everything," he wrote, urging her to stay with Judson. ". . . For God's sake Marian please be a woman and be stable in mind and realize that none of these people who surround you know conditions in America like you do."[33]

Anderson knew all too well what Billy King was suggesting: In the glare of the European spotlights, she had forgotten that she was a black woman from the streets of South Philadelphia. Ambition was one thing, but a foolhardy disregard for the realities of race and class was something else again. The world might appear to be different from the perspective of the European stage, but back home traditional rules still applied. To get along in life, a black person in America, North or South, had to respect the power and privileges of the white man. Anderson's European advisers—Horowitz, Enwall, and Vehanen—clearly knew next to nothing about the realities and limitations of black life, and Hurok was a Russian émigré who had spent most of his thirty years in the United States surrounded by other Jewish immigrants. Since his arrival in 1906, he had lived in Philadelphia and New York, but he had hardly set foot in the South. Despite his considerable experience as a promoter, he had never dealt with the world of black churches and colleges, and he had never had to navigate the treacherous subtleties of Jim Crow. Judson had some of the same limitations, but at least he was a known quantity who had remained loyal to Anderson despite her European dalliances. A white man of his stature was not to be trifled with, especially when the nation was in the throes of an economic depression that made survival itself a challenge.

Anderson knew all of this, of course. But something about Hurok inspired her trust and confidence. She had never met anyone quite like him, a larger-than-life character who exuded charm, charisma, and authority. Without being overly pompous, he acted as if the normal rules of society did not apply to him. He was bigger than that, a force of nature who set his own limits. Flying high, he encouraged his clients to hang on for the ride of their lives. While he could be overbearing and self-serving, he knew how to promote all manner of attractions, including himself. Anderson was understandably a bit frightened by his reputation for bluster, but after a summer of rest in Sweden with the Enwalls she was ready to commit. Just before the start of the 1934 fall tour, she asked her attorney, Hubert Delany, to finalize a contract with Hurok Productions. The die was cast.[34]

During the remainder of the year, she maintained a frenetic schedule, spending most of October and November in Scandinavia before delivering a whirlwind of pre-Christmas concerts in Holland, Belgium, France, and Switzerland. Along the way she sang with the some of the best orchestras in Europe. Some of this made her a little uncomfortable, since she was accustomed to singing with a lone accompanist. But, whatever the format, she delighted concertgoers and critics alike. In early January she began one of the great adventures of her life as she, Kosti, and the Enwalls crossed over the Finnish border into the Soviet Union. Warned that Soviet ideology was rigidly secular and that Soviet authorities might be offended if she sang spirituals before a Russian audience, Anderson decided to take the risk during a brief series of six concerts in Leningrad and Moscow. After the intermission of the first concert in Leningrad, an official translator told the crowd what to expect during the second half of the recital. What happened next shocked Anderson and Kosti, who thought they had seen everything in nearly two years of touring in Scandinavia.

"When the time came for the spirituals she did not say much about them to the audience beyond giving the names," Anderson remembered. "I would guess that she mentioned their Negro origin, but I doubt that she stressed their sacred meaning. I went out and sang them, and then the concert was presumably over. It was quite a distance from the piano to the stage exit, and as Kosti and I walked off, not looking back, we heard a swelling noise. It grew in volume and intensity, and when we reached the artist's room it had mounted to horrifying proportions. It sounded as if the building were being torn up by its roots. 'What on earth is going on?' I asked. 'I don't know,' said Kosti, looking as bewildered as I surely did. The young woman came into the room and asked us to go out on the stage again. We did, and what we saw astonished us. Half the audience—the half that had sat in the rear of the house—had rushed down the aisles and had formed a thick phalanx around the stage. Those nearest the stage were pounding on the board floor with their fists. Deep voices were roaring in Russian accents, 'Deep River' and 'Heaven, Heaven.' We did several encores with the throng almost underfoot. It was disconcerting for a few moments, but how could one resist such enthusiasm?"[35]

Following the Russian tour, Anderson traveled throughout Central and Eastern Europe, threading her way southward with stops in several capital cities, including Warsaw, Vienna, Prague, and Budapest. By early April she was in Monte Carlo, and from there she headed to Italy for a month of concerts. After singing in Rome, where she gave a special command performance for Crown Princess Marie-José, she turned north to Milan, Trieste, and Venice. In May she returned to Russia for a second and longer tour, which was scheduled to end in Leningrad on June 5. By this point she was approaching exhaustion, but Soviet authorities, grateful for Anderson's willingness to return for an extended second tour, arranged a "vacation" in the remote Caucasus mountain resort town of Kislovodsk that entailed an added mini-tour of concerts in the Ukraine and adjoining republics, including Joseph Stalin's home republic of Georgia. The traveling conditions in these regions were challenging at best, and the vacation trip soon lost whatever charm it might have held. "By the time we reached our destination I wished we had never started," she later confessed, "in fact, I wished by then that I had never journeyed so far from home."

Though thankful for all the plaudits and attention, Anderson had grown weary by late summer. The experience at Kislovodsk, which included a brief but torrid love affair with a Russian actor named Emmanuel Kaminka, did little to stem the feeling that she had been away from home too long. Hurok had begun to talk about a grand concert tour that would take the United States by storm, but with or without stardom she wanted to spend some time on South Martin Street in Philadelphia. Although she had no firm plans for the coming year, she wanted to be home by Christmas. However, she hoped to accomplish at least one additional thing before leaving Europe: to appear at the famous Salzburg Music Festival in August. When she had performed in Vienna during the spring tour, Archbishop Sigismund Waitz of Salzburg had come backstage to see if he could persuade her to participate in the annual festival. He suggested a benefit concert to be held in the towering Salzburg Cathedral, and both Anderson and Enwall were pleased to accept the invitation. Unfortunately, when Enwall followed up on the offer, working through the Viennese concert promoter Wilhelm Stein, he ran into a brick wall of Nazi opposition. On May 21, Austrian authorities denied the request for a concert on the grounds that non-Aryans were no longer welcome at the Salzburg Festival. When the denial hit the press, festival organizers tried to sidestep a rising chorus of criticism by pleading ignorance. Enwall persisted and eventually pushed the organizers into a compromise that would allow Anderson to sing at the Mozarteum, one of the festival's main venues, as long as she did not appear on the official festival program.

When Anderson sang at the Mozarteum on August 28, neither she nor Enwall knew quite what to expect. Shielded from the behind-the-scenes negotiations, she was most anxious about a rumor that the maestro Arturo

Toscanini planned to attend her recital. "I was hoping that he would not," she later confessed. "I held him in such high esteem that I felt I could not possibly do anything of interest to him." Just before she went onstage, she learned that Toscanini was indeed in the audience. "I was as nervous as a beginner," she recalled. Somehow she made it through the first half of the program, which included several difficult songs by Schubert and Sibelius, but during the intermission Toscanini, escorted by Madame Charles Cahier (aka Sarah-Jane Layton Walker), a prominent contralto and voice teacher whom Anderson had known for several years, suddenly appeared in her dressing room.

What happened next became a staple of musical lore. According to Anderson's own account, "The sight of him caused my heart to leap and throb so violently that I did not hear a word he said. All I could do was mumble a thank you, sir, thank you very much, and then he left. Madame Cahier, however, was not so nervous. She had heard and told me of Maestro's words: 'Yours is a voice such as one hears once in a hundred years.' It was enough, more than enough, that he addressed such words to me. If it had been up to me I would not have allowed his comment to be made public. I certainly would not have allowed it without asking his permission. But it was already news before I had any power to intervene. I had the other half of the concert to sing, and there were people clamoring to find out and report what Maestro Toscanini had said. He was the dominant personality in Salzburg and the musical world at large, and it was news that he had seen fit to come to a concert by a singer who was not yet well known."[36]

Anderson's life would never be the same again. In any context, Toscanini's comment would have been newsworthy. But its being uttered about a contraband performer against the backdrop of the most famous music festival in the world magnified the impact of his words. The greatest magnifier was, of course, Sol Hurok. Although he was not in Salzburg to hear the magical words of Toscanini, he immediately grasped the significance of what had happened. He and his new client had received the gift of a lifetime. The publicity value of Toscanini's endorsement was incalculable, a perfect framing mechanism for Anderson's impending reintroduction to America. The outline for what would soon be known as the "Anderson fairy tale" was now set. Following a series of farewell concerts in the fall of 1935, the young woman with "the voice of the century" returned to her native land with the imprimatur of European musical royalty and the fervent hope that talent and hard work would triumph over racial prejudice.[37]

CHAPTER 3

Deep Rivers

Deep River, My home is over Jordan.
Oh, Deep River, Lord, I want to cross over into campground.
—FROM THE SPIRITUAL "DEEP RIVER," ARRANGED BY HARRY
T. BURLEIGH[1]

M ARIAN Anderson returned to the United States in late December 1935. Accompanied by Kosti Vehanen, she crossed the Atlantic on the luxury liner *Île de France*, arriving in New York just before Christmas. On the third day of the passage, she injured an ankle while falling down a stairway as the ship lurched in rough seas. But, after clearing customs, a beaming Anderson limped down the gangplank to an adoring coterie of family and friends that included the noted composer and arranger Harry T. Burleigh. While the subsequent discovery that her ankle was broken cast a shadow over her Philadelphia homecoming, she seemed to take everything—from her temporary physical limitations to the challenge of reengaging with American culture—in stride. The triumphant experiences in Europe had given her a new confidence, deepening her maturity and sense of self. Though still gracious and unpretentious, she was not the same woman who had departed for Europe in September 1933.[2]

The nation, too, had undergone significant changes during Anderson's twenty-seven months abroad. Six years after the Great Crash of 1929, economic depression still dominated the lives of most Americans, black and white. But the political culture of hard times had become harsher and more polarized as the economic crisis had lengthened. For a time the legislative activism of Franklin Roosevelt's First Hundred Days brought a measure of hope, but the persistence of unemployment and dire circumstances soon spawned a number of radical and even desperate responses to the nation's plight. On Roosevelt's right, the "Radio Priest," Father Charles Coughlin, the silver-tongued leader of the National Union for Social Justice, issued a steady stream of quasi-fascist nostrums, while the reactionary and vitriolic Republicans and ultraconservative Democrats of the American Liberty League called for a return to traditional, pro-business values, demonizing both the president and his "socialistic" New Deal. On the left, Roosevelt faced a sharp challenge from socialists and Communists, as well as from ascendant movements led by the famed muckraker Upton Sinclair, the founder of the End Poverty in California (EPIC) campaign; Dr. Francis Townsend, the originator of the Townsend Old Age Revolving Pension Plan; and Senator Huey Long, the bombastic Louisiana "Kingfish," whose popular Share Our Wealth program threatened to sweep the nation prior to his assassination in September 1935.[3]

Responding to these and other challenges, Roosevelt nudged his administration to the left following the Democrats' landslide victory in the congressional elections of 1934. In January 1935 he launched the Second New Deal, a reformulated program of federal activism that recognized the special problems of the poor, the unemployed, the elderly, farmers, and organized labor. From May to August, in an unprecedented flurry of legislation, Congress established the Works Progress Administration (WPA), the Rural Electrification Administration (REA), the National Labor Relations Board (NLRB), and the Social Security Administration (SSA). Collectively, these new agencies promised to transform the profile of the federal government, though the expansionist spirit of the Second New Deal was quickly countered by a landmark Supreme Court decision in late May that struck down the two-year-old National Industrial Recovery Act (NIRA) as an unconstitutional infringement of private property rights. Both the success and the constitutionality of the Second New Deal remained an open question as 1935 drew to a close. If this were not enough to keep the president and much of the nation on edge, a deadly Labor Day hurricane left hundreds dead in the Florida Keys, and a series of drought-induced dust storms threatened life and labor in the Southwestern plains. Nature itself seemed to be conspiring with the forces of despair and disruption.[4]

Marian Anderson had returned to a nation with a troubled present and an uncertain future. Human misery and high anxiety were rampant in virtually every community from Maine to California, a general malaise manifested in the broken dreams of young and old, and in the vacant faces that dotted every street corner and country road. For black Americans the situation was especially dire, if not altogether new. For them the Great Depression had simply compounded the dual burdens of race and class, all but wiping out the social and economic gains of the past three decades. With few exceptions, they were mired among the "mudsills and bottom rails" of American society, and by the mid-1930s the bottom rail itself seemed on the verge of collapse. The gravest crisis was in the Deep South, where millions of black sharecroppers and laborers were being pushed off the land into a migration stream that held out little promise of improvement, despite the recent proliferation of New Deal agencies designed to facilitate economic recovery. In many cases New Deal agricultural and relief policies—invariably implemented and controlled by local whites opposed to black advancement—actually made matters worse for black farmers and laborers.

In Southern towns and cities, legally codified cradle-to-grave segregation, along with race-based economic exploitation, remained in full force. In the North, where black migrants were generally regarded as unwelcome economic competitors and social pariahs, the customary patterns of racial discrimination and de facto segregation were stronger than ever. North and South, racial tensions were on the rise as blacks and whites vied for limited resources, sometimes in a move for uplift and upward mobility, but more often in a vain effort to sustain a way of life that appeared to be slipping away.[5]

Later in the decade the New Deal would initiate a Second Reconstruction that would bring a measure of hope and opportunity to black Americans. But in late 1935, as Anderson prepared to renew her American career, there was little hint of impending progress. The agents of change remained hidden in the inner world of the New Deal, where a racial revolution of sorts was slowly making its way to the surface of public life. The prime movers of this revolution were four public figures who became friends during the first two years of the Roosevelt era and who eventually transformed their personal connections into a vanguard for racial justice. Two of these figures—First Lady Eleanor Roosevelt and Secretary of the Interior Harold L. Ickes—were white; and the other two—the Florida-based educator Mary McLeod Bethune and NAACP executive secretary Walter White—were black. All four would play a prominent role in Anderson's eventual emergence as a civil rights icon, a development made possible by the groundwork laid during the mid-to-late 1930s.[6]

Eleanor Roosevelt was perhaps the most unlikely member of the quartet that turned the New Deal toward civil rights. In her early years, living either among the wealthy land barons of New York or among privileged schoolgirls in England, she became familiar with a small circle of black house servants, gardeners, and other laborers. The rest of black America, however, was a complete mystery to her. In 1905, just prior to her marriage, she became a volunteer at the Rivington Street settlement house on the Lower East Side of Manhattan. But the desperate circumstances of the impoverished blacks sprinkled among the immigrant masses in New York did not seem to make much of an impression on her. For the next twenty years, as a wife, mother, and society woman, she displayed a compassionate and generous nature toward friends and family. But nothing indicated that her compassion extended to the least fortunate members of American society or that she was troubled by the racial discrimination that circumscribed the lives of black citizens. During the Wilson administration, when her husband served as undersecretary of the navy with the notorious white supremacist Josephus Daniels of North Carolina as his superior, she politely but firmly refused to join a campaign led by First Lady Ellen Wilson and Charlotte Everett Hopkins to combat slum conditions in Washington's poorest black neighborhoods.[7]

The first sign of a change of heart came in the mid-1920s when the Roosevelts became frequent visitors to Warm Springs, Georgia, where FDR had established a therapeutic center for polio victims. Appalled by the casual cruelty of the racial mores of southwestern Georgia, Eleanor went out of her way to treat the black workers at Warm Springs with a kindness and respect normally reserved for white people. Some local whites seethed with resentment, one recalling many years later that the meddling woman from New York "ruined every maid we ever had." Unlike her husband, who made every effort to accommodate the racial sensibilities of his Georgia neighbors, she paid little attention to the time-honored etiquette of Jim Crow. Her racial apostasy became even more pronounced after 1927, the year she met and befriended Mary McLeod Bethune, the irrepressible president of the National Association of Colored Women (NACW). Born in Mayesville, South Carolina, in 1875, Bethune had long been the nation's most prominent black female educator. Having founded the Literary and Industrial Training School for Negro Girls in Daytona, Florida, in 1904, she later arranged a merger with the Cookman Institute for Men in 1923. For the next twenty years, she used the presidencies of Bethune-Cookman College and the NACW as a bully pulpit for educational and social reform. As the first educated and accomplished black woman that Eleanor Roosevelt had ever known, she introduced her new friend to a restless world of activism and racial striving.[8]

By the time the Roosevelts entered the White House in March 1933, the first lady, though not quite the crusading reformer of later years, was ready to take a public stand on issues related to race and poverty. Less than three weeks after her husband's inauguration, and twenty years after her refusal to become involved with the Washington slum issue, she toured Washington's notorious inner-city alleys with the aged Charlotte Everett Hopkins at her side. Shocked by the miserable living conditions that she and Hopkins observed within walking distance of the Capitol, the first lady offered whatever help she could give to the beleaguered Washington Committee on Housing. By early 1934 she was the committee's staunchest advocate and "honorary Chairman," and for the next decade she worked tirelessly to eradicate the "back alley slums" of black Washington.[9]

At roughly the same time, in August 1933, she plunged into an extended effort to combat poverty in the coal-mining towns of West Virginia. Following an eye-opening visit to the severely depressed region surrounding Morgantown—a visit arranged by her close friend Lorena Hickok and American Friends Service Committee (AFSC) leader Clarence Pickett—she lobbied successfully for the creation of a model community known as Arthurdale. The Arthurdale project absorbed much of her time and energy, and she developed a deep bond with the impoverished and malnourished mining families of northern West Virginia. But she soon learned a hard lesson about the depth of racial prejudice among working-class Americans. In February 1934, with Arthurdale still under construction, a representative group of white miners known as the Homesteaders Club voted to exclude black families from Arthurdale. The first lady urged them to reconsider, but to her dismay they refused to lift the proposed color bar. When Arthurdale opened in June, she swallowed her pride and blessed the new community with her presence.

But the episode only steeled her determination to fight for racial justice elsewhere. "Arthurdale," biographer Blanche Wiesen Cook later observed, "propelled the issue of race to the top of ER's agenda."[10] One early offshoot of the Arthurdale project was a historic civil rights meeting held at the White House on January 26, 1934. Convened on the eve of an inaugural National Public Housing Conference, at which Eleanor Roosevelt and several black leaders were scheduled to speak, the after-dinner meeting brought together the AFSC's Clarence Pickett, the presidents of Howard University, Atlanta University, and the Tuskegee Institute, the noted Fisk University social scientist Charles S. Johnson, North Carolina Mutual Life Insurance Company president Charles C. Spaulding, and NAACP executive secretary Walter

White. For nearly five hours, the conversation ranged across a wide range of racial issues, from unemployment and unequal education to substandard housing and lynching. Throughout the evening the common thread of complaint was the New Deal's refusal to deal with the pressing problems of racial discrimination and black poverty. The president was not present, except for a brief round of greetings and handshakes at the close of the evening. But the first lady was there for every minute of the discussion, listening intently and eventually pledging to do whatever she could to move her husband's administration toward active cooperation with black organizations. Never in the long history of the White House had such words been spoken by a first lady or anyone else close to the seat of power.[11]

At the housing conference the next morning, she underscored her pledge with a public denunciation of slumlords, insisting that "holders of property who exploit human beings must be made to feel that they are bad citizens." Black leaders sensed an opening, and later in the week Melvin Chisum, the field secretary of the National Negro Press Association, wrote the first lady to suggest a new departure in the administration's relationship to black America. Among other suggestions, Chisum proposed the appointment of "a capable, intelligent Negro woman of fine training" to a government position from which she could monitor the New Deal's commitment to racial justice and equal treatment. The first lady immediately embraced the idea and turned to her friend Mary McLeod Bethune as the obvious choice for the position. At her urging, Bethune moved to Washington in October 1934, and with the help of Harry Hopkins, the head of the Federal Emergency Relief Administration (FERA), the Florida educator became a member of the board of advisers for the recently created National Youth Administration (NYA) in early 1935. A year later she left the board to become the director of minority affairs at the NYA, where she worked closely with executive director Aubrey Williams, a passionately liberal white reformer from Alabama. Formerly a lifelong Republican, Bethune was by then an avid New Deal Democrat, symbolizing the shifting partisan loyalties of much of the black electorate.

At the NYA, Bethune had considerable success extending the agency's efforts on behalf of black youth. But her greatest impact on New Deal policies came as the organizer of the Federal Council on Negro Affairs, widely known as the Black Cabinet. By 1936, the federal bureaucracy included approximately forty-five black officials or advisers, the largest number to date and large enough to serve as an unofficial advisory board on racial and civil rights issues. With the approval of the Roosevelts, the members of the Black Cabinet held weekly meetings at Bethune's apartment, usually gathering on Friday evenings to share their thoughts on the plight and prospects of black America. More often than not, the meetings included other black leaders such as Walter White, Charles H. Houston, Judge William Hastie, and A. Philip Randolph, the head of the Brotherhood of Sleeping Car Porters. On occasion, the conversation turned to matters of racial integration and unrestricted participation in American life, but for the most part Bethune and the Black Cabinet stopped short of challenging the "separate but equal" doctrine enshrined in the 1896 *Plessy v. Ferguson* decision. White and several others were clearly dissatisfied with this moderate approach, but the focus on equalization rather than desegregation helped to insulate the Black Cabinet from the objections raised by white supremacists both inside and outside the administration. As long as Bethune and her friends avoided a frontal assault on the legal and social foundations of Jim Crow, the Roosevelts protected and sanctioned the Black Cabinet's largely behind-the-scenes advocacy of racial equality.

Bethune represented the only direct link between the Black Cabinet and the Roosevelts, but her frequent visits to the White House were more than enough to keep conservative tongues wagging. Over time, as the personal and political relationships between Bethune and Eleanor Roosevelt deepened, their effort to lobby the president on matters of racial policy intensified. From the outset, however, the president's strong political ties to powerful Southern leaders, including Vice President John Nance Garner of Texas and the most senior Democrats in both the House and Senate, limited his willingness to take risks on behalf of racial progress.[12]

FDR's fear of alienating white supremacist politicians and voters was never more apparent than during the bitter and protracted struggle to enact a federal antilynching law from 1934 to 1940. Even though the first lady and Bethune, along with Walter White, implored the president to direct his congressional lieutenants to support the Costigan-Wagner Anti-Lynching Bill, FDR could not bring himself to do it. On several occasions the bill passed the House, only to be killed in the Senate by Democratic leaders allied with the president. "I did not choose the tools with which I must work," he explained to White in 1935. "Had I been permitted to choose them I would have selected quite different ones. But I've got to get legislation passed by Congress to save America. The Southerners by reason of the seniority rule in Congress are chairmen or occupy strategic places on most of the Senate and

House committees. If I come out for the anti-lynching bill now, they will block every bill I ask Congress to pass to keep America from collapsing. I just can't take that risk."

The failure to pass a federal antilynching law was the biggest disappointment of White's long career with the NAACP. As a young boy, he had witnessed the Atlanta race riot of 1906, cowering behind darkened windows as white supremacist marauders roamed through his neighborhood. He never forgot the terror of that experience. Later he devoted himself to investigating lynchings across the South. With his blue eyes and with skin light enough to pass for white, he visited more than forty lynching sites without being identified as an NAACP official. After becoming executive secretary of the NAACP in 1931, he established the antilynching campaign as the organization's highest priority, which it remained for the rest of the decade.[13]

FDR's refusal to intervene in the antilynching-bill controversy did not endear him to White and other civil rights leaders. But it did not forestall progress on other, less sensational fronts. From the mid-1930s on, the Black Cabinet, with Eleanor Roosevelt's help, won a series of quiet victories on issues related to racial justice. Most of these victories were a by-product of what historian Harvard Sitkoff has called the Second New Deal's "concern for the dispossessed and for the underdog," a concern generated by a growing political mobilization on the left. Yet in a few instances New Deal officials also took a forthright stand for racial equality.[14]

The most obvious example of racial liberalism at the highest levels of the New Deal bureaucracy was Harold Ickes's leadership of the Department of the Interior and the Public Works Administration (PWA). A crusading social worker from Illinois and a close friend of Jane Addams's, Ickes was the president of the Chicago branch of the NAACP from 1922 to 1924. When he arrived in Washington in 1933, he wasted no time in desegregating the Interior Department's cafeteria and other facilities, and in appointing a special adviser to deal with the "economic status of the Negro." While the selection of a liberal white Southerner, Clark Foreman, as the adviser drew stinging criticism from black leaders, the appointment of the Harvard-educated black economist Robert C. Weaver as Foreman's assistant (and ultimate successor) and of the young black attorney William H. Hastie as the department's assistant solicitor helped to solidify Ickes's reputation as a proponent of civil rights. Ickes eventually persuaded FDR to appoint Hastie to a federal judgeship, making him the first black member of the federal bench. At both the Interior Department and the PWA, Ickes ultimately added a number of black appointees. He also did everything he could to encourage other New Deal agencies to hire black officials and desegregate their facilities and operations. As he told the Chicago Urban League in 1936, he had "always felt it to be my privilege, no less than my duty, to do everything in my power to see that the Negro was given that degree of justice and fair play to which he is entitled."

Despite such sentiments, Ickes had limited success in liberalizing the agencies under his control when it came to matters of race. Racial equalization rarely extended to operations outside Washington, where local officials and citizens stymied efforts to combat discrimination and exclusion. Ickes's strategy of emphasizing economic relief as a prerequisite for social change often preempted more deliberate attempts to enforce racial equality, and without a broad base of public support among whites, he could do only so much to alleviate long-standing inequities. The PWA tried to implement public housing contracts that required a share of black laborers equal to the black proportion of the population recorded in the 1930 federal census, and black families occupied more than a third of the units constructed by the agency. But the hard realities on the ground in the South and elsewhere frequently fostered a lack of compliance and cooperation with Ickes's directives. For most blacks in need of relief or shelter, the result was something less than the revolution envisioned by the secretary and his outnumbered allies.[15]

ICKES shared the expansive view of racial justice espoused by Bethune, White, and Eleanor Roosevelt. But, as the Second New Deal took shape in 1935, this view showed no sign of gaining ground in American popular or political culture. The wholesale denigration of blacks remained a national pastime, rooted firmly in long-standing presumptions about race and society. Neither Ickes nor anyone else had found a way to convince white America that black citizens had anything to contribute other than menial labor and occasional moments of quaint or escapist entertainment. Few whites believed that blacks could successfully compete in any field, from show business to competitive sports to grand opera. They doubted that blacks could add anything significant to the nation's storehouse of intellectual or political capital, or to the high- or middle-brow culture that many Americans craved. Even some blacks, after a lifetime of being told that they were intellectually and culturally inferior, questioned their race's capacity to excel in the "higher" forms of art, theater, science, literature, sports, entertainment, and music.

Many others rejected the theory that their failure to make notable contributions in these areas was natural or innate. Yet that realization did not alter the relative position of blacks and whites in American life.[16]

No amount of talent, creativity, and hard work, it seemed, could overcome the obstacles of race. In a rigidly segregated society, black achievement did not lead to national, regional, or even local prominence. In the world of sports, for example, black athletes rarely competed against whites. The only significant exceptions were the Olympics, where three black Americans won medals at the 1932 games in Los Angeles; professional boxing; and a handful of college football, basketball, and track-and-field programs. As strange as it may seem to later generations, blacks could not imagine sports as a road to fame and fortune in the 1930s, when the "cult of the black athlete," to use sports historian John Hoberman's apt phrase, was not yet in vogue. The mainstream worlds of tennis, golf, and horse racing—where black jockeys had been banned since 1912—were lily-white, and in the popular sport of college football only five blacks played on predominantly white teams in 1935. No black football player had been named as a first-team all-American since 1923, and virtually all of the black talent in college football resided in all-black conferences unknown to the white press and public.[17]

Aside from boxers, black athletes did not participate in major professional sports. The National Football League, which had tolerated a smattering of black players during its first thirteen years, imposed a whites-only policy in 1934 that would last until 1946; and in professional basketball the black presence in 1935 was limited to two barnstorming teams, the New York Renaissance Big Five and the Harlem Globetrotters, and Hank Williams, who played center for the Buffalo Bisons in the fledgling Midwest Basketball Conference. Most important, the national pastime of baseball maintained a strict color bar that had been in force since the mid-1880s. Even the most talented black ballplayers had no choice but to spend their careers in the Negro National League, which white fans all but ignored and regarded as decidedly inferior to the major leagues. The best Negro League teams more than held their own in exhibition games against barnstorming white major leaguers, and a few black stars such as Satchel Paige and Josh Gibson drew considerable attention from the black press and earned handsome salaries. But white sportswriters routinely dismissed black baseball players as comic showboaters who lacked the intelligence, discipline, and training needed to compete at the highest level. Even Paige, who would later become an American folk hero, had little stature outside the black community at this point. In the Jim Crow context of the mid-1930s, occasional confrontations with barn-storming white sluggers were simply not enough to establish a reputation as one of the best pitchers in the game or to inspire the admiration of white fans.[18]

During the mid-1930s, the only professional sport that regularly fostered interracial competition was boxing. In January 1935, John Henry Lewis won the world light-heavyweight title, defeating the white fighter Bob Olin in a fifteen-round decision, and William "Gorilla" Jones and Henry "Homicide Hank" Armstrong were leading contenders in the middleweight and feather-weight divisions respectively. But in the heavyweight division, where most of the glory and the money was to be had, black boxers labored in the long shadow of Jack Johnson, the defiant and controversial champion of the pre–World War I era. Johnson's uncompromising assertions of privileged celebrity, including sexual dalliances with white women, had provoked white suprema-cist outrage on both sides of the Mason-Dixon Line. Consequently, no black heavyweight, including the great Harry Wills, had been permitted to fight for the heavyweight championship since Johnson lost his title to Jess Willard in 1915.

The restrictions on black heavyweights would eventually give way to the talent and mystique of Joe Louis, the "Brown Bomber" from Detroit. But in 1935 Louis was only in his second year as a professional. Despite his June 25 victory over the towering, Italian ex-champion Primo Carnera, which some observers saw as a symbolic triumph over Benito Mussolini's fascist ideology, Louis was not yet a national hero. The Johnson specter still troubled white America, and even after Louis's knockout of a second ex-champion, Max Baer, in late September, he had no guarantee of ever getting a shot at the title.[19]

A dearth of black celebrities and a disregard for black achievement ex-tended to virtually every aspect of American public life. Perhaps most obvi-ously, political office-holding at all but the lowest level was the exclusive province of whites. The lone exception was Arthur W. Mitchell, a Demo-cratic congressman from Chicago who in 1934 had defeated the three-term incumbent, Republican Oscar De Priest, the first black elected to Congress in the twentieth century. Elsewhere the white political monopoly held firm. In 1935, no blacks were senators, cabinet members, big-city mayors, gover-nors, or statewide officials of any kind. Nor were any blacks on the federal or state judicial bench. Indeed, in the professions, from medicine and engineer-ing to journalism and law, literally no blacks were in positions of national or even regional visibility. Readers of the *Chicago Defender*, the *Pittsburgh Courier*, the *Baltimore Afro-American*, and other black newspapers could find stories of black accomplishment in all of these fields. But the individuals featured in the black press had succeeded in the closed world of Jim Crow and were thus all but invisible to white Americans, who had little knowledge of what was going on inside black institutions.[20]

The same invisibility characterized the nation's leading black businessmen, none of whom appeared in mainstream accounts of economic enterprise. Similarly, in the field of art no works by contemporary African-American painters or sculptors graced the halls of the nation's major museums and galleries. In science, the only black researcher known outside the world of historically black colleges was George Washington Carver, the renowned Tuskegee botanist who had conducted experiments with peanut oil. And even his accomplishments were often downgraded as the work of an applied scientist rather than the work of a true genius advancing the frontiers of basic research. In other areas of academic life, black scholars fared even worse. With no hope of teaching at elite or predominantly white institutions, and with few opportunities to present their ideas in scholarly journals or even in popular magazines, blacks rarely participated in the major intellectual or policy debates of the day. Nearly all of their intellectual energy was spent addressing each other in black venues inaccessible to white Americans.[21]

In the world of literature, the Harlem Renaissance of the previous decade had produced a rash of memorable poetry and prose, as Jean Toomer, Langston Hughes, and others interpreted the black experience with style and probity. Yet no black writer in living memory had cracked the bestseller list or been considered for a major literary prize. In 1935, black literature was just that—literature written by and for blacks. Later in the decade and in the 1940s, Richard Wright and Zora Neale Hurston would attract a relatively broad range of readers, winning some respect from white critics. But, with the exception of the popular novelist Frank Yerby, neither they nor any other black writer of their era garnered a large audience outside the black community. Nor did they command sustained attention from the white academy. As late as 1955 the standard compendium of Southern literature, Willard Thorp's *A Southern Reader*, did not include a single line of fiction written by a black American. Only in a nonfiction section entitled "The Negro Speaks" and in a brief selection of "Negro Spirituals and Songs" did Thorp acknowledge the black experience. Even Ralph Ellison's 1952 novel, *Invisible Man*, destined to be a classic, escaped his attention.[22]

The situation was little better in the world of entertainment. For white

Americans, the realms of radio, film, and theater presented a dazzling array of popular idols, glittering stars, and cultural affirmation. But for black Americans, exposure in the popular media of the day invariably meant typecasting, marginalization, and cultural denigration. In the relatively new medium of radio, the only black stars in the mid-1930s were the heavily stylized characters of the wildly popular *Amos 'n' Andy* show. In 1935, radios could be found in 70 percent of American homes, and *Amos 'n' Andy* was the highest-rated show in the nation, drawing an estimated thirty to forty million listeners every evening. Freeman Gosden and Charles Correll, the voices of Amos and Andy, offered a steady stream of dialect and malapropisms as they represented two native Georgians who had migrated first to Chicago and later to Harlem. Following a culturally cued script that appealed to stereotypic conceptions of African-American life, the show drew its humor from a lampooning of black pretense, especially the foibles of Amos's and Andy's pompous friend George "the Kingfish" Stevens. While white listeners rolled with laughter at the comic adventures of Amos, Andy, and the Kingfish, blacks experienced yet another assault on the ideas of racial equality and black competence. The characterizations of race in *Amos 'n' Andy* generally lacked the mean-spirited hyperbole of the white supremacist caricatures fashionable in the minstrel shows of the early twentieth century. But although many whites "laughed with, not at" Amos and Andy, as one critic noted, the show did not alter the basic calculus of inequality.[23]

Blacks played a larger role in the film industry of the 1930s. Yet here, too, their celebrity did little to dispel notions of black inferiority. As the film historian Donald Bogle has written, on-screen the 1930s was "the Age of the Negro Servant." With the advent of talking pictures, "Hollywood had found a new place for the Negro—in the kitchens, the laundry rooms, and the pantries." Black actors had more work than ever before, and the stock character of the black domestic was raised to an art form by talented men and women such as Stepin Fetchit, Louise Beavers, Hattie McDaniel, Mantan Moreland, Willie Best, and Clarence Muse. With rolling eyes and foolish grins, they shuffled their way through some of the most popular films of the mid-1930s, including *It Happened One Night, Stand Up and Cheer, Belle of the Nineties, Steamboat 'Round the Bend, Little Miss Marker, The Littlest Rebel,* and *The Little Colonel.* The last two of these films, both released in 1935, featured the interracial duo of Shirley Temple, the nation's most beloved child star, and Bill "Bojangles" Robinson, a celebrated tap dancer from Richmond, Virginia, who had been playing Uncle Tom roles since the late 1920s. As Temple's faithful servant and guardian in Old South melodramas, Robinson became an iconic symbol of "moonlight and magnolias" nostalgia, much to the dismay of black leaders who longed for more progressive representations of black virtue.

Blacks who regarded Robinson's fame with ambivalence found Stepin Fetchit's celebrity even more troubling. The only true black movie star in Hollywood, the Florida-born Fetchit appeared in twenty-six films from 1929 to 1935, always playing a slow-witted, stammering, head-scratching "coon." As one of Fox Pictures' biggest moneymakers, he lived a lavish lifestyle that belied his bowing and scraping on-screen. Film magazines and Fox press releases dazzled movie fans, white and black, with tales of Fetchit's six houses, twelve cars, sixteen Chinese servants, and two-thousand-dollar cashmere suits. The first black celebrity whose excesses rivaled those of white movie stars, he enjoyed a high-rolling career that depended on the perpetuation of demeaning racial images that almost certainly deepened white contempt for black Americans.[24]

During these years, black actors had few opportunities to reach white moviegoers with images and performances that challenged conventional views of racial difference. One of the rare exceptions was *Imitation of Life*, a critically acclaimed 1934 film about interracial cooperation and intergenerational conflict amid the hard times of the Great Depression. Starring Claudette Colbert and two talented black actresses, Louise Beavers and Fredi Washington, the film tells the story of two widows, one black and one white, who move in together in a joint effort to save their daughters from the clutches of poverty. Beavers, as Aunt Delilah, develops a homemade pancake mix that Colbert, as Miss Bea, markets to the public. Both women become prosperous but ultimately suffer disappointments as their daughters make bad choices. Washington, as Delilah's light-skinned daughter, Peola, tries to pass for white, explaining, "Mama, I want the same things in life that other people enjoy." In the end, following Delilah's death, Peola recognizes the error of her ways and closes the film weeping next to her mother's casket.[25]

White critics hailed *Imitation of Life* as a breakthrough film that recognized the dignity and humanity of the black race. But the film literally and figuratively communicated mixed messages about the realities of race, class, and color. Other Depression-era films, created by blacks for blacks, offered clearer alternatives to traditional racial stereotypes. Yet few, if any, whites ever saw them. Bringing realistic images of black culture to a mainstream white audience was all but impossible during these years, and nothing demonstrates this sad truth better than the film career of Paul Robeson. For nearly a decade Robeson had been a towering figure on the theater and concert stages of London and New York, but when he turned to film, he experienced frustration after frustration. Having developed both a deep appreciation for African culture and a radicalized political vision that clashed with complacent American pieties, he looked to movies as a means of inculcating a new respect for historical and contemporary black achievements. By 1935, he had appeared in a half dozen films, mostly in Europe, all of which showcased his talents without advancing his political and cultural agenda. His performance in the cinematic version of Eugene O'Neill's *Emperor Jones* (1933) came closest to what he had hoped to find in the film industry, but most critics and moviegoers came away with more fear than respect for the homicidal Brutus Jones, an imprisoned Pullman porter who kills a chain-gang guard and escapes to Jamaica, where he becomes a brutal autocrat. Two years later, Robeson starred in *Sanders of the River*, a British film that promised to portray colonial Africans as the dignified and resourceful heirs of a rich cultural heritage. But when the film was actually released, Robeson and everyone else realized that the final cut simply dramatized "the sacredness of British colonial rule," as one critic put it. According to an admiring reviewer in the London *Times*, the film offered "a grand insight into our special English difficulties in the governing of savage races."[26]

Robeson made six more films during the next seven years, including the popular musical *Show Boat* in 1936. But he later confessed that he took no pride in any of his cinematic ventures. He felt much more comfortable in the theatrical world, where he had first gained fame in the early 1920s. Yet even on the stage, he and other black actors found few opportunities to educate whites about the myths and realities of black America. Both on and off Broadway, predominantly white audiences flocked to a series of black-themed plays and musicals during the early and mid-1930s, including *Blackbirds of 1930*, *Shuffle Along*, *Show Boat*, and *Fast and Furious*. All of these productions demonstrated a range of black talent, but the roles and scripts that captivated Depression-era audiences rarely deviated from the romantic racialism that had dominated black theatrics since the early days of minstrel shows and vaudeville. While singing, dancing, and smiling blacks were welcome, the financial constraints and cultural traditions of the American theater precluded dramatic representations of black striving or achievement, except in minor or foreign venues. Robeson's extraordinary success with Shakespeare's *Othello* in 1930–31 took place in London and did not cross the Atlantic. And the 1935 New York production of *Stevedore*, in which he played Lonnie Thompson, a black laborer who narrowly escapes a lynch mob after being falsely accused of rape, closed after a brief run.[27]

BLACK contributions to serious drama received little attention or respect in white America. But in the theater and other places of popular amusement, whites readily acknowledged the musical talent of black Americans. Since the early days of ragtime and jazz at the turn of the century, black singers, dancers, and musicians had entertained black and white audiences in a wide variety of clubs and concert halls. As early as the 1870s, the Fisk Jubilee Singers of Nashville, Tennessee, conducted extended tours featuring Negro spirituals, attracting national and international attention. In the turn-of-the-century heyday of vaudeville and minstrel shows, black musicians gained increasing visibility, and by the 1920s a few had even achieved something akin to celebrity status. In the world of jazz, blues, and popular music, Joe "King" Oliver, Jelly Roll Morton, Bessie Smith, Ethel Waters, Louis Armstrong, and the pianists Earl "Fatha" Hines and Fats Waller were an important part of the scene. Some, such as Alberta Hunter and Josephine Baker, spent most of their careers as expatriates and were better known in Europe than in the United States. But most remained in America despite the burdens of racial condescension and Jim Crow. With the emergence of swing and big-band music in the early 1930s, the list of black musical stars expanded to include bandleaders Edward "Duke" Ellington, William "Count" Basie, and Chick Webb, one of the era's most acclaimed drummers. And later in the decade they were joined by John "Dizzy" Gillespie, Cab Calloway, the jazz vibraphonist Lionel Hampton, and singers Ella Fitzgerald and Billie Holiday.

Jazz singers and musicians were among the most famous blacks in America during the Great Depression. Blacks and whites alike admired, mimicked, and even loved them. Only Joe Louis, Stepin Fetchit, Amos and Andy, and the flamboyant black preacher Father Divine enjoyed a higher public profile. Yet their rising fame and celebrity had surprisingly little impact on white supremacist mores and the standard critiques of black culture. Many whites, and some middle-class blacks, regarded jazz and blues musicians with a strong undertone of condescension. Grounded in time-honored distinctions between highbrow and lowbrow culture, and between superior and inferior races, popular black music was the music of the back alley and the street, or at best the dance hall. While it was fun to listen or dance to and merited a measure of admiration, black musical achievement lost most of its stature when interpreted through the lens of romantic racialism. Black musicians were simply doing what came naturally, re-creating the primitive rhythms and melodies of the African jungle or the Old South. Blacks were born to dance and sing and shout, whites told themselves without any sense of irony or concern. The music was exotic and alluring, but beautiful voices singing bluesy compositions and trumpet players playing heart-stopping solos did little or nothing to disturb traditional notions of racial and cultural hierarchy. For some whites, popular music actually reinforced the sense of racial difference, providing blacks with an acceptable but tightly defined outlet for creativity. Certainly it was preferable to black success in other areas of American life, such as politics, business, the professions, and competitive sports. For the social order to remain intact, blacks had to know their place, and the world of popular music was one of the places where they allegedly belonged.[28]

Classical music, however, was another matter altogether. Even among those who knew little about the intricacies of classical music, the genre had a certain mystique. Mastery of classical technique required superior intelligence, discipline, and years of training. The world of classical music was the province not only of natural talent but of cultivated genius. Here the barriers to black achievement were thought to be both cultural and physiological. Conventional wisdom held that blacks did things naturally and impulsively without much thought or deliberation. Classical music, by contrast, was intellectual, highbrow, and European in origin. As such, it was deemed inappropriate for African Americans three or four generations removed from the jungles of Africa. Black success in the world of classical music would be tantamount to beating whites at their own game, something that could not be tolerated or even contemplated in white supremacist circles. It would represent an affront to white sensibilities, upsetting expectations based on multiple layers of observation and socialization. Most white Americans had never encountered a major black composer, opera singer, or virtuoso violinist. Indeed, one suspects that few whites could even imagine such a thing.

In reality, notwithstanding the currents of racial prejudice and condescension that diminished the achievements of black musicians, the actual number of black contributions to classical music should have given whites pause. Elizabeth Taylor Greenfield (1824–76), a Mississippi-born slave adopted as an infant by a family of Philadelphia Quakers, drew rave reviews from music critics during a career that spanned the Civil War. Dubbed the Black

Swan, Greenfield mastered a twenty-seven-note range that she demonstrated in scores of concerts in England and the northeastern United States. Her 1853 New York City debut in Metropolitan Hall drew several thousand listeners, even though black patrons were barred from the hall. During the 1860s and 1870s, she operated a Philadelphia music studio that supported an all-black opera troupe. But her early death at the age of fifty-two curtailed both her career and a local black classical tradition that would not recover until Marian Anderson's emergence a half century later.

Though less well-known, the Hyers sisters, Anna and Emma, enjoyed considerable popularity during the 1870s, first in their hometown of Sacramento, California, and later in a string of Western and Midwestern cities where they sang either in tandem or as the leads in choral and theatrical productions. Other notable black singers of the Gilded Age included Nellie Brown of New Hampshire, a soprano best known in New England but who also performed recitals in Baltimore and Washington, and Marie Selika (Williams) (1849–1937), a gifted coloratura soprano who gained a reputation as "the queen of staccato" and who even sang at the White House in 1878 during the administration of President Rutherford B. Hayes. Like Greenfield and Brown, Selika struggled against racial discrimination and never received her full due as an artist. The White House invitation, the first ever to a black singer, provided a measure of hope for aspiring black artists, and Selika later delivered a command performance for Queen Victoria in 1883. But, sadly, neither the rave reviews from Buckingham Palace nor the fleeting triumph at the White House had any noticeable impact on a color bar that kept the nation's opera houses lily-white until long after her retirement in 1916. Confined to Jim Crow theaters and vaudeville halls, Selika's extraordinary voice never reached the ears of mainstream America.[29]

Gilded Age America was more receptive to a curious figure known as Blind Tom, the most celebrated and successful black musician of his day. Born on a plantation near Columbus, Georgia, Thomas Greene Bethune (1849–1908) was an ex-slave and child prodigy who dazzled audiences with his sightless piano performances. Though his vocabulary was reportedly a hundred words or less, Blind Tom learned to play approximately seven thousand pieces of music from memory. This made him one of the wonders of the Gilded Age and attracted fans as sophisticated as Mark Twain. Unfortunately, his classification as an idiot savant left him well outside the classical mainstream. Other nineteenth-century black composers and musicians such as the Louisiana Creoles Edmond Dédé (1827–1903) and Charles Lucien

Lambert Sr. (1828–96), and the Virginia-born classical guitarist Justin Holland (1819–87), generally avoided classification as freakish oddities. But—with the exception of Holland, who published two bestselling guitar manuals in the 1870s—their popularity remained limited and regional in scope; relatively few whites, then or later, had any awareness of their talents and ambitions.[30]

The best black classical musicians and composers of the next generation fared little better. In the 1880s, the aspiring black violinist and composer Will Marion Cook (1869–1944) studied music at Oberlin College before becoming a protégé of the great Czech composer Antonin Dvorak. Cook took Dvorak's suggestions to heart, grounding his African-American "nationalist" compositions in traditional European musical forms such as symphonies, art songs, and marches. But his eventual collaborations with the poet Paul Lawrence Dunbar and minstrel stars such as Bert Williams led him away from the world of classical music. In 1919, his New York Syncopated Orchestra gave a command performance before King George V, though there was nothing classical about the "Negro songs" that delighted the king and his court. Harry T. Burleigh (1866–1949)—Dvorak's personal assistant and close collaborator, and later Marian Anderson's mentor and friend—had more success than Cook in tying his "race music" to a classical tradition. But he, too, failed to achieve full acceptance among the arbiters of classical taste and convention, even after Dvorak proclaimed "Go Down, Moses" to be every bit as "great as a Beethoven melody."[31]

During the early twentieth century, most African Americans with classical training eventually looked elsewhere for professional fulfillment after discovering that careers within the classical music establishment were essentially closed to them. Despite years of classical training, talented musicians such as R. Nathaniel Dett (1882–1943), the choral director of the Hampton Institute from 1913 to 1932, William Levi Dawson (1898–1990), the longtime director of the Tuskegee Institute Choir, and the New Jersey–born James Price Johnson (1891–1955), the master of stride piano and composer of the 1921 jazz classic "Carolina Shout," turned to semiclassical and popular genres for their livelihood. Some, such as Dawson, tried to keep at least one foot in the classical world, but such efforts invariably drew more condescension than respect. In 1934 the Philadelphia Orchestra performed the premiere of Dawson's *Negro Folk Symphony*, but even the white critics who praised the symphony's "dramatic feeling" and "racial sensuousness" were reluctant to acknowledge it as a serious piece of classical music.[32]

Florence Beatrice Price (1887–1953), who left her native Little Rock to study at the prestigious New England Conservatory of Music, was one of the few black composers who remained committed to the classical mainstream, and in 1932 her *Symphony in E Minor* took top honors in the Wanamaker "Negro Artists" competition. In 1933, the Chicago Symphony Orchestra performed her prize-winning symphony at the Chicago World's Fair. But this proved to be the end rather than the beginning of a promising career. During the last twenty years of her life, no major orchestra showed any interest in her work.[33]

Price's contemporary William Grant Still (1895–1978) fared somewhat better, living long enough to become the acknowledged "dean" of African-American composers. Born in Woodville, Mississippi, and raised in Little Rock, Still studied both at Oberlin and the New England Conservatory before apprenticing himself to the modernist master Edgard Varèse. In 1931, the Rochester Philharmonic Orchestra premiered Still's *Symphony no. 1 "Afro-American,"* the first black composition to be performed by a regional symphony orchestra. Five years later he conducted the Los Angeles Philharmonic Orchestra, making him the first African American to wield a baton in front of a major American orchestra. Nevertheless, he remained a marginal figure in the classical world for at least another decade. Throughout the 1930s and early 1940s, he was known primarily as an arranger and staff composer of popular music for WNBC and WCBS radio. At the same time, his habit of including adaptations of W. C. Handy and George Gershwin in his classical compositions undercut his image as a serious composer. Only in the late 1940s, after Leopold Stokowski praised him as "one of our greatest American composers," did Still begin to receive anything approaching proper recognition.[34]

The hybrid quality of Still's music was hardly unique, of course. The practice of adapting folk melodies and popular tunes had a long history in classical music, predating and foreshadowing the "nationalist" motifs embodied in Dvorak's *New World* symphony. This was true in both Europe and the United States and was especially evident in the colonial societies of the Caribbean and South America. Among colonial black composers, incorporating racial and folk themes into classical European forms became a dominant, almost irresistible tradition. The earliest black composers—Ignatius Sancho (1729–80), who was born on a slave ship bound for Colombia and who later worked as a house slave in Greenwich, England, and Joseph de Bologne, aka the Chevalier de Saint-Georges (1745–99), a Guadeloupe-born mulatto who became the toast of Parisian musical circles in the late 1770s as a violinist and composer of sonatas and concertos—were orthodox musicians who downplayed their racial and colonial heritage. But later figures, such as the Afro-Brazilian composer and organist José Mauricio Nunes Garcia (1767–1830), the Afro-Cuban violinists José Silvestre White (1835–1918) and Amadeo Roldán (1900–39), and the great Haitian pianist/composers Occide Jeanty (1860–1936), Ludovic Lamothe (1882–1953), and Justin Elie (1883–1931), infused their music with colonial exoticism. Haiti alone produced as many as sixty classical composers during the nineteenth and twentieth centuries. Most, of course, attracted little attention beyond their native land. Like other artists of the international African diaspora, they were virtually unknown in the United States, even among African-American musicians. By the 1930s, many Americans had acquired at least a passing familiarity with African percussion, Latin syncopation, and Negro spirituals. But few had any inkling that black composers, domestic or foreign, had put these elements to good use in classical compositions.[35]

Black operatic performers were somewhat more visible than black composers. Yet they too languished on or beyond the margins of American music. All-black opera companies dated back to 1872, when the Colored American Opera Company was founded in Washington, and during the half century following Reconstruction, scores of promising operatic singers trained to sing at the highest level. Unfortunately, such artists found relatively few opportunities to sing in black productions, and no opportunities at all to perform with the nation's white opera companies. Unlike the worlds of jazz and blues, the classical world showed few signs of liberalization during the early twentieth century. For black opera singers, the best, and in many cases the only, options during this era of Jim Crow and ethnocentrism were church, choral, and theatrical music. Singing opera on a grand scale was essentially foreclosed for black singers until the late 1920s, when a few individuals found employment with European opera companies. The first to do so was the coloratura soprano Lillian Evanti (1890–1967), a Howard University graduate who began singing with the Nice Opera Company in 1927 and who later performed in *La Traviata, Rigoletto*, and *Romeo and Juliet*. Caterina Jarboro (1903–86), a Wilmington, North Carolina, native trained in France and Italy, followed Evanti's lead in 1930 when she sang the lead role in *Aida* at the Puccini Opera House in Milan. Three years later, she made history by performing the same role with the Chicago Opera, the first major American opera company willing to hire a black singer.

Jarboro and others hoped that this groundbreaking performance would prompt a general suspension of the unofficial color bar in American opera.

But old ways died hard. The other leading black sopranos of the day—Abbie Mitchell, Florence Cole Talbert, Anne Brown, and Etta Moten—waited in vain for invitations to sing in mainstream opera productions. Even Roland Hayes, Anderson's dear friend and mentor, widely recognized as one of the world's great tenors, could not find work on the American operatic stage. Todd Duncan (1903–98), the great baritone and the first to sing the role of Porgy in George Gershwin's *Porgy and Bess* in 1935, was the first black male to sing with a major American opera company. But his debut with the New York City Opera did not come until 1945. In the years that followed, the New York City Opera would become a haven for black opera singers. Yet its cross-town rival, the Metropolitan Opera, the greatest of all American opera companies, did not lower its color bar until 1955, when Anderson sang a minor role in Verdi's *Ballo in Maschera*.[36]

Anderson's debut at the Met came at a special moment, a time of hope and renewal sandwiched between the landmark *Brown* school-desegregation decision of May 1954 and the yearlong boycott triggered by Rosa Parks's refusal to give up her seat on a Montgomery, Alabama, bus in December 1955. Twenty years earlier, at the depths of the Great Depression, the situation was decidedly different for a young black woman looking for success outside the narrow world of Jim Crow. Anderson had already proven that the barriers of racial prejudice could be breached in many parts of Europe, even in the face of rising totalitarianism. But those same barriers remained all but inviolate in her own country. For all its faults, the United States in 1935 did not have jackbooted dictators or a looming Holocaust. Yet, in its own way, America was a deeply troubled society that rivaled Nazi Germany in its racial fixations and fantasies. Though masked by a national creed of democracy and freedom, these racist pathologies posed enormous challenges to any person of "color" seeking to cross the deep rivers of discrimination and segregation that defined the boundaries of African-American identity and ambition.

The American race problem was political and economic, but it was also cultural and even psychological. Before whites could envision blacks as fellow citizens deserving a full complement of rights and respectful attention, they had to see them as fully developed human beings. In the intellectual world, the relativist revolution begun by the anthropologist Franz Boas and others had already eroded the presumptions of black inferiority. But in the wider world of public opinion and popular culture, the time-honored shibboleths of white supremacy still held sway. The persistence of racism was most obvious in the white South, where political demagogues such as Theodore Bilbo and Eugene Talmadge touted the virtues of the "Southern way of life" and fulminated against those who doubted that the Negro's God-given "place" was at the bottom of society. Yet, in a somewhat subtler form, racist attitudes also dominated popular thought and behavior in the white North. Such attitudes did not go unchallenged in either region, but the forces of racial tolerance awaited a general cultural awakening that would put white supremacist institutions and values on the defensive.

In some quarters, the rise of race-based anti-Semitism in Nazi Germany had discredited any ideology based on racial prejudice, prompting a reformulation of America's commitment to democratic principles of inclusion. But, for most Americans, the philosophical connection between totalitarian intolerance and American bigotry would remain vague until the closing weeks of World War II, when the full horror of the Holocaust was revealed. In the mid-1930s, most whites, North and South, practiced racial discrimination without much sense of the damage that they were inflicting upon their black neighbors. They did so, in part, because they did not believe that proper race relations could be based on anything other than an ordered hierarchy of ability, accomplishment, and character. While most whites had some awareness of the negative effects of racial prejudice, they believed that blacks were at the bottom because they deserved to be there.

One way to break this Gordian knot of racial stasis, some argued, was through a combination of economic uplift and educational progress. This was the gospel of Booker T. Washington, to which many Americans, black and white, paid tribute. An alternative model of racial progress, associated with W. E. B. Du Bois and many other civil rights activists, emphasized political mobilization and protest. Unfortunately, after several decades of hard work and agitation, neither of these strategies had achieved fundamental change, much less broken the Gordian knot. This failure had multiple causes, but one critical reason was the inability of black leaders to find a way to gain whites' respect without making the dominant race feel uncomfortable or threatened. Time and again, signs of racial progress backfired as whites interpreted black success as a personal threat or as an assault on social order. The response was either white supremacist violence or the mobilization of enough political and economic power to keep blacks in their place, or in many cases a combination of the two.

The second critical factor crippling black leaders was their failure to convince the American public that racism was a stain on the national honor and a threat to the realization of American democracy. As long as racism could be explained away as a regional peculiarity—as something that plagued Mississippi and Alabama, but not mainstream America—the idea that the national government had a responsibility to correct the situation lacked urgency and legitimacy. The full activation of this responsibility was decades away, but to get there civil rights advocates needed a starting point, some dramatic event that would point the nation in the right direction. For a time, it appeared that sports, which yielded national heroes such as Jesse Owens and Joe Louis, might provide such a moment. But, as much as athletic exploits helped, the seminal event, when it finally materialized in 1939, occurred not in the ring or on the playing field but rather at the Lincoln Memorial, where a single voice became a clarion call for freedom.[37]

MARIAN Anderson was well aware that she had deep rivers to cross. But with Hurok's encouragement she decided to return to her native land in late 1935, not as a "race" singer but as an American. The hearth of a close and nurturing family drew her home. Yet, as she later insisted, "The family was not all. There were other people to be considered—all the friends and neighbors who had believed in me. They had not helped me and had faith in me just to see me run away to Europe. I had gone to Europe to achieve something, to reach for a place as a serious artist, but I never doubted that I must return. I was—and am—an American." By that self-definition she did not mean a second-class American. Somehow, in her quiet but determined way, she had come to believe that she and others of her race deserved first-class citizenship and a full measure of opportunity.[38]

Even so, she must have realized that the odds were heavily against her. Roland Hayes—who had become a popular concert performer despite his operatic frustrations—was her model. But, as she knew all too well, Hayes had endured decades of disappointment before receiving his due from white critics and concertgoers. Having already had her share of disappointment, she could only hope that racial mores had changed enough to allow an easier transition to the wider arena of the mainstream American concert stage. The American concert hall circuit, where most of the patrons and virtually all of the artists were white, represented a great unknown to Anderson. Could she really do what no other black female performer had ever attempted? Could a black woman from Philadelphia win the admiration and respect of white Americans, many of whom, she suspected, would shrink from acknowledging her full humanity or even letting her pass through their front door? Was mainstream America ready for someone like her, a black woman singing predominantly "white" music? Was there another America, an emergent nation of justice and equality, that would judge her on the basis of merit without regard to race or skin color? If the answers to these questions turned out to be no, she could forgo her highest ambitions and still make a decent living performing at black colleges and churches; and she always had the option of returning to Europe, where she was already an established star. But as a matter of personal pride she was determined to challenge the traditional restrictions of a race-conscious nation.[39]

The chances of success, and the underlying likelihood of change, were unclear as Anderson, at the age of thirty-eight, prepared for the most ambitious American tour in the history of classical black artistry. Brandishing Anderson's European press clippings and Toscanini's endorsement, Hurok had put together a nine-week tour consisting of fifteen concerts in fifteen cities, primarily in the Northeast. The tour included a stop in Washington and two concerts in the Deep South, one in Atlanta and a second in Tuskegee. Leaving as little as possible to chance, Hurok had carefully selected venues and had prepared the way with clever press releases emphasizing Anderson's recent acclaim. MARIAN ANDERSON RETURNS TO NATIVE LAND FRESH FROM EUROPEAN TRIUMPHS, a planted *New York Age* headline proclaimed on December 14. "Still blessed with the modesty and simplicity of manner that so ingratiated her to church audiences as a young girl," the *Age* assured its readers, "Marian Anderson returns . . . with honors unprecedented in musical history." Anderson herself recoiled from such Horatio Alger–style hyperbole, but Hurok knew what he was doing. By the time his client arrived in America, the stage was set for a celebration of talent and virtue that transcended race.[40]

The first stop was New York's Town Hall, where Anderson performed on December 30. Ten years earlier Town Hall had been the scene of Anderson's first public humiliation at the hands of New York's fearsome critics. But there would be no humiliation this time. Singing to a full house, with one ankle still in a cast, she rose above her nervousness, and her injury, to deliver a stunning performance. "Let it be said at the outset: Marian Anderson has returned to her native land one of the great singers of our time," the critic Howard Taubman wrote in the *New York Times*. "The Negro contralto who has been abroad for four years established herself in her concert at the Town Hall last night as the possessor of an excelling voice and art . . . There was no doubt of it, she was mistress of all she surveyed." A discerning critic who later ghostwrote Anderson's autobiography, Taubman expressed his admiration not only for "a contralto of stunning range and volume, managed with suppleness and grace," but also for an extraordinary depth of feeling. "Miss Anderson has the transcending quality of all authentic art," he insisted, "a genuine emotional identification with the core of music . . . It was music-making that probed too deep for words." In closing, Taubman urged his readers to embrace Anderson as a national treasure: "In the last four years Europe has acclaimed this tall, handsome girl. It is time for her own country to honor her, for she bears gifts that are not to be feared. Born of poor parents in Philadelphia, Miss Anderson has made something of her natural endowment. If Joe Louis deserves to be an American hero for bowling over a lot of pushovers, then Marian Anderson has the right to at least a comparable standing. Handel, Schubert and Sibelius are not pushovers."[41]

Taubman did not ground his praise in romantic racialism. But several of the critics present at the Town Hall concert could not resist characterizing Anderson as a "colored" artist. "Her voice is of amazing richness with that magnetic quality so often found in her race," Henriette Weber wrote in the *New York Journal*. Samuel Chotzinoff, writing in the *New York Post*, went a bit further, praising her racial gifts while criticizing perceived lapses of natural behavior. "Miss Anderson has the emotional intensity of her race," Chotzinoff observed, "from which the voice catches fire, and which colors every word she enunciates. It may be that the lapses in taste so frequently exhibited by white singers are due to their assumptions of feelings they do not actually experience. The Negro, on the other hand, easily and naturally identifies himself or herself with every variety of poetic emotion, and the identification is so absolute that there can be no room for false sentiment. If Miss Anderson failed at several points in her recital to do justice to a song it was only because she abandoned her instincts and trusted to her head."

Such racial condescension was not the response that Anderson had hoped for, but she was heartened by the few commentators who managed to look beyond traditional stereotypes. B. H. Haggin, the music critic of the *New York Daily Eagle*, complained that Town Hall was too small to accommodate "all those who should have been there, the millions of white Southerners who regard the Negro as an innately inferior being fit for nothing better than exploitation as a beast of burden." To Haggin, Anderson's performance "proved again that the Negro is blessed with the same innate endowment, the same capacities as the white man, and that thereafter he can be brutalized by the treatment he receives from the South, or can be made into a great singer and artist, with all that this implies in depth and richness and subtlety of feeling." W. J. Henderson, the music critic for the *New York Sun*, offered a somewhat more ambiguous judgment: "She is a singer of whom her race may well be proud, in spite of the indisputable fact that there is not a trace of the mannerisms of her people in her singing."

The critics' tendency to infuse musical criticism with racial commentary troubled Anderson. But, on balance, she was pleased with the response to the Town Hall concert. Not only did the critics praise her voice and showmanship; to her relief, they also regarded her white accompanist, Kosti Vehanen, as a welcome addition to the American concert stage. No critic, nor anyone else in the audience for that matter, expressed any objection whatsoever to his presence. Despite the unprecedented match of a black singer with a white pianist, there was no organized boycott, and no one walked out in protest. On the contrary, the demand for tickets was so great that Hurok scrambled to schedule a second New York concert at Carnegie Hall on January 20.[42]

The only thing that marred Anderson's return to the American stage, other than her broken ankle, was an ugly incident that occurred the day before the Town Hall concert. A white friend who was absent from the city had graciously offered Anderson the use of her suite at the fashionable Algonquin Hotel. But, unfortunately, she had failed to notify the management ahead of time. When Anderson showed up at the hotel, the desk clerk nearly turned her away because of her race. In typical fashion, Anderson shrugged off the "cool reception," maintaining her dignity in the face of callous prejudice. But the incident confirmed that the spirit of Jim Crow was alive and well, even in a cosmopolitan city such as New York.[43]

In mid-January, as Anderson prepared for her Carnegie Hall concert, admiring profiles appeared in *Time* and the *New Yorker*. Both articles praised Anderson, giving her valuable national exposure, but they did so with more than a hint of racialist presumption. "One Viennese critic described her as 'a black Lilli Lehmann,'" the *Time* critic pointed out. "That she is not. But she is an exciting, sure-voiced singer who would make any race proud." Under the title "Dark Contralto," the *New Yorker* described Anderson's voice as "the latest sensation of the musical world," but went on to emphasize her physical characteristics as a Northern Negress: "She has coffee-colored skin, black hair, wide-set eyes, a large and mobile mouth. There's no trace of a Southern Negro accent in her voice."[44]

Anderson, despite her determination to excel in a classical European genre, made no effort to downplay her racial identity. While she did not want to be typecast as a singer of Negro spirituals, she was proud of her black heritage, especially her close personal connection to the black community of Philadelphia. The second stop on her 1936 tour, a homecoming concert held at the Academy of Music on January 16, attracted a capacity crowd dominated by black Philadelphians eager to embrace one of their own. Sponsored by the black sorority Alpha Kappa Alpha, Anderson's recital drew an emotional response from the audience, and from several Philadelphia music critics, who reported that the woman who had dazzled European audiences with songs sung in German and Swedish was still Marian of Martin Street. "She returns an artist of rare distinction to be ranked not only with those two other famous American singers of her race, Roland Hayes and Paul Robeson, but with any of the great American artists of our time," Edwin Schloss of the *Philadelphia Record* acknowledged. Yet he and other local critics seemed relieved that she was still at her best singing spirituals. "In the songs of her people the singer came into her own superbly," Schloss observed, adding, "You will not hear Negro spirituals often sung as Miss Anderson sings them, beautiful in their proud humility—never vulgarized—rich with the ring of native authenticity." Another critic, writing in the *Philadelphia Bulletin*, suggested that Anderson's rendition of lieder songs was too refined for an audience that had come to hear her sing familiar melodies in English. Only with the spirituals and with a closing encore of "Home Sweet Home," he insisted, did the crowd's emotional intensity match the high expectations raised by Anderson's long-awaited homecoming.[45]

The notion that Anderson was both an international star and an unspoiled, unpretentious, working-class girl from South Philadelphia was crucial to Hurok's promotional strategy. Put simply, he wanted to appeal to America's traditional deference to European high culture without sacrificing Anderson's identification with hard work and humble origins. Trumpeting her accomplishments without provoking the traditional fear of "uppity Negroes" required a careful balancing of themes related to race, class, and culture. Accordingly, Hurok's widely distributed press releases stressed the "fairly tale" quality of Anderson's life, a saga of luck and pluck that took her from childhood poverty to international acclaim with no loss of modesty and humility along the way. This moral tale had special resonance during the Great Depression, and many editors and reporters responded just as Hurok hoped they would.

Three days after the homecoming concert, on the eve of the Carnegie

Hall recital, the *Philadelphia Record* ran a feature story on Anderson under the headlines AT HOME IN MARTIN STREET OR IN PARIS and WORLD ACCLAIM FAILS TO KILL NEGRO SINGER'S LOVE FOR HOME, NEIGHBORS AND SIMPLE LIFE. "All the plaudits of Europe and America have not changed her," the *Record* reported. On the same day, the *Brooklyn Eagle* published an admiring profile by Irving Kolodin entitled AN ANDERSON FAIRY TALE, and two days later, in a *New York Herald Tribune* review of the Carnegie Hall recital, the noted music critic Lawrence Gilman expounded on the ennobling legend of Marian Anderson: "Miss Anderson is the sort of person, the sort of artist, about whom legends gather. As a child she lived with her family in a single room in the Negro quarter of South Philadelphia, and her mother took in washing. Today she is called a priestess of lyric art, and her selflessness and consecration are compared with those of a few transcendent artists . . . No one can see and listen to Miss Anderson for two minutes without realizing that one is in the presence of an artist of extraordinary devotion, intensity, and self-effacement. Her poise, her simplicity, her spiritual transparence, the mood of exaltation that enwraps her, are immediately influential upon all who sit before her."[46]

Fairy tale or not, Anderson's life took an almost magical turn at Carnegie Hall. The January 20, 1936, concert was not her first appearance on America's most celebrated concert stage. She had performed there on four occasions between 1921 and 1930, twice as a supporting artist and twice as a featured soloist. To her dismay, the solo performances had drawn less than capacity crowds and decidedly mixed reviews that faulted her interpretation of German lieder, which, according to one reviewer, were "considerably beyond Miss Anderson's imaginative and emotional scope." Six years later, buttressed by Hurok's publicity campaign, the recent triumph at Town Hall, and the plaudits of several seasons in Europe, Anderson received an entirely different reception. The hall was packed, the audience responded to her performance with unbridled enthusiasm, and admiring critics anointed her one of the greatest artists of the day.

Success at this level was a milestone that few black artists had dared to contemplate. As recently as December, Anderson had sung in several of Europe's grandest concert halls, but the Carnegie Hall concert was different. This was America, where the top rung of virtually every institution was reserved for whites, and where Carnegie Hall was indisputably the top rung of classical venues. Opened in 1891, the acoustically perfect hall had showcased some of the world's finest musicians and composers, from Tchaikovsky and

Dvorak to Gershwin and Rachmaninoff, while serving as the home of the venerable New York Philharmonic. Any performance at Carnegie Hall was sure to attract a celebrity-laden audience, and Anderson's 1936 recital was no exception. The crowd included movie stars such as Katharine Hepburn and Gloria Swanson and scores of other celebrities, all of whom seemed to revel in Anderson's triumph. Other black artists had performed at Carnegie Hall over the years, but seldom as soloists or featured performers, and never with the advance billing that Anderson enjoyed. Less than a month after her return to the United States, she had reached the top of the American concert world.[47]

The remainder of the 1936 tour brought a string of successes. After completing several recording sessions for Victor Records in late January and early February, Anderson sang before capacity crowds in Chicago, Utica, Atlanta, Tuskegee, and Hampton, Virginia. At Tuskegee and Hampton, and in Atlanta, where she performed at the Spelman College chapel, the audiences were overwhelmingly black. But both the Chicago and Utica concerts attracted predominantly white audiences. In Utica, where a large number of students from nearby Colgate and Hamilton Colleges attended the concert, the local press reported, with a measure of amazement, that Anderson "sings without a trace of an accent and her vocabulary is much above average." Following the Chicago concert, which drew four thousand music fans despite frigid, subzero conditions, white critics raved about the "flawless beauty" and "radiant sonority" of her voice, which *Chicago American* music writer Herman Devries pronounced "undisputedly the greatest contralto of the hour."

Neota Dyett, the music critic of the black *Chicago Defender*, agreed, characterizing Anderson's voice as "indescribable." "Miss Anderson," Dyett pointed out, with considerable pride, "has not been content with her unusual talent, but has developed scholarly musicianship and an artistry that is unsurpassable, and of which the race in general should be proud. Her German lieder, especially as displayed in the Schubert group, was something which should have compelled the admiration of the most discerning critic." At the same time, Dyett reassured her readers that Anderson remained a loyal race woman: "The gorgeous quality of her voice, her thorough understanding of the traditions of Race folklore, as well as the high regard which she holds for the spirituals, have made her one of the greatest living exponents of Race folksongs."

In a follow-up interview, Anderson revealed her conviction that no amount of learning or musicianship should obscure the importance of singing spirituals in "Negro dialect." "We do not change Schubert or Beethoven to suit our audience, why change the dialect of our people?" she asked. "Nothing seems more ridiculous than to hear a Negro spiritual sung in pure English accent . . . The Negro spiritual must be held dear by all singers of the race and the traditions guarded closely. That is the only tradition we have."[48]

Anderson's determination to include both European and African-American music in her recitals complicated the racial dynamics of her American concert tour. Whatever the venue, balancing the expectations of black and white concertgoers in a nation sharply divided along racial lines was never easy. Yet, more often than not, she somehow achieved just such a balance. In concert after concert, she defied convention, breaking down traditional racial barriers, which no longer seemed to apply to her. "Nothing like the success of Miss Anderson . . . has been seen in concert circles in many years," reported the *Philadelphia Daily News*. "Homage and tribute," as one admiring observer put it, followed her wherever she went, including the nation's capital, where she spent a memorable week in mid-February.[49]

SINGING in Washington carried special meaning for Anderson. In addition to being the nation's capital, the city harbored one of the largest and most sophisticated black communities in America. It was the home of Howard University, the nation's most prestigious black college, which harbored a number of leading black intellectuals and music lovers. Only Harlem and Chicago rivaled Washington as centers of black cultural life, and no American city had a longer heritage of racial consciousness and striving. Anderson had sung there many times over the years in a variety of venues, amassing a large and loyal capital-city following that grew with every concert. Indeed, by the early 1930s Washington had hosted more Anderson concerts than any other American city, aside from her hometown of Philadelphia.[50]

Anderson insisted that she always looked forward to her Washington concerts with special anticipation, even though the city was rigidly segregated by both custom and law. As Anderson discovered, racial segregation in Washington during the 1930s was not the unremitting, cradle-to-grave style of enforced separation that could be found in Deep South cities such as Birmingham, Jackson, and even Atlanta. Instead, the nation's capital offered a curious mixture of discrimination and relative tolerance that baffled and confounded local citizens and visitors alike. Every American city had its own peculiarities regarding race and segregation, but Washington seemed to revel in its labyrinthine system of discrimination. One source of this confusing mix was the unusually sharp economic and class lines that divided the city. As the historian Constance McLaughlin Green pointed out in 1965, there have always been at least two Washingtons: the seat of government symbolized by "stretches of greensward and the gleaming white marble facades of public buildings"; and "'the Other Washington'—the city of slums and broken homes, of unemployed fathers, of wretched living conditions, and of drab streets where vice, disease, and hopelessness were ever-present." That there was still another Washington—a restless and proud community of middle-class blacks—further complicated the traditions and mores that dominated the city.

In a 1937 study commissioned by the Federal Writers' Project, the black poet Sterling Brown captured the inconsistent spirit of Washington's race relations. While noting that "segregation in Washington seems an accepted fact," he also observed that as a general rule "public buildings and public conveyances are not segregated." Yet, "Negroes are not served in restaurants, saloons, hotels, movie houses, and theaters, except those definitely set aside for them. Some stores will not accept their trade. Some governmental departments have separate accommodations, and some discriminate in the type of work offered to Negroes." A number of bright spots appeared amid this dark picture: the city's taxicabs, trolleys, buses, railroad-terminal waiting and dining rooms, public libraries and parks were integrated; a black judge served on the municipal court; and several local hotels and restaurants were willing to host interracial meetings, an opportunity virtually unknown farther south. But Brown's overall assessment of Washington race relations was dismal: "The Negro of Washington has no voice in government, is economically proscribed, and segregated nearly as rigidly as the Southern cities he condemns."[31]

This was the capital city that Anderson and Hurok encountered in February 1936. Earlier in her career, Anderson's Washington concerts had been held either in black churches or at the Lincoln Theater, a black vaudeville house that doubled as a classical concert hall, for want of a more suitable auditorium. Consequently, her Washington audiences had been almost entirely black, with a scattering of white critics and a few others who suppressed the common fear of being in a black-majority setting. The opportunity to reach a wider and more diverse audience had not emerged until 1933, when the pianist and Howard faculty member Charles Cohen established the Howard University Lyceum Concert Course, an annual series designed to showcase black artists. Cohen hoped to attract a broad audience of music lovers, including any whites who cared to attend. But for a number of years, his efforts were stymied by his inability to secure a racially integrated venue large enough to accommodate major artists such as Anderson.[52]

During the 1930s and 1940s, Washington was the only major city in the United States without a municipal auditorium, a sad reality that many observers attributed to the city's long-standing lack of political independence and meaningful representation in Congress. The only concert venue of any size in the city was Constitution Hall, a privately owned facility run by the National Society of the Daughters of the American Revolution (DAR), an all-white heritage organization devoted to an aggressively atavistic style of American patriotism. Opened in 1929, the nearly four-thousand-seat auditorium hosted a wide variety of lectures, theatrical productions, and concerts, including performances by Roland Hayes and the Hampton Institute Choir in 1931. Predictably, the Hayes and Hampton Choir concerts attracted a sizable number of black patrons—and considerable controversy. By the time Cohen began making the arrangements for the inaugural season of the Howard concert series in late 1932, Constitution Hall had imposed a "white artists only" policy that effectively barred his series from the hall. Two years earlier, in December 1930, the DAR executive committee had turned down the Metropolitan Musical Bureau of New York's request to schedule a Paul Robeson concert in the hall. But in rebuffing Robeson the DAR had not relied on a formal color bar.

Unbeknownst to all but a few DAR insiders, a 1925 preconstruction agreement between the DAR and one of the major donors to the Constitution Hall building fund mandated a whites-only policy for performers. No one enforced the agreement, however, until 1932, when Fred Hand, the manager of Constitution Hall, tried to assuage the feelings of white subscribers who complained that the 1931 Hayes and Hampton Choir concerts had attracted too many black patrons. Even though the management did its best to steer black ticket holders toward an unofficial Jim Crow section of the hall, the racial mix at both concerts offended the sensibilities of whites who regarded Constitution Hall as an elite enclave. Some whites wanted to ban black concertgoers altogether, which was the policy of many Washington theaters and halls, including the National Theater, the home of Washington's second-largest concert stage. But the new policy worked out by the DAR and Hand followed the original 1925 agreement: blacks could continue to sit in the audience, but they could not appear onstage. Of course, the clear expectation among all concerned was that few if any blacks would purchase tickets to see white performers, and that every effort would be made to seg-regate the few blacks who did show up at the hall.[53]

The precipitating event behind the change in policy was a bitter con-frontation between Hand and Hayes in January 1931. When Hayes walked onstage to begin his recital, he discovered a segregated audience, with blacks sitting in an obvious cluster separated from whites. Visibly upset, he returned to his dressing room, refusing to sing until the crowd was "properly mingled." Hand, an avid segregationist with a hot temper, readily accepted the chal-lenge. In an obvious attempt to intimidate anyone in the audience thinking of moving, he strode toward the empty stage and "stood with his arms folded in the middle of the aisle." To Hayes's dismay, Hand's threatening presence kept the black patrons "silent in their seats, not venturing to move." After a few minutes of indecision, Hayes reluctantly returned to the stage to give his performance. But this change of heart failed to mollify Hand, who report-edly vowed that as long as he was manager "no Negro would ever again ap-pear" at Constitution Hall. The one exception, which he could not avoid, was the already scheduled appearance of the Hampton Choir on March 21.[54]

The Hampton Choir sang as scheduled on that night, but not without disappointment. The attendance was sparse and little money was raised for the National Memorial Association, the sponsor of the benefit concert. The sole reason for this poor showing, according to the *Washington Daily News*, was an "odd ruling" by the DAR that "kept many colored people away from the event." As the *News* explained in a stinging editorial, "The DAR man-agement ruled that only two blocks of seats, those on the corners of the sur-rounding tiers, might be sold to colored people. After these were disposed of, hundreds of colored people were turned away with the information that the seats were sold out . . . consequently the Hall was two-thirds empty. The seats assigned to colored people were packed; beside them were empty blocks. Here and there through the hall, a few other colored people sat, doubtless in seats sold personally by members of the memorial association." Foreshadow-ing the reaction to Anderson's situation eight years later, the editorial char-acterized the DAR's seating policy as an insult to one of the nation's finest musical ensembles: "The choir that has sung in the music centers of Europe, that sang by invitation in Westminster Abbey, that was entertained at a for-mal tea in Berlin by Ambassador Frederick Sackett, a Kentuckian; that choir sang to empty seats because only two hundred of its own people were per-mitted to come into the DAR's Hall and hear it."

News of the incident soon spread, prompting Walter White to send an open letter to the *New York Herald Tribune*. Writing on behalf of the NAACP, White castigated the DAR for practicing racial discrimination and undermining the efforts of an important organization dedicated to the construction of a national memorial celebrating the achievements of the black race. White suggested that an apology was in order, but the leaders of the DAR felt otherwise. The mistake, in their view, was not racial segregation but rather the unwise decision to allow black performers of any kind to enter the hall. This hardening of attitudes became apparent in April, when the Columbian Educational Association's request to hold a convention at Constitution Hall was turned down. A highly regarded black educational organization, the CEA, as the group was known, received no formal explanation for the refusal. But any doubt that race was the root of the problem disappeared a few months later when the DAR began to include a "white artists only" clause in all Constitution Hall contracts.[55]

Four years later this racial restriction posed a serious problem for Charles Cohen and Sol Hurok, both of whom hoped to present Marian Anderson to as large an audience as possible. Anderson's last recital in Washington, held in 1933 under the auspices of Cohen's new Howard concert series, had taken place in a church auditorium, where, according to Alice Eversman, the music critic of the *Washington Star*, "her extraordinary singing was enjoyed by only a small audience." Writing in early February 1936, Eversman urged the concert organizers to find a venue that would allow a far larger number of Washingtonians, black and white, to hear "one of the greatest artists of the day." Eversman reminded her readers, "She is not a specialist, as might be supposed, in music of her own race, but a true interpreter of the great music of all nations . . . She represents, more than any other artist before the public today, the strength of genius which finds its way through all obstacles. To hear this simple young colored woman with the glorious voice sing the great German lieder, the dignified classics, or the ingratiating French songs is an experience not likely to be soon forgotten."

Eversman made no mention of Constitution Hall in her plea for a larger venue. But she applauded the announcement that Anderson's upcoming concert had been moved from the beautiful but small Rankin Chapel at Howard to a much larger auditorium at Armstrong High School. On an earlier visit, Anderson had performed at Paul Dunbar High School, and Armstrong, like Dunbar, offered one of the largest venues in Washington open to black performers. Ironically, the largest such venue, the National Theater, did not allow blacks in the audience.

When Anderson arrived at the Armstrong auditorium on Tuesday evening, February 18, every seat was filled, including perhaps a hundred seats occupied by whites. Several music critics were also on hand, and Anderson did not disappoint them. In a hyperbolic review bursting with community pride, a black reporter for the *Washington Tribune* proclaimed that Anderson was the "Greatest Singer of All Times." The reporter explained, "We know now why teachers put aside their own homework early; we know why preachers cut short their pastoral calls and adjourned their conferences; we know why doctors, dentists, lawyers and business men shut tight their office doors and hurried home to jump into smart tuxedos . . . We know why dinners were hurriedly eaten, dishes left unwashed and children hustled to bed. We know why the Armstrong auditorium was far too small to hold the crowd that wanted so badly to get in. We know why thousands of Europeans had hailed the smart young singer, why the great Toscanini stood up and cheered when the crowd went wild in New York. And we know why Washington (as long as it has its monuments and memorials) can never forget Marian Anderson." White critics employed less fulsome language, but they too lavished praise on Anderson's talent and artistry. To Eversman, Anderson's performance was "a rare concert by a simple and sincere artist." In a city where blacks rarely encountered kind words or respectful consideration from the white establishment, no one had anything negative to say about the golden-voiced woman from Philadelphia. Segregation notwithstanding, she was the toast of the town.[56]

Even so, few observers expected what came next. On the morning after the Armstrong High School concert, Hurok proudly announced that Anderson had been invited to sing at the White House later in the day. While Anderson was not the first black to receive such an invitation, the list of black artists who had performed at the White House was, as Walter White pointed out on several occasions, embarrassingly short. Marie Selika and Sissieretta Jones were the first, singing for a string of presidents from Rutherford B. Hayes in the late 1870s to Theodore Roosevelt just after the turn of the century. But the New Deal era marked the first time that a series of black artists appeared during a single administration. At White's urging, Eleanor Roosevelt went out of her way to invite several black performers during her husband's first term, including Todd Duncan, Dorothy Maynor, Lillian Evanti, and the South Carolina–based Sedalia Quartet.[57]

Anderson's invitation—graciously accompanied by invitations for her mother and Kosti Vehanen, plus a trip to and from the White House in the president's limousine—represented "the crowning achievement in a career that has been over ten years in the making," according to the *Philadelphia Independent.* The occasion was a private dinner party for Circuit Court of Appeals judge William Denman and his wife, close personal friends of the Roosevelts'. Held in the intimacy of the Monroe Drawing Room, Anderson's after-dinner performance featured six songs, divided between spirituals and selections from Schubert. In deference to her husband—who had recently complained about the stodginess of most White House musical selections, declaring, "I wish that once, just once, these musicians would play or sing a tune I've heard before"—the first lady had requested a spirituals-only program. But Anderson politely but firmly proposed a more eclectic program. Even in such an awe-inspiring venue, she refused to be typecast as a mere singer of black music.

Vehanen, who had considerable experience performing for heads of state, described the scene that night as "a dignified atmosphere of tradition and also of the democratic spirit." The Finnish pianist recalled, "There was a large, comfortable sofa at one side of the fireplace, on which the President was sitting and enjoying the great fire. His sure and strong handshake gives one a feeling of confidence, and his friendly, warm glance is good for the heart. That we were in the presence of a big personality no one could doubt." Yet somehow the evening belonged to Marian and Eleanor. "On this occasion," Vehanen declared, "Marian sang with a special fire. I have often noticed that when a well-known person, or one she especially honors, is before her, she sings with exceptional brilliance and fullness." As good as she was, perhaps the most important part of the evening had nothing to do with her voice. "After she sang," Vehanen continued, "there was a very touching scene. Mrs. Roosevelt, our charming hostess, took Marian's mother by the hand, and led her over and introduced her to the President. I shall never forget seeing these two ladies enter the room. Mrs. Roosevelt's manner was sure and free, as becomes a woman of the world, happy to welcome the mother of America's best-known singer. In all of Mrs. Anderson's being, there was evident the feeling that this was one of the greatest moments in her life. Her face reflected her gratitude and the pride she felt."[58]

The feeling of gratitude was no less evident in the countenance of her daughter, who immediately forged a powerful personal connection with the first lady. Indeed, as the nation and the world discovered three years later, the bond of friendship and mutual respect that began that evening in the Monroe Drawing Room proved strong enough to sustain an inspiring dramatization of democratic promise. Together, this unlikely pairing, so different in cultural heritage and background, found themselves at the core of a mass mobilization of engaged citizens. Drawing black and white into a movement for racial justice, these two modest but strong-willed women became inextricably linked in a chain of events that altered the course of American history.

CHAPTER 4

The Heart of a Nation

Dear to the heart of the shepherd, Dear are the lambs of His fold.
Some from the pastures are straying, Hungry and helpless and cold.
—FROM THE HYMN "DEAR TO THE HEART OF THE SHEPHERD"[1]

Two days after the White House recital, Marian Anderson woke up to a pleasant surprise. As smiling friends and family members streamed into her South Philadelphia kitchen with newspapers in hand, she discovered that her fame had suddenly ascended to a new level, thanks to a gracious review by the first lady. "My husband and I had a rare treat Wednesday night listening to Marian Anderson, a colored contralto, who has made great success in Europe and this country," Mrs. Roosevelt reported in her nationally syndicated column *My Day*. "She has sung before nearly all the crowned heads and deserves her great success, for I have rarely heard a more beautiful and moving voice or a more finished artist." Such words of praise, coming from the most celebrated of sources, represented a milestone in a nation where favorable publicity was rare for black men and women. During the 1930s black news coverage in the mainstream press represented little more than a crime report, and most newspapers, North and South, still restricted the use of courtesy titles such as *Mr.* and *Mrs.* to whites. With a long record of glowing reviews, "Miss" Anderson, as she was often called, had already breached this disrespectful tradition. But the first lady's public endorsement carried the added weight of the White House, quashing any doubt that Anderson's 1936 concert tour was making history.[2]

The final three weeks of Anderson's 1936 American tour, which ended in mid-March with a farewell concert in Philadelphia, were nothing less than triumphant. In concert after concert, she attracted sellout crowds and lavish praise from a wide variety of critics, confirming her status as a unique and potentially transcendent figure in the annals of American classical music. Nowhere was this more evident than in Boston, where the entire scene challenged the racial etiquette of Jim Crow. Beginning with her arrival in the city on February 28, two days before her debut at Symphony Hall, Anderson attracted the kind of attention that was traditionally reserved for white celebrities. After Roland Hayes and a large contingent of fans met her at the railway station, she accompanied Hayes to his Brookline mansion, where they treated reporters to a series of impromptu piano duets. Writing in the *Boston Globe* the next morning, a starry-eyed reporter assured his readers that Anderson was as virtuous as she was talented. "Unflustered by the plaudits of a dozen European capitals, as modest and as studious as in the hard penny-pinching days back in Philadelphia when her mother had to take in washing and success in the musical world seemed only a dream," she was still "the girl who made an Anderson's fairy tale come true." The *Globe* reporter insisted that Anderson was the rarest of artists, one who had the power to change lives. To prove his point, he repeated an apocryphal story that had made the rounds in Europe the previous fall. Unable to tolerate a shrewish wife who "had no soul," a music lover in Budapest had reportedly committed suicide after leaving a note commanding his wife to attend a Marian Anderson concert as the first step "toward acquiring a soul."

The number of souls regenerated by Anderson's recital at Boston's Symphony Hall went unrecorded. But, surely, no one who was there that night could have left without some sense of enlightenment or renewal. The black New Englanders who made up nearly half of the audience found pride and empowerment in Anderson's performance. The whites who sat nearby, some of whom were undoubtedly experiencing a racially mixed audience for the first time, had a sense of discovery bordering on wonder. The lessons learned undoubtedly varied from individual to individual, but for at least one observer the evening's events pointed to cultural achievement as the best path to racial harmony. "As one scrutinized this artist's large and highly mixed audience and noted its decorum, its discrimination and fine quality—and above all, the superlative talents of the singer," a *Boston Herald* reporter declared, "the question arose whether . . . the way to advance in the respect of community of one's fellow citizens, must not be through quiet penetration in the fields of art and intellect rather than through greedy grasping for political power and the ruthless exploitation of it." The necessity of choosing between culture and politics was, of course, a highly debatable point. But the notion that Anderson's artistic success transcended the world of music, carrying a broader meaning for advocates of racial uplift and civil democracy, was a prescient observation.[3]

On a more mundane level, the 1936 tour was a commercial success that rewarded Hurok's decision to reintroduce Anderson to the American public. With one exception, all eighteen concerts sold out, and the clamor for return engagements and additional concerts signaled a bright future for Anderson's career. Prior to the Town Hall triumph in December, a close friend of Hurok's had questioned the impresario's judgment, predicting, "You won't be able to give her away." Yet, by the end of the tour, Hurok had earned a substantial commission, calling into question the common belief that representing black artists was a losing proposition. Anderson herself grossed $6,800, a considerable sum for less than three months of work. As she well knew, this was more money than most Americans, black or white, expected to see in three years. Against all odds, and in defiance of racial convention, she was edging her way into the economic elite at a time when many Americans were headed in the opposite direction.[4]

Both Hurok and Anderson were well aware that, in the past, black success had often bred resentment and even violence. Accordingly, they eschewed the *diva* label so common in the world of classical music, making every effort to reassure the public that money and fame had not gone to Anderson's head. Carefully orchestrated press releases and interviews stressed her unpretentious manner and lifestyle. Fortunately, there was more than enough truth in this characterization to sustain her wholesome, nonthreatening image. Without exception, the national press embraced this portrayal of the singer, emphasizing the steady continuities of hard work and humility that marked her life story. As the *Boston Herald* reported in late February, even with all of her accolades Anderson "remained the same, simple, modest, unaffected girl she has always been."[5]

This view was especially prevalent in Philadelphia among the people who knew her best. Scheduled to return to Europe in early March, she postponed her departure to participate in a benefit concert sponsored by the United Campaign, a citywide coalition of 141 charitable organizations. Enhancing the participation of several black charities, Anderson gave a bravura performance that, according to one observer, provoked "pandemonium" one moment and reverential silence the next, leaving some members of the audience looking like "glued waxed figures with not a muscle moving, nor an eyelash drooping." Even if we allow for hyperbole, it seems evident that she ended her three-month stay in America with both her musical and personal reputations intact.[6]

Sailing for Europe brought only a brief respite from the demands of the concert stage. By early April, Anderson and Kosti Vehanen were back on tour, this time in Italy. Anderson admired Italian culture, especially its baroque masters and the lyrical language of its opera and folk songs. But the spring of 1936 was not the best time for a person of color to venture into a nation still crowing over its recent conquest of Ethiopia. Benito Mussolini's fascist followers were seemingly everywhere, spouting the slogans of a hard-edged national chauvinism that left little room for racial tolerance. Fortunately, none of this intruded into Italy's grand concert halls, where Anderson encountered nothing but warm welcomes and adoring fans. Even so, the lingering fear that racial politics would disrupt her three-week-long Italian tour cast a shadow over an otherwise pleasant visit.[7]

Anderson maintained a grueling pace throughout the spring, giving a series of concerts in Spain, France, England, Belgium, Holland, the Soviet Union, and Austria. Singing before capacity crowds in city after city, from Barcelona to Moscow, she offered a musical salve to Europeans looking for joy and comfort in a continent veering toward totalitarianism and war. Everywhere she went, her music provoked unbounded enthusiasm. But she could not help but notice the rising force of militarism and fascism all around her. In Spain, where civil war between Republican Loyalists and Generalissimo Franco's Nationalists would break out later in the year, a mixture of fear and hope dominated an anxious populace. Kosti Vehanen, who gallantly tried to shield Anderson from as much unpleasantness as possible, later confessed that the situation in Barcelona reminded him of "Finland before the Russian Revolution." "There was much confusion and excitement in the streets which were crowded with people," he wrote of the city where Anderson gave her first Spanish concert. "I could see the dark expression in many faces and a frantic look in many eyes." Canceled trains and civil disorder made the Spanish tour the adventure of a lifetime, but Anderson remained outwardly calm and resolute, fulfilling all of her contractual engagements, even in the isolated Basque city of Bilbao. Exhibiting the same poise and quiet strength that had sustained her since childhood, she did not shrink from her responsibilities even in the face of danger.[8]

This intrepid spirit was even more evident in June when Anderson refused to cower before Austrian authorities. Eager to return to the scene of the 1935 recital that had charmed Arturo Toscanini, she gave two concerts in Salzburg, even though once again local officials prohibited her from participating in the Salzburg Festival. The German army's occupation of the Rhineland in March 1936 had emboldened Austria's Nazi sympathizers, but the situation was complicated by a rising tide of musical refugees from Berlin and other German cities. In a nation that loved classical music above all else, even the most zealous Nazis were reluctant to use their full authority to impose racial and ethnic restrictions on performing artists. The result was a policy of harassment that stopped short of outright persecution. When Bruno Walter, a distinguished Jewish conductor who had fled the Reich soon after Hitler's rise to power, came out of retirement in early 1936 to direct the Vienna State Opera, he had to brave death threats and, on at least one occasion, stink bombs released into the concert hall. Undeterred, he fought back by defiantly announcing that he had invited the great "Negro contralto" Marian Anderson to sing Brahms's *Alto Rhapsody* during the Vienna Music Festival. While it is doubtful that Anderson had full knowledge of the politics swirling around Walter's gesture, she did not hesitate to accept an invitation to sing a piece of music that had long interested her, a piece that she would later record with great success in collaboration with Eugene Ormandy and the Philadelphia Orchestra. For her, musical considerations were always paramount, even in the throes of political or racial controversy.

Anderson's performance at the 1936 Vienna festival drew rave reviews, including a memorable account of her triumph by Herbert Peyser in the *New York Times*. According to Peyser, Anderson had earned a special dispensation from Viennese music lovers, who normally voiced serious doubts about foreigners of any color doing justice to the works of German and Austrian composers. Politics and race notwithstanding, they accepted her interpretations of Schubert and Brahms "without challenge," uncharacteristically but graciously overlooking minor errors of language or inflection. Peyser himself was of a similar mind, praising her "intuitive grasp" of Brahms's "poignantly human message." At the Vienna festival, as in her earlier performances of Germanic music, "the complete subordination of herself to the end of the composition" was compelling.[9]

In Germany itself, subordination of a different kind was the order of the day, with alleged racial inferiors facing exploitation or, in Anderson's case, exclusion. In 1930 and 1931, the economic and political instability of the Weimar regime had prompted Anderson to leave Berlin for the more promising venues of Scandinavia. But she had done so voluntarily. Five years later, racial discrimination had become an inescapable dictate of German public policy, and performing in the Reich was no longer an option for her or any other African-American artist.

In July 1936, Anderson once again escaped to the relative calm of Scandinavia, and from there she observed the racial drama of the Summer Olympics in Berlin. Staged as a demonstration of Aryan superiority, the Olympics ultimately produced a symbolic struggle between Adolf Hitler and Jesse Owens, a twenty-two-year-old African-American track star from Ohio State University. Born in the Black Belt plantation region of Alabama as the grandson of slaves, Owens won four gold medals in Berlin, setting Olympic records in all four events, including the hundred-meter dash and the long jump. This unprecedented feat established Owens as a national hero in the United States, especially after Hitler failed to acknowledge his accomplishment. Faced with the evil specter of the Fuehrer's increasingly aggressive mixture of racism and militarism, most Americans chose democratic nationalism over racial solidarity. Earlier in the year the celebrated heavyweight boxing match between Joe Louis and Max Schmeling had foreshadowed this reversal of tradition, but unlike Owens, Louis lost to his German opponent. In a rematch held two years later, Louis defeated Schmeling, earning his dual status as a national hero and foil to Nazi theories of invincibility. But in the summer 1936 Jesse Owens stood alone at the peak of black accomplishment, an inspiring example of what African Americans could achieve on a level playing field.[10]

Anderson, like Louis, would eventually rival and even surpass Owens as a civil rights icon. But securing popular acclaim took a bit longer in the music world, where there was no single event to focus attention on the struggle against racial hierarchies. When such an event did present itself, albeit unexpectedly, in 1939, Anderson made the most of her opportunity. Yet she could never have done so if she had not prepared the way with years of steady achievement. In the fall of 1936, as Owens basked in the glory of his recent achievements and as newsreels and newspaper stories made his name a household word around the world, Anderson resumed her grand tour of Europe. Traveling to Copenhagen, Stockholm, Paris, London, Geneva, Budapest, and Prague, she extended and deepened her reputation, achieving a public profile in the European classical world that no previous black artist had ever enjoyed. Releases from extensive recording sessions enhanced her popularity, and by the time she and Vehanen returned to the United States in

January 1937, few music lovers on the European continent had not heard her ethereal voice in one medium or another.[11]

WITH the help of Hurok and NBC radio, Anderson reached roughly the same level of fame in America by the end of her 1937 tour. Beginning in late January, she performed no less than forty-four recitals over three months. Some of the concert venues were repeats from 1936, but the addition of a number of cities, mostly in the Midwest, brought her greater exposure and a host of new fans. In customary fashion, she offered a mixture of German lieder and spirituals, drawing capacity crowds and critical acclaim wherever she went. "If there is such a thing as perfect singing in this world," Marjory Fisher, the music editor of the *San Francisco News*, declared, "Miss Anderson is its leading exponent. She has everything: voice, technique, artistry, intelligence, and humility." Lawrence Mason, writing in the *Toronto Globe and Mail*, concurred: "It is difficult to imagine a more nearly perfect sound produced by a human throat than many of the notes in Miss Anderson's upper and middle registers . . . Sweeping superlatives are uncritical and usually meaningless, but it is hard to believe that any other voice now before the public on the concert stage is as beautiful as Miss Anderson's."[12]

Many critics went beyond praise of her performances, offering admiring accounts of her personal life and character. "No one can see and listen to Miss Anderson for two minutes," insisted the *New York Herald Tribune*, "without realizing that one is in the presence of an artist of extraordinary devotion, intensity and self-effacement." Echoing Hurok's press releases, the *New York Amsterdam News* described her life as "a twentieth-century fairy tale," marveling at her "world acclaim" and "how she has hurdled almost every barrier and given to the world one of the greatest voices of the age." "Miss Anderson's life has been quiet, deliberate and free from the temperamental hysteria of the usual accomplished artist," another New York critic noted approvingly.[13]

Mixed among the superlatives and personal comments were racial digressions that strained to explain her unique appeal and style. "The quality of the voice is peculiarly captivating," mused a reporter for the *New York Evening Journal*, "with something elusive in its color as the inhered mystery of an unfamiliar race." Similarly captivated, the Chicago critic Eugene Stinson hailed Anderson as "the Supreme vocal entertainer in the world" but struggled mightily with the racial and intellectual aspects of her artistry. "It is not her voice alone that is remarkable," he concluded, "but that the mind behind it is too alert, too inventive and too original in its musicianship not to haunt one with curiosity as to its secret . . . Most of her individuality is due to the fact that she is of Negro birth. Her frankness, her concentration upon a single thing, her imagination, her emphasis, her quality of voice and the prodigality of her gift are all within the birthright of her people. Yet we must grant that in her we do not hear her people singing; she is too gigantically individual for that. We hear Marian Anderson; there is only one of her." Following an Anderson concert in San Francisco, one local critic noted that her voice was "fresh, free and strong, as only Negro voices can be," while another found it "amazing that music of the simple Negro folk should enter the symphony master repertory and suffer no whit in comparison." Writing in the *Houston Chronicle*, Cora McRae reported that Anderson had brought something "fresh and new" to Texas—"a voice that transcended all barriers of race and color."[14]

By 1937, the musical world had grown accustomed to musings about the racial origins and characteristics of Anderson's artistry. But, except for occasional comments on the value of spirituals, Anderson herself did not betray any strong feelings about these matters. Instead, she concentrated on the practical challenges of singing in front of predominantly white audiences in a wide variety of settings. One can only imagine her apprehension when she learned that Hurok had added Houston and Oklahoma City to the 1937 tour. Though not in the Deep South, both communities adhered to strict codes of racial segregation, presenting Anderson and her white accompanist with potentially unpleasant complications. At the same time, several of the other new cities on the tour, including Salt Lake City and Des Moines, had little experience with black artists. Much to their relief, Anderson and Vehanen made their way through the mid-South and across the country without incurring the wrath of vigilant white supremacists. In several instances, they did so by performing in segregated halls, but their mere presence onstage as an interracial duo often represented the first such experience for Jim Crow communities.

Ironically, the closest brush with racial discord during the 1937 tour came in the North, in the university town of Princeton, New Jersey, where the only local hotel, the tony Nassau Inn, maintained a strict color bar. Fortunately, within minutes of being turned away from the inn, Anderson found alternative lodging with Albert Einstein, Princeton's most famous resident, who graciously invited the distressed singer to spend the night at his home. Thus began a remarkable friendship that brought Anderson to the eminent physicist's residence at least once a year until his death in 1955.[15]

The Princeton situation was unusual in that it involved the kindness of a world-famous celebrity. But the necessity of avoiding or sidestepping the dictates of racial segregation was a stark reality for Anderson and other touring black performers. Sometimes the realities of Jim Crow rendered certain places off-limits for black performers, as in most of the public venues in the Deep South. For Anderson, however, the racial situation was often subject to some negotiation and mitigation. In many, though by no means all, instances, she could take advantage of a combination of factors: Hurok's careful planning; her growing fame and fortune; and a unique public image that confounded racial stereotypes. Thus, from the mid-1930s on, she frequently received special treatment that shielded her from the worst indignities of Jim Crow.

Anderson herself attributed this treatment almost solely to the careful travel plans prepared by Hurok Productions. "Thanks to the skill and thoughtfulness of my manager and his staff," she recalled years later, "I have been spared and shielded. They have not told me every hazard they have encountered and overcome in arranging things for me . . . I know, of course, that there have been difficulties and problems. I look at the itinerary, see that I am scheduled to stay at a certain hotel in a certain city, and sense that an exception has been made. It is better not to know for sure. It is more comfortable not to think about it if I can avoid it. I have a performance to give, and if my feelings are divided I cannot do my best. If my mind dwells even partly on the disconcerting thought that I am staying where I am not really welcome, I cannot go out and sing as though my heart were full of love and happiness. And yet the work must be done. If I suspect that an exception is being made for me I go into the hotel not with triumph but out of necessity."

As this statement suggests, Anderson approached the challenges of racism with a spirit of pragmatism. Though mindful of her position of privilege and genuinely concerned about the harsh realities that dominated the lives of less fortunate members of her race, she took full advantage of her celebrity and economic circumstances. She did so because she was first and foremost a musician, a professional performer who realized that she could not maintain a grueling concert schedule without insulating herself as much as possible from the draining diversions of Jim Crow. Earlier in her career she had put up with more than her share of filthy railway coaches and substandard lodgings. But as a forty-year-old woman trying to keep up with Hurok's ever-increasing bookings, she had no qualms about preserving her energy and peace of mind any way she could.[16]

Anderson's unswerving dedication to her musical career placed severe limitations on her public involvement in politics and civil rights. Much of her quiescence was voluntary and in keeping with her personal style and beliefs. But she also had to deal with Hurok, who actively discouraged her from identifying with controversial causes, especially those that called attention to her race or that could be characterized as subversive. Hurok had strong views on anti-Semitism, racism, and international affairs and was an early and vocal critic of Hitler and the Nazis. But he did not want his clients mixing art and politics, which he felt was bad for business. For Anderson anything that detracted from the "fairy tale" image was off-limits. The closest she came to violating this proscription was her public love affair with the Russian people. "They are the finest people in the world," she told a reporter after her triumphant 1935 tour of the Soviet Union. While she never offered an opinion on the merits of Stalin's leadership or Soviet communism, even casual comments on life and culture under a totalitarian regime carried some risk.[17]

Public advocacy of racial justice was also risky, and Anderson trod softly there as well. In private she often expressed strong feelings about her rights as an American citizen, but she showed no inclination to draw public attention to specific acts of racial discrimination. Instead, she liked to think of herself as a role model, a one-woman vanguard who had been given the opportunity to advance her race through individual determination and strength of character.

During the 1930s, and to some extent throughout her life, Anderson's approach to social change was more in line with the racial-uplift policies of Booker T. Washington than with the race-conscious protest tradition advocated by W. E. B. Du Bois. "I try to leave behind a conviction in those [white supremacists] with whom I have had contact that their attitudes were not based on knowledge," she explained. "It may be that if they discover they are wrong about an individual they will begin to realize that their judgment of a group is equally fallacious . . . the only hope for all of us is that we will attempt in good faith to rid ourselves of unknown fears in matters where it is possible to discover that the fears are often groundless and unreasonable. Fear is a disease that eats away at logic and makes man inhuman."

While Anderson conceded that "there are some people around whose minds never change, and . . . are not in the least bit interested in having them changed," she claimed that she had witnessed enough progress to sustain her faith in the widening impact of an entering wedge. Even though she often found the pace of change to be frustrating, she maintained her commitment to a slow and steady style of amelioration. A prime example was her willingness to take meals in her room while on tour. "That is my preference," she insisted. "If I wanted to take them elsewhere I would. I assume that there are hotel managements that are happier to have me dine in my room. It is not because they have any objections but they feel other guests might complain— or so the explanations would go. If I were inclined to be combative, I suppose I might insist on making issues of these things. But that is not my nature, and I always bear in mind that my mission is to leave behind me the kind of impression that will make it easier for those who follow."[18]

This explanation of Anderson's racial "mission" appeared in her 1956 autobiography, *My Lord, What a Morning*, making it somewhat less authoritative than a contemporary statement. Yet these mature reflections, filtered as they were through her ghostwriter, Howard Taubman, undoubtedly reflect the basic ideas and experiences that informed her life prior to World War II. Early in her career she demonstrated care and compassion in welcoming opportunities to serve both the Philadelphia and the broader black community—through benefit concerts, contributions to scholarship funds, and a host of church-related activities. But none of these philanthropic endeavors led her to view herself as a social and political activist in the tradition of Paul Robeson. Not only did she avoid making public statements on controversial issues, but the thought that anyone other than her closest friends had the slightest interest in her politics probably never entered her mind in these years. As she told the journalist Leon Jaroff in 1989, "Certainly, I have my feelings about conditions that affect my people. But it is not right for me to mimic someone who writes, or who speaks out against segregation. That is their forte . . . What I had was my singing, and if my career has been of some consequence, then that's my contribution."

Anderson was an accomplished singer, a celebrity to an ever-widening circle of music lovers, a world traveler, and a proud black woman with a social conscience. But for a black woman living in the late 1930s, no résumé, however impressive, translated into political or intellectual currency. Interviewers inquired about her family, her musical tastes, her fashion choices, and even her love life. But they rarely veered into questions of racial justice or public policy. Hemmed in by social conventions of gender and race, she was perceived as a talented female star who represented her race in cultural, not political, terms. As a February 1937 *Life* magazine profile put it, Anderson was "a quiet unassuming Negro" who "speaks four languages." This was just what Hurok wanted: publicity that made his talented client appear exotic but nonthreatening.[19]

The combination of a remarkable voice and a carefully cultivated rags-to-riches biography was enough to guarantee a degree of celebrity. But the mystique that accompanied Anderson's fame also rested on uniqueness. Among the nation's leading classical performers, she was the only African-American woman, the only singer to perform recitals in multiple languages, the only contralto to venture into the high soprano range, and virtually the only female idol to eschew the diva persona. She was, in sum, a singular figure who inspired unending curiosity and genuine awe. It is little wonder that neither the concert-going public nor the press could get enough of her.

ANDERSON closed her 1937 American tour at the renowned May Music Festival in Ann Arbor, Michigan, where she shared the stage with the Philadelphia Orchestra and two of the world's greatest vocalists, Kirsten Flagstad and Lauritz Melchior. This was a fitting end to a season that confirmed her status as a bright and shining star in the world of classical music. No other black performer, past or present, had achieved as much, and no one doubted that the best was yet to come.[20]

In the summer of 1937, Anderson returned to Europe, where she enjoyed a stellar though somewhat abbreviated season of recitals in a half dozen countries. At Hurok's suggestion, she shortened her European tour by several weeks, substituting a series of concerts in South America. Taking her far from the troubles of a continent drawing ever closer to war, the South American tour was a wondrous and enlightening experience. During an extended stay in Brazil, Argentina, and Uruguay, she drew record crowds that enhanced her international reputation. She also gained a new perspective on race, observing a form of racial assimilation almost unknown in the United States or Europe. Here color, not race, was the primary arbiter of relations among blacks, browns, and whites, with discrimination often following lines of economic and social class. Accustomed to the stark racial dichotomy between black and white that prevailed in the United States, Anderson found colonial Latin mores to be both intriguing and liberating. Not only did the South American concertgoers shower her with affection, but with her light brown skin she encountered little overt prejudice in her hotel and travel arrangements. Underscoring the artificial and gratuitous nature of the Jim Crow system that she had known since childhood, Anderson's experiences in South America opened her eyes to a world that few African Americans were privileged to see.[21]

The wildly successful South American tour buoyed Anderson's confidence, setting the stage for her most ambitious American season to date. The 1938 tour included more than sixty recitals spread from coast to coast. In less than five months, from January to May, Anderson sang to more than a quarter million American concertgoers, and to millions more over the radio. As in the past, the tour skirted the Deep South, but Hurok found new bookings in three Texas cities—San Antonio, Dallas, and Fort Worth—plus Richmond, Virginia, the onetime capital of the Confederacy. The addition of these cities to the schedule forced Anderson to deal with new variations of Jim Crow culture, but the experiences of past seasons had hardened her to the inevitable aggravations of segregated concert halls, hotels, and railway cars. Too proud to reveal her discomfort to the press or anyone else, she suffered in silence. Smiling sweetly for the cameras, she reserved her voice for the stage.[22]

At the peak of her craft, cloaked in beautiful Parisian gowns, looking and sounding like the "Queen of Song," as one New York critic described her, Anderson elicited a string of hyperbolic superlatives during the 1938 tour. In San Francisco she was hailed as "the greatest singer of her generation," and in Dallas she was cast as "one of the supreme song recitalists of all time." The *Daily Worker* dubbed her "the Negro Nightingale," and the noted critic Glenn Dillard Gunn seconded Toscanini's judgment that she was "the Voice of the Century."[23]

As in the past, some critics went beyond musical appreciation, registering observations of what they perceived as an unprecedented social phenomenon. To the San Francisco critic Alfred Frankenstein, Anderson was "like some idealized piece of sculpture representing her race at its finest." But others detected something else, an artistic presence that confounded traditional limitations of race. "For some two hours 2,000 persons knew neither creed, race, color, pettiness, political prejudice," a New York critic declared after attending a concert at the Metropolitan Theatre in March, adding that Anderson "somehow sends each one in her audience exploring in his own private world." Writing in the *Houston Post*, the veteran music critic Hubert Roussel claimed that Anderson had given Houstonians the "thrill of a lifetime" with her rendition of "Ave Maria." "She has made this number her own," he insisted. "Hearing it as it comes from the dark woman who stands tall and immobile, as impersonal as a tree or a mountain and yet throbbing with the passion of all human inspiration and yearning for sign of divine guidance, is the most dramatic experience I have had in 30 years of attending the theater." After observing the crowd's reaction to Anderson's encore, Roussel marveled at the scene and added a note of social commentary: "Still the audience wouldn't go home. People clotted around the stage, slamming their hands, as though to beg for a mere sight of the woman who had moved their emotions. She returned again, simple and cool in a gold dress against the empty stage. And there, you thought, but for the Grace of God, stood somebody's negro cook."[24]

For Roussel, and perhaps for many others, the Anderson mystique seemed to prompt a reconsideration of racial mores. Following a recital in early March, the *St. Louis Globe* critic Harry Burke observed, "St. Louis, if the memory of the oldest concertgoers may be trusted, has never witnessed such a triumph of song as when Marian Anderson . . . made her debut before a mixed audience which, regardless of race or color, refused to leave when her program was over, which cheered vociferously and called for more; which thronged to the platform to thank her personally and beg for just one more to an already generous list of encores. Surely in 20 years of concert attendance here this reviewer has never witnessed such a remarkable tribute as that paid to that Negro singer by a city south of the Mason and Dixon line." Thomas Sherman, the music critic for the rival *St. Louis Dispatch*, had virtually the same reaction, noting that "a large and diversified audience" had "found a common meeting place on the top level of esthetic experience." Marveling at the interracial audience's behavior, Sherman concluded, "They had had a glimpse into an ordinarily invisible realm whose proportions and perspectives are but faintly suggested by the anarchy and irrelevancies of the external world. In short, it was the miracle of art—a miracle according to definition because it transcended the natural order of things." In a postconcert interview with another *Dispatch* reporter, Anderson acknowledged that her singing often had a spiritual effect on members of the audience. "I don't know of a greater thrill," she said, "than the one I get when some harried individual, with care written on his face, comes to me after a concert and says, 'Miss Anderson, I can't put this into words, but you've done something for me here,' pointing to his heart."[25]

For many of those in the hall that night, the miraculous transcendence of social and racial conventions witnessed by Burke and Sherman was undoubtedly a fleeting phenomenon. But for others, one suspects, the concert was a profound and perhaps even life-altering experience. Many white Americans, it seems, had great difficulty placing Anderson in the normal hierarchy of race. Neither her talent nor her appearance fit the expectations of racial inferiority. Attending an Anderson concert could be mystifying, not only in the emotional intensity of her voice, but also in disrupting and contradicting a lifetime of racial socialization.

What were white Americans to make of a woman whose beauty, manner, and talent violated the perceived limitations of racial progress? Some may have dismissed her as the proverbial exception that proved the rule, and others undoubtedly attributed her gifts to whatever white lineage she could claim. Yet, as Anderson's fame grew, neither of these options proved adequate as an acceptable explanation for her success.

Anderson provoked less confusion among black Americans. But even in the black community she defied easy categorization. Unlike most jazz and blues artists, she cultivated a style of music that did not always resonate with a majority of her own race. While she inspired deep devotion among her many black fans, relatively few shared her enthusiasm for German lieder and Sibelius. Many took pride in her mastery of European classical music, but most came, first and foremost, to hear her haunting renditions of Negro spirituals. Judging by commentary in both the black and the white press, Anderson's association with the spirituals endeared her to the black public. When one white critic expressed surprise that Anderson's spirituals seemed to reflect "more the objective approach of an artist than an innate racial expression," the singer responded, "I know exactly what you mean. I did not live in the time or place that gave birth to spirituals, but I can remember my mother and grandmother hum some of them and they are dear to my heart. I sing them as I feel them . . . not in imitation of the way they must have been sung at the time of their origin, but in accordance with what they mean to me today."[26]

Of course, not even the sweetest evocation of slave culture could eliminate all of the complications raised by Anderson's attempt to bridge the music of antebellum America and nineteenth-century Europe. She was, after all, a curious mixture of cultural and class traditions—a black woman from South Philadelphia who not only sang songs in German, Italian, and Swedish but who also spent much of her life in Europe surrounded by members of the continental elite, who vacationed in the south of France, and who wore high fashion and expensive jewelry. In 1938 alone she grossed nearly a quarter of a million dollars from concert fees, making her one of the wealthiest black women in America. Newspaper and magazine reporters insisted that none of this had gone to her head, that she was still the same humble girl who had sung in the Union Baptist choir. But no amount of virtue could camouflage her entrenched involvement in the white world beyond Jim Crow. For many black women she was a role model of sorts, but not one who offered an easily imaginable path to liberation or upward mobility. As a December 1938 *Collier's* magazine profile put it, "When she stands on a platform, exquisitely dressed by Paris in white or a gleaming brocade, her strong, slender figure and poised bearing proclaiming in every detail the ripened mistress of a great art, she is one of the proudest ornaments of this country." For better or for worse, Anderson was an extraordinary individual, and no aspiring black artist of the late 1930s could reasonably expect to duplicate her rise to fame and fortune.[27]

Anderson was acutely aware of the racial and class implications of her ascension and did everything she could to maintain strong ties with black institutions. Despite pressure from Hurok, who tried to limit her engagements to lucrative commercial venues, she continued to perform benefit concerts at black churches and other community institutions, including Hampton and Tuskegee Institutes and Howard University, which presented her with an honorary degree in June 1938. The Howard degree, the first of many honors that would adorn the last five decades of her life, lifted Anderson's spirits at the end of a grueling concert season. The presentation, which marked her long and special relationship with Howard, turned the university's commencement ceremony into bedlam when hundreds of well-wishers rushed the stage to congratulate the guest of honor.[28]

Earlier in the spring, the university had faced a similar situation when Anderson had returned to the Howard Lyceum series for the third straight year. In 1936 and 1937, university officials had secured special permission from the school board to hold Anderson's recital in the auditorium of the all-black Armstrong High School. By 1938, however, the Armstrong auditorium was no longer big enough to accommodate the expected throng of Anderson fans. Charles Cohen, the musical director of the Lyceum series, was confident that Anderson could fill Constitution Hall's four thousand seats, but the largest Washington venue open to black artists was the Rialto Theater, which seated approximately two thousand. To no one's surprise, the Rialto concert attracted an overflow crowd. But Cohen and others were stunned by the number of whites in the audience. For the first time, a Lyceum series concert had drawn more whites than blacks, indicating Anderson's unique status as a crossover artist. Anderson herself was accustomed to predominantly white audiences, but the presence of so many whites at a concert sponsored by a black university was a milestone worth noting.[29]

ANDERSON'S close relationship with Howard and the obvious implications of the Rialto concert would have profound consequences in the weeks and months ahead. The sequence of events leading to the epochal Lincoln Memorial concert of April 1939 began innocently enough the previous June when Hurok and Cohen came to terms. The contract stipulated that Anderson would participate in the 1939 Lyceum series on Easter Sunday, April 9, a choice of dates that all but ensured unprecedented ticket sales. Once again, Cohen faced the challenge of securing a venue large enough to meet the expected demand. Clearly, neither the Rialto Theater nor the Armstrong auditorium would suffice. During the fall, as Cohen and his colleagues, including the noted baritone Todd Duncan, mulled over the situation, the discussion inevitably turned to the availability of Constitution Hall. Three years earlier Cohen's request to book the hall had been rebuffed by manager Fred Hand and the DAR. But, with Hurok's support, Cohen decided to try again, hoping that the DAR would either abandon its restrictive policies or at least grant a waiver to one of the world's most popular singers.[30]

On January 6, Cohen summoned up the courage to approach Fred Hand with a request for an April 9 booking. Predictably, Hand wasted little time in issuing a terse rejection, informing Cohen that the National Symphony Orchestra had already reserved the hall for Easter Sunday. He also reminded the Howard professor that a long-standing policy prohibited black artists from performing at Constitution Hall. Discouraged but unwilling to let the matter drop, Cohen sought the counsel of several friends and colleagues, including the university's treasurer, V. D. Johnston. On January 12, the *Washington Times-Herald* published a carefully worded and somewhat cautious "open letter" written by Johnston on behalf of the Lyceum-series committee. "The question arises," Johnston maintained, ". . . whether there are not a sufficient number of persons in Washington and vicinity interested in hearing Miss Anderson and what she represents to impress upon the D.A.R. that this restriction may not represent public opinion in Washington." Three days later the *Times-Herald* followed up with a stinging editorial entitled "We Must Hear Marian Anderson." Condemning the DAR's restrictive policies, the editorial noted the bitter irony of Constitution Hall's proximity to American democracy's most sacred monuments. "It stands almost in the shadow of

the Lincoln Memorial," the *Times-Herald* pointed out, "but the Great Emancipator's sentiments about 'race, creed or previous condition of servitude' are
not shared by the Daughters." At Constitution Hall, the editorial lamented,
"Prejudice rules to make the Capital of the Nation ridiculous in the eyes of
all cultured people and to comfort Fuehrer Hitler and the members of our
Nazibund."[31]

Cohen and Johnston appreciated the *Times-Herald*'s support. But they
had already concluded that the situation called for more than friendly press
coverage. Earlier in the week Cohen had contacted Walter White, hoping
that the NAACP executive secretary could mobilize an organizational challenge to the DAR's policies. The moment White learned of Cohen's dilemma
and the apparent snub of a beloved black singer whom White had admired
since the 1920s, he immediately initiated a behind-the-scenes deliberation on
how to proceed. Within hours the discussion spread by phone and in person
to the Black Cabinet and beyond, as Mary McLeod Bethune, NAACP special counsel Charles Houston, and several others, including Eleanor Roosevelt, became part of an ongoing and sometimes spirited conversation. While
the consensus was that something had to be done, developing a strategy that
would force the DAR to reconsider its decision was complicated by the first
lady's membership in the organization.[32]

A public confrontation with the DAR carried considerable risk, with
the potential of embarrassing the Roosevelts at a critical time for the New
Deal. Eleanor Roosevelt's widely publicized activities on behalf of civil
rights, especially her appearance at the November 1938 meeting of the left-
wing Southern Conference for Human Welfare (SCHW) in Birmingham,
had already stoked the fires of controversy. After discovering that Birmingham's pugnacious public-safety commissioner Eugene "Bull" Connor had
ordered the biracial SCHW to maintain segregated seating at the city auditorium, the first lady defiantly took a seat in the section reserved for black
delegates. When a police officer informed her that she was in the wrong section, she agreed to move, but only to a folding chair placed in the aisle between the black and white sections. This gesture, later a staple of civil rights
lore, further endeared her to black Americans. But it did not help her husband's political situation in the white South, where conservative Democrats
were busy forging a powerful congressional coalition with like-minded Northern Republicans.[33]

For this and other reasons, White favored a subtle, indirect means of
undercutting the DAR's position. Instead of attacking them, he decided to

offer further proof of Marian Anderson's elevated stature. If DAR leaders would not bow to the principle of equality, perhaps they would shy away from the negative publicity that would accompany a public confrontation with a popular and virtuous celebrity. Perhaps they would do the right thing out of self-interest. Accordingly, he persuaded an NAACP committee to present Anderson with the Spingarn Medal, the organization's most prestigious annual award. First awarded in 1915 and named for Joel Spingarn, a Jewish liberal from New York who helped found the NAACP and who served as its president from 1913 to 1939, the Spingarn Medal signified "the highest or noblest achievement by an American Negro during the preceding year or years." The announcement of Anderson's selection on January 16 placed her in rare company. Previous winners included George Washington Carver, James Weldon Johnson, and W. E. B. Du Bois. She was only the third musician to receive the medal, joining her dear friends and mentors Harry T. Burleigh and Roland Hayes, who had been honored in 1917 and 1924, respectively. She was also the third woman chosen, following Mary Talbert (1922) and Mary McLeod Bethune (1935). In the formal statement accompanying the announcement, the NAACP selection committee declared, "Marian Anderson has been chosen for her special achievement in the field of music." But, in an unusual gesture, the statement, sounding much like a Hurok press release, went on to praise her modesty: "Equally with that achievement, which has won her world-wide fame as one of the greatest singers of our time, is her magnificent dignity as a human being. Her unassuming manner, which has not been changed by her phenomenal success, has added to the esteem not only of Marian Anderson but of the race to which she belongs."

By all accounts, no one was more thrilled by the news of Anderson's selection than Eleanor Roosevelt, who graciously agreed to present the medal in person at the upcoming NAACP national convention scheduled to meet in Richmond, Virginia, in July. Anderson herself could hardly have been more pleased by the award and by the first lady's involvement. Yet Anderson was clearly troubled by the prospect of a public controversy over the DAR's restrictive policies. On tour in the Midwest, she not only received official notice of the award from White but also word of a plan to solicit public statements from artists who opposed the DAR's position. Despite his concern for the Roosevelts, White decided to step up the pressure when the Spingarn announcement failed to produce an immediate response from the DAR. Adopting a scheme suggested by Mary Johnson, a close friend who worked for *Time* magazine and who had recently interviewed the president general of the DAR, White wired a dozen musical luminaries, including Arturo Toscanini, Leopold Stokowski, and Lily Pons, on January 19. "Marian Anderson has been denied use of Constitution Hall in Washington, D.C., by Daughters of the American Revolution," the message explained, before asking them for an "opinion on this ban." Over the next week the expected expressions of outrage arrived at the NAACP office, but White was not quite sure how to use them. Neither he nor anyone else, it seems, was quite ready to go to war with the DAR.[34]

Seeing few signs of progress, Cohen enlisted Hurok's help in a plaintive letter written on January 19. Playing to Hurok's ego, he suggested that the impresario's unmatched experience with concert hall managers was just what the negotiations needed. Never one to shrink from a challenge or a compliment, Hurok promptly dispatched a carefully worded letter to Hand. As a racial liberal and a Jew who had suffered his share of ethnic prejudice, Hurok was offended by the DAR's restrictive policies. But he was also a shrewd businessman capable of setting aside his anger and indignation when money or influence was on the line. Accordingly, his letter to Hand argued on behalf of his client without explicitly expressing his outrage toward Constitution Hall's general policy of restricting "Negro artists from appearing there."

"Without attempting to discuss the justification of such a policy," Hurok wrote, "we are asking whether you would waive that restriction in the case of Miss Anderson. It need not be pointed out to you, we hope, that Marian Anderson is one of the greatest living singers and the application of such a restriction would be to deny a great musical experience to the people of your city, since it is impossible to present her in any other hall in Washington." Hurok closed the letter with a thinly veiled threat, asserting "that there is not a single artist or performer of high or lowly station in America today who would not be grieved and possibly outraged by your decision to exercise the restriction above-mentioned." Unmoved, Hand issued a curt response reiterating that the April 9 date was already booked and advising Hurok that any questions relating to "the matter of policy under which Constitution Hall operates" should be addressed to "Mrs. Henry Robert, Jr., President General of the National Society of the DAR."[35]

On January 27, with his ire rising, Hurok sent a letter to Robert with virtually the same wording as his earlier letter to Hand, adding only a plea for a quick decision "since upon it will depend our touring plans for Miss Anderson." Robert would, in fact, convene a meeting of the DAR's Board of

Management to discuss the matter five days later. But during those five days the interjection of other critical voices heightened the board's sense that the DAR was under attack. On the same day that Hurok wrote to Robert, Walter White, apparently acting independently of Hurok, issued a press release trumpeting the responses from the artists solicited a week earlier. As White explained in a letter to Robert on January 31, "The refusal to permit Miss Marian Anderson, distinguished Negro contralto, to sing there in April has shocked musicians, music-lovers and fair-minded Americans generally. Barring a world famed artist because of color from a building named by the Daughters of the American Revolution 'Constitution Hall' violates the very spirit and purpose of the immortal document after which the hall is named."[36]

In actuality, at the time that White made this statement there had been very little public outcry about the DAR's decision and even less press coverage. But White's hyperbole may have helped to push Robert and the DAR into a siege mentality just the same. At the very least, the DAR leaders began to brace themselves for an escalating public controversy, especially after Harold Ickes weighed in on January 30. Following a disturbing conversation with Howard University's president, Mordecai W. Johnson, the secretary of the interior could hardly contain his outrage. "This is such an astounding discrimination against equal rights," he informed Robert in a brief but blistering letter, "that I am loath to believe that the Daughters of the American Revolution should invoke such a rule."[37]

When the DAR board met on February 1, the Ickes letter was a major topic of conversation. The DAR was no stranger to public controversy, having incurred widespread criticism during the late 1920s for maintaining a blacklist of allegedly subversive organizations that included the NAACP, the YMCA and YWCA, the ACLU, and the Federal Council of Churches. To the dismay of civil libertarians both inside and outside the DAR, a list of the ninety organizations considered to be a threat to America's civil order appeared in a pamphlet entitled "The Common Enemy," along with the names of dangerous individuals such as the social worker Jane Addams, Harvard Law School dean Roscoe Pound, the presidents of Smith, Vassar, and Mt. Holyoke Colleges, Senator Robert La Follette of Wisconsin, and the black intellectual W. E. B. Du Bois. Over the years the DAR had also raised more than a few eyebrows by periodically expelling members who dared to dissent from organizational orthodoxy, and by generally endorsing an array of reactionary political and social views. Being upbraided by a cabinet officer, however, was a new and jarring development.

To Sarah Corbin "Sally" Robert, who had been president general less than a year, Ickes's letter appeared to be part of an unprecedented assault on the DAR's autonomy. Destined to play a major role in the Anderson concert controversy, Robert was a gracious but forceful woman with an acute sense of propriety. Though intelligent and well educated, she had grown up in a family of modest means, one that boasted a long American heritage but something less than the elite status often associated with the DAR. A native of Williamsport, Pennsylvania, she studied at Syracuse University before undertaking a ten-year career as a public high school history teacher in Brocton and Rome, New York, and Atlantic City, New Jersey. Following her marriage to the mathematician Henry Martyn Robert Jr., the son of the founding editor of *Robert's Rules of Order*, in 1919, she moved to Annapolis, Maryland, where she became a leading figure in the state conference of the DAR. Widowed in 1937, she later divided her time and energy between serving as a trustee and parliamentarian for *Robert's Rules* and promoting the interests of the DAR. A cultural and political conservative, she had little sympathy for proponents of social change, especially those who appeared to flout convention.[38]

In the absence of official minutes, which were reportedly destroyed to protect organizational privacy, we cannot be certain about what transpired at the most important meeting in DAR history. But all available evidence suggests that Robert exercised strong leadership in forging a consensus asserting the DAR's authority to protect itself from outside interference. The vote to sustain the "white artists only" policy was 39 to 1. The rationale for rejecting the request for a waiver, as Robert explained to Ickes two days later, was practical and contractual.

"In reply to your letter of January 30," she wrote, "Constitution Hall had already been engaged for Easter Sunday for use by another musical organization. Dr. Johnson was informed of the existence of a policy of several years' standing limiting the use of Constitution Hall to white artists. The artistic and musical standing of Miss Marian Anderson is not involved in any way. In view of the existence of provisions in prevailing agreements with other organizations and concert bureaus, and the policy which has been adopted in the past, an exception cannot be made in this instance." Interestingly enough, Robert sent a somewhat different letter to Hurok on the same day, emphasizing the problem with the April 9 date but making "no mention of the discriminatory clause."[39]

Whether deliberate or inadvertent, Robert's failure to mention the "white artists only" policy to Hurok encouraged the impresario to explore the option of alternative dates. Adopting an indirect strategy, he asked a friend to inquire about open dates on behalf of a white artist. At Hurok's request, Mark Levine, an agent for the National Concert and Artists Corporation, wrote to Hand asking if any dates were available in early April when the pianist Ignaz Paderewski could perform at Constitution Hall. Unaware that the request had anything to do with the Anderson controversy, Hand promptly sent Levine a list of ten open dates that included April 8 and 10, though not April 9.[40]

This was a startling turn of events for Cohen and the Lyceum-series committee. Prior to Hurok's intervention in early February, they had all but given up on Constitution Hall. During the previous two weeks, they had undertaken a desperate search for alternative venues, albeit with little success. Preliminary inquiries about the availability of commercial theaters went nowhere; the Rialto was in the midst of bankruptcy proceedings and had closed its doors, and neither the Belasco nor the National Theater could guarantee an April 9 booking. Check back with us in late March, the managers counseled Cohen, who suspected that he was being given the runaround. Unwilling to wait, he turned instead to the District of Columbia public schools for help.[41]

ON January 31, just prior to the DAR meeting, Cohen filed a booking application with the Washington School Board's Community Center Department for the use of a two-thousand-seat auditorium at Central High School, one of the city's largest white schools. Though rigidly segregated, the District school system had a long history of opening its facilities to the public for after-hours use. The practice dated back at least to 1915, when Congress passed an act authorizing the supplemental use of school buildings for civic and community events. The Community Center Department's implementation of the act generally maintained racial separation, with black and white officials empowered to regulate community use within their respective sectors of the dual school system. The act did not prohibit black use of white facilities, and on rare occasions such racial crossovers had occurred. But Cohen's request was unusual enough to warrant the involvement of Superintendent Frank W. Ballou, an imperious white paternalist who had guided the District's dual school system since 1920.

The news that the request would be handled by Ballou and not by

Elizabeth Peeples, the director of the Community Center Department, or by her black assistant Garnet Wilkinson, did not bode well for the Howard committee's prospects. The superintendent was a controversial and unpopular figure in Washington's black community, where he had gained a reputation as a firm segregationist with close political ties to conservative Southern congressmen. Neither Cohen nor anyone else could be sure about Ballou's racial sensibilities or about how much white supremacist pressure was being brought to bear on his decision. But from the outset, Cohen and his colleagues were less than sanguine about the likelihood of gaining Ballou's assent.

Their primary concern, aside from the overriding issue of race, was a loosely enforced School Board policy that prohibited "the use of school facilities . . . for any purpose which will result in a financial profit." In 1936 and 1937, when the Community Center Department had granted permission for Anderson to sing at Armstrong High School, Cohen had sidestepped the commercial-exclusion policy by promising to funnel all concert profits into a scholarship fund. He made the same offer in 1939, hoping that Ballou would ignore Anderson's heightened profile as a commercially successful artist. But he worried that the commercial-exclusion policy provided the superintendent with the opportunity to reject the Central High proposal without confronting the deeper issue of segregation.[42]

In the weeks to come, Ballou would indeed follow a path of indirection that relied on the commercial issue. But his initial rejection of the Howard committee's proposal did not offer a rationale for the decision. Writing on behalf of Ballou, Elizabeth Peeples dispatched a two-sentence letter to Cohen on February 3: "In the opinion of the school officers, it is not possible under the law for the Community Center Department to grant your request for the use of Central High School auditorium to present Miss Marian Anderson. I trust that you may be able to make some other satisfactory arrangement for her appearance in Washington as I appreciate fully all that you say in regard to her place among the popular artists of the day."

For Cohen and the Howard committee that had worked so hard to arrange the April concert, the acknowledgment of Anderson's popularity did not soften the blow of what amounted to a summary rejection. Though no one was shocked by Ballou's decision, the seemingly dismissive nature of his communication with the committee provoked a strong reaction among Howard faculty members and administrators, who were accustomed to a modicum of respect.

Over the next few days their disappointment turned to anger and a firm

The Anderson Family, c. 1910. From left to right,
Alyse, Anna, Marian, and Ethel.

Marian Anderson
in 1920.

Roland Hayes, internationally acclaimed tenor and Marian Anderson's friend and mentor, 1954. (*Courtesy of the Library of Congress*)

Giuseppe Boghetti, Marian Anderson's voice teacher, 1937.

Harry T. Burleigh, Pennsylvania-born singe composer, and arranger of African-Americi sprituals, c. 1940.

rian Anderson and her
nish accompanist, Kosti
hanen, performing at
Mozarteum, Salzburg,
stria, 1935.

rian Anderson and Terese
Enwall, wife of Anderson's
Scandinavian promoter,
Helmer Enwall, gathering
hay in Sweden, 1934.

Marian Anderson and Kosti Vehanen on board the Ile de France, bound for the United Sta
December 1935.

Marian Anderson in an academic procession at Howard University just prior to receiving an honorary degree, June 1938.

The Daughters of the American Revolution host a tea party for the patriotic organization's president general, 1947. (*Courtesy of Getty Images*)

Sidney Katz and Charles Houston, representing the Marian Anderson Citizens Committee, at the District of Columbia School Board hearing on the request to hold a Marian Anderson concert at Central High School, March 1, 1939. (*Courtesy of Getty Images*)

Walter White, executive secretary of the NAACP, 1950. (*Courtesy of the Library of Congress*)

Assistant Secretary of the Interior Oscar Chapman talks with Marian Anderson and her mother just prior to the Lincoln Memorial concert, April 9, 1939. (*Courtesy of Getty Images*)

Secretary of the Interior Harold L. Ickes welcomes Marian Anderson after introducing her to the crowd at the Lincoln Memorial, April 9, 1939.

Marian Anderson
in midsong,
April 9, 1939.

A photograph of the crowd surrounding the reflecting pool, taken from the east facade of the
Lincoln Memorial, April 9, 1939.

arian Anderson singing in front of seventy-five thousand people at the Lincoln Memorial,
pril 9, 1939. (© *Thomas D. McAvoy/Stringer/Time & Life Pictures/Getty Images*)

Marian Anderson poses with her mother, Anna Anderson, in front of Daniel Chester French's statue of Abraham Lincoln, April 9, 1939.

Eleanor Roosevelt presents the Spingarn Medal to Marian Anderson at the annual meeting of the NAACP, Richmond, Virginia, July 1939.

Marian Anderson sharing a moment with her mother after receiving the Bok Philadelphia Award, March 1941.

Marian Anderson bowing to the crowd at Constitution Hall, January 7, 1943. (*Courtesy of Getty Images*)

A snowy but gleeful exit from Constitution Hall, January 7, 1943. From left to right, Sol Hurok, Franz Rupp, Marian Anderson, and Hurok Productions traveling manager Isaac Jofe.

Mitchell Jamieson's Marian Anderson Mural, Department of the Interior, dedicated January 1943. (*Courtesy of the Fine Arts Program, U.S. General Services Administration; Photograph by David Alliso*

Marian Anderson visiting
soldiers at Fort Logan Army
Air Force Base, Colorado,
March 1943.

Marian Anderson as
Ulrica in *Un Ballo in
Maschera*, Metropolitan
Opera, 1955.

Marian Anderson and her husband, Orpheus "King" Fisher, in Hong Kong, October 1957.

Edward R. Murrow, Marian Anderson, and Sol Hurok discussing the television show *The Lady from Philadelphia*, December 1957.

arian Anderson as a U.S. delegate to the United Nations, 1958.

arian Anderson receives the Presidential Medal of Freedom from President Lyndon Baines
hnson, December 6, 1963.

Marian Anderson ends her farewell tour at New York's Carnegie Hall, April 18, 1965.

Marian Anderson rehearsing with Aaron Copland, composer of *A Lincoln Portrait*, in Saratoga Springs, New York, 1976.

resolve to force Ballou and the School Board, which included three black members, to reconsider the Central High request. At a minimum, they wanted a public exposition of the rationale behind the rejection of the proposal. If the proposed concert had been rejected as a threat to racial segregation, they wanted Ballou and the School Board to say so in a public forum.[43]

As word of Ballou's decision spread beyond the Howard campus, some members of Washington's black community called for a no-holds-barred confrontation with the School Board. But at Howard itself cooler heads prevailed, as Cohen and others recognized that the short-term goal of finding a place for Anderson to sing took precedence over settling scores with Ballou and the board. At this point, during the first week of February, the Howard committee had all but given up on Constitution Hall, leaving the reconsideration of the Central High proposal as their last hope. In this situation, burning bridges with the school system was hardly a viable option. Instead, Cohen formed a special negotiating committee consisting of himself; Gustav Ausenne, the treasurer of the university; Dorothy Cline, a researcher at the U.S. Housing Authority; Glenn Dillard Gunn, the music editor of the *Washington Times-Herald*; and Doxey A. Wilkerson, a highly respected professor of education at Howard. With Wilkerson taking the lead, the committee prepared a detailed proposal to be submitted to the School Board at its next meeting on February 15.[44]

In the meantime, as Wilkerson and the committee drafted and refined the new proposal, Hurok resurrected the Constitution Hall option, having learned that alternative dates were available. On February 8, Cohen resubmitted his application to Fred Hand, changing the requested date from Easter Sunday, April 9, to either Saturday the eighth or Monday the tenth, two of the dates offered to Paderewski. Hand wasted no time in replying, advising Cohen on February 10 "that Constitution Hall will not be available on either April 8th or April 10th for the Marian Anderson recital." Hand offered Cohen no explanation for the lack of availability, but when Hurok called a few days later, the defiant manager shouted into the phone, "No date will ever be available for Marian Anderson in Constitution Hall!"

On February 13, the DAR issued its first press release regarding the Anderson matter. The text repeated the arguments about unavailable dates and long-standing policy, but the organization's primary rationale for discrimination had shifted to community standards. "The rules governing the use of Constitution Hall," the press release asserted, "are in accordance with the policy of theaters, auditoriums, hotels and public schools of the District of Columbia." When reporters and other interested parties inquired about the details of the DAR's adherence to a communitywide pattern of segregation, they discovered that President General Robert was unavailable for comment, having boarded a train for a seven-week national tour of DAR state conferences. Aside from a couple of terse statements to reporters, Robert maintained her silence until her return to Washington in mid-April, giving the distinct impression that she and the DAR considered the Constitution Hall controversy to be all but over.[45]

Sally Robert had ample reason to believe that the controversy would soon fade from view; after all, no one in American history had ever sustained a civil rights protest involving such a seemingly trivial matter. Nonetheless, her judgment rested on an understanding of an America that was passing from view. She, along with most of her DAR colleagues, saw the situation through the narrow lens of privilege, hierarchy, and tradition. What she did not see was the unique configuration of factors gaining strength and coordination just beyond her vision: the devotion inspired by Anderson's mystique; the gathering determination of Washington's black community to assert its right to full participation in the life of the nation's capital; the ascendance of the NAACP and the Black Cabinet; the general recasting of the American creed in an age of rising totalitarianism; the creative energy of restless émigrés such as Hurok; and the moral conscience of a DAR member who lived in the White House. Somehow, from mid-February on, all of these factors aligned to produce the equivalent of a two-front war fought over issues both simple and profound. As civil rights advocates challenged the entrenched authority of the School Board and the DAR, the Anderson campaign became much more than an effort to sustain a university concert series by defending Marian Anderson's right to sing. For many of those engaged in the struggle, the campaign had become nothing less than a fight for self-respect and human dignity.

The public phase of the struggle began in earnest on February 15, when Doxey Wilkerson appeared before the School Board. Despite inclement weather, the meeting room was filled to overflowing, mostly with black citizens who had come to support the Howard committee. Unfortunately, only seven of the nine board members were on hand to hear Wilkerson's presentation, and John Wilson, one of the board's three black members, left before the matter came to a vote. Wilkerson began by presenting a memorandum signed by all five members of the negotiating committee. Describing the difficulty of finding a suitable venue for the Anderson concert as "a problem of considerable significance to the cultural life of our entire community," the memorandum went on to make the case, procedurally and culturally, for over-turning Superintendent Ballou's decision.

With the elimination of Constitution Hall and the city's commercial theaters from the list of available venues, Central High auditorium was the only hall in the District large enough to accommodate "one of the most pop-ular concert artists before the American public." The memorandum contin-ued, "Just two weeks ago she sang to a capacity audience of 4,000 persons at the Mosque in Pittsburgh. She is booked already to render seventy-five recit-als this season, more than any other American artist has ever been engaged for in advance. Unquestionably, because of her incomparable excellence, Miss Anderson is now one of the greatest artists in the musical world. That such an artist be brought to our community is a matter of general civic importance."

The strategy throughout was to emphasize the citywide importance of the concert, not the particular interests of the black community. After re-minding the school board that Anderson's 1938 concert at the Rialto had attracted "considerably more white than Negro persons," the memorandum insisted that Howard was applying "for use of the public schools for a musi-cal project whose appeal is truly to the community as a whole." The negotiat-ing committee also reassured the board that the Central High proposal was "quite unrelated to the existence of a dual system of schools in this commu-nity, and would not affect in any manner the relationships which there ob-tain." The memorandum declared, in a concession that the committee would later retract, "Our request is made to meet a specific emergency situation. We do not raise with you any question of continuing policy. Rather, we ap-peal for the use of a particular building for a particular occasion, our appeal being prompted by an unforeseen exigency."

All of this fell on deaf ears. The board members listened politely, asked a few questions, then promptly rejected the Howard committee's request by a vote of 5 to 1. The only member in favor of holding the Anderson concert at the Central High School auditorium was West A. Hamilton, the lone black member at the meeting. At the close of the meeting, as the disappointed crowd filed out of the room, murmurs of anger signaled that the fight was not over. Indeed, it soon became clear that the School Board's decision had ignited a firestorm of indignation among black Washingtonians, as well as a good deal of consternation among local white liberals. Prior to the decision, most close observers of the situation had regarded Superintendent Ballou as the biggest obstacle to overcome. But following the School Board's nearly unanimous vote, virtually everyone recognized that the root of the problem was an institutional mind-set that relegated blacks to second-class citizenship. As Patrick Hayes, a white theatrical agent close to the scene, recalled years later, "The issue was now larger than the DAR–Constitution Hall denial: The entire city was closed to the committee and the artist. It was now more than a concert booking. It was a moral and ethical issue, a sacred cause with repercussions reaching far beyond the city limits." Speaking for the NAACP, Walter White called the School Board's action "contemptible" in a telegram sent to the chairmen of the House and Senate District committees on February 17. Drawing a comparison between American racism and fascism that would become a major theme among Anderson's supporters in the weeks ahead, he maintained, "Such childish discrimination makes ridiculous and hypocritical American protestations against outrages suffered by minorities in Nazi Germany and other parts of the world."[46]

Closer to home, several community groups in Washington held emergency meetings to consider a course of action against the School Board. The first to do so was the Washington agency of the black-owned North Carolina Mutual Life Insurance Company, which sent a letter of protest to Ballou on February 17 alleging that his opposition to the Central High concert "shows a narrowness of thought, and is based purely on race prejudice." The first protest meeting of any size took place on the eighteenth, when the local chapter of the American Federation of Teachers assembled at a downtown YWCA. But the most important development occurred the next day when Charles Edward Russell, a white attorney who presided over the city's Inter-Racial Committee, convened a meeting that led to the formation of a group tentatively called the Citizens Committee for Protesting the Exclusion of Marian Anderson. Claiming to represent "fifteen organizations and . . . thousands of the District's citizens of all races," the Citizens Committee began its campaign to counter the School Board's decision with a letter of censure to John Wilson, the black board member who had skipped out before the vote, and a letter of appreciation to West Hamilton. "We feel that you alone have voiced the sentiments of all of us who look forward to a world of progress and peace, and not backward to the dark days of prejudice and oppression," the letter read. "For many years, problems of an interracial nature growing out of our dual education system have been left hanging fire. We pledge our support to assist you in getting those problems solved."

Drawing upon long-standing resentment against the School Board's prejudicial policies, the Citizens Committee assembled a picket line in front of the board's headquarters on the morning of the twentieth. The School Board had not faced this kind of protest since the early 1920s, but the committee was just getting started. Streamlining its name to the Marian Anderson Citizens Committee (MACC), the group soon elected an interim set of officers and formed a steering committee representing twenty-four organizations that ranged from labor unions to fraternal orders. It also began collecting signatures on a petition to be presented to the School Board at its next meeting on March 1. Filled with soaring rhetoric, the petition took the board to task for "shutting the doors of the schools in the face of an artist of world renown because of the separate school system." It also declared that since the board members had been elected to serve as "the guardians of the public schools which are the bulwark of American democracy, it scarcely behooves them to endorse what every civilized person regards as the worst form of intolerance, especially in these times when the forces of intelligence and civilization are combating racial intolerance and oppression."[47]

During the last week of February, as the number of signatures and affiliated organizations mounted, the MACC took on a more formal structure. After electing Charles Houston chairman, the committee established an office at Houston's law firm, located at 615 F Street, Northwest. Houston was the perfect choice to lead the MACC. An honors graduate of Amherst College and Harvard Law School, and the former dean of Howard Law School, he had close ties to the Black Cabinet and the national leadership of the NAACP. He also had experience on the District of Columbia School Board. After serving a two-year term on the board earlier in the decade, he had come away with a deep sense of frustration with a dual school system that routinely shortchanged black students. Thus, he welcomed the Anderson controversy as an unexpected opportunity to expose the school system's shortcomings. The MACC was also fortunate to have Bertha Blair, of the League of Peace and Democracy, as vice chair; John Lovell Jr., an energetic young Howard instructor, as secretary; and James E. Scott, an official with Kappa Alpha Psi, as treasurer. Under Lovell's daily supervision, the MACC office was soon producing a steady stream of correspondence and press releases related to the Anderson controversy.[48]

The result was a noticeable increase in press coverage, first in Washington and later nationally. Most of the coverage was favorable, such as the *Philadelphia Record*'s call for a congressional investigation of the Washington School Board. But there were important exceptions. On February 21, the *Washington Post* ran an editorial defending both the DAR and the School

Board, prompting Lovell to write a scathing letter to the editor: "Your editorial in Tuesday's newspaper is a disheartening example of a device used for many years to justify discrimination, namely, the interposition of petty issues between a fact and the great issues it throws into bold relief . . . You say that the D. A. R. have the same unquestionable right to decide in these matters as a private club. But is a private club tax-exempt? If the D. A. R. wish to exercise their personal views above those of the community they serve, they should pay for such freedom by the rebate in taxes to the government." Turning to the School Board controversy, Lovell asked plaintively, "Does the dual school system mean that artistic standards in Washington must be halved up into white and black?" He warned the *Post*, "The Negro people of Washington are squarely behind those of us who challenge this discrimination, to the bitter end, and they are encouraged that, seeing as they do hundreds of their white friends in the ranks beside them, this is one battle against discrimination they will not have to fight alone."[49]

The broad nature of Anderson's local support became apparent when the MACC held its first mass meeting on Sunday, February 26. Two days earlier Cohen had resubmitted the Howard committee's application to the School Board with additional argumentation, and the MACC hoped that a public protest would encourage the board to reconsider its position. A widely distributed broadside urged concerned citizens of all races to come to the meeting to DEFEND OUR DEMOCRATIC RIGHT TO HEAR MARIAN ANDERSON SING! "Even as in Naziland," the broadside insisted, "superb art is here crucified upon the altar of racial bigotry. Shall we permit the D. A. R. and the Board of Education to impose this unwholesome policy upon our community? Shall the people of Washington dictate, or be dictated to?" Employing this kind of rhetoric was politically risky, but when the doors opened at the Lincoln Temple Congregational Church on Sunday afternoon, the onrush of ordinary citizens confirmed that the appeal to democratic values had tapped a deep strain of outrage in Washington. The original plan had been to hold the meeting at Mt. Pleasant Congregational Church, one of the city's largest and most prestigious white churches. But when the organizing committee learned that Mt. Pleasant's minister faced stiff opposition from a conservative faction within his congregation, the site of the meeting was moved to Lincoln Temple, a black church located on Seventeenth Street, in the heart of downtown Washington.

By the time the meeting started at four o'clock, more than fifteen hundred people, approximately a third of whom were white, had jammed into the church to hear a succession of speakers denounce the School Board and the DAR. As the afternoon progressed, the crowd discovered that they were not alone. MACC leaders reported that, although only a week old, the organization had already received words of support and encouragement from scores of individuals and organizations, including the NAACP, the United Mine Workers, the Brotherhood of Sleeping Car Porters, and the Washington council of the liberal Descendants of the American Revolution. In Anderson's hometown, the entire Philadelphia Orchestra had endorsed a statement declaring that "a great injustice has been done to one of America's foremost artists. Such discrimination, we feel, is contrary to the musical and cultural life of our country and not in keeping with the American spirit of fairness." Sylvan Levin, the director of the Philadelphia Opera Company, had termed the DAR racial ban "so terrible that I really find it difficult to express my feelings"; and Anderson's longtime teacher, Giuseppe Boghetti, had compared the ban to the "prejudice and bigotry . . . rampant in other parts of the world." He had told a Philadelphia reporter, "The whole thing is deplorable. I had thought this kind of race prejudice was a thing of the past in this country . . . Mrs. Boghetti, who is a member of the DAR, is entirely in sympathy with my feelings in the matter, and is seriously considering resigning from the organization." The assemblage also learned that the noted violinist Jascha Heifetz had expressed deep remorse after completing a recent concert at Constitution Hall. "I was really uncomfortable on that platform," Heifetz confessed to reporters gathered in his dressing room, "uncomfortable to think that this very hall in which I played has been barred to a great singer because of her race; it made me feel ashamed. I protest, as the entire musical profession protests, against such a sad and deplorable attitude."⁵⁰

Heifetz's words stirred the crowd, but even the organizers of the meeting had to concede that they faced a steep uphill struggle. Neither the School Board nor the DAR showed any sign of reversing their opposition to the Anderson concert, and it seemed unlikely that the situation would change anytime soon. The MACC was a fledgling organization representing a local movement with little visibility or leverage outside the District of Columbia and Philadelphia. Despite a few editorials in the black press, the Anderson controversy had not yet captured the attention of the national press or, even more important, the imagination of the American people. The *New York Times*, one of the best barometers of national interest, had run only one brief article on the Anderson controversy, on February 23, and had buried it on page 24. Even with Anderson's rising popularity, a heated School Board meeting and an uncharitable decision by the DAR were apparently not enough to secure front-page or sustained coverage.[51]

As February drew to a close, the MACC, for all its local success, needed a catalyst, some defining event that would focus the attention of mainstream America on the manifest injustice of denying Marian Anderson's right to sing. For weeks everyone from Hurok to Houston and the Black Cabinet had puzzled over what it would take to generate a national groundswell of support, but so far they had failed to come up with anything. In late January, Lulu Childers, the director of music at Howard, floated the idea of arranging an outdoor concert for Anderson, vowing, "She'll sing here—even if we have to build a tent for her." And a month later, on February 24, an exasperated Hurok picked up on the idea, informing the NAACP that Anderson would perform "out in the open air in front of Constitution Hall. She will sing for the people of Washington and there will be no charge, because the concert will be held out in the open. Our only stage decoration will be two American flags." Weeks later this plan would evolve into the Lincoln Memorial concert, but at the time Hurok's bluster roused little attention or enthusiasm.[52]

THE defining event, when it burst upon the scene on February 27, came from an unlikely source. For nearly two months Eleanor Roosevelt had remained in the background, biding her time and contemplating how she could help the talented young woman who had charmed the president and everyone else at a White House recital three years earlier. In mid-January the first lady had embraced the opportunity to present Anderson with the Spingarn Medal at the NAACP national convention in July, following up with a second invitation for Anderson to sing at the White House, asking her to perform before the king and queen of England in June. But otherwise the first lady had remained silent as the DAR and School Board controversies unfolded. By all accounts, she had kept close tabs on the developing situation through periodic conversations with Houston, White, Bethune, and other members of the Black Cabinet. Yet when Howard officials pleaded with her to speak out against the discriminatory policies of the DAR in early February, she politely but firmly refused. As a DAR member, she was understandably hesitant to criticize a powerful organization capable of mobilizing opposition to her husband's agenda for reform. But Anderson's plight tore at her heart, ultimately forcing an act of conscience.[53]

The first sign that she had decided to join the fray was a one-line tele-

gram delivered to Lovell a few hours before the mass meeting: I REGRET
EXTREMELY THAT WASHINGTON IS TO BE DEPRIVED OF HEARING MARIAN
ANDERSON, A GREAT ARTIST. Disappointed that the first lady would not be at
the meeting to deliver the message in person, Lovell read her brief statement
to the crowd without thinking much of it until the next morning. On February 27, less than twenty-fours after the Lincoln Temple meeting, Eleanor
Roosevelt broke her silence in the most dramatic way possible. Without
mentioning Anderson or the DAR by name, her nationally syndicated *My
Day* column announced her resignation from a patriotic organization that
had violated the principles of American democracy. In a brief but somewhat
oblique statement, she explained why she could no longer be a member of
such an organization:

> I have been debating in my mind for some time a question which I have
> had to debate with myself once or twice before in my life. Usually I have
> decided differently from the way in which I am deciding now. The
> question is, if you belong to an organization and disapprove of an action
> which is typical of a policy, shall you resign or is it better to work for a
> changed point of view within the organization? In the past when I was
> able to work actively in any organization to which I belonged, I have
> usually stayed in until I had at least made a fight and been defeated. Even
> then I have as a rule usually accepted my defeat and decided either that I
> was wrong or that perhaps I was a little too far ahead of the thinking of
> the majority of that time. I belong to an organization in which I can do no
> active work. They have taken action which has been widely talked on in
> the press. To remain a member implies approval of that action, and
> therefore I am resigning.[54]

At a press conference later in the day, she continued to avoid specific
mention of the DAR, though when asked point-blank whether she had "resigned from the DAR," her answer left no doubt as to the organization in
question. "Mrs. Robert better answer that question," she responded, offering
a sly smile to the reporters in the room. The actual resignation letter had
been mailed to DAR headquarters on the twenty-sixth, though Sally Robert
was not there to receive it. Only later would she read the first lady's stinging
words: "You had an opportunity to lead in an enlightening way, and it seems
to me that your organization has failed." The president general's response
was courteous, but it offered nothing specific or substantial to counter the

argument for resignation. "Your letter of resignation reached me in Colorado upon my return from the far West," Robert wrote. "I greatly regret that you found this action necessary. Our society is engaged in the education for citizenship and the humanitarian service in which we know you to be vitally interested. I am indeed sorry not to have been in Washington at this time. Perhaps I might have been able to remove some of the misunderstanding and to have presented to you personally the attitude of the Society."[35]

The resignation was not altogether surprising. Eleanor Roosevelt had only been a DAR member since 1933 and had never been entirely comfortable affiliating with an openly elitist organization. Predominantly Republican, the DAR was staunchly conservative and generally opposed to much of what her husband's administration was trying to accomplish. Thus, in a strictly political sense, she had no reason whatsoever to have anything to do with the Daughters. Nevertheless, in the early days of the New Deal it had seemed prudent to accept the entreaties of a high-profile organization that professed to do good works and defend the nation's honor. Edith Scott Magna, the president general of the DAR at the time, who was in the midst of a factional struggle to rescue the organization from its most extreme right-wing members, pleaded with Roosevelt to aid the forces of moderation by accepting a life membership. Against her better judgment, Roosevelt agreed. Elated, Magna waived the normal initiation fee and presented the first lady with a special "embossed certificate inscribed with the names of her six Revolutionary ancestors." Despite Magna's hopes, over the next six years Roosevelt's role in the DAR was completely ceremonial, limited to an annual White House reception that welcomed the Daughters to Washington each spring. Even though the organization continued to drift to the right, the first lady had no involvement in the DAR's internal politics prior to her resignation.[36]

The DAR's initial response to the resignation was a firm denial that the organization had received anything in writing from the White House. And the organization continued to downplay the significance of the resignation for several weeks. Others, however, wasted no time in hailing Roosevelt's gesture as a seminal event. Suddenly the Anderson controversy was front-page news from coast to coast. Reporters were accustomed to writing about Eleanor Roosevelt, the social reformer, but nothing comparable to the DAR resignation had ever come across the newswires. No first lady had ever interjected herself into a public controversy in such a personal and forthright way.

As a political act, the resignation was largely symbolic, with no guarantee that it would have any impact on the DAR's policies. Yet it seemed to strike a deep chord among those who had been waiting for a sign that at least some white Americans were ready to live up to their professed ideals of freedom and equality. For them the realization that the most famous white woman in the nation had done so was no small matter. Black journalists, rankled not only by the mistreatment of Marian Anderson but also by the DAR's earlier denigration of the NAACP as a subversive organization, could hardly contain themselves.

To James Wooton of the *Philadelphia Tribune*, the situation was now clear: "A group of tottering old ladies, who don't know the difference between patriotism and putridism, have compelled the gracious First Lady to apologize for their national rudeness to one of the world's greatest living artists." Finding sweet irony in the DAR's misbehavior, he sarcastically thanked the Daughters for enabling Anderson's "transition from mortality to immortality, while very much alive. She is now more than Marian Anderson the singer. She is now Marian Anderson, a beauteous symbol." In the *Pittsburgh Courier*, a front-page story on the resignation carried a picture of Anderson under the headline STORM CENTER. The caption read, "While Germany looks on, Miss Anderson is on the threshold of becoming an 'international incident.'" Arthur Huff Fauset, a black columnist from Philadelphia who had known Anderson for years, explored the same theme with less restraint. Calling for a boycott of Constitution Hall as the first step in countering America's racist hypocrisy, he pointed out, "Uncle Sam's Negro children, like the little chicks, have a way of coming home to roost on America's much vaunted democratic perch, and making the United States look rather ridiculous—especially to those bad fellows, Germany, Italy, and Japan." He asked, "Where else in the world is a Jim Crow car? Where else are there hotels and eating places by the thousands, North, East, South, and West, where Negroes dare not so much as enter the door to eat? . . . Where else in the world are people barred from employment solely on account of the color of their skins? . . . What other democracy or dictatorship boasts of a Constitution granting the franchise to all citizens, then deliberately turns round and restrains millions of black citizens from enjoying this prerogative, and gets backing from the Supreme Court to disqualify these Negroes? We could go on indefinitely."[57]

Not every black commentator was as candid, or as angry, as Fauset. But the DAR resignation seemed to unleash feelings that had previously been held in check—and not only in the black community. For several weeks, the controversy surrounding Anderson, the DAR, and the first lady served as racial touchstone for millions of Americans. To Carleton Smith, a cynical feature writer for *Esquire*, the resignation simply "released the gutters of publicity. Club women wrote letters, columnists wisecracked, newspapers editorialized, Congressmen and Senators jumped on the bandwagon. L'affaire Anderson rivaled Hitler's coups as a front-page item." But Smith missed the deeper story of racial reflection; the public discussion of the resignation provided a rare and valuable opportunity to explore the meaning of the American creed, in the press, in the halls of government, around the breakfast table, and wherever Americans gathered.[58]

The rhetoric in the mainstream press was more subdued than in the black press. But, with a few notable exceptions, the nation's leading dailies wasted no time in lining up behind the first lady. The *New York Times*, which had steadfastly ignored the Anderson controversy prior to the resignation, led the way with a carefully worded March 1 editorial: "Those who love music and are unable to perceive any relationship between music on the one hand and political, economic or social issues on the other will regret, as Mrs. Eleanor Roosevelt does, that Washington may be deprived of the pleasure of hearing this artist. If Miss Anderson's inability to find a suitable hall in the national capital is due to social or racial snobbery, all that can be said is that such an attitude is inconsistent with the best American traditions, including those that were born in the fires of the American Revolution. It is hard to believe that any patriotic organization in this country would approve of discrimination against so gifted an artist and so fine a person as Miss Anderson. In fact, no organization could do so and still merit the adjective patriotic."[59]

Heywood Broun, writing in the *New York World-Telegram*, expressed roughly the same sentiment without mincing words: "When the Daughters of the American Revolution refused to permit Miss Marian Anderson to give a concert in Constitution Hall in Washington it seemed to me one of the most monstrous and stupid things which have occurred within America in years . . . But let us forget the Daughters. It is up to some radio chain or musical organization to offer, and indeed, to plead with Miss Anderson to accept the facilities of a national hookup so that everyone in our nation can hear one of the most glorious voices now vital in the world. At such a celebration no mention should be made of the erring organization, and I do not think it is necessary to place any emphasis upon the fact that Miss Anderson is a Negro. The answer to the bigots both here and abroad can be most eloquently expressed in her own singing voice. In the extraordinary notes within her range there are sounds which make the whole world kin . . . Let us . . . join with Marian Anderson in a celebration of the international unity of art and the artists. And to me it would seem most fitting if Eleanor Roosevelt should act as chairman for this evening of fellowship and fraternity."[60]

Across the Hudson River, the *Newark Evening News* offered a similar judgment, praising the first lady for addressing a "vulgar and degrading situation." The *Evening News* advised its readers, "Let us reexamine our patriotism, and let those who do formal obeisance to their patriotic ancestors reinspect the ideals for which those patriots fought. God has given a Negro woman a great voice—an American voice. Perhaps in time . . . with the return of a modicum of common sense and perspective . . . that voice will be heard in the capital of the United States." The *Philadelphia Record* was more succinct but no less impassioned: "Shameful this affair is. But the American way is to fight intolerance. That fight is now on. We all may be proud that the First Lady is leading it."[61]

In one way or another, virtually all of the editorials picked up on the theme of hypocrisy and false patriotism. In a piece entitled "Un-American Daughters," the *Cleveland Plain Dealer* insisted that the first lady's "fair-minded countrymen are emphatically on her side in resentment of the snobbish and undemocratic attitude of this purportedly patriotic organization . . . It is ironic as well as outrageous that in the capital of her own country she [Anderson] is Jim Crowed, and by an organization which pays lip service to liberty." Cal Tinney, writing in the *Washington Post* on March 7, couched his criticism of the DAR in a satirical letter to Arturo Toscanini. Referring to April 9, he speculated, "I don't know what Constitution Hall will be used for that night. Probably for a lecture on how everybody is free and equal in the United States." Always looking for the dark comedy in contemporary events, the *New Yorker* magazine found "a neat if rather elementary irony" in the "decision to bar Miss Anderson, a distinguished Negro singer, from Constitution Hall, which, of course, takes its name from a document guaranteeing Miss Anderson freedom from racial discrimination."[62]

Constitutional scholars could quibble over whether the Fourteenth Amendment to the Constitution actually provided such a guarantee, but, revealingly, some Northern papers tried to explain the situation in both regional and national terms. According to the *Boston Evening Transcript*, "The First Lady need offer no apology for her action . . . No less than the President, himself, she represents the country as a whole and she cannot permit her name even by implication to be linked with a policy of racial discrimination." Turning to the DAR, the editorial speculated that the organization "is probably more guilty of inertia than deliberate discrimination. A spokesman for the organization explained that a similar policy was followed by the management of other auditoriums in the capital, which, geographically at least, is a southern city, and the D. A. R. merely adopted the accepted practice. But this circumstance will not serve as an excuse if the D. A. R. fails to remedy the evil, now that it has resulted in such a scandal. Since the organization is national and dedicated to the promulgation of patriotic principles, it should, of course, have broken with the Jim Crow tradition in the capital and made its auditorium available to all artists regardless of color or creed."[63]

Similarly, the *Springfield (MA) Daily Republican*, after lamenting that "it takes the resignation of the 'first lady' to force the broadcasting from coast to coast of the shabby treatment of Marian Anderson at the national capital," reminded its readers that "the issue raised cannot be confined to the D. A. R. Almost every other auditorium management in Washington enforces the same rule against rentals for concerts or other performances by Negro artists. Even a public school hall was denied for Miss Anderson's song recital. From this point of view, Washington is as race-conscious, it is as far out on the color line, as almost any southern city. The D. A. R.'s rule for its Washington auditorium was almost certainly dictated by its own southern membership even more than by the sentiment of a large part of the population of the national capital."[64]

Criticizing the benighted South was, of course, a popular pastime in many Northern communities, where manifestations of racial prejudice closer to home often received less attention than they deserved. But in the Anderson episode the obvious identification of the DAR and the District of Columbia as national institutions made it difficult to view the race problem as a regional phenomenon—especially after it became clear that many white Southerners were less than enthusiastic about the decision to bar Marian Anderson from Constitution Hall.

To the dismay of conservative white supremacists, the editorial reaction in the South to the resignation was decidedly mixed. While some white Southern editors took a hard line against liberal agitation, a surprising number went out of their way to support the first lady's decision to challenge the DAR. "We cannot agree with the decision of the D. A. R.," a March 8 editorial in the *Ocala (FL) Banner* declared. "While most of the barrage of protests which have followed the action come from north of the Mason and Dixon line, even around here most people seem to consider the decision unwarranted." "Why there should be any objection to the appearance of Marian

Anderson in Constitution Hall at Washington passes all human understanding," Grover Hall, the politically moderate editor of the *Montgomery Advertiser* wrote on February 28. "If as it would appear Mrs. Roosevelt has resigned from the D. A. R. against this amazing policy, *The Advertiser* thinks she has done a courageous and honorable thing." Another Southern moderate, Hodding Carter of the Greenville, Mississippi, *Delta Democrat-Times*, agreed, "We fail to see how the D. A. R. achieved a single worthy purpose in denying the Hall to a negro woman whose voice brings pleasure to men and women of every race . . . Mrs. Roosevelt's resignation from the D. A. R. in protest against this discrimination was, we think, a merited rebuke."[65]

Virginius Dabney went even further in a March 1 editorial in the influential *Richmond Times-Dispatch*: "In these days of racial intolerance so crudely expressed in the Third Reich, an action such as the D. A. R.'s ban upon potential Negro lessees of Constitution Hall seems all the more deplorable. That this ruling has not been relaxed or repealed is a rather sad commentary on the descendants of those men who helped to create a democracy which strongly cries out against gross racial discrimination in other countries . . . It could be suggested that while members of the D. A. R. are restoring the dwellings of their Revolutionary forebears, they might give some thought to the restoration of their ideals as well."[66]

For Dabney, the dean of Southern liberals, the Anderson controversy represented a step on the path to increased interracial contact and a New South. But most of the editors who criticized the DAR saw no contradiction between allowing Anderson to sing at Constitution Hall and sustaining the systemic traditions of Jim Crow. "We are without sympathy with the 'drawing of the color line' against a negro artist who has something worthwhile to offer to white and black people alike," the conservative editor of the *Charleston News and Courier* wrote on March 1, reassuring his readers, "This we say without budging an inch from insistence upon social separation of the races. No such question is involved in renting a hall to a negro."[67]

Drawing this kind of distinction often baffled outsiders unfamiliar with the shibboleths of the South's paternalistic style of racism. But in the context of Southern culture and politics it made sense. Blacks who kept their social place could come physically close to whites, as long as whites remained confident that they were setting the acceptable limits of contact. This helps to explain why Southern politicians were virtually mute on the Anderson controversy; indeed some undoubtedly enjoyed the DAR's discomfort, feeling that it revealed the hypocrisy of white Northerners, who often identified racism as an exclusively Southern phenomenon. But the politicians' silence following the resignation was also a function of partisanship; as leaders of the Democratic Party, they were in no position to criticize the first lady, which would have been interpreted as an indirect attack on a Democratic president. In private, they could say all they wanted about the meddlesome Roosevelts. But political propriety prevented conservative Democratic politicians, Southern and Northern, from speaking their mind on the resignation and related issues.

A few politicians tried to straddle the line on the Anderson controversy. New Jersey governor A. Harry Moore, for example, defended the DAR after Bishop Francis J. McConnell of the Methodist Episcopal Church suggested that the heritage organization "might better be called the Mothers of Fascism." Speaking to a New Jersey state DAR convention, Moore insisted that Bishop McConnell's "statement is not at all applicable to the work you have been doing to make America great." Yet, the governor did not endorse the DAR's color bar, which received no mention whatsoever in his speech.

The politicians who spoke out forcefully were the most liberal members of both parties. One of the most passionate critics of the DAR was Mayor Fiorello La Guardia of New York City. "No hall is too good for Marian Anderson," he exclaimed a few days after Eleanor Roosevelt's resignation. "She is one of the most outstanding singers of our time, if not all time. The Washington decision does not detract one bit from the artistic standing of this young cultured gentlewoman." His fellow New Yorker, Senator Robert F. Wagner, agreed: "The Marian Anderson case is not a local issue. It is a matter of the foremost national and international importance. If art can be stifled and racial lines drawn so tightly in our own capital city, then it would be well for us to ponder the fate of democracy in the United States." Henry A. Wallace, the secretary of agriculture, put it more simply, reminding Americans, "Artistic ability is not measured by the color of the skin." Of the same mind but a different party, Republican Senator William E. Borah of Idaho declared on March 3, "It seems intolerable that this cultured woman should be denied an opportunity to be heard."[68]

Some politicians did not stop at words. Senator Robert M. La Follette Jr., an independent from Wisconsin, announced on March 7 that the Bronson M. Cutting Memorial Lectures, a congressionally sponsored series named for a popular New Mexico senator who had died in a plane crash in 1935, would no longer be held at Constitution Hall; and Representative Joseph P. McGranery, a Pennsylvania Democrat, called for a congressional investigation of the Washington School Board. Joseph A. Gavagan, a liberal

Democratic congressman from New York City who had sponsored antilynching legislation earlier in the decade, also called for congressional action. "The whole country has been shocked by the spirit of intolerance manifested toward Miss Marian Anderson by the D. A. R. and the Board of Education of the District of Columbia," Gavagan wired the NAACP's Charles Houston on March 25. "We need the practice of American principles as well as their preachment." At the state and local level, little could be done, but Mrs. Clarence Hand, a Republican assemblywoman from Essex County, New Jersey, who was also a former regent of the Essex County DAR, introduced a resolution at the state DAR conference "condemning the national organization" for barring Anderson from Constitution Hall. The conference rejected the resolution, but Mrs. Hand continued to speak out against Sally Robert and other conservative DAR leaders. "The action of the national society was definitely not Americanism and absolutely against the principles for which the DAR stands," she told an interracial Newark audience on March 19. "I believe in practicing what you preach."[69]

Other politicians, including Republicans such as Senator Henry Cabot Lodge Jr. of Massachusetts, expressed public support for Anderson in the wake of the resignation but made no explicit mention of the first lady. Whether this reflected partisanship or common courtesy, such omissions were cold comfort for the DAR. Whatever their motivations, the politicians who chose to speak out on either Anderson's or the first lady's behalf were not taking much of a risk. By mid-March, public opinion was clearly running squarely against the DAR. A Gallup poll released on March 18 revealed that 67 percent of those polled approved of the first lady's resignation. The pollsters reported that the "most frequent reason given by those who back up Mrs. Roosevelt's decision is: 'There shouldn't be any race prejudice in this country.'" The pollsters expressed surprise that Republicans (63 percent) supported the decision almost as firmly as Democrats (68 percent), but the explanation could be found in the regional peculiarities of Southern Democrats. The regional rates of approval ranged from 80 percent in the West to 43 percent in the South. "Southerners dissented by an average vote of 57%," the pollsters explained, "but even some of the dissenters declared they had no objection to Marian Anderson's singing as a paid performer. It was Mrs. Roosevelt's 'making a fuss about it' that they disliked."[70]

One white American who had every reason to welcome the "fuss" was Sol Hurok, who issued a press release on February 27 describing the first lady as "a woman of courage and excellent taste." The unexpected announcement, he declared, represented "one of the most hopeful signs in these troublesome times for democracy." In later years Hurok would make every effort to downplay the importance of Eleanor Roosevelt's resignation, elevating his own role to Herculean proportions. Indeed, in his recasting of the saga, the first lady, Walter White, Charles Houston, and everyone else became secondary players in a drama masterminded by Hurok Productions. "I took over the Washington Hotel, a whole floor upstairs," he recalled in 1974, "and I brought in my press agent and all to start to bombard the whole country, you know— artists, actors, and so on and so on. A big campaign we made . . . The whole thing was just a question of mass protest. I raised the sentiment all over the country, as a matter of fact. The world protested." Perhaps so, but there is no solid evidence that he ever rented a room, much less a whole floor, of the Washington Hotel for the purpose of mobilizing opposition to the DAR. In January and February, he tried to negotiate with Hand and Robert and periodically made public statements that helped to sustain the momentum of the Anderson protests. But neither he nor his staff made any attempt to solicit letters and telegrams from famous artists and celebrities until February 27, the day of Eleanor Roosevelt's resignation announcement. This was more than a coincidence. From a publicity standpoint, the first lady's resignation changed everything, establishing an almost unassailable Anderson ally and creating a perfect foil in the DAR. Like any good promoter—and he was among the best—Hurok simply seized the opportunity of a lifetime. In the week following the resignation, he mobilized his many contacts across the musical and theatrical world, convincing dozens of prominent celebrities to speak out against the DAR. But this overwhelming response was as much a testament to the resignation's influence as it was to his skills as a promoter.[71]

It was also, of course, a tribute to Marian Anderson. The first lady did not mention Anderson in the resignation announcement or in her press conference later in the day. Yet the image of a wholly innocent victim, a supremely talented woman who had asked for nothing but the right to share her gift with as many people as possible, was crucial to the empathetic reaction that was sweeping the nation. To this point, Anderson had taken no active role in the DAR controversy, or in the School Board fight, and Hurok wanted to keep it that way. Realizing that his client, on tour in San Francisco three thousand miles away, was about to face an onslaught of questions, he wired Anderson instructions on how to deal with the press. The prescribed answer to all questions about the resignation was "For details of the case, please refer to my manager in New York, who is arranging an outdoor concert in Washington on April ninth free to the public." Hurok urged her to make "only the briefest statement in this vein" and suggested a two-line acknowledgment of the first lady's gracious gesture.

To Hurok's relief, Anderson followed his instructions without missing a word. "I am not surprised at Mrs. Roosevelt's action because she seemed to me to be one who really comprehended the true meaning of democracy," she calmly told a group of reporters gathered in a San Francisco hotel lobby. "I'm shocked beyond words to be barred from the capital of my own country after having appeared in almost every other capital in the world." In the days and weeks that followed, Anderson did her best to remain aloof from the gathering controversy surrounding the DAR. But it was not easy. "As we worked our way back East, continuing with our regular schedule," she recalled years later, "the newspaper people made efforts to obtain some comment from me, but I had nothing to say. I really did not know precisely what the Hurok office was doing about the situation and, since I had no useful opinions to offer, did not discuss it. I trusted the management. I knew it must be working on every possible angle, and somehow I felt I would sing in Washington."

Some evidence suggests that Anderson knew more than she let on and that she actually had strong feelings on the racial and social matters at hand. But she kept these feelings to herself. What she felt in her heart can only be imagined, but undoubtedly the first lady's willingness to stand up to the DAR solidified their friendship. Indeed, less than three weeks after the resignation, Anderson accepted Mrs. Roosevelt's invitation to entertain King George VI and Queen Elizabeth of England when they visited the White House in June. Once again, the irony of being welcomed by royalty but banned from Constitution Hall underscored the absurdity of Anderson's situation, compounding the political problems of the DAR.[72]

THE tidal wave of criticism that engulfed the DAR in early March left the organization sharply divided over how to respond. Neither the DAR nor any other heritage organization had ever been the subject of such intense controversy, so it had no precedent or protocol to follow. Publicly, Sally Robert and the National Board of Management said as little as possible, but in private there was considerable discussion of how best to deal with the crisis. Robert let it be known that she would not tolerate any overt criticism of the first lady, even though she knew full well that the membership's anger was palpable. Behind the scenes, in all regions of the nation, a solid majority of Daughters rallied to the society's defense. In mid-March, Mrs. A. W. Eason, the general chairman of the DAR's Chickasaw District, announced at a meeting in Memphis, Tennessee, that she had urged all of the society's chapters to join the fight against the "indiscriminate mixing of white and Negro actors on the screen." Robert did not comment publicly on Eason's clarion call, but she and other national officials did not want to be drawn into another highly publicized racial controversy.

Most of those who spoke out were actually among the minority who agreed with the first lady, dissidents such as Assemblywoman Hand. In Texas a group of two hundred Daughters registered their dissent from the board's decision by requesting a bloc of tickets for Anderson's Lincoln Memorial concert. Others went even further and emulated Roosevelt by resigning. While no precise record of resignations in 1939 exists, the number almost certainly reached into the hundreds. Prior to the Anderson controversy, the DAR's membership rolls had been increasing, but the 1940 figures showed a one-year drop of 256 members. The society's membership, which totaled approximately 150,000, increased by 316 in 1941, and by 146 in 1942, indicating that 1939, the year of the Roosevelt resignation, had interrupted an upward trend. One resignation that received considerable press attention was that of Dr. Elsie Reed Mitchell, a sixty-seven-year-old woman from Berkeley, California, who had been one of only two honorary life members in the DAR's West Coast affiliate. On the opposite coast, in Washington and Boston, a new organization calling itself the Descendants of the American Revolution openly recruited dissident DAR members as well as men belonging to the Sons of the American Revolution. The ringleader of insurgency was Mrs. J. Anton DeHaas, described in the press as a "Belmont club woman" and "the wife of a Harvard professor." The Descendants, among the first groups to affiliate with the MACC in mid-February, were heartened by the first lady's resignation and hoped for a mass defection by the DAR's more liberal members. But the exodus never reached the magnitude of a full-scale revolt.[73]

In characteristic fashion, DAR leaders essentially ignored the Descendants of the American Revolution and the other dissenters who either left the society's ranks or tried to effect reform from within. The leaders also made no sustained effort to mobilize their supporters, either inside or outside the organization. Instead, they exhibited an air of supreme confidence, giving the impression that they were unconcerned about the loyalty of the people who mattered. Embattled as it was, the DAR did indeed have its supporters, especially in the South. While no groundswell of public support for the society's action occurred, periodic letters to the editor indicated that many conservatives approved of the "white artists only" policy. Some even saw the outline of a dark conspiracy behind the campaign to discredit the DAR.

"The entire controversy would be silly," one irate supporter wrote to the *Washington Times-Herald* in late March, "but for the source of its inspiration, and its ultimate implications. There can be little doubt that the entire row was inspired by Communists, and a few self-appointed agitators of the colored race, who have little regard for the future welfare of their people in trying to force them upon the whites and promote social equality, which is not only undesirable for both races, but is as impossible as it is to mix oil and water. The attacks upon the D. A. R. for refusal to permit the use of Constitution Hall for the singer have been unjust and outrageous." Another, less literate DAR supporter wrote a letter of complaint to the Rand School in New York after the school's radio station broadcast a pro-Anderson news show on March 10: "I listen in to hear you all speak for Marian anderson I think of you speakers must have broken loose from the mad house I sat the D. A. R. were reight my believe is to let the nigers stay for themself & the white For themselfs if the nigros are allowed to mix with the white Thay will be getting so bold we'll Be having so much mixed Breed that every white mother will Have collored children without Brains you better have better Judgment and use better brains and let the niggers stay by themselfs. I hoped you'll send this to the D. A. R." The letter was signed "From a good American."[74]

Eleanor Roosevelt's resignation exerted its most direct influence on the campaign to liberalize the racial policies of the DAR. But it also had an immediate and lasting impact on the simmering School Board controversy. Coming on the heels of the mass meeting, the resignation had the dual effect of emboldening the MACC and undercutting Superintendent Ballou and his segregationist allies. Considering that the school system depended upon federal funding and congressional oversight, Washington school officials could not afford to ignore the political implications of the first lady's action, even though she scrupulously avoided any public involvement in the Central High debate. Anderson's supporters were eager to exploit this vulnerability, ensuring a tense and politically charged atmosphere when the School Board met at the Franklin School on March 1 to reconsider the MACC's proposal. This time the MACC was represented by two speakers, MACC chairman Charles Houston, and Sidney Katz, a union official with the Washington-area CIO, one of the eighty-two organizations that had endorsed the Central High proposal.

Bearing a petition signed by more than three thousand local citizens, Houston spoke boldly and passionately without a hint of deference to the segregationists on the board. He began by reading a telegram of support from Senator Henry Cabot Lodge Jr., a prominent Massachusetts Republican, before reciting a long list of artists and politicians who had spoken out on Anderson's behalf. Turning to the commercial-exclusion issue, he cited numerous examples of profit-oriented events held at District schools. Both the New York Philharmonic and Sergei Rachmaninoff, among others, had appeared at Central High, and profitable athletic contests, such as a 1934 exhibition tennis match between Bill Tilden and Ellsworth Vines, held at McKinley Technical High School, had been sanctioned by the board without controversy. The issue at hand, Houston insisted, was not profit but prejudice. "It seems to me a travesty on democratic principles," he declared, "to say that Marian Anderson in the capital of the nation at night can't give a concert in a public building." By the time he sat down, the crowd was abuzz as the board members shifted nervously in their seats. But the airing of grievances was not yet over.

If anything, Katz was even more emphatic in his denunciation of the board, which had foolishly followed the DAR's lead "accepting the backward level which DAR leaders are trying to set for this community." Turning Anderson away from Central High School, he insisted, with an unexpected twist, "represents an insult to the white community . . . It implies that in public buildings, the Board of Education will set the standard that it is improper for white and Negro people to sit together at meetings and concerts. In essence the discrimination is no different from that which the fascists in Germany and in Italy are exercising against the great Jewish artists whom they are driving from their own country . . . The Board of Education cannot deal lightly with such a vital issue in a period of history as important as we are now passing through. If the Board of Education reaffirms its ruling, it will be hailed as a victory for cultural backwardness, for barbarism, for the absurd race theory of Nazi Germany and Fascist Italy."[75]

The next speaker was Superintendent Ballou, who summarized a thirteen-page report justifying the rejection of the MACC proposal. But neither he nor the chair of the board could forge a consensus favoring a second rejection. Unable to overcome the fear among several members of the board that the political cost of barring Anderson from Central High had risen too high, the best the die-hard segregationists could do was a resolution referring the matter to the Committee on the Community Use of

Schools. Houston and other MACC leaders were not sure what to make of this development, but when the biracial committee met two days later, the mood was surprisingly conciliatory. After a brief discussion, the committee reversed the School Board's decision, stating their conviction "that a concession now, as a proof of good will to Marian Anderson and the colored people of the District, will serve to remove this question from public discussion." The only condition, which proved to be a deal-breaker, was the committee's insistence that the concert application would be granted "only under positive and definite assurance and agreement that the concession will not be taken as a precedent and that the Board of Education will not in the future again be asked to depart from the principle of a dual system of schools and schools facilities."

The committee's report cited Doxey Wilkerson's February 15 statement, which as a tactical matter had agreed to such a condition. But it failed to acknowledge that the national implications of the Anderson controversy had escalated considerably during the past two weeks. Once personal and collective expectations had risen to levels inherent in a broad movement for social change, the MACC could no longer countenance a compromise that aided Anderson while precluding others from breaching the barriers of Jim Crow. As Houston reported to the NAACP national office the day after the meeting, "I wanted Marian Anderson to sing in Central, but not at the cost of my dignity and self-respect." He and others suspected that whoever drafted the committee's report had made it "deliberately provocative," realizing "that some elements in the school administration really hoped the Negroes would indignantly reject it, so that the elements could go to the public and say: see, the radicals don't want Marian Anderson particularly, they are just using her concert as an opening to attack segregation."[76]

Two weeks of confusion followed. After the School Board ratified the committee's decision by a vote of 6 to 2, Cohen and his Howard colleagues consulted with Houston and NAACP officials in New York, but no one could come up with a statement that met the board's requirements without yielding, in Walter White's words, "vitally important principles." On March 6, after rejecting a draft crafted by Houston, White declared, "We all are strongly of the opinion that it would be far better for Marian Anderson not to sing in Washington this year than to accept such conditions as the School Board has laid down. We do not see that Howard University, Marian Anderson and, least of all, the NAACP should participate in any fashion in an agreement binding upon the future and upon other artists . . . Incidentally,

Hubert Delany as Marian's lawyer and Hurok are unequivocally opposed to acceptance of the hall on such conditions."[77]

Nevertheless, three days later, on March 9, Cohen, acting independently of the NAACP and the MACC, notified the School Board that he was ready to sign a contract. In his acceptance letter, he made every effort to reassure the board without actually capitulating to its demands. But his effort only angered Ballou, who ruled that the letter's language fell far short of the required assurances. On March 17, acting on behalf of the board, Ballou formally withdrew the offer. In a curt letter to Cohen, he declared, "The responsibility for making the Central High School auditorium unavailable for the concert of Miss Marian Anderson on April 9 must be assumed by you and your associates of Howard University." Hurok, among others, flatly rejected Ballou's assertion, assuring reporters that the School Board was simply "manipulating a variety of smoke screens to conceal its original impulses." Speaking for the MACC, John Lovell chided the board for twisting "a simple emergency request for use of a public building into an attempt to involve the local dual school system. The dual system is not in issue. The issue is the community use of a public building on a holiday." Many observers agreed, and MACC leaders scheduled a mass meeting on March 26 to vent their feelings and to call for a congressional investigation of the board's behavior. Whatever the truth of the matter, Ballou and the School Board had effectively foreclosed the possibility of compromise. The Dark Contralto would not sing at Central High School on Easter Sunday 1939.[78]

CHAPTER 5

Sweet Land of Liberty

My country, 'tis of thee,
Sweet land of liberty,
Of thee we sing.
—MARIAN ANDERSON'S "AMERICA," APRIL 9, 1939[1]

WHETHER Marian Anderson would sing anywhere in Washington on Easter Sunday 1939 remained an open question as her winter tour drew to a close. The public outcry on her behalf was still rumbling as she made her way eastward from Portland, Oregon, to Fort Worth and a string of other Texas cities. But with less than one month to go before the Washington recital date, her options were dwindling. The campaign to book Central High School had failed, and the DAR showed no signs of reversing the "white artists only" policy at Constitution Hall. For a few days in mid-March, the Belasco Theatre reemerged as an option, and Cohen and the Howard committee, in desperation, seriously considered signing a contract with the Belasco's manager. But they backed off when MACC and NAACP leaders strongly advised against it. As Walter White wrote to Cohen on the twenty-fourth, the booking "would be a let-down since the Belasco is a dilapidated old theater which is not highly regarded in Washington." After all they had gone through, after all the petitions and letters and protest meetings, holding the Anderson concert there would be seen as a defeat, not a victory, by many of those who had embraced the search for a proper venue as a matter of self-respect and pressing social significance.[2]

The only viable option left—and seemingly the only means of salvaging the Anderson affair as a civil rights campaign—was an outdoor concert, an idea first suggested by Howard music professor Lulu Childers in January. Since late February Hurok had been telling reporters that his client would sing in the open air at a park adjacent to Constitution Hall, but no formal arrangements had ensued. Why Hurok failed to follow through is unclear, though part of the reason was undoubtedly his reluctance to lose the added publicity generated by continued speculation about the concert site. He also had to deal with Walter White, who, among others, was cool to the idea. "I think it would be undignified," White told Charles Houston on March 21, "and too much like a small boy thumbing his nose at the back of a larger boy who has beaten him up."[3]

For weeks White and Houston had worried that either Hurok or Cohen would settle the matter in a manner that would abandon the broader goals of the NAACP and the MACC. But their concerns began to recede with the emergence of a powerful idea that eventually drew everyone involved into its orbit: that the recital should be held at the Lincoln Memorial. No one knows for sure who first proposed the idea, but the possibility of using the Lincoln Memorial was already being discussed by Cohen and the Howard committee at the beginning of March in the immediate aftermath of Eleanor Roosevelt's resignation from the DAR. By March 6, Hurok, Houston, and White had entered the discussion, with White taking the lead. In all likelihood, White and other NAACP leaders had considered the Lincoln Memorial site prior to the discussions at Howard. But, whatever the details of authorship, White had seized the idea as his own by mid-March. At an NAACP Board of Directors meeting on the thirteenth, he pushed through a resolution designating the Lincoln Memorial as the only proper site for Anderson's recital. Fittingly, the resolution was introduced by Hubert Delany, Anderson's longtime attorney and close friend.[4]

White was convinced that the site was a perfect match for the Spingarn Medal winner, but the letter that he sent to Hurok later that day betrayed concern that the impresario would regard the resolution as presumptuous. "I would like to offer the suggestion that should an open-air concert by Miss Anderson be held in Washington the possibility of holding it at the Lincoln Memorial be considered," he wrote, with uncharacteristic understatement. "This would have a particular significance, which you will readily see."[5]

How readily Hurok saw the significance of the site became apparent a week later when he told a *New York Times* reporter that Anderson would sing at the Lincoln Memorial on Easter Sunday "as a rebuke to all who have snubbed the Negro singer." Though taken aback by Hurok's impulsive statement, White wasted no time in mobilizing the Anderson coalition. In his 1948 autobiography, White characterized the Lincoln Memorial as "the most logical place" for the Anderson recital. But the logic of holding a gathering at the seventeen-year-old Memorial was not as obvious in 1939 as it would later become.

Over the coming decades, the Memorial would host literally hundreds of mass meetings, including the August 1963 March on Washington for Jobs and Freedom, which drew a quarter of a million people to the west end of the National Mall. But the notion of holding a civil rights rally, a concert, or any other mass assemblage at the site was definitely novel in the spring of 1939. The federal agencies with the responsibility of managing the site, the National Park Service and the Department of the Interior, had never granted a permit for a large gathering at the Memorial, and the only black organization of any size to have used the site was the AME Zion Church, which held a mass religious service for two thousand people in 1926.

The principal speaker at the AME Zion service, Bishop E. D. W. Jones, paid homage to Lincoln, insisting, "The immortality of the great emancipator lay not in his preservation of the Union, but in his giving freedom to the Negroes of America." But that is not the way most Americans, black or white, viewed the sixteenth president during the early twentieth century. When Congress formed a commission to create a Lincoln memorial in 1911, government officials, historians, and most of the public viewed him as a symbol of national unity. In some parts of the South, he was still the "Black Republican" who had forced the issues of secession and the defense of slavery. But many white Southerners, like most Northerners, had come to see him as a moderate alternative to the Radical Republicans, who had foisted the carpetbagger regimes upon the South during Reconstruction. The Lincoln commission, chaired by Ohio Republican William Howard Taft, did everything in its power to embed this image in the Memorial, which was constructed during the politically turbulent era of World War I and its immediate aftermath. Even the location of the Memorial symbolized intersectional harmony, lying just across the Potomac River from the Arlington home of Robert E. Lee, another icon of reunion.[6]

At the dedication of the Memorial in early June 1922, the commission unveiled Daniel Chester French's striking sculpture of Lincoln perched inside a marble, columned temple. The inscription above the statue read IN THIS TEMPLE, AS IN THE HEARTS OF THE PEOPLE FOR WHOM HE SAVED THE UNION, THE MEMORY OF ABRAHAM LINCOLN IS ENSHRINED FOREVER. On the interior side walls, the texts of the Gettysburg Address and the Second Inaugural Address gave testament to a war that had led to emancipation. But the

absence of any other mention of slavery or abolition communicated a message
of "national consensus, linking North and South on holy, national ground,"
as the historian Scott Sandage once observed. In his dedication address,
President Warren G. Harding assured the crowd—which was seated in racially segregated sections—that Lincoln was not an abolitionist, but rather a
unionist who favored emancipation only as "a means to the great end" of
"union and nationality." The other principle speakers, including Taft, followed the president's lead, studiously avoiding the historic issues of slavery
and emancipation. The only exception was Robert Russa Moton, the black
president of Tuskegee Institute, who gently reminded the platform party and
the audience that it was Lincoln who "spoke the word that gave freedom to a
race, and vindicated the honor of a nation conceived in liberty and dedicated
to the proposition that all men are created equal."[7]

Critical accounts of the dedication ceremony appeared throughout the
black press, which registered strong disapproval of the Jim Crow atmosphere
at the Memorial. In the *Crisis*, the official organ of the NAACP, W. E. B.
Du Bois mocked the ceremony in an article entitled "Lincoln, Harding,
James Crow, and Taft." No one had expected the Memorial to represent
Lincoln as a black hero. But the assembled dignitaries' utter disregard for the
historical importance of emancipation was deeply troubling. Over the next
fifteen years a number of black intellectuals and liberal white historians attempted, with some success, to restore Lincoln's image as the Great Emancipator. But for most Americans, including many in the black community, he
remained a national hero with only a tangential connection to the liberation
of African Americans. By the late 1930s, the increasingly conservative Republican Party was no longer the "party of Lincoln," and the Democratic
Party, with its strong ties to the white South, had yet to embrace him as a
symbol of racial justice. Some of the hundreds of thousands of black voters
who shifted from the Republican to the Democratic Party in 1936 may have
brought their pictures of Lincoln with them, but far more seem to have put
up pictures of FDR, the man who had given them a measure of hope during
hard times.

In this context, the choice of the Lincoln Memorial as the backdrop for
the Anderson recital was a calculated gamble. The organizers could not be
certain how the American public would respond to the juxtaposition of a
black concert singer and a white Republican president from Illinois. Physically and aesthetically, the Memorial and the adjacent rectangular reflecting
pool stretching eastward toward the Washington Monument represented a

stunning site. But the political and cultural implications of staging a controversial concert on sacred ground were complex and potentially dangerous. The situation called for careful planning and just the right touches to ensure that the event communicated the right messages to the right people.[8]

Prior to the planning, however, the organizers faced the task of gaining permission to use the Memorial for such an unprecedented purpose. Here Walter White proved to be the indispensable link to the Department of the Interior. Not only had White known Secretary Ickes since the early 1920s, when Ickes, then a young social worker, had served as president of the Chicago branch of the NAACP, but White was even closer to Assistant Secretary Oscar L. Chapman. Prior to his appointment as Ickes's assistant, Chapman had worked for Senator Edward Costigan of Colorado, the cosponsor, with Senator Robert F. Wagner of New York, of the Costigan-Wagner antilynching bill. While the antilynching bill was under consideration, White met with Costigan and Chapman on several occasions and came away with enormous respect for both men. In a letter written to Anderson the week before the concert, White described Chapman as "a protégé of one of the greatest human beings who ever lived," giving him much of the credit for securing permission for her to sing at the Lincoln Memorial. Some accounts even suggest that Chapman prompted White to consider using the Memorial for the Anderson concert. "Oh, my God," White supposedly responded, "if we could have her sit at the feet of Lincoln!"[9]

While this particular story may be apocryphal, the Virginia-born assistant secretary certainly smoothed the way for White and his colleagues. Following an early conversation with White, Chapman consulted Felix Cohen, one of the department's attorneys, to make sure that holding the concert at the Memorial would be legal. When Cohen came back with the judgment that "There is nothing that stands in your way except courage," Chapman was off and running. Within minutes, he was in Ickes's office making the pitch for the Memorial concert. By all accounts, Ickes, who had already interjected himself into the DAR controversy, hardly needed persuading. In White's words, "Mr. Ickes was equally excited over the prospect of such a demonstration of democracy." Even so, Ickes felt that such an audacious departure from convention required presidential approval, especially in a situation indirectly involving the first lady. Rushing to the White House, Ickes caught up with the president just as he was leaving for a two-week vacation at Warm Springs, Georgia. Breathless, but confident that Roosevelt would see the political as well as the ethical value of holding the Anderson concert at the Lincoln Memorial, Ickes pressed the departing president for an immediate answer. Roosevelt was more than obliging. Having heard enough about Anderson from his wife to last a lifetime, he was as anxious as anyone else to bring the concert-hall controversy to a close. "She can sing from the top of the Washington Monument if she wants to," he declared before heading for Georgia.[10]

With the president's approval in hand, Ickes moved quickly. On Thursday, March 30, he announced to the world that Marian Anderson would sing at the Lincoln Memorial on Easter Sunday, April 9. The announcement, which appeared in newspapers across the nation on the thirty-first, provided no particulars other than that the concert would be free and open to the public, and that it would be broadcast over the Blue Network of NBC radio. At that point, the NAACP, the MACC, Hurok Productions, and the National Park Service were feverishly working out the other details large and small. With only ten days to go before the concert, there was no time to waste—and no time to bicker over competing visions of the event.[11]

THE most pressing challenge was the question of sponsorship. Who would sponsor the concert, and who would pay for it? The Park Service would absorb most of the cost for security and crowd control, but that still left a host of financial burdens, including the cost of programs and publicity. As the original promoter of the event, Hurok agreed to assume the responsibility for these costs and other incidentals, though he later complained that he was left with a staggering bill. However, he did not feel comfortable acting as Anderson's sole sponsor. Recognizing that the Lincoln Memorial affair would be perceived as more than a mere concert, he asked White if the event could be held "under the auspices of the NAACP." White was tempted to say yes, but after discussing the matter with his staff he declined Hurok's offer. "It would have meant publicity for the Association which could not have been bought for many tens of thousands of dollars," White later explained. "But there was a broader issue involved than publicity. Because the NAACP is known as a fighting propaganda agency, its sponsorship of the concert might have created the impression that propaganda for the Negro was the objective instead of the emphasizing of a principle. I, therefore, proposed that the concert be given under the most distinguished and nonpartisan auspices possible—namely, a sponsoring committee on which would be asked to serve such persons as members of the Cabinet and the Supreme Court, senators, congressmen, editors, artists, and others who believed that art should show no color line."[12]

With Hurok and Houston in agreement, White began to assemble a list of potential sponsors, though his initial task was to find an appropriate chairperson for the committee. His first thought was to turn to the first lady, but upon reflection he "did not feel that Mrs. Roosevelt should put herself on the spot, particularly since reactionaries in the South were already pillorying her for her attitude on the Negro." Instead, he approached Caroline O'Day, a liberal Democratic congresswoman from New York. A native of Georgia, a former social worker, and an accomplished painter who had studied art in France and Germany, O'Day seemed the perfect choice to lead a committee devoted to protecting artistic expression and equal opportunity. To White's relief, she not only agreed to chair the committee but also allowed him to turn part of her congressional office into a makeshift telegraph room.

During the first week of April, the O'Day office sent out more than five hundred telegrams to prospective sponsors. The typical telegram read: "Will you join me in sponsoring an open-air free concert by Marian Anderson under the auspices of Howard University from the steps of the Lincoln Memorial, at 5 p.m., Sunday, April 9? No expenses of any nature whatever involved in your acceptance. Seats on platform provided for sponsors. Please wire answer collect, Room 440, House Office Building—Caroline O'Day, M.C." The wire went out to a wide variety of individuals, but the primary goal was to recruit a blue-ribbon list of political and governmental figures, sponsors who would reinforce the civic meaning of the event. The organizers did not want the concert to be a partisan affair, or to give the appearance of liberal New Dealers using the Lincoln Memorial for political purposes. They wanted it to be a celebration of democracy in which all Americans could take pride.[13]

To this end, they paid particular attention to the Supreme Court, the ultimate seat of constitutional integrity. Fortunately, one of the first potential sponsors to respond affirmatively was Chief Justice Charles Evans Hughes, a former presidential candidate and the nation's most distinguished Republican. Acceptances from Associate Justices Hugo Black, a former Klansman from Alabama, and Stanley Reed, a moderate Democrat from Kentucky, soon followed.

By the end of the week they were joined by the first lady, Secretary of the Interior Ickes, Secretary of the Treasury Henry Morgenthau, Secretary of Commerce Harry Hopkins, Secretary of the Navy Claude Swanson, and Attorney General Frank Murphy. Five representatives and fourteen senators also signed on as sponsors. The senators, whose political leanings ranged across the ideological spectrum, included six Democrats: Bennett Champ Clark of Missouri, Joseph Guffey of Pennsylvania, Pat McCarran of Nevada, Elmer Thomas of Oklahoma, and James Mead and Robert F. Wagner of New York; six Republicans, William Barbour of New Jersey, William Borah of Idaho, Arthur Capper of Kansas, James Davis of Pennsylvania, Senate minority leader Charles McNary of Oregon, and Robert Taft of Ohio; and two independents, the maverick ex-Republicans Robert La Follette Jr. of Wisconsin, and George W. Norris of Nebraska. Both Taft and Capper were staunch conservatives, and Capper had even sponsored a controversial antimiscegenation bill in 1923, during his first term in the Senate. But nonetheless they stepped forward when asked to endorse a fundamental principle of fairness.[14]

The list of political sponsors was strikingly bipartisan, but even more striking was the noticeable absence of several prominent individuals that the concert organizers had hoped to enlist. Chief among them was Vice President John Nance Garner, a prickly Texan who had earned the nickname Cactus Jack. Notoriously conservative on matters of race, Garner, along with Postmaster General James A. Farley, was the biggest challenge for Ickes, who delighted in making them squirm. "I am trying to smoke these two men out on this Negro issue and probably they find it embarrassing," he wrote in his diary on April 6. "Others, too, have found it embarrassing, I do not doubt," he concluded, adding, ". . . on the whole there has been a very good response but significantly some people prominent in public life have failed to reply at all to Mrs. O'Day's invitation." One of the biggest disappointments was the recalcitrance of Henry Wallace, the New Deal's economically liberal secretary of agriculture. When White inquired about Wallace's failure to respond, he was told that the secretary had a blanket policy prohibiting the use of his name as a sponsor. But White and others suspected that the former Iowa farmer was simply unengaged in issues related to race.

Garner's absence from the list, though less surprising, caused the biggest stir, especially after Ickes leaked the story to the investigative reporters Drew Pearson and Bob Allen. A likely contender for the Democratic presidential nomination in 1940, Garner became apoplectic when criticism of his apparent lack of courage appeared in Pearson and Allen's *Washington Merry-Go-Round* column. Pearson and Allen often skewered Southern politicos, and in this instance Garner had plenty of company among his political allies south of the Mason-Dixon Line. With the exception of the two border-state senators, Clark and Thomas, not a single Southern Democrat had joined the sponsor list. The difference in Garner's case was that, with the president off in Warm Springs, he was the highest-ranking official in the capital. While neither the president nor the first lady pressured him to become a sponsor or to attend the concert, his responsibility was clear. Avoiding the issue was an obvious affront not only to Anderson and black Americans but also to the New Deal administration.[15]

By the time the official program was printed, the names of 132 sponsors appeared on the back cover. The list—which included such luminaries as Katharine Hepburn, Fredric March, Tallulah Bankhead, and Leopold Stokowski—was impressive and a tribute to the organizers' efforts. But anyone looking closely at the list could detect some padding. More than a dozen of the "sponsors" were MACC and NAACP leaders, including Mr. and Mrs. Walter White, Mr. and Mrs. Charles Houston, Charles Cohen, and Doxey Wilkerson. The Huroks were also on the list, suggesting that the organizers had come up a bit short in their search for sponsors. Too many individuals, it seems, had responded with some version of the excuse "My position makes it unwise for me to participate in controversial issues of this character." The organizers were disappointed, but the hesitancy of some to embrace the concert gave them all the more reason to tend to the details with care and precision.[16]

White, in particular, pored over every detail, weighing the probable reactions to everything from the choice of music to the design and distribution of the printed program. The goal, as White kept reminding his colleagues, was to project an air of dignity that would underscore the importance of the occasion. The front cover of the program, for example, featured the simple announcement "Howard University and Associated Sponsors Present Marian Anderson at the Lincoln Memorial in Washington, Sunday, April 9, 1939, Five O'clock" on the top half of the page and the opening line of Lincoln's Gettysburg Address on the bottom half. While waiting for Anderson to sing, members of the audience would have the opportunity to ponder the address's immortal words: "Fourscore and seven years ago our fathers brought forth on this continent a new nation, conceived in liberty and dedicated to the proposition that all men are created equal." In case anyone missed the point, White also arranged to have the programs distributed throughout the crowd by a mix of black and white Boy Scouts.[17]

A great deal of thought and deliberation also went into the choice of music. On March 30, Gerald Goode, the head of publicity for Hurok Productions, sent White a tentative list of the songs to be sung, suggesting the national anthem as the opening number. White immediately shot back his opinion that "'America' should be sung instead of 'The Star Spangled Banner' not only for the ironic implications but because more people know the words and it is more singable." Goode eventually ran the idea by Anderson, who agreed that "America" was the best choice. She also approved the other five songs on the proposed program, undoubtedly pleased that someone had finally consulted her on at least one aspect of the concert.[18]

During the previous two weeks, as the arrangements for the concert had taken shape, Hurok had deliberately kept Anderson in the dark. Part of his motivation resided in a sincere concern for her mental condition, especially her ability to focus on the ongoing concert tour in Texas. But he also feared that she might have serious reservations about some of the things that were being done on her behalf. Accordingly, after his initial public statement on the Lincoln Memorial concert on March 21, he somehow failed to notify her. Apparently no one informed her that she was scheduled to sing at the Memorial until the twenty-fourth, when White sent a letter to her hotel in Waco, Texas.[19]

Hurok had good reason to act as he did. Years later Anderson confessed in her autobiography that she had been deeply conflicted during the days leading up to the concert. As she put it, "the weight of the Washington affair bore in on me." The decision to sing came only after a difficult period of soul-searching. "I was informed of the plan for the outdoor concert before the news was published," she recalled. "Indeed, I was asked whether I approved. I said yes, but the yes did not come easily or quickly. I don't like a lot of show, and one could not tell in advance what direction the affair would take. I studied my conscience. In principle the idea was sound, but it could not be comfortable to me as an individual. As I thought further, I could see that my significance as an individual was small in this affair. I had become, whether I liked it or not, a symbol, representing my people. I had to appear." Even with this realization, it took a conversation with her mother, always her most trusted counselor, to bring the matter to closure. "You know what your aspirations are. I think you should make your own decision," her mother counseled. According to Anderson, her mother "knew what the decision would be. In my heart I also knew. I could not run away from this situation. If I had anything to offer, I would have to do so now."[20]

While Anderson steeled her courage, White, Houston, Goode, and Chapman finalized the arrangements for Easter Sunday. With Hurok still in New York, Goode and White set up shop in Washington, where they worked closely with the MACC, the Howard music-series committee, and Mike Straus, the head of publicity for the Department of the Interior. Straus assumed the task of coordinating the publicity for the concert, but he relied heavily on the MACC to get the word out to the many Washington-area organizations that had been drawn into the Anderson campaign. If each organization could persuade a majority of its membership to attend the concert, the area around the Memorial and the reflecting pool would be filled to capacity. If the organizations didn't come through, the concert organizers faced a potentially embarrassing situation. Fearing the worst, White made a concerted effort to encourage black organizations in Philadelphia and New York to send large delegations to Washington by train.

Since this was the first concert of its kind, no one had a firm sense of how many people were likely to show up on Sunday afternoon. Although the capital was jammed with Easter-season tourists, no one could be sure how many would wander over to the Memorial to hear Anderson sing. Even so, by early April the organizers were confident enough to request a significant police presence. National Park Service officials, also anticipating a large turnout, realized that park rangers and security personnel alone could not provide sufficient crowd control. With Chapman's approval, the Park Service recruited approximately five hundred federal building guards and several squads of metropolitan policemen to ensure that things didn't get out of hand. Neither the Park Service nor the organizers had any reason to believe that the concert presented a threat to public order, but provocation by white supremacist extremists was always possible. Indeed, ten days before the concert Howard president Mordecai Johnson warned White that it was not inconceivable that the Ku Klux Klan would "do something" to disrupt the event.[21]

During the first week of April, the organizers faced disruption, but not from the Klan. Kosti Vehanen, the scheduled accompanist at the Lincoln Memorial concert, suddenly became seriously ill while on tour with Anderson in St. Louis. Earlier symptoms had been treated by a Washington physician, who advised Vehanen to return to Washington for special treatment. With her longtime friend and accompanist in a Washington hospital, Anderson turned to Franz Rupp, a gifted, young German pianist under contract with Hurok, to continue the tour. Anderson and Rupp appeared in Birmingham and Atlanta before heading north to New York. Along the way, they stopped off in Washington to visit Vehanen in the hospital. Goode, fearing that Anderson would face a crush of Washington reporters as soon as she arrived in the capital, met the singer's train in Annapolis. As they traveled to

Washington, Anderson finally received a briefing on what to expect on Easter Sunday, only a few short days away. "Mr. Goode filled me in on developments as we rode into Washington," she recalled years later, "and he tried to prepare me for what he knew would happen—a barrage of questions from the newspaper people. They were waiting for us in the Washington station. Questions flew at me, and some of them I could not answer because they involved things I did not know about. I tried to get away; I wanted to go straight to the hospital to see Kosti. There was a car waiting for me, and the reporters followed us in another car. I had some difficulty getting into the hospital without several reporters following me. They waited until I had finished my visit, and they questioned me again—about Kosti's progress and his opinion of the Washington situation. Finally we got away and traveled on to New York."[22]

The Washington visit deepened Anderson's respect for Goode—she called him "a tower of strength"—but the most important development was Kosti's apparent recovery. Barring a relapse, he would be by her side at the Lincoln Memorial after all. Anderson regarded Kosti's recovery as a godsend. Rupp was a fine pianist, as he would prove again and again over the next twenty-five years as her primary accompanist. But, as she prepared for the most difficult challenge she could imagine, Anderson clung to the comforting presence of a man who knew her every mood and musical idiosyncrasy. The prospect of singing outdoors in indeterminate weather, to a crowd ten or more times the size of any she had ever sung to before, was intimidating enough without having to worry about technical adjustments to a new accompanist. Even on a day devoted to democracy, she remained, above all else, a musical perfectionist. For April 9 to be the best day of her life, as Hurok and White assured her it would be, the recital had to be a musical as well as a political triumph.

This was a tall order even for a world-class performer, and understandably Anderson began to panic as the recital date drew near. Back home in Philadelphia for the first time in several months, she immediately nestled into the bosom of her family, which made her less than eager to go back on the road again, especially to a place where she faced an uncertain welcome. Only recently she had learned that no respectable hotel in Washington was willing to rent her a room for Sunday evening. Goode had arranged for her entire entourage—which included her mother and sisters—to stay at the home of Cornelia and Gifford Pinchot, a venerable seventy-four-year-old progressive Republican who had been the first chief of the U.S. Forest Service before serving two terms as governor of Pennsylvania. She appreciated the Pinchots' generosity, but it did not salve her anxieties about the racial atmosphere in the capital. At midnight on Saturday, less than eight hours before she was scheduled to board a train for Washington, she telephoned Hurok to ask if she had to go through with her commitment. But, fortunately for her and the millions who would draw inspiration from her appearance at the Lincoln Memorial, his enthusiasm and confidence assuaged her fears. Recognizing what was at stake, she promised to make her rendezvous with destiny.[23]

W H I L E Anderson was wrestling with her anxieties, Walter White was on the road to Washington, nervously eyeing the weather. When he and his family left New York on Saturday afternoon, "the weather was crisp and cold but heavy with the promise of approaching spring." As they approached Washington, "sleet began to fall." He later recalled, "With it fell our hopes. We went to bed low in spirits because of the snow piling up on the streets outside. Weeks of thought and all our hard work seemed about to be thwarted by nature. I was almost afraid to look out of the window when I awoke early the next morning. I shouted with happiness to see the sun." As the day progressed, the sun darted in and out, with more drizzle and cold wind than anything else. But the streets were now clear of snow and ready for the final preparations for an expected onslaught of concertgoers.

The probable size of the crowd was still anybody's guess, but the relatively small turnout at the traditional Arlington National Cemetery sunrise service early that morning suggested that Secretary Ickes's prediction that fifty thousand would show up at the Lincoln Memorial was a bit optimistic. Of course, even if only ten thousand crowded around the Memorial, the parking and security details would still have their hands full. So no one was surprised when officials closed the streets around the Memorial Circle. By noon, there was a scattering of people near the base of the Memorial steps, early comers who wanted to secure a seat as close to the stage as possible. But the biting wind coming off the Potomac was enough to discourage all but the hardiest enthusiasts. In the early afternoon, Anderson herself, accompanied by Kosti Vehanen, arrived at the Memorial for a sound check. Setting up a battery of six microphones and a makeshift amplification apparatus had posed a stiff technological challenge to Mike Straus's staff, but everything seemed to be in working order as Anderson and Kosti tested the system.

After examining her sheet music, Anderson took a moment to look out over the reflecting pool, a site she had not visited in years. At that moment it was quiet and beautiful with little hint of what was about to unfold.

When she returned three hours later, it was an altogether different scene. As she stepped out of a limousine at the back of the Memorial, she caught a glimpse of the multitude gathered on the other side. At that moment, she had no way of estimating the size of the crowd. Only later would she learn that as many as seventy-five thousand people had braved the cold to hear her sing. Neither she nor anyone else had ever seen anything quite like it—a gathering of black and white, young and old, rich and poor that stretched for hundreds of yards around and beyond the reflecting pool. In later years she often encountered individuals who explained that they had been somewhere in the crowd on that Easter Sunday—men and women who tried to explain why they had come and what the experience had meant to them. But at the time she could only imagine the stories lost in the multitude.

She did not know, for example, that Bob Carter, a second-year law student at Howard who later became a leading NAACP legal strategist and distinguished federal judge, was in the crowd. Despite warnings that he would be fired from his job as a hotel busboy if he did not show up to work that Sunday afternoon, Carter went anyway, witnessing what he later called "a historic event that signaled a new era in race relations." Also in the crowd were the young Sanderlin brothers—Willis, Ray, and Jim—who had recently lost their father and who had come to the concert with their grieving mother, partly out of curiosity and partly in search of solace. Others came in groups of friends, or under church or NAACP sponsorship. But from the outset, even before Anderson began to sing, the gathering suggested a common purpose that drew people together, a spirit that disrupted and confounded the normal divisions of race, class, and culture. "The whole setting was unique, majestic, and impressive," Ickes wrote in his diary the following Saturday, after reflecting on what he had seen, "and I could not help but feel thankful that the D. A. R. and the school board had refused her the use of an auditorium."

It is little wonder that the scene nearly took Anderson's breath away. "I had sensations unlike any I had experienced before," she later declared in her autobiography. "The only comparable emotion I could recall was the feeling I had when Maestro Toscanini had appeared in the artist's room in Salzburg. My heart leaped wildly, and I could not talk. I even wondered whether I would be able to sing." It took a line of policemen to hold back the throng as Hurok, Anderson, and Hubert Delany made their way into the building.

"We entered the monument," Anderson remembered, "and were taken to a small room. We were introduced to Mr. Ickes, whom we had not met before. He outlined the program. Then came the signal to go out before the public."

Oscar Chapman and Caroline O'Day shared the honor of escorting Anderson to the stage. Emerging from the shadows of the Memorial, Anderson encountered the platform party for the first time. The stage, which had been empty earlier in the afternoon, was now filled with Supreme Court justices, cabinet secretaries, senators, representatives, and other dignitaries, more than two hundred in all. Her mother and sisters were also there, but few faces were familiar other than those of Walter White, Mary McLeod Bethune, and Sol Hurok. Ickes, sensing that she felt a little disoriented, grasped her hand warmly before delivering what he later termed "the best speech" of his life. His introduction was both gracious and eloquent, offering a history lesson on democratic piety:

> In this great auditorium under the sky all of us are free. When God gave
> us this wonderful outdoors and the sun, the moon and the stars, He made
> no distinction of race or creed or color. And 130 years ago He sent to us
> one of His truly great in order that he might restore freedom to those from
> whom we had disregardfully taken it. In carrying out this task, Abraham
> Lincoln laid down his life, and so it is as appropriate as it is fortunate that
> today we stand reverently and humbly at the base of this memorial to the
> great emancipator while glorious tribute is rendered to his memory by a
> daughter of the race from which he struck the chains of slavery. Facing us
> down the Mall beyond the Washington Monument, which we have
> erected as a symbol of the towering stature and fame of him who founded
> this Republic, there is a rising memorial to that other great democrat in
> our short history, who proclaimed that principle of equality of opportunity
> which Abraham Lincoln believed in so implicitly and took so seriously. In
> our own time, too many pay mere lip service to these twin planets in our
> democratic heaven. There are those, even in this great Capital of our
> democratic Republic, who are either too timid or too indifferent to lift up
> the light that Jefferson and Lincoln carried aloft. Genius, like justice, is
> blind. For genius has touched with the tip of her wing this woman who, if
> it had not been for the great mind of Jefferson, if it had not been for the
> great heart of Lincoln, would not be able to stand among us today a free
> individual in a free land. Genius draws no color line. She has endowed
> Marian Anderson with such a voice as lifts any individual above his

fellows, as is a matter of exultant pride to any race. And so it is fitting that Marian Anderson should raise her voice in tribute to the noble Lincoln, whom mankind will ever honor. We are grateful to Miss Anderson for coming here to sing to us today.[24]

Ickes's remarks drew thunderous applause, but now all eyes were on Anderson. Wrapped in a fur coat to shield her from the wind, with her hair tied back, she slowly walked to the bank of microphones before looking out over the crowd. "She looked slender and beautiful when she emerged between the high marble columns, directly in front of the great Lincoln Memorial which was filled with shadow in the late afternoon light," Kosti Vehanen later recalled. ". . . No one who saw her walking that day down the marble steps will ever forget this unusual and wonderful sight, and few can recall it without tears springing to their eyes." Turning to Kosti, Anderson gave a nod that she was ready to sing. But for a moment or two there was no sound but the whir of newsreel cameras. "My head and heart were in such turmoil that I looked and hardly saw, I listened and hardly heard," she later recalled, with a poignant sense of wonder. "All I knew then as I stepped forward was the overwhelming impact of the vast multitude. There seemed to be people as far as the eye could see. The crowd stretched in a great semicircle from the Lincoln Memorial around the reflecting pool on to the shaft of the Washington Monument. I had a feeling that a great wave of good will poured out from these people, almost engulfing me. And when I stood up to sing . . . I felt for a moment as though I were choking. For a desperate second I thought that the words, well as I know them, would not come. I sang, I don't know how." Sitting a few feet away on the viewing stand, Hurok shared her sense of awe. Years later he remembered the crowd's warmth and immensity, especially the "upturned faces, expectant, quiet, attentive." "Looking down at them," he had felt "a kind of buoyancy, as though one were floating on a sea—and it was a sea, with a tide of strong feeling flowing from them to the erect figure of a woman standing composed and ready by the piano on the platform. When she opened her lips and sang, it was as though the tide flowed back to them."[25]

With her eyes closed and her head tilted upward, Anderson began with the opening line of "America": "My country, 'tis of thee, sweet land of liberty." But as she completed the line, some in the crowd realized that she had substituted *we* for *I* at the end. Either out of stage fright or premeditation—she never divulged which—she sang "Of thee *we* sing." Most of the crowd, it seems, did not catch the change of words. All they heard was the most haunting rendition of "America" imaginable, sung against a backdrop dripping with symbolism. Years later those who were there would try to tell their children and grandchildren what it was like to hear the lyrical words of democracy from such a beautiful voice while looking up at Lincoln's statue. But the emotional intensity of the experience was difficult, if not impossible, to convey. By the time she had finished the last line of "America"—"Our starry flag unfurled, The hope of all the world, In peace and light impearled, God hold secure!"—she had the assembled multitude firmly in her grasp. And she never let go for the rest of the afternoon.[26]

The second selection was the aria "O mio Fernando" from Gaetano Donizetti's beloved opera *La Favorita*. The song meant a lot to her; she had sung it many times, and fifteen years earlier she had chosen it for her debut with the Philadelphia Orchestra. The closing cadenza was one of the most demanding in all of classical music, and as her voice rose and fell, the crowd seemed to gasp in collective wonder. By the time she had moved to the third and final selection before the intermission, "Ave Maria," the sun had darted out from the clouds, bathing the Memorial in an eerily sweet light. As she made her way through Franz Schubert's glorious stanzas, some in the crowd began to weep, either out of joy or in recognition of the supreme irony of the situation.

After a brief, five-minute hiatus, she returned to the stage for the "spiritual" half of the program. The selections were three of her favorites. She began with "Gospel Train," arranged by her old friend Harry Burleigh, and ended with "Trampin'," a work song popularized by Edward Boatner, and "My Soul Is Anchored in the Lord," a classic spiritual adapted by Florence Price, the first African-American woman to have gained wide acclaim as a composer. Though each selection had its own appeal, the spirituals were more familiar to many in the crowd, especially to the thousands of black families that had come out to hear one of their own. When she came to the end of "My Soul Is Anchored in the Lord," the crowd erupted with applause. Anderson was close enough to the front rows to see tears in the eyes of some of those who could hardly believe what they had just witnessed. Some held up their children, and others bent down to lift their sons or daughters onto their shoulders, all in an effort to help them see the woman responsible for the joyous commotion. Not knowing quite how to respond, and with tears in her own eyes, Anderson regained her composure by singing the spiritual "Nobody Knows the Trouble I've Seen" as an encore. Once again, as her voice trailed off, the crowd broke out in thunderous applause. Moments passed, and the crowd was still clapping and cheering. But somehow she managed to say a few words before leaving the stage. "I am so overwhelmed, I just can't talk," she exclaimed into the bank of microphones. "I can't tell you what you have done for me today. I thank you from the bottom of my heart."[27]

By then those in the crowd nearest to the stage had surged forward, with others filling in behind, all trying to get into position to thank Anderson personally. Walter White, who was on the stage throughout the ensuing melee, later offered a vivid description of the scene:

> As the last notes of "Nobody Knows the Trouble I've Seen" faded away the spell was broken by the rush of the audience toward Miss Anderson, which almost threatened tragedy. Oscar Chapman ploughed through the crowd and directed me to the microphone to plead with them not to create a panic. As I did so, but with indifferent success, a single figure caught my eye in the mass of people below which seemed one of the most important and touching symbols of the occasion. It was a slender black girl dressed in somewhat too garishly hued Easter finery. Hers was not the face of one who had been the beneficiary of much education or opportunity. Her hands were particularly noticeable as she thrust them forward and upward, trying desperately, though she was some distance away from Miss Anderson, to touch the singer. They were hands that despite their youth had known only the dreary work of manual labor. Tears streamed down the girl's dark face. Her hat was askew, but in her eyes flamed hope bordering on ecstasy. Life which had been none too easy for her held out greater hope because one who was also colored and who, like herself, had known poverty, privation, and prejudice, had, by her genius, gone a long way toward conquering bigotry. If Marian Anderson could do it, the girl's eyes seemed to say, then I can, too.[28]

Anderson's recollection, though simpler, echoed White's observation. "There were many in the gathering who were stirred by their own emotions," she recalled, with a measure of understatement. "Perhaps I did not grasp all that was happening, but at the end great numbers of people bore down on me." She added that "they were friendly; all they wished to do was to offer their congratulations and good wishes." Even so, the crush of the surging crowd endangered both her and the platform guests, who scrambled to get out of the way. Fortunately, a coterie of policemen blocked the crowd long enough to allow her to escape into the recesses of the Memorial, where she sat in the shadow of Daniel Chester French's towering sculpture of Lincoln. She remained there for several minutes posing for photographs, as a swarm of photographers ignored the long-standing Park Service rule that prohibited taking pictures "from within the sanctum where the statue stands." She also mingled with a number of fans who had sneaked through the cordon of security guards. But by six o'clock she was gone, having joined her mother and sisters in a rented limousine that whisked them away to a private dinner at a Pennsylvania Avenue mansion.[29]

The entire event, including the postconcert activities, had lasted less than an hour. But in that brief time Anderson gained a new life and identity. By merging her image with Lincoln's in such a dramatic way, the thirty-minute recital placed her on a path that few public figures had ever followed. Already renowned as a singer, she was forever after an iconic symbol of racial pride and democratic promise. "No one present at that moving performance ever forgot it," the historian Constance McLaughlin Green wrote in 1966. The meaning of the experience was difficult to articulate, but Mary McLeod Bethune came as close as anyone to capturing the essence of what had happened. In a letter to Charles Houston written the morning after the concert, she confessed that she was having difficulty expressing "what we felt and saw yesterday afternoon." She insisted, "It cannot be described in words. There is no way. History may and will record it, but it will never be able to tell what happened in the hearts of the thousands who stood and listened yesterday afternoon. Something happened in all of our hearts. I came away almost walking on air. We are on the right track—we must go forward. The reverence and concentration of the throngs . . . told a story of hope for tomorrow—a story of triumph—a story of pulling together—a story of splendor and real democracy. Through the Marian Anderson protest concert we made our triumphant entry into the democratic spirit of American life."[30]

Bethune spoke for the thousands who were actually at the Memorial, but Anderson's performance was probably only slightly less moving for those who listened to the live broadcast on NBC radio. The distinguished historian John Hope Franklin, for one, could hardly rein in his emotions nearly seventy years later when reflecting upon the impact of the broadcast, which he listened to in a Goldsboro, North Carolina, parlor. "I couldn't believe my ears," he told an interviewer in 2007. "The thought of Marian Anderson singing at the Lincoln Memorial, with all those dignitaries seated at her feet, stretched my imagination and touched my heart." For Franklin, as for other radio listeners, the music was captivating. But they also had the benefit of a lead-in provided by the organizing committee. In a brief but carefully worded statement, the NBC radio commentator framed the event as something more than a concert. He began, "Marian Anderson, one of the greatest artists of this generation, whose superb voice Toscanini has acclaimed as a voice heard once in every hundred years, is about to lift her voice in song on the steps of the Lincoln Memorial." He ended, "It is fitting and symbolic that she should be singing on Easter Sunday on the steps of the memorial to the Great Emancipator, who struck the shackles of slavery from her people seventy-six years ago. Miss Anderson faces the greatest audience ever assembled in Washington in one spot. Cabinet members, justices of the United States Supreme Court, senators and representatives, diplomats from foreign countries, the great in music and arts, and over sixty thousand citizens are gathered to hear a great artist and give a living testimonial to the spirit of democracy."

With such an opening, it is not surprising that thousands of listeners perked up their ears.[31]

IN the days and weeks following the concert, millions more read about it in newspapers and magazines or watched the newsreel footage in movie houses. Panoramic shots of the crowd and close-ups of Anderson singing into the microphones with Lincoln in the background appeared in the black press and many of the major dailies, giving visual aid to Americans trying to comprehend an unprecedented event. Readers looking closely at the photographs could see that the crowd was unsegregated and more or less evenly divided between blacks and whites. Some of the celebrities on the platform were recognizable, confirming the suspicions of several Southern congressmen who had reportedly canceled their plans to attend the concert after learning that the seating would be racially mixed. The cancellations did not appear in most accounts of the concert, but virtually every other aspect of what had transpired at the Lincoln Memorial on Easter Sunday received close scrutiny from reporters and editorial writers.

Journalists covering the concert noted the unprecedented size and diversity of the crowd, and some made a point of surveying the viewing stand, remarking on who was there and who was not. The most obvious names among the missing were President and Mrs. Roosevelt and Vice President Garner. Few observers had expected the president to be at the concert, since it was widely known that he planned to spend the Easter holidays at Warm

Springs, Georgia; and Garner's decision to stay home was no surprise considering his conservative racial views. But the first lady's conspicuous absence was another story. Prior to the concert, there had been widespread speculation—indeed, a general expectation—that she would be on hand to witness the event closely associated with her resignation from the DAR. On April 6, a headline in the *Washington Star* announced, MRS. ROOSEVELT EXPECTED TO ATTEND ANDERSON CONCERT. In some circles it was even rumored that the first lady had invited the black dancer Bill "Bojangles" Robinson to sit next to her on the viewing stand. But on the day of the concert the best she could do was to send Anderson a large bouquet of roses and an apology for not being in Washington for the big event. She had been away from the capital for more than a month, traveling all the way to the West Coast on a cross-country lecture tour and family visit. As she explained in her *My Day* columns, a long-standing commitment to be on hand for the birth of her daughter Anna's third child required her to be in Seattle, Washington, in late March and early April. She left Seattle on April 6, returning to Washington via Hyde Park, New York, where she spent Easter Sunday. Clearly, she could have returned to Washington in time for the Sunday afternoon concert but instead chose to return on Monday, April 10, the same day that the president returned from Warm Springs.

Why the first lady chose Hyde Park over Washington on Easter Sunday remains something of a mystery, but at least one Eleanor Roosevelt scholar, Allida Black, has speculated that the decision to forgo the concert was based on a creditable impulse: put simply, the always gracious first lady did not want her presence to upstage Anderson; she wanted the music and the celebration of democracy, not the DAR resignation, to be the center of attention at the Lincoln Memorial. This explanation seems plausible and is consistent with her desire to keep the DAR controversy in the background later in the month. On April 16, after just five days in Washington, she returned to Seattle, ostensibly to spend more time with her new grandchild and to attend her grandson Curtis's ninth birthday party. While family matters were certainly an important consideration in the decision to return to the West Coast, she also wanted to avoid the unpleasantness of a scheduled White House reception for the DAR later in the week. By returning to Seattle, she avoided a face-to-face meeting with Sally Robert and the other Daughters attending the organization's Continental Congress. Though somewhat awkward, and despite some grumbling from her critics in the DAR, the first lady's unexpected absence allowed her to sponsor the annual reception for the Continental Congress without actually being there. Indeed, her desire to extricate herself and Anderson from the shadow of the DAR controversy became clear in an exchange of letters with Walter White several days after the concert. "Thanks in large measure to you," White insisted on April 12, "the Marian Anderson concert on Sunday was one of the most thrilling experiences of our time. Only one thing marred it—that you couldn't be there. But I understand thoroughly the reason you could not come." White went on to reference her expressed fear that an MACC plan to picket the DAR's upcoming Continental Congress would reopen the resignation controversy to no one's benefit.

Whatever its origins, Eleanor Roosevelt's decision to remain in the background encouraged the press to focus less on the White House and more on the scene and meaning of Anderson's history-making triumph. "Easter Sunday in Washington was a day to be remembered," Howard Vincent O'Brien of the *Chicago Daily News* wrote in his syndicated column, *All Things Considered*, in mid-April, "for on that day was enacted one of the most moving dramas in American history." Ignoring the cold wind, O'Brien, a former novelist and literary critic, painted a vivid word picture of the scene: "It was a gorgeous Sunday," with "only a few blossoms left on the Japanese cherry trees around the tidal basin, but the grass and the foliage rich in April green. The sun was at its cheeriest, with just the right amount of fleecy clouds in the blue sky . . . It was a well-dressed crowd and as decorous as a church congregation. There was no shouting, no jostling, no hilarity, even among the children . . . There was symbolism in the Easter finery, for it was worn by the children and grandchildren of people who had been slaves. On faces black, brown and indeterminate one could read the fact that behind those faces were souls ecstatically aware of freedom."

O'Brien went on to describe the reaction to Anderson's voice—"an absolutely breathless hush, as if everyone in that multitude was thinking in awe of the contrast between the land of which she sang and the tortured lands elsewhere. It was a tearful, rapturous moment, and I have not met anyone who was not made tremulous by it." The close of the concert confirmed O'Brien's feeling that he had witnessed an extraordinary and telling event. Unfortunately, he reported, the radio broadcast had ended too soon, depriving listeners of hearing Anderson's "speech of thanks, delivered in what I think was the most beautiful speaking voice I ever heard. Had there been microphones to pick up the noise of the crowd as it melted away afterward listeners would have heard nothing, for the throng was as silent as if it had come from a benediction." He gave Oscar Chapman the last word. "Surely, we have nothing to fear," Chapman had told him moments after the concert, "as long as such things as this are possible in the United States."

O'Brien was hardly alone in his enthusiasm. A headline in the *Washington Star* on April 11 predicted EASTER, 1939, MAY INSPIRE HISTORIANS, and on the same day the *Washington Herald* ran an editorial suggesting that the Marian Anderson Easter Sunday concert should become an annual event. A day earlier a *Washington Daily News* headline had sarcastically asked its readers to THANK THE DAR. Other papers, both in Washington and elsewhere, voiced similar sentiments. In the South most editors simply ignored what had happened at the Memorial, but almost everywhere else, even in towns and cities dominated by Republican papers, the press response was favorable. One of the few negative responses came from the left, from the skeptical editor of the *New Negro Alliance,* the journal of a militant protest organization that often challenged discriminatory hiring practices in the District of Columbia. "The golden voice of Marian Anderson poured forth from the Lincoln Memorial as seventy-five thousand citizens, black and white, stood shoulder to shoulder in peace and harmony to enjoy its moving beauty," he acknowledged, before arguing that the concert had changed nothing: "Leaving the majestic natural setting, this multitude returned to gross discrimination and vicious segregation . . . Negroes were still unable to attend theaters, use Central High School or Constitution Hall, or to exercise their rights as American Citizens. The pent-up emotions of thousands of Negroes were discharged quietly over the Reflecting Pool and then the straight-jacket of social policy and racial prejudice was quickly made secure and operative again."[32]

Front-page press coverage of the concert, whether positive or negative, soon subsided, of course, as other stories—everything from Hitler's latest saber rattling to the hitting exploits of a young rookie outfielder named Ted Williams—competed for public attention. But Anderson herself remained an object of considerable curiosity, though she did her best to dodge it. One week after the Lincoln Memorial concert, she appeared at Carnegie Hall, where she was nearly mobbed by adoring fans. At a postconcert reception and dinner for three hundred guests, which included Walter White, Ethel Waters, and the black poet Countee Cullen, Mayor La Guardia called Anderson "one of America's greatest artists," before ironically chiding her for complaining about the DAR's lack of hospitality. "I've been in public life fifty-five years and haven't been invited by the DAR," quipped the mayor.[33]

Two days later, the Department of the Interior announced its intention to install a mural commemorating the Lincoln Memorial concert. To be hung in the Interior Department building, the mural would be sponsored by a national committee chaired by Edward Bruce, the chief of the Treasury Department's fine arts section, who was the first to suggest the project. Bruce had been present at the concert and had been brought to tears by Anderson's rendition of "America." He hoped that the mural, to be selected in a national competition, would "capture for posterity, the solemnity, grandeur and challenge of that moment." He declared, "This enterprise honoring the famous contralto is a further step in the cultural development of our colored people. It is an outgrowth of her recital recently at the Lincoln Memorial, a program which so wonderfully exemplified the progress of her race." Whether Anderson was offended by Bruce's well-meaning but condescending words is unclear, but she was noticeably embarrassed by all of the attention. During the rest of April and most of May, she took a well-earned vacation in Philadelphia, resting her voice and reconnecting with friends and family. She granted a few interviews, but for the most part she tried to avoid public appearances where she would face a battery of questions. Now that the concert was behind her, she was reluctant to talk about the meaning of it all. Others, however, were more than happy to fill the void.[34]

For the MACC, the Lincoln Memorial concert was a potential springboard for reforming the reactionary racial policies of both the DAR and the School Board. On April 12, three days after the concert, the MACC board approved a plan to picket the DAR's upcoming national conference unless notification of a change in policy arrived by April 17. The following day Houston and Lovell sent a letter to Sally Robert insisting that the "open air concert" had not solved "the fundamental issue of the ban on Negro artists in Constitution Hall." Their letter listed three demands:

1. That Constitution Hall be opened to Marian Anderson and other Negro artists.

2. That no reputable and responsible organization be barred from sponsoring a concert in Constitution Hall on account of race.

3. That the management of Constitution Hall be instructed to advise the Marian Anderson Citizens Committee as to dates available for concerts by Marian Anderson and other Negro artists in the Concert Season of 1939–1940.[35]

Eleanor Roosevelt, like most MACC supporters, had no problem with the demands. But she was horrified by the thought of a picket line at the DAR convention. In a frantic special-delivery letter, she pleaded with Walter White to intervene: "I do not know if there is anything you could do to prevent this but it worries me very much to have anything of this kind done. In the first place, Washington is a city where one could have serious trouble and I think it would not do any good to picket the D. A. R. It would only create bad feeling all the way around. At present the D. A. R. Society is condemned for the stand it took and if picketing is done it may result in the sympathy swinging to the other side. I would strongly urge you to use your influence against this and to leave well enough alone." On the thirteenth, Lovell distributed a public letter that described the picketing plan, vowing, "We are determined that the Marian Anderson incident of 1939, with all its terrible implications, shall not be repeated." But the first lady's objections, channeled through White, were enough to kill the picketing idea. After sending Houston an urgent telegram, White followed up with a letter reiterating the argument against picketing: "Let's don't do anything to pull the D. A. R. out of the deep hole into which they have sunk themselves." He added, "I talked with Hubert Delany this morning and he authorized me to say that Miss Anderson would very strongly agree with Mrs. Roosevelt's position as a matter of strategy." Less than twenty-four hours later MACC leaders held an emergency meeting, at which a majority agreed to honor the wishes of the two women they could not afford to alienate.[36]

As an alternative strategy, the MACC decided to flood the DAR with letters of protest on the eve of the national convention, and to ask for a hearing at the convention. Fredric March, Pennsylvania congressman James McGranery, Doxey Wilkerson writing on behalf of the American Federation of Teachers, Mary McLeod Bethune, Hubert Delany, and Walter White all participated in the campaign, as did Clarke and Mairi Foreman, two of the New Deal's most progressive activists and recent sponsors of the Lincoln Memorial concert. With obvious passion, the Foremans wrote, "We feel that the refusal of Constitution Hall to the greatest American singer, because she happened to be colored, is so completely contrary to the best American ideals that it casts a shadow on all the undertakings of your organization. Surely Americanism, like charity, begins at home; and if your organization wishes to be taken seriously by the rest of the country it should practice what it preaches and show by example that it really is an American organization."

A member of Ickes's inner circle with close ties to the Black Cabinet, Clarke Foreman was also a native Georgian and the grandson of Evan Howell, the influential publisher of the *Atlanta Constitution* during the post-Reconstruction era. The Howells had descended from wealthy colonial slaveholders, some of whom had fought in the Revolution, and were just the kind of people that the DAR hoped to recruit. But there is no record that the DAR ever responded to the Foremans' plaintive letter. As the embattled Daughters gathered in Washington on April 17 for their annual convention—known in the organization as the Continental Congress—they were in no mood to acknowledge their racial sins, past or present.[37]

Five days before the convention opened, Emmeline Street, an ill-informed Connecticut woman who served as the DAR's national vice president general, muddied the waters of an already confusing situation by telling a local DAR chapter in Willimantic that her organization had acted as it did because the U.S. Congress had passed a law prohibiting black performers from appearing in "white" auditoriums in the District of Columbia. Her remarks, though never validated by anyone else in a position of authority in the DAR, drew considerable press attention, and probably a private reprimand from Sally Robert. No such law existed, and no one, inside or outside the DAR, had ever mentioned it before. With little or no time to address the gaffe, Street and Robert had an embarrassing situation on their hands as the DAR delegates streamed into Washington.[38]

Robert, in characteristic fashion, refused to acknowledge any diversions. When reporters asked about Constitution Hall, she advised them to wait for her speech. Always a paragon of order, she had prepared a carefully worded address, which she delivered on the first afternoon of the Continental Congress. Only part of the speech dealt with Constitution Hall, but that part engaged the delegates, many of whom were puzzled by certain aspects of the Anderson controversy. Robert began her explanation with a reminder that Constitution Hall and other DAR buildings represented "a contribution to the cultural life of Washington." She continued, "If Constitution Hall, this building, had been built commercially, the income has not been sufficient to cover interest alone on the investment, even without maintenance and repairs. If it were operated commercially, thus requiring return on investment, the cost for its use for practically all events now held there would be prohibitive. Only because those who built it for their own use ask no return upon a great investment is it possible for the people of this community to share at all in its advantages. The only reason the building exists and that it can be opened to others, is that women in every State and in chapters in other countries through years of hard and united effort brought their gifts to Washington."

With many in the room nodding their approval, she moved on to the more difficult topic of restricted access to the building: "In the beginning there were no rules, except that all events should be of dignity and refinement and not in contradiction to the ideals of the society. With experience, a number of rules developed. If certain plans proved impractical, they could not be continued. As a result of actual experience, a rule was adopted which has remained in force through parts of four administrations and which has recently been under discussion. That rule arose because of unpleasant experiences in attempting to go contrary to conditions and customs existing in the District of Columbia, as a result of which the society was widely criticized in letters and comments in the press for not cooperating, even though all restrictions had been waived. Statements were incorrect and were not based upon facts. Experience showed the society that it could not go contrary to nor further than the customs existing in the city in which its properties were located. There was no question of prejudice, personality, or discrimination. This society has consistently through its nearly fifty years been a friend of, and has worked for, many minority groups. It will continue to do so."

If the delegates were not thoroughly confused by this time—they had been told that the DAR abided by the segregationist customs of Washington yet at the same time waived the racial restrictions at Constitution Hall in keeping with the organization's liberal traditions—the next section of the speech took them through a labyrinth of doublespeak. "The question was merely this," Robert intoned: "Could the society by continuing a practice contrary to accepted custom cope with its difficulties? In business, if any venture is accompanied with results detrimental to the company or corporation, the practice is discontinued. The rule under question was simply that, under the conditions in the District of Columbia, the community did not accept the step which the society had taken. Experience proved that it could not proceed further than local conditions warranted. The very fact that the rule attracted no attention through parts of four administrations indicated that it was in accordance with existing customs." In other words, during the early 1930s the DAR had tried a bold experiment in racial integration that had alienated white subscribers who did not want to share the hall with black concertgoers. Why she didn't just say this in clear and straightforward language is unclear, though her motivation probably had something to do with her continuing attachment to the original rationale for turning Anderson away—the claim that the April date had already been booked by the National Symphony Orchestra. Despite what she had just said about the "white artists only" rule, she then repeated the argument that the problem was primarily a matter of an unreasonable request for a booking date that was already filled.

Only in the closing minutes of her speech did Robert get to the real crux of the DAR's determination to hold the line against racial integration at Constitution Hall. The root of the problem, she insisted, was external pressure unduly and unfairly applied. Shortly after the Howard committee's informal request was received, "with no request yet in writing, letters began to appear in the press. Comment and adverse criticism gathered like a snowball." What is more, "information and letters received during this period clearly indicated that the question was not one regarding a single artist, but involved far-reaching changing social forces." According to Robert, acceding to the Howard committee's demands would inexorably have led to financial ruin and crushing legal liability: "An important consideration was that, to make an exception, would be in direct contradiction to existing agreements with concert bureaus who have regularly used the hall for some years and whose agreements cover a period of years. The society therefore would have opened itself to legal responsibility for violation of its own agreements."[39] This particular argument had little basis in fact, according to Peggy Anderson, an investigative journalist who later did a careful study of the DAR's contractual agreements.

As Anderson put it, Robert "was apparently unaware that the DAR had few if any long-standing agreements for future use of Constitution Hall. Her implication was that the Society had already signed contracts for events scheduled over 'a period of years,' but most DAR contracts at that period provided for events that would take place within a few months." Thus, Robert was either misinformed or using the contractual issue as a smoke screen for what was really at stake, namely the DAR's right to control its own affairs, in matters of race or anything else. Either way, the autonomy issue seems to have been paramount in her mind. Robert said as much in her closing remarks: "The membership should distinctly understand that to have made an exception would not only have been in violation of signed agreements and customs for all similar properties in Washington, but would have meant that the society retreated under fire of widely scattered groups and organizations, many of whom knew nothing of the facts, and whose interest had nothing to do with the real question. To have changed the rule while it was entangled with so many factors having nothing to do with the rule would have been to surrender the society to influences inimical to its purposes and efforts. When independence of action is threatened, and when fog beclouds real issues, there can be no surrender."[40]

The military analogy, though a bit melodramatic, was fitting for an organization so closely tied to the American Revolution. But Robert also wanted the delegates, and the wider world, to recognize that no heritage organization should be burdened with the responsibility of winning the war against racial prejudice. "Is it reasonable," she asked, "that one group of women alone, whose properties are privately owned, whose buildings were possible only through voluntary contributions of its members in all parts of the country accumulated during nearly fifty years of effort, be expected to work out the problems of vast groups backed by great changing social forces? . . . Conditions are the same as when experience dictated the need of the rule. This is not a question for the Daughters of the American Revolution alone to solve. When the community at large has worked out its problem, the Daughters of the American Revolution will be willing, as at all times, to adapt its policies to practices and customs in accordance with the highest standards of the community."

Robert's words were striking, not only for what they said, but also for what they did not say. In her long speech, not a single mention was made of Marian Anderson's stature, Eleanor Roosevelt's resignation, or Vice President General Street's congressional-mandate argument. Nor did Robert offer even so much as a hint that racial prejudice was inconsistent with the ideals of the republic. For her, and by implication for the entire DAR, the primary issue at hand was the organization's right to do as it pleased without any interference from the outside. At the deepest level, the "real principles involved" were "keeping free from entanglements" that might violate the sensibilities of mainstream America. Clearly, Marian Anderson and her allies were not part of that America.[41]

The leaders of the MACC were not privileged to hear President General Robert's speech, and they did not meet with DAR officials during the Continental Congress. But they did contact Robert through Anson Phelps Stokes, the liberal but diplomatic dean of the National Cathedral. Beginning in late March, Stokes wrote a series of letters to Robert suggesting a face-to-face meeting with a delegation from the MACC. He also consulted with Houston throughout the crisis, periodically counseling the MACC leader to tone down his organization's rhetoric. "When you are asking a group of citizens to modify their action," he wrote Houston on April 16, "it seems to me that you defeat your purpose in quoting with apparent approval statements in certain parts of the country to the effect that the D. A. R.'s action is 'an expression of bigotry and intolerance, shameful in any group.'" Stokes favored a softer approach, one that would avoid unnecessary references to the DAR's past sins. With this in mind, the MACC sent a letter to Robert on April 17 proposing a meeting with an eight-person interracial delegation led by Stokes, Congresswoman Caroline O'Day, Rosamond Pinchot, and the Reverend R. W. Brooks, the pastor of the Lincoln Memorial Congregational Church. After some hesitation, Robert agreed to meet, but not before the end of May. This gave the MACC delegates more than a month to prepare their case.[42]

In the meantime, the MACC turned its attention to the unresolved School Board controversy. Ballou's withdrawal of the Central High School offer on March 17 had left several issues hanging, angering a broad cross-section of Washington's black community. While few Washington activists showed any interest in challenging the dual school system, many were troubled by the policies that had barred Anderson from Central High School. In the weeks following the Lincoln Memorial concert, Houston and others redoubled their efforts to change a set of School Board policies that they considered blatantly discriminatory. As early as the mass meeting of March 26, Herbert Marshall, the president of the Washington branch of the NAACP, had insisted that the "denial of the use of the Central High School auditorium is the very antithesis of democracy," and nothing that had happened since had dissuaded him or any other MACC leader from this belief. The Marian Anderson controversy that had spawned the MACC was over, but the battle for equal justice in the nation's capital was just beginning. Appealing to several cabinet secretaries, including Harold Ickes, and enlisting the support of several congressmen, MACC leaders called for a federal investigation of the school system. But political and institutional inertia frustrated them at every turn. Despite the best efforts of Houston and his colleagues, it would be years before black Washingtonians achieved anything approaching fundamental reform in the District's schools.[43]

By comparison, the campaign to strike down the color bar at Constitution Hall seemed fairly straightforward. Yet here, too, racial tradition proved intractable. Nervous about the potential fallout from the upcoming May 31 meeting, Sally Robert warned Houston, "This is to be strictly a private meeting," and advised the MACC delegation to enter the DAR building through the side entrance on D Street. Troubled by this directive, Houston responded by expressing the hope that the D Street request "has no element of furtiveness about it." He acknowledged, "I can appreciate that you may not wish the press to have the details of the conference, but I hope you have no objection to the press being advised that the conference is being held."

With this spirit of distrust, the meeting was doomed from the start. Although Robert and her lieutenants listened politely to what the delegation had to say, they didn't engage in a meaningful dialogue. As John Lovell wrote to Houston after the meeting, "Nobody on the D. A. R. side made any attempt at argument, either in attack or defense," and the delegation "found it very difficult to get Mrs. Robert to state an opinion or to answer a direct question or to pretend that there were two sides to the matter in any respects." On a more positive and lighthearted note, Lovell reported, "The Marian Anderson delegation was treated with the greatest courtesy and if Mrs. Robert was wincing inside at our taking possession of her fine office furniture, she did not show it in her face. (Somewhere I have read a woman is trained to show her emotions; a lady to hide hers.) It seems to be that the sum total of testimony indicates that the conference was a success in only one particular, namely Mrs. Robert is a lady." Whenever one of the delegates asked Robert about a specific point, she reached forward with a copy of her address to the DAR Congress. This document, she seemed to think, answered all questions or concerns. After two awkward hours, the delegates had extracted no concessions from Robert other than a promise to read and distribute a brief prepared by Anson Phelps Stokes. Entitled "Art and the Color Line," the twenty-six-page brief was later submitted to the DAR's Executive Committee and Board of Management for consideration at a scheduled October meeting.[44]

WHILE the DAR was digging itself a deeper hole, Anderson was reemerging from her post–Lincoln Memorial vacation. Over the next few months she would discover just how famous she had become. On May 28, she drew a huge crowd when she sang at the World's Fair in New York, and two days later she was in Springfield, Illinois, for the Memorial Day premiere of the Twentieth Century–Fox film *Young Mr. Lincoln*. As director John Ford and leading man Henry Fonda looked on, she sang "America" and three other songs, reinforcing her new association with the Great Emancipator. A few days later, she repeated the performance at the Hollywood premiere held at the posh Fox Wiltshire Theatre. Though surrounded by celebrities, she received as much press attention as the stars of the film. Realizing that many

Americans regarded her as a living expression of Lincoln's ideals, reporters put her on the same pedestal as Fonda, who didn't seem to mind. Anderson seemed a bit overwhelmed by it all, but she would soon discover that serving as Lincoln's surrogate was an inescapable responsibility.[45]

Another responsibility, which she embraced wholeheartedly, was her increasingly public friendship with Eleanor Roosevelt. Back in March she had agreed to appear at the White House as part of a program on American music following a state dinner honoring the visiting king and queen of England. The royal couple's two-week tour of Canada and the United States had turned into an epochal event, drawing huge crowds along parade routes in New York and Washington. The Roosevelts spared no effort in welcoming the titular heads of state of America's most important ally, and the state dinner and program on June 8 represented the climax of the effort. The program, "American Songs as Played and Sung," offered a diverse selection of "Negro spirituals, cowboy ballads, and mountain tunes" plus "folk dances" performed by the Soco Gap square-dance team of North Carolina. Anderson's recital came near the end of the program, sandwiched between Kate Smith's "When the Moon Comes over the Mountain" and Lawrence Tibbett's operatic rendition of "The Pilgrim's Song," by Tchaikovsky. How the Russian composer's work found its way into a program of American music was unclear, but Anderson began the European detour with a stirring performance of Schubert's "Ave Maria," before closing with two spirituals.

Anderson did not meet the king and queen until after the program, and when she did, her nerves got the better of her. "It occurred to me that it might be the right thing to curtsy," she later explained. "I had seen people curtsy in the movies, and it looked like the simplest thing in the world. I practiced a few curtsies in Mrs. Roosevelt's room. An aide came to call me, and I happened to be the first woman in line to meet Their Majesties. I remember that I was looking into the queen's eyes as I started my curtsy, and when I had completed it and was upright again I had turned a quarter- or half-circle and no longer faced the queen. I don't know how I managed it so inelegantly, but I never tried one again, not even for the king." Embarrassed by the failed curtsy, Anderson managed only a few words of greeting when she encountered the first lady in the receiving line. But three weeks later she had a second opportunity to spend some time with the woman who had been instrumental in arranging her appearance at the Lincoln Memorial.[46]

On July 2, both Anderson and Eleanor Roosevelt traveled to Richmond to attend the annual convention of the NAACP. They were there for the 1939

Spingarn Medal award ceremony. As Walter White and an audience of five thousand looked on, the first lady, as promised, personally presented the medal to Anderson, paying tribute to a woman who "had the courage to meet many difficulties." She assured Anderson, "Your achievement far transcends any race or creed." Earlier in the program, the first lady had offered a few words along the same lines, reminding the crowd that "people cannot grow up good citizens unless we provide good environment for all the people." In accepting the medal, Anderson was almost overcome with emotion, tearfully acknowledging the "significance it carries" and how honored she felt to receive it "from the hands of our first lady, who is not only a first lady in name, but in every deed." That all of this took place in the former capital of the Confederacy added to the meaning and symbolism of the ceremony, particularly for African Americans, who had waited a long time for such a moment.[47]

The Spingarn Medal was the first of several awards that confirmed Anderson's new status. No longer just a singer, she had become a public figure in the broadest sense. In February 1940, after conducting a nationwide poll, the Schomburg Collections of the New York Public Library, in conjunction with the Association for the Study of Negro Life and History, included Anderson on a short list of individuals who had done the most to improve American race relations. With Eleanor Roosevelt, Harold Ickes, Joe Louis, George Washington Carver, and the novelist Richard Wright also on the list, Anderson was in good company. A few months later, Temple University awarded her an honorary doctorate, and a committee of educators selected her as one of the ten most "outstanding young women of America," along with such notables as Anne Morrow Lindbergh, actresses Helen Hayes and Deanna Durbin, authors Carson McCullers and Clare Boothe, and Mildred McAfee, the president of Wellesley College.[48]

The most consequential honor came in March 1941, when Anderson received the Bok Award. Established in 1921 by Edward W. Bok, the Pulitzer Prize–winning editor of the *Ladies' Home Journal*, the annual award, which included a $10,000 stipend, honored "a Philadelphian who had done some service that redounds to the credit of the city." Anderson was the first black Philadelphian to be so honored, making the 1941 award ceremony at the Academy of Music a milestone in the city's racial history. To the delight of a mixed audience, Anderson announced that she would use the Bok prize money to establish the Marian Anderson Scholarship Fund, which would sponsor an annual vocal competition for young singers between the ages of sixteen and thirty. Prize money from the competition, Anderson explained, "shall enable some poor, unfortunate but nevertheless very talented people to do something for which they have dreamed all of their young lives."[49]

The scholarship fund was just one manifestation of Anderson's growing sense of civic responsibility. While she had always been generous with her time and money, from 1939 on she devoted more and more of her energies to benefit concerts and other charitable activities. In New York City alone, she performed a half dozen benefit concerts in 1940, adding to the coffers of such organizations as the NAACP, the National Urban League, the International Committee on African Affairs, the Division of Colored Work of the YMCA, and the National Association of Day Nurseries. Whenever she agreed to perform, concert organizers were virtually guaranteed an overflow crowd. On July 18, 1940, twelve thousand people showed up for an outdoor concert at Philadelphia's Fairmount Park, and two days later more than twenty-five thousand attended a recital in New York's Lewisohn Stadium, the largest crowd in the history of the city's stadium concert series.[50]

Whatever the venue, large or small, Anderson somehow found time for those in need. Despite frequent radio appearances and a grueling schedule of between sixty and eighty concerts a year, she rarely said no to anyone who sought a favor. Those in her debt included Franklin Roosevelt, who received Anderson's enthusiastic support during his 1940 presidential race against Wendell Willkie. While she did not feel comfortable speaking out on issues of public policy, she made no effort to conceal her admiration for the Roosevelts and the New Deal. On the eve of the election, *New York Times* editor Arthur Krock assembled a list of politically salient celebrities, naming Anderson— along with bandleader Benny Goodman, dancer Bill "Bojangles" Robinson, composer Irving Berlin, and historian Carl Sandburg—as the president's principal cultural boosters. Although the heavyweight champion Joe Louis was among the celebrities in Willkie's corner, Anderson and the Brown Bomber would soon find themselves on the same team.[51]

With America's entry into World War II in December 1941, the American creed came into tight focus as federal authorities emphasized the stark contrast between Allied virtues and the evil designs of the Axis powers. Part of this emphasis became manifest in the influential "Why We Fight" series of patriotic propaganda films, which included the film *The Negro Soldier*. But there was an even broader effort to distinguish between the Nazis' totalitarian anti-Semitism and America's racial and ethnic pluralism. Along with Louis, Anderson became a potent symbol of racial pride and inclusion, and government officials made every effort to keep them in the public eye. On January 9, 1942, barely a month after Pearl Harbor, Louis fought a benefit championship bout against Buddy Baer, donating most of his winnings to the Navy Relief Fund, and the next morning he enlisted in the U.S. army. Anderson's contributions to the war effort, though less spectacular than Louis's, were no less substantial, surpassing anything one could reasonably expect from a forty-five-year-old woman.

For three years, she interrupted her concert tours with hundreds of visits to hospital wards and military bases, sometimes for casual conversations with wounded soldiers and sailors and often for impromptu bedside or mess-hall concerts. In one instance, she had the honor of christening a new Liberty ship named the SS *Booker T. Washington*, and in another she tried to lift the spirits of wounded soldiers at a military hospital in Topeka, Kansas. As she later recalled, the "wounded men . . . I was warned, could not remain seated and listening for more than fifteen minutes. But they would not permit me to leave after fifteen minutes, and their medical guardians thought it would be good for them if I continued. That performance lasted forty-five minutes, and I was more touched than the audience." From Boston to Seattle, she sang for white servicemen and servicewomen, and for their black counterparts, usually to crowds as segregated as the army and navy units they represented. But occasionally, as in Topeka, elements of racial mingling offered some hope that the nation might eventually live up to its professed ideals.[52]

For Anderson, the war brought many surprises, both good and bad. But one of the biggest surprises came in September 1942, when the DAR invited her to sing at Constitution Hall. It had been more than three years since Anderson had sung in Washington, though each year Hurok had renewed his request for an Anderson concert in Constitution Hall. Each time he had been rebuffed or ignored. Anderson played no part in this behind-the-scenes drama, leaving the negotiations to Hurok's staff, though she was aware of the continuing desegregation effort by Charles Houston and the remnants of the MACC. Thus, she was as shocked as anyone when Hurok informed her of the invitation. Not one to hold a grudge, she was open to the idea of singing at Constitution Hall, though she and Hurok were somewhat reluctant to accept the invitation under the conditions stipulated by the DAR. The invitation asked her to sing the first of several special war-relief concerts, with the understanding that her appearance would not set a precedent for future performances at the hall by her or any other black artist. For the good of the nation, the DAR wanted her to perform a single recital, but the color bar would remain in force.

Anderson supported the war-relief effort and was determined to sing in Washington again, but Walter White soon reminded her and Hurok that more than war relief was at stake. Anderson had become a symbol of racial justice and should not become involved in anything that detracted from her image or the ongoing struggle for civil rights. "Acceptance under such humiliating conditions" would not only be "most unfair to Miss Anderson," White counseled Hurok, but in all likelihood, it would also be a setback for the causes of justice and equality. Combined with spirited commentary in the press, White's adamant opposition to accepting the invitation as offered was enough to delay Hurok's decision. But, on October 3, the impresario thought he had found a way to sidestep the color-bar issue without incurring the disfavor of the NAACP or the general public, which clearly valued war relief above racial equality. "Miss Anderson will give this concert," Hurok informed Fred Hand, "subject to the specific agreement by the Executive Committee that no segregation in the seating arrangements be exercised" and with the understanding that "her appearance in Constitution Hall is to be construed as a precedent that hereafter Constitution Hall will be open to her in the normal course of her annual tours." In other words, the general color bar could stand, but Anderson would be granted a permanent exemption, with no segregated seating at any of her Constitution Hall concerts.[53]

Hurok's counteroffer led to a month of nervous speculation as Hand forwarded the letter to the DAR Executive Committee, which was scheduled to meet on October 30. Anderson was distracted by the deteriorating condition of her sister Ethel's husband, James DePreist, who died on October 7. But Hurok's staff and White had a protracted discussion of just how much they were willing to risk to set a firm precedent or to combat segregated seating. Much of the discussion concerned competing definitions of racial separation and discrimination. To White, any form of enforced separation was unacceptable. To Hurok and Anderson, only unequal seating, where blacks were forced to sit in a balcony or in the back of the hall, was out of bounds. For them, "vertical segregation," achieved by dividing the hall into racially restricted sections on the left and the right, was an acceptable compromise.

In many Southern venues even this modified form of segregation was unachievable, but both Hurok and Anderson reasoned that periodically accepting horizontal segregation was better than not singing at all. White disagreed, and as he and the others waited for the DAR's decision, he offered his opinion on an upcoming concert in Louisville, Kentucky. When the local hall manager insisted on the traditional form of segregation, White advised Anderson to cancel the recital. Considering that Hurok had just demanded integrated seating at Constitution Hall, White's position seemed reasonable. But the response from Gerald Goode, ostensibly writing on behalf of Hurok and Anderson, indicated that Hurok Productions was ready to accept different restrictions in different places. Goode's telegram to White insisted that "public relations strategy requires that issue of segregation be concentrated for present in Washington where moral victory is in sight."[54]

The exact meaning of Goode's position was difficult to decipher other than the obvious message that Anderson would sing in Louisville, segregated hall or not. In any event, the DAR's rejection of Hurok's counteroffer at the October 30 meeting soon overshadowed White's concerns about Louisville. Hand's letter to Hurok in early November amounted to nothing less than an ultimatum: accept the original offer as tendered, as "the other artists for War Benefit Concerts" had agreed to do, or consider the invitation withdrawn. "No appearance of any artist, attraction or event can ever be considered as a precedent," Hand continued, "insofar as future engagements in Constitution Hall are concerned." In response, a furious Hurok lashed out in the press on November 4. "The DAR is persisting with its original theory, isn't it?" he asked rhetorically. "It has not become one bit wiser since it was taught a lesson by public opinion on Easter Sunday in 1939."

Two days later, however, he reversed course and accepted the DAR's original invitation. "Because Miss Anderson is very much concerned that the issue of her future performances at Constitution Hall shall not be a cause of deprivation to the Army Emergency Relief Fund," Hurok informed Hand, "she is ready to make plans immediately to sing in accordance with your letter of invitation which you addressed to her on Sept. 28." As to the matter of segregated seating, Hurok took the risk of asserting that the DAR had already capitulated on that issue. "Since the executive committee has not referred in its letter to the matter of segregation in the seating arrangements," he contended, "Miss Anderson understands that this is no barrier." In making this claim, Hurok was, in effect, whistling as he walked by the graveyard. But the DAR did not challenge his assertion. Both Hurok and Anderson were surprised and pleased, feeling fortunate to emerge from the negotiations with a Solomonic compromise. Neither singer nor manager revealed any of the back-and-forth between them, but Anderson had clearly made her wishes known, and Hurok had acted accordingly. Perhaps for the first time in their eight-year relationship, they were more or less equal partners in deciding the best course of action in a high-profile public setting.[55]

Hurok and the DAR agreed to hold the benefit concert on the evening of January 7, 1943. But when they announced their mutual agreement on December 2, no one foresaw that the concert would be upstaged by another related event. For more than three years, Edward Bruce's mural committee had been raising funds and soliciting artistic expressions of Easter Sunday 1939. The winner of the competition had been chosen, the mural was ready to be unveiled, and the plans for the unveiling ceremony were set. The only task left was to choose a date for the ceremony. After consulting with the committee, Secretary Ickes chose January 6, the traditional holiday of the Epiphany and the eve of Anderson's Constitution Hall concert. Suspecting that Anderson was too polite to remind the DAR of the significance of her belated appearance at the hall, Ickes was determined to do so indirectly. When the official ceremonial program was printed, the back cover included the notice: "Miss Anderson will make her initial appearance at Constitution Hall, Thursday, January 7, at 8:30 P.M., for the United China Relief." A few lines up, the program copy reminded readers, "On Easter Sunday, 1939, at the invitation of the Secretary of the Interior, Miss Anderson gave a people's concert, singing from the steps of the Lincoln Memorial 'in God's great out-of-doors where all men are free.'"[56]

Purposeful rhetoric of this kind was the order of the day on January 6 as an array of dignitaries witnessed the mural's unveiling. Although Edward Bruce was ill and unable to attend, Assistant Secretary Oscar Chapman, Secretary Ickes, and Charles Houston, representing both the mural committee and the MACC, were on hand to provide the expected oratorical flourishes for the audience at the Interior building and a national radio audience. Chapman set the tone with a sobering but stirring introduction laced with allusions to the trials of war and the dangers of totalitarianism: "For men of goodwill and tolerance these are indeed difficult and heart-trying times . . . We are in a period in which it appears that the enlightenment of the human spirit that has been developed through generations of painful toil toward a civilized way of life has been subjugated completely to brutal selfishness. A period where the forces of brutality stir up currents and eddies of intolerance." But, turning to the subject of the hour, he assured the gathering that all was not lost: "While grave doubts are natural and moments of discouragement are not uncommon, a calm appraisal shows abundant manifestations of the inherent desire of man to live peacefully and humanely. This meeting . . . is but one expression of this humane spirit. At times when we may have grave doubts, it is heartwarming to recall the sincere expression of tolerance which typified the concert at the Lincoln Memorial four years ago. All who were present on that occasion could not help but be impressed with the dignity of the human spirit. At that time instead of giving mere lip service to our democratic ideals we gave active allegiance to the greatest of all those ideals—tolerance. Intolerance in any form we must hate and fight—for it is the evil cancer which seeks to destroy our spiritual and moral being."[57]

To prove his point, Chapman introduced "a group of young Negro seamen who are preparing to take an active part in the people's worldwide fight against bigotry and intolerance." Among the first African-American sailors to take advantage of the navy's new policy of "opening enlistment to Negroes in other than the messman's rating," eight recruits from the Great Lakes Naval Training Station in northern Illinois sang as a "double quartet." Both the music and the intended symbolism set the stage for Houston's formal presentation of the mural.

With obvious pride in his long involvement in the Anderson controversy, Houston spoke passionately about the meaning of both the Lincoln Memorial concert and the mural that commemorated it. "The occasion was more than a concert," he insisted, his voice cracking with emotion, "it was almost a trial of the American people . . . Everything about that Marian Anderson concert was significant. The day was Easter Sunday, the day when the Christian world rises in spiritual rebirth. The place was the Lincoln Memorial, sacred to the memory of the Great Emancipator, whose love for the common people knew no bounds. There was no time for recriminations at that concert. No one mentioned the Daughters of the American Revolution, or the Board of Education. After the briefest introduction, Miss Anderson sang to the people. Under the marvelous gift of her art, seventy-five thousand persons were bound together throughout an afternoon in ties of a great spiritual experience of common sympathy and understanding."

Shifting to the mural, Houston explained that "many persons present were so touched that they felt the occasion was too historic to pass away unmarked." Hence, the formation of the mural committee and the conclusion "that whatever was done should be an expression of the people themselves." When the committee "launched its campaign to raise funds for the mural, it made no effort to obtain large donations; it purposely held down the size of the individual contributions so that the fund might represent as many people as possible. Thousands of schoolchildren and others contributed to the fund. A national contest of artists was held, and the design of Mitchell Jamieson selected as most faithfully portraying the spirit of the day. Four years have now passed, but the inspiration of that Easter Sunday concert is still quietly at work in many ways."

Perhaps the most obvious way was through Jamieson's art, which captured the spirit of the concert in a Thomas Hart Benton–like representation of ordinary people sitting and standing on the edge of the crowd. But Houston could not resist adding a gracious mention of the impending Constitution Hall concert: "Tomorrow night the Daughters of the American Revolution are donating Constitution Hall free for a benefit performance, and on the invitation of the Daughters of the American Revolution this same Marian Anderson is singing in Constitution Hall as the guest artist of the evening, the entire proceeds of the concert going to the United China Relief. This is not the answer to all our problems, but it is a step forward which we gladly acknowledge. We are glad that it includes not only white and black but the Chinese people as well." What Houston left out, for obvious reasons, was the probable explanation for the designation of United China Relief as the concert's beneficiary. After being notified that the army relief fund was no longer accepting civilian contributions, Anderson was asked to substitute the beneficiary of her choice. She chose United China Relief, and while she never revealed her motivation, many suspected that it had something to do with the DAR's earlier refusal to rent Constitution Hall to Paul Robeson for a United China Relief benefit concert.

Houston knew this but diplomatically kept the focus on the mural, which, in his words, commemorated "a milestone in the progress of the United States along the pathway of democracy." Before turning the podium over to Ickes, he voiced the committee's hope that the mural would not become "a museum piece for musty halls where people would have to make a special trip to see it. We conceive of the mural as a living document which we trust may always be kept in a public building at a spot where the greatest number of people may see it as they go about their daily lives. It is our message to them that we believe in the inherent decency and integrity of the American people."[58]

In accepting the mural on behalf of the U.S. government, Ickes returned to the theme of democracy versus totalitarianism. After recalling that Easter Sunday 1939 "was one of those soul-stirring moments when we plumbed the depth of emotion," he acknowledged that "since that day humanity has undergone convulsive changes. A mighty struggle for freedom, not of one race or of one people, has gripped the globe. Two mutually exclusive ideologies have engaged in mortal combat that will not end until one or the other has been destroyed." Assuring the audience that "each of us has his or her part to do," he conceded that "we can not all do great things." The few who were able to rise to that level deserved special praise and thanks. "There is only one Marian Anderson," he insisted, "whose voice . . . has given life to a new concept of human relationships in millions of hearts . . . Marian Anderson's voice and personality have come to be a symbol—a symbol of American unity at a time when a lack of it might well prove fatal to us as a people; a symbol of the willing acceptance of the immortal truth that 'all men are created equal' . . . She used the rich gift with which genius has endowed her to make an indifferent people realize that if the possession and cultivation of a voice are not related to the color of one's skin, then the same must be equally true of other human gifts and qualities."[59]

As Ickes's eloquent words trailed off, Anderson rose to sing three carefully chosen spirituals. Still a bit tired from a Monday-night concert at Carnegie Hall and a Tuesday-night ceremony in Philadelphia during which she accepted an award from a local Jewish group, she prefaced the spirituals with a brief but moving statement on the personal meaning of the mural and the concert it depicted. Struggling to keep her composure, she began by assuring everyone present and the radio audience listening in that she was "deeply touched" by the suggestion that she had become "a symbol of democracy." She continued, "That Easter Sunday concert was more than a concert for me. It was a dedication. When I stood on the steps of the Lincoln Memorial with the statue of President Lincoln at my back and seventy-five thousand of my fellow countrymen before me, it seemed that everyone present was a living witness to the ideals of freedom for which President Lincoln died. When I sang that day, I was singing to the entire nation. I have carried the inspiration of that Easter Sunday with me ever since. When I have sung in army camps to entertain the soldiers, I have felt I was looking in the same faces I saw before me at the Lincoln Memorial." With the German refugee Franz Rupp at the piano, she then sang "Let Us Break Bread Together" and two other spirituals before asking the double quartet to join her at the podium for the singing of "The Star-Spangled Banner." In a nation awash in patriotic rhetoric, it was a genuine moment of hope and solidarity that few of those privileged to be there ever forgot.[60]

The next day Marian Anderson finally saw the inside of Constitution Hall. Years later she insisted that breaching the hall's color barrier carried no special meaning for her. "May I say that when I finally walked into Constitution Hall and sang from its stage I had no feeling different from what I have in other halls," she declared in her autobiography. "There was no sense of triumph. I felt that it was a beautiful concert hall, and I was happy to sing in it." Perhaps so, but one suspects that her words masked a bittersweet reality. Considering all that she had gone through to get there, it seems highly likely that her actual feelings were anything but neutral. Coming on the heels of the highly emotional mural ceremony, entering the inner sanctum of white Washington must have evoked a somewhat confusing mixture of satisfaction and sadness. If she had such feelings, she did not let them interfere with her dedication to the music of the evening. On that night, she sang gloriously to a capacity crowd. All 3,844 seats were filled, and by all accounts no one went away disappointed. Blacks made up more than half of the crowd, and to Anderson's relief there was no discernible pattern of segregation. Blacks sat in all parts of the hall, not just in the balcony. According to the *New York Times*, "present . . . throughout an audience as unique as it was distinguished were scores of Negro music lovers, ranging from Dr. Mordecai Johnson of Howard University to humble house servants who turned out to hear and applaud Miss Anderson." Many, like Anderson, were experiencing the hall for the first time, though a good number had been at the Lincoln Memorial four years earlier. Aware of the special nature of the benefit concert, they seemed to applaud with unusual fervor at the end of every song, and they literally roared when Anderson dedicated "Ave Maria" to the memory of George Washington Carver, the acclaimed black scientist who had died two days earlier.

Some of the loudest applause came not from black concertgoers but from the box seats in the front of the hall, where an array of New Deal dignitaries sat with family members and friends. Four U.S. senators—Lister Hill of Alabama, Hattie Caraway of Arkansas, William Smathers of New Jersey, and Robert Reynolds of North Carolina—all Democrats, were in the audience, as were Associate Justices Hugo Black and William O. Douglas. Ickes and Chapman were also there, joined by the secretary of agriculture, the undersecretary of war, and the Chinese ambassador to the United States. Sitting in the box that attracted the most attention was the first lady and a group of guests who had just come from a White House dinner party. The guests included the Jewish wife of Secretary of the Treasury Henry Morgenthau Jr., and Admiral Sir Percy Noble, the head of the British naval delegation in Washington, and Lady Noble. They had come to see Eleanor Roosevelt's friend and fellow American, a forty-five-year-old woman from Philadelphia who had seemingly done the impossible, reawakening a nation's sense of fair play and tolerance with the sound of her voice and the force of her character.[61]

As Eleanor Roosevelt knew all too well, it was not that simple. Yet she also knew that she had been party to a historic milestone that had changed America forever. She gloried in the concert that night. But this time she didn't have to explain who Marian Anderson was when describing the concert in her *My Day* column. She didn't have to. Everyone already knew who Marian Anderson was, and some were even beginning to comprehend the meaning of what she had done, how she had opened the minds and hearts of a troubled nation at odds with the highest ideals of freedom and democracy. Some hearts and minds remained closed, of course, as Anderson would discover again and again over the last fifty years of her life. But she and her many supporters, black and white, had moved the nation closer to the day when all Americans could take pride in a broad-based and ongoing struggle to realize the long-deferred dreams of "liberty and justice for all."[62]

An American Icon, 1943–93

There is hope for America. Our country and people have every reason to be generous and good . . . All the changes may not come in my time; they may even be left for another world. But I have seen enough changes to believe that they will occur in this one.

—MARIAN ANDERSON, 1956[1]

MARIAN Anderson's life as a civil rights icon continued for half a century. From the early years of World War II until her death on April 8, 1993, at the age of ninety-six, she retained her status as a powerful symbol of racial pride and democratic promise. While never close to the center of the struggle, she resided on the margins of the civil rights movement as a unique historical figure. To many Americans she was an individual of uncommon dignity and consummate artistry who represented the union of personal courage and cultural achievement. Music remained her first love and primary concern, and she did not seek fame beyond the concert stage. Yet, in her own quiet way, she shouldered the broader responsibilities thrust upon her. Whatever her private wishes, she accepted the reality that her public life was inextricably bound with the Lincoln Memorial and the Daughters of the American Revolution. As the years passed, she rarely mentioned the Constitution Hall controversy in public, reserving her comments and reflections for a handful of magazine interviews and a few guarded passages in her 1956 autobiography. But others were more forthcoming, seeing her story as an essential element of civil rights lore.[2]

Beginning in the immediate postwar era, but especially after the emergence of a national freedom struggle in the mid-1950s, Anderson's name was linked with a handful of other cultural figures who doubled as movement pioneers, most notably Jesse Owens, Joe Louis, Jackie Robinson, and Rosa Parks. She was also part of an expanding universe of black celebrities, from Louis

Armstrong and Duke Ellington to Harry Belafonte and Sidney Poitier. Some, especially Belafonte, had more direct involvement in the civil rights movement than she had. But no celebrity activist could match the iconic power of the legendary Lincoln Memorial concert. Despite an unfortunate pattern of scholarly neglect, no popular discussion of racial equality as a national issue was complete without some mention of Easter Sunday 1939. Along with the individual feats of Owens, Louis, Robinson, and Parks, the concert stood as a milestone of black accomplishment and national progress.[3]

During the last fifty years of her life, Anderson devoted most of her time and energy to music and family. When she was not on tour, she lived with her husband, the architect Orpheus "King" Fisher, whom she married after a long courtship in July 1943. Surrounded by a menagerie of cats, dogs, sheep, pigs, and other farm animals, they lived on Marianna Farms, a sprawling rural estate in Mill Plane, Connecticut, just outside Danbury. Light-skinned enough to pass for white, Fisher was an object of considerable curiosity, with many neighbors and others speculating that Anderson had entered into an interracial marriage. Over time the speculation died down, and the couple settled into a comfortable life at Marianna Farms. As one of the wealthiest black women in the nation, Anderson could have retired from the concert stage in her forties or early fifties, as was common in the singing profession. Yet she continued to tour the United States, Europe, and on occasion Asia and Latin America for another twenty years. Although she was in constant demand, she gave fewer recitals than she had given in the mid and late 1930s. But her increased involvement in the recording industry added to her professional burdens and responsibilities. Recording and concert artists half her age spent less time in the studio or on tour than she did, and friends and other observers marveled at her seemingly boundless energy and enthusiasm. While critics and fans sometimes noted that the quality of her voice was declining, Anderson's matchless stage presence and moral stature ensured overflow audiences and continued popularity.[4]

By the mid-1950s, annual surveys revealed that Anderson was among the most admired women in the world. Along with Eleanor Roosevelt, Mamie Eisenhower, and a handful of others, she was a perennial favorite, and invariably the only black woman on the list. This elevated status rested upon her supreme artistic talent and memories of the Lincoln Memorial concert. But her continuing efforts to break down racial barriers and pave the way for aspiring young black artists also added to her reputation. Many individuals and communities benefited from the expansion and widening influence of the

Marian Anderson Scholarship Fund as well as her generous gifts of time and money to scores of other charitable projects. All of this received considerable play in popular magazines, and occasionally in the new medium of television, as her mystique and selfless image were passed on to postwar generations.[5]

Those who had a distinct memory of Easter Sunday 1939, and those who were born in the 1940s—a bit too late to hear the first sounds of freedom at the Lincoln Memorial—shared an appreciation for her periodic contributions to interracial understanding and tolerance. Of course, not everyone saw her as a positive influence. As racial and sectional tensions intensified during the early 1950s, some segregationists in the South lumped her with the other alleged "outside agitators" intent on disrupting the vaunted Southern way of life. This was particularly true after NAACP leaders persuaded her to abandon her policy of singing to "vertically" segregated audiences. Despite their discomfort with all forms of racial segregation, both Hurok and Anderson were reluctant to do anything that threatened to disrupt her Southern tours, and they continued to resist the entreaties of Walter White, Mary McLeod Bethune, and a host of local black activists as late as the fall of 1951. It took Anderson several months to make up her mind, but after the Richmond branch of the NAACP picketed her performance in January 1951, reducing an expected crowd of four thousand to fourteen hundred, White and his allies were confident that she would soon eventually see the light.

To step up the pressure, White surveyed sixteen black leaders on what advice they would give Anderson; in response all but one urged her to take an unequivocal stand against segregation. Bethune spoke for the nearly unanimous consensus when she counseled, "The time has come when people like Marian Anderson and others who believe in the complete annihilation of segregation and discrimination should make the public announcement that they would not appear before any segregated audience. Marian Anderson has come a long way up the ladder with her marvelous voice and her economic security is such that it could be done without any loss to her. If she cannot do it today, I am sure I do not know when she or anyone else in her position can do it." When even this chastening language was not enough to bring Anderson and Hurok around, White undertook a second survey, this time of white officials and attorneys in Texas, where Anderson was scheduled for a multicity tour the following year. The response was encouraging, with virtually all of the white Texans downplaying the potential social and legal barriers to integrated concerts. They could not see any major reason why Anderson could not sing in front of fully integrated audiences in Texas.

This information, which surprised even White, did the trick, and Anderson soon agreed to end her long-standing policy of compromising with Jim Crow, not only in Texas but across the South.

The new policy went into effect in January 1952, when she became the first black artist to break the color line in Jacksonville and Miami, Florida. She performed without incident in front of integrated audiences in both cities, though there were a few tense moments in Jacksonville, a city known for its strict adherence to Jim Crow. When several hundred irate whites demanded refunds after Colonel Edward Henry reversed his opposition to integrated seating at the Duval County Armory, more than a few seats were empty. But no violence or attempts to disrupt the concert took place. Two days later, Anderson was taken aback by her reception in Miami, which included a motorcycle escort from the train depot and a street parade featuring Anderson in a convertible draped in red, white, and blue bunting. When *Jet* magazine later reported that Anderson received massive police protection during her stay in Miami, some readers must have wondered how far race relations had progressed in southern Florida. But, whatever the underlying realities, the two Florida concerts marked a new era in Anderson's career, and in the racial dynamics of black entertainment in the South.[6]

As the 1952 tour progressed, the normally cautious Anderson began to embrace the task of breaking racial barriers. But in early February, midway through the tour, her transition to the new era was interrupted by the death of seventy-eight-year-old Harold Ickes. The old New Dealer's many friends thought it was appropriate to remind the nation of his finest hour, and on April 20, Anderson found herself back at the Lincoln Memorial singing a tribute to the man who had done so much to make her first appearance at the Memorial possible. It was her first return to the Memorial steps in thirteen years, and all of the memories of struggle and triumph came flooding back. President Harry S. Truman, who as a junior senator from the racially conservative state of Missouri had not seen fit to attend or sponsor the 1939 concert, had announced his intention to attend the ceremony, but at the last minute he dispatched his press secretary, Joseph Short, to the Memorial as a replacement. The family was disappointed, but their spirits were buoyed by Oscar Chapman, who had agreed to deliver the principal eulogy, and the unexpectedly large crowd of ten thousand that showed up at the Memorial. Many came to pay their respects to an honorable and influential public servant, but others almost certainly came to revisit the spectacle of Anderson singing in the shadow of Lincoln. The ceremony began in the late afternoon, following the model of the 1939 concert. Dressed in a blue taffeta gown and carrying a bouquet of red roses, Anderson sang two groups of songs, opening with Johann Sebastian Bach's "Come, Sweet Death" and closing with "Ave Maria" and "America."[7]

The entire scene, with its emotional intensity and loud applause, evoked memories of 1939. But Ickes's passing was just one of many signs that change was in the air. Nowhere was this more evident than in the areas of race relations and politics. The NAACP had already shifted its legal strategy from reluctant acceptance of "separate but equal" to a frontal assault on the half-century-old *Plessy* doctrine. Within a year a new president, Dwight Eisenhower, would be in the White House, and soon thereafter a new chief justice, Earl Warren, would take the helm of the Supreme Court. The new alignment, along with the NAACP's updated strategy, would lead to the *Brown* school-desegregation decision in May 1954, and ultimately to a siege mentality and massive resistance in the white South. But, before the reaction set in, indications were clear that racial democracy was on the rise in other areas of the nation. Black ascendance in the entertainment industry and the worlds of collegiate and professional sports, combined with the successful desegregation of the armed services, heralded new attitudes and possibilities.[8]

Even the national leadership of the DAR softened its position on racial integration in 1951, after the new manager of Constitution Hall, Harold Maynard, made a concerted effort to overturn the hall's "white artists only" policy. In April 1951, the DAR Board of Management consented to an experimental concert by the black soprano Dorothy Maynor, temporarily reversing its long-standing opposition to even minor adjustments in policy. Six years earlier, May Erwin Talmadge of Georgia, the first Daughter from the Deep South to serve as president general, and other conservative DAR leaders had fended off an internal challenge from a group of liberal dissenters led by Connecticut congresswoman Clare Boothe Luce. When the black soprano Hazel Scott was denied access to Constitution Hall in September 1945, several DAR chapters filed resolutions of protest, and Luce threatened to resign from the organization. But Fred Hand and the Board of Management refused to budge, even after the controversy became the subject of public debate.

In the tradition of the MACC, Scott's outraged husband, Democratic congressman Adam Clayton Powell Jr. of Harlem, criticized the DAR in a letter to President Harry Truman demanding government sanctions against the organization, and in a second letter to Mrs. Truman urging her to boycott an upcoming DAR tea. The president responded sympathetically, and even compared the DAR's exclusionist policy to Nazism, but he refused to interfere in the affairs of a private organization that he claimed was beyond the reach of governmental authority. After quoting from the exchange of letters, a *New York Times* editorial admonished the president, reminding him that the DAR's original incorporation by Congress granted the organization a special tax-exempt status that effectively made it a semipublic institution. The Trumans were unmoved, despite their professed opposition to DAR policy, and Mrs. Truman, a longtime DAR member, attended the tea as planned.

In protest, Congressman Powell promptly organized a "People's DAR" rally, proclaiming that the initials of his DAR stood for "Drive Against Reactionaryism." Reminding the public that the Roosevelts had stood by Marian Anderson in 1939, he blasted the Trumans for failing to maintain the same standard of moral courage and responsibility. "I don't see how anyone can compare the action of the DAR with Nazism," he declared, "and then let his wife sit down and have tea with the Hitlers." To drive home his objection, Powell dispatched a telegram to the White House calling for the repeal of the DAR's tax-exempt status, and within a week two anti-DAR bills were being debated in the House of Representatives. One bill, introduced by the liberal New York congressman Emmanuel Celler, threatened to revoke the DAR's charter, and a second, sponsored by California congresswoman Helen Gahagan Douglas, would have removed Constitution Hall's tax exemption until the DAR adopted an open booking policy that processed applications without regard to "race, creed, color or national origin." Both bills provoked a raucous exchange on the House floor, including charges that Communists were behind the attack on the DAR, but neither ever had a realistic chance of becoming law.

By the end of the year, the Scott episode had receded from view, but in early 1946 opposition to the color bar at Constitution Hall reignited when Hand turned down a booking request from Eddie Condon, the white leader of an interracial jazz band. This time Luce made a nationwide radio appeal for repeal of the "white artists only" policy. She also spearheaded the formation of a ten-member Committee Against Racial Discrimination in Constitution Hall, which introduced a reform resolution at the DAR's 1946 Continental Congress. When DAR leaders refused to allow one of the protest committee's members to present the resolution to the delegates, the committee angrily withdrew the resolution, and Luce, along with Frances P. Bolton, a Republican congresswoman from Ohio, resigned. The color bar remained in force for commercial artists for the rest of the decade, and the only black performers allowed to sing in the hall were the members of the Cardozo High School choir. Having won a District of Columbia choir competition, the Cardozo singers were allowed in the hall but not onstage. For reasons known only to Fred Hand and the inner circle of the DAR, the black boys and girls of Cardozo were ordered to sing while standing in front of their seats.[9]

Whatever its origins, such rude treatment turned out to be the death rattle of segregation at Constitution Hall. Hand's retirement and an infusion of moderates into the leadership of the DAR set the stage for Maynor's groundbreaking 1951 concert, and within two years the "white artists only" policy quietly disappeared. Fittingly, Anderson was one of the first artists to take advantage of the new policy, On March 14, 1953, less than a year after the Ickes funeral at the Lincoln Memorial, she sang at Constitution Hall under the sponsorship of an American University concert series. As in her previous concert ten years before, the seating arrangements were fully integrated. But this time there was no need for a special appeal to the management.

Harold Maynard, unlike Fred Hand, wanted to make amends and do the right thing, which in postwar Washington was no longer dictated by a single-minded belief in the sanctity of Jim Crow. Life in the nation's capital was changing, and in the fall of 1954, fifteen years after the Board of Education had denied Anderson access to Central High School, the District of Columbia's dual school system was dismantled. It would take years to wipe out many vestiges of the old system, as white flight and other factors complicated desegregation. Yet by June 1955 more than 75 percent of the District's schools had achieved at least token integration. Fortunately, the predictions of mass disruption and violence proved unwarranted, as the city eased into a more open system of racial coexistence and interaction. In many areas of the capital, a city beset by crushing poverty and residential segregation, true integration remained an unrealized ideal. But the desegregation of Constitution Hall and the public schools, the two institutions that had tried to block Marian Anderson's access to the American mainstream in 1939, represented an important thrust in the right direction.[10]

T H E racial makeup of the American classical music scene was also changing during the early and mid-1950s, especially in the traditionally all-white bastion of opera. Anderson had no experience with operatic artistry, but from time to time she had entertained the idea of singing opera on a limited basis.

During her first trip to the Soviet Union in 1935, the famed actor and theater director Konstantin Stanislavsky had approached her about singing the lead role in *Carmen*, but she was not in a position to accept the role on the spot. "I was touched and thrilled by the offer," she recalled. "I told him I would like to think about it. And I did think about it . . . I was young, and time stretched invitingly before me. What was the hurry? I would return when there was more time . . . I told Stanislavsky that I would be interested, but time passed too quickly . . . Stanislavsky died. I lost an invaluable opportunity, and I have so regretted it." It would be twenty years before her next opportunity to sing opera. In September 1954, Anderson met Rudolf Bing, the general manager of the Metropolitan Opera, at a New York dinner party hosted by Hurok. After drawing Anderson into a quiet corner, he stunned her with a simple question: "Would you be interested in singing with the Metropolitan?" "I think I would," Anderson blurted out in response, realizing the significance of his gesture. Seconds later he introduced her to Max Rudolf, the Met's artistic administrator, who revealed that both he and Bing had discussed the matter with Hurok the previous year. Anderson knew nothing of this prior to the conversation at the party, but she did not let her surprise interfere with the golden opportunity at hand.[11]

Bing and Rudolf had in mind the role of Ulrica, the aged sorceress in Giuseppe Verdi's *Un Ballo in Maschera*, known in the United States and Britain as *The Masked Ball*. Anderson wasted no time in poring over the score to see if she was a good fit for the part. Her initial impression was that Ulrica's part "lay too high" for her contralto voice. But, upon further reflection and following a few sessions with the opera's conductor, Dimitri Mitropoulos, she agreed to accept the role. Despite her considerable reputation, this was a daring decision for a fifty-seven-year-old singer well past her prime. During the past decade, the nation's leading music critics, especially those in New York, had become increasingly harsh in their assessments of her voice. While no one questioned her stage presence and performance skills, the tonal quality of her voice had declined to the point where some critics were urging her to retire while her reputation was still intact. Few were as venomous as Claudia Cassidy of the *Chicago Tribune*, who asserted, "Miss Anderson is now in the pitiful dusk of a glorious career and her once-noble voice is now a ravaged ghost, rusted, unsteady, often (painfully) out of tune." But there were enough doubters to make her think twice about making a risky foray into the musical minefield of opera.

She did so because she could not resist the challenge, and because she wanted to be the first singer to break the color barrier at the Met. No black performer had ever sung with the Metropolitan Opera in its seventy-one-year history; indeed, no one thought such a thing was even possible until Bing took over the management of the nation's greatest opera company in 1950. Soon after his arrival, Bing made it clear he intended to diversify the opera's staff. "I shall be happy to engage Negro singers," he announced in April 1950, "if I can find the right voice for the right part." This proved to be more difficult than he had imagined, as several auditions by black singers over the next years failed to produce what he considered a good match. During his first year at the Met, he recruited the black pianist Sylvia Olden as a rehearsal coach, and a year later he hired a talented black ballerina from New Orleans named Janet Collins, who had recently starred in Cole Porter's Broadway musical *Out of This World*. But the prospects for a black singer at the Met looked dim until Anderson accepted Bing's offer in the fall of 1954, four months after the *Brown* decision.[12]

The pressure on the Met to hire a black singer had been mounting for a decade, ever since Lazslo Halasz had founded the rival New York City Opera in 1944. Halasz, who spent several days as Anderson's companion and chaperone during her 1931 visit to Prague, was determined to make the New York City Opera a haven for dispossessed and overlooked artists, especially African Americans and displaced European refugees like himself. By 1948, several black soloists had appeared in New York City Opera productions, including the baritones Todd Duncan and Lawrence Winters and the soprano Camilla Williams. Halasz also approached Hurok about the possibility of Anderson performing in the New York City Opera's production of *Lohengrin*. But the impresario put him off. If his famous client was going to sing opera, she was going to start at the top, which in New York City meant the Met.[13]

Strictly speaking, the role of Ulrica, even when sung at the Met, was not exactly the top of the opera world. But a supporting role was probably as much as Anderson could manage, considering her age and lack of operatic experience. No one knew this better than Anderson herself, who did everything she could to prepare for her debut. When the big night finally arrived, on January 7, 1955, coincidentally the twelfth anniversary of her debut at Constitution Hall, she was nervous but ready to prove that she deserved the honor of being the first black to breach the color line at the Met. As Bing had hoped, Anderson's appearance attracted a capacity crowd and a large coterie of critics and reporters. Anderson did not appear onstage until the second scene of act 1, but as soon as the crowd spied a black Ulrica "stirring the witch's brew" in a steaming cauldron, a long and thunderous ovation filled the hall, delaying the scene's opening for nearly five minutes. Anderson would later appreciate this tribute, but at the time it unnerved her. "When the audience applauded and applauded before I could sing a note," she recalled, "I felt myself tightening up into a knot. I had always assured people that I was not nervous about singing, but at that moment I was as nervous as a kitten. I was terribly anxious that this of all things should go well, but there were things that happened to my voice that should not have happened. With all the experience that I had behind me, I should have been firm and secure, but my emotions were too strong . . . I know I tried too hard. I know I overdid. I was not pleased with the first performance. I know it was not the best I could do."

Self-deprecating reflections notwithstanding, both the cast members and those in the audience showed their appreciation at the end of the performance as she was singled out for round after round of applause. A week later she sang the part of Ulrica a second time when the Met took the production to her native Philadelphia. Returning in triumph to the city that had provided her start carried special meaning for her. "The Philadelphia performance, for me, went better," she reported. "I felt happier and securer. It was good that this was so. I wanted to do well for this audience that included people who had helped to raise money to pay for my early training." Many of those who had helped and nurtured her decades earlier had already passed on, but in Philadelphia she would always be "our Marian." Anderson did not sing opera again until the following year, when she returned as Ulrica. But her two 1955 performances were soon followed by those of a second black performer at the Met, Robert McFerrin, who sang the role of Amonasro in *Aida* in mid-January. The barrier had been broken, and over the coming decade black singers at the Met became commonplace. Anderson herself only sang at the Met during the two productions of *Un Ballo in Maschera*, as both she and Bing realized that younger and better operatic voices were available.[14]

If 1955 marked the beginning of a new era at the Met, it also saw a changing of the guard in the civil rights movement. The death of her old friend and comrade-in-arms Walter White in March signaled a new departure for the NAACP, and six months later the national reaction to the brutal murder of fourteen-year-old Emmett Till by two Mississippi white supremacists created a sobering backdrop to the rising expectations of the immediate post-*Brown* era. In December, the quickening pace of the civil rights struggle became manifest in the unexpected emergence of nonviolent direct action in

Montgomery, Alabama. As the Montgomery bus boycott enlisted thousands of nonviolent foot soldiers and dragged on for more than a year, Dr. Martin Luther King Jr. and Rosa Parks, the forty-two-year-old black seamstress who started it all, became important figures in the march toward freedom. In later years Parks and Anderson would often fall into the same unenviable category of "accidental" historical catalysts. But both women exercised more historical agency than popular mythology gave them credit for. Both were indispensable figures, in part because they found themselves at the right place at the right time. But both made themselves into who they were, activating the contingency of history. They did not just appear on the scene offering weary feet or a transcendent voice. They were historical agents in their own right.[15]

Like Parks, Anderson was never fully comfortable in the role of an activist. Yet within the limits of her personality and professional commitments, she maintained and deepened her connections to the ongoing struggle for civil and human rights. Her status as a national icon often complicated and inhibited her capacity to criticize the state of American race relations. But she learned to walk the tightrope between the demands of conscience and perceived national interest. The peculiar difficulties that she faced became apparent in 1957 when she agreed to undertake a two-month-long cultural exchange tour of Southeast Asia.

Sponsored by the American National Theater and Academy (ANTA), an agency that had been sending American artists abroad for more than a decade, usually as a subcontractor for the State Department, the tour included twenty-six concerts in twelve different nations, beginning with Korea in late September. Anderson's tour represented one of ANTA's most ambitious efforts in cultural diplomacy, with scores of public appearances scheduled in between the concerts. In effect, she was being asked to serve as a cultural ambassador and spokesperson for the U.S. government at a time when the government's commitment to racial justice was uncertain. Just prior to Anderson's departure, the school desegregation crisis in Little Rock, Arkansas, had produced spectacular headlines as Governor Orval Faubus flouted court orders and ultimately defied President Eisenhower. To assert constitutional authority and to protect the interests of the nine black children enrolled at Central High School, Eisenhower dispatched federal troops to Little Rock on September 24, the day of Anderson's first concert in Seoul.

Adding to the pressure on Anderson, a CBS television crew had accompanied her to Southeast Asia to film a special episode of Edward R. Murrow's popular news program *See It Now*. Later broadcast as "The Lady from Phila-delphia," the program captured the excitement and some of the angst of Anderson's first experience with international diplomacy. At virtually every stop, she encountered questions about Little Rock and the condition of American race relations, controversial subjects that made her noticeably un-comfortable. Without saying too much, she tried to communicate both her disappointment in Faubus and her faith in American institutions. In the only news-conference clip to appear in the television program, she told a group of reporters in Rangoon, Burma, that, despite her firm opposition to segrega-tion, she would be willing "to sing for Governor Faubus in Little Rock." She declared, "If it could help at all, I should be very delighted to. If Governor Faubus would be in the frame of mind to accept it for what it is, for what he would get from it, I should be very delighted to do it." Some mistakenly in-terpreted this statement as appeasement, but Anderson was only being true to herself. For her, the value of song was always deeper than political consid-erations.[16]

Anderson had a strong sense of right and wrong grounded in religious faith, and when the situation called for it, she could be forthright in her criticism of public officials. Prior to leaving for Seoul, she had become en-tangled in a controversy surrounding the great black trumpeter and singer Louis Armstrong. Familiar to Voice of America listeners and other interna-tional audiences, Armstrong, or Ambassador Satch as he was sometimes called, was normally the smiling face of jazz diplomacy. But on the night of September 17, while on tour in Grand Forks, North Dakota, he offered a shockingly candid view of the federal government's apparent refusal to respond to Faubus's white supremacist antics. Grand Forks was the hometown of Judge Ronald Davies, who had reissued the desegregation order in Little Rock, warning Faubus to cease and desist. Whatever the provocation, Arm-strong took aim at the Eisenhower administration. "It's getting almost so bad a colored man hasn't got any country," he told a young reporter for the *Grand Forks Herald*, adding that Eisenhower had shown himself to be a "two-faced" coward with "no guts." Admitting to having second thoughts about a possible goodwill tour of the Soviet Union sponsored by the State Department, Armstrong offered an obscenity-filled version of "The Star-Spangled Banner" before lashing out at Secretary of State John Foster Dulles. "The way they are treating my people in the South, the government can go to hell," he growled. The sensational story soon spread across the country, ap-pearing on the evening news and eliciting widespread outrage and censure, including calls for boycotts of Armstrong's concerts and records. Even *Jet* magazine joined the chorus of criticism. Only a few black celebrities were courageous enough to come to his defense—notably the recently retired baseball great Jackie Robinson, the boxer Sugar Ray Robinson, the jazz singer Lena Horne, and the actress and cabaret star Eartha Kitt—but one of them was Marian Anderson.[17]

This act of conscience did not endear her to the Eisenhower administration, but as soon as the Armstrong flap blew over—Satchmo publicly recanted as soon as the president sent troops to Little Rock—State Department officials could not help touting her potential value as a Cold War ambassador. The wildly enthusiastic crowds in Southeast Asia confirmed her status as an international celebrity, and the administration began looking for a public role for her to fill. In July 1958, one New York congressman suggested that she would make a great assistant secretary of state for African affairs, but administration officials had already decided to nominate her to be an alternate delegate to the United Nations. After an initial refusal to accept the nomination, Anderson changed her mind after reflecting upon the human misery that she had encountered in India and other impoverished areas of Southeast Asia, talking with Eleanor Roosevelt, and learning that she would be only the third black to serve on the United Nations delegation. With the recent birth of independence in Ghana and the looming decolonization of much of Africa, there was a lot of work to do at the UN, especially for someone with a deep interest in racial progress. The mixed reaction to the December 30 broadcast of "The Lady of Philadelphia" indicated that even restrained criticism of American racism could provoke a strong reaction from the white power structure in the South. So, at the age of sixty, Anderson had little to lose by asserting herself on matters of civil and human rights at the international level.[18]

Anderson's international experience was extensive, primarily in Europe, South America, and Japan. But she had only been to Africa once, on a brief stopover en route to South America in 1938. A whirlwind tour of Dakar, Senegal, had left her with lasting impressions of the economic problems and cultural vitality of West Africa. She would encounter both during her tenure as a UN delegate. Assigned to the Trusteeship Council, she dealt with issues of independence and self-governance among eleven territories, most of which were in Central and West Africa. Following her first day as a delegate, the *New York Times* ran a revealing profile of the "New Voice at the U.N." "There are great areas where people overseas need to know and meet equivalent people in America," she told the *Times* interviewer. "There are so many misconceptions. The main feeling is that America has a lot of money and is attempting to buy what it likes. A lot of people don't want to be bought. They resent it. Especially since we give people what we think they ought to have, not what they should have. One mustn't give people things because we happen to think they need them. The important thing is to find out what they really need."

This plea for cultural autonomy, according to the profile, was rooted in her recent experiences in Southeast Asia. "Wherever she went," wrote the reporter, "she was greeted as if she were royalty. She did more than sing. She met people, discussed their problems with them, presented her own point of view and explained her music and her philosophy of life." The reporter claimed, "Qualified observers have called her the best ambassador the United States has ever sent overseas," but Anderson herself was more modest. "I had not been taught enough about them," she confessed. "Cities were dots on maps, far away and terribly sort of impersonal, you know. Then one goes there and sees the buildings and the seething mobs of people, and sings to them, and also talks to people as intelligent as one finds anywhere. Naturally one comes away with different ideas."[19]

Anderson's commitment to cultural sensitivity served her well during her brief tenure at the UN. She became a popular figure among African diplomats, entertaining them at receptions held either at her apartment or at UN headquarters. Her many friends included the prime ministers of Togoland and the French Cameroons, two of the territories preparing for national independence. The leaders of both territories were growing impatient with the pace of nationalization and suspected that colonial powers such as France and England were using their influence behind the scenes to delay the day of independence. Some Africans also worried that the U.S. delegation was secretly working in concert with the Europeans, a suspicion that placed Anderson in a difficult position when Ghana and several other countries introduced resolutions calling for a special session to speed up the granting of full independence to the French and English Cameroons.

To Anderson the difference between a special or regular session appeared to be little more than a technicality, so she didn't think she was doing anything especially controversial when, as instructed, she introduced a motion to cut off debate on the Cameroons resolutions. When the motion went down to defeat, she realized that she had been party to a maneuver perceived to be anti-independence. Offering a statement of explanation just made matters worse, as several African delegates vented their anger at the United States and its delegation. Despite her personal prestige, Anderson received stinging criticism for her naïveté, prompting her to ask for a few moments to address the assembly. "There is no one in the room who is more interested in the people whose fate we are trying to determine than I," she insisted, her hands trembling with emotion. "Like many of the representatives, I am a member of an instructed delegation and we are here to carry out what is wanted, otherwise we would not be here." The obvious implication that she did not agree with her instructions sent several American diplomats scrambling to shield her from reporters looking for further statements that would add fuel to the fire. Anderson said nothing more on the matter, but when the dust settled in early December, the press credited her with advancing the cause of African independence. Thanks to her involvement, the United States had little choice but to reverse course and support an extension of the general session that would focus exclusively on the Cameroons issue. The French trust territory became the Republic of Cameroon on January 1, 1960, and twenty-one months later it joined with the former British colony to its south to form the Federal Republic of Cameroon. No one was more pleased than Anderson, though she had long since retired from the baffling world of post-colonial diplomacy.[20]

THE early 1960s brought new opportunities and challenges as Anderson, like other Americans, learned to deal with the tumult of change. She now had enough medals and plaques to fill several rooms. She received so many Woman of the Year awards that she lost count of the organizations honoring her, and an honorary degree from Princeton in 1959 was only one of many such tributes. The flood of awards only heightened her sense of responsibility. As the civil rights movement gathered strength, she stepped up her philanthropic support of the NAACP, which celebrated its fiftieth anniversary in 1959. The NAACP's legalistic approach to the civil rights struggle was consistent with her acute sense of propriety, but she tried to keep an open mind on the more assertive direct-action tactics of the Congress of Racial Equality and the Student Nonviolent Coordinating Committee. Any reservations that she may have had about the wisdom of the sit-ins and Freedom Rides were kept private.

In the political arena, she welcomed the election of John F. Kennedy and the onset of the New Frontier, which she regarded as a reprise of the

New Deal. Braving the cold, she sang the national anthem at Kennedy's inauguration, and soon thereafter she accepted the new administration's invitation to resuscitate her involvement in international affairs. In May 1961, she traveled to the Black Sea to attend a Soviet-American conference on cultural exchanges and mutual understanding, and in November she became a founding director of the Freedom from Hunger Foundation, a government-sponsored organization designed to combat hunger and famine in underdeveloped nations. A month later, she participated in a United States Information Agency television project aimed at an East German audience. Traveling to West Berlin with her accompanist Franz Rupp, she returned to the scene of her Rosenwald-sponsored training to sing two spirituals and "The Lord's Prayer."[21]

After celebrating her sixty-fifth birthday in February 1962, Anderson resumed a full schedule of touring and recording, making her first trip to Australia and New Zealand in May and June. The crowds down under were large and enthusiastic, but the critics were less kind. She had become accustomed to harsh criticism from American commentators, who had been noting her declining voice for years. But the Australian and New Zealand critics, having waited so long to hear her perform live, made no effort to conceal their disappointment. Stung by the criticism, Anderson considered retirement, but Hurok talked her out of it.

Following her return to the United States, she faced the added burdens of family illnesses, including her favorite nephew James DePreist's bout with polio. A promising young conductor, DePreist was like a son to Anderson, who later reveled in his hard-won success with the baton. His illness drew Anderson even closer to her youngest sister, Ethel DePreist, as both women tended to him and his aging and increasingly fragile grandmother. As the ailments mounted, Anderson tried to balance familial and career responsibilities, but this became more difficult with every passing month. In November 1962 she mourned the death of Eleanor Roosevelt, with whom she was immensely proud to be associated. Publicly acknowledging her debt to the century's most remarkable first lady, Anderson sang through her tears.[22]

Anderson's spirits rebounded in 1963, when she completed a successful tour of Texas—her first Southern tour in more than a decade—received a cluster of honors, and reconnected with the civil rights movement. In July, she learned that President Kennedy had selected her as one of thirty-one recipients of the Presidential Medal of Freedom, and later in the same month she hosted an NAACP fund-raiser for two hundred guests at Marianna

Farms. A week after the highly successful event, a grateful Roy Wilkins, the NAACP's executive secretary, invited Anderson to sing the national anthem at the upcoming August 28 March on Washington. Held at the Lincoln Memorial, the march was the greatest assemblage in the Memorial's history, roughly three times the size of the Easter Sunday 1939 crowd. The organizers were eager to exploit Anderson's historic connection to the site and the theme of the march, and she was thrilled at the opportunity to accommodate them. Unfortunately, caught in a traffic jam of epic proportions, she arrived too late to sing the anthem. She did sing "He's Got the Whole World in His Hands" midway through the proceedings, but her appearance was overshadowed by Mahalia Jackson's rousing performance of "I Been 'Buked and I Been Scorned." Like everyone else at the gathering, Anderson felt privileged to hear Dr. King's soul-stirring "I Have a Dream" speech, but her experience at the Memorial was bittersweet at best.[23]

She also had mixed feelings about retirement, but by late 1963 she and Hurok agreed that she could not go on much longer. As she was the first to admit, her singing voice no longer met her own exacting standards, and her mind and body were weary from decades of traveling. Both Anderson and Hurok wanted her to go out in style with a lavish world tour, and they finally set a date of December 12 for a public announcement that she was retiring. In the classic Hurok tradition of working every angle, the date was chosen as a natural follow-up to the Presidential Medal of Freedom award ceremony, scheduled for December 6. Unfortunately, the assassination of President Kennedy on November 22 cast a pall over both events. The award ceremony— which honored two other musicians, Pablo Casals and Rudolf Serkin, as well as Anderson and a host of nonmusical medal winners—produced more tears than smiles. The citation on Anderson's medal—"Artist and citizen, she has ennobled her race and her country, while her voice has enthralled the world"—captured the spirit of her accomplishments, and a picture of her and President Lyndon Johnson appeared in the *New York Times* the next morning. Johnson, however, respectfully declined Hurok's request for a letter that could be read at the retirement press conference.

Even so, the December 12 press conference went ahead as planned. Standing in front of an array of reporters at the St. Regis Hotel in New York, Hurok and Anderson announced plans for a farewell tour to begin in the fall of 1964 and discussed their long and "joyous association." Hurok made a point of recounting Anderson's struggles against Jim Crow and the DAR before opening the floor to questions. When asked if she still harbored hard

feelings about the Constitution Hall controversy, Anderson answered de-
murely, "I forgave the DAR many years ago. You lose a lot of time hating
people." Responding to a second question about how she planned to spend her
retirement years, she declared that she hoped to become "more active in the
civil rights struggle." She also announced her intention to spend more time
with her husband and family. But her mother's death less than a month later
scrambled all of her plans. The passing of Anna Anderson, who had always
been her daughter's closest confidant and dearest friend, was a heavy blow.[24]

In 1964, Marian Anderson did indeed mark her retirement with a grand
tour, even though family obligations ruled out the original plan for a world-
wide celebration. The farewell tour began, fittingly, at Constitution Hall on
October 24, 1964, and ended at Carnegie Hall on Easter Sunday, April 18,
1965. The six-month-long tour took her from coast to coast and to fifty cities
across the nation. But the Southern part of the tour was noticeably thin,
limited to four concerts in Alabama, North Carolina, and Florida. Passage
of the Civil Rights Act in August had renewed hope that American democracy had come of age, but in the short term regional tensions were inflamed.
In planning the tour, Hurok wanted to avoid any unpleasant racial incidents,
so caution was the order of the day. Anderson did sing in Tuscaloosa, the site
of Governor George Wallace's 1963 pronouncement in favor of "segregation
now, segregation tomorrow, segregation forever." But her recital there was at
all-black Stillman College, not at the recently desegregated University of
Alabama.

The tour had already narrowly escaped a brush with racial controversy
when RCA had negotiated a recording contract with Harold Maynard, the
longtime manager of Constitution Hall. The DAR was pleased that RCA
wanted to record the opening concert of Anderson's farewell tour, Maynard
declared, but permission to record the recital rested on assurances that there
would be "no language anywhere in the recording and liner pertaining to
past recitals and experiences." When RCA's attorneys balked at this restriction, the DAR made the language of the proposed contract even more specific, insisting that "there would be no reference made in publicity, liner or
newspaper releases dealing with the unfortunate incident that resulted in
Miss Anderson's historic Lincoln Memorial concert." With no sign that the
DAR was willing to engage in any further negotiations, RCA attorneys informed Hurok's agents that they were no longer interested in recording the
concert. But a last-minute intervention by Anderson, who had no interest in
embarrassing the DAR, convinced RCA to comply with the stated terms.

The recording would document Anderson's last concert at Constitution Hall without any historic references.[25]

Reminding the music-loving public of Anderson's past associations with the DAR was hardly necessary. While Anderson rarely broached the subject, the 1939 Lincoln Memorial concert remained a milestone in the history of American democracy. Many of those who heard her sing on Easter Sunday, either in person or over the radio, were still alive; and in many cases they were not shy about sharing memories of the event with their children and grandchildren. Like Jackie Robinson's first season with the Dodgers, the mythic Lincoln Memorial concert was a story to be retold and retold. The essential elements of the saga lived on as an instructive morality play, as Anderson's extraordinary longevity and continuing accomplishments, combined with the maturation of the struggle for civil rights, reinforced and expanded the meaning of what had happened in 1939. As long as the struggle continued, the contrasting images of Anderson's dignity and the DAR's hypocrisy retained direct relevance to the realization of national ideals.

The DAR itself played no small part in perpetuating the Constitution Hall controversy. The mistakes of 1939 were unfortunate but understandable. DAR leaders justifiably resented being singled out as racists at a time when white supremacy was the national norm. But that was no excuse for the pattern of vacillation and haughty disdain initiated by Sally Robert and others. One minute they insisted that the problem was a simple misunderstanding about open dates, a miscommunication that had nothing to do with racial exclusion; the next minute they defended segregation as a necessity dictated by custom and community standards. From the outset, DAR leaders fostered more confusion than clarity, but their biggest problem was a lack of historical and political awareness. Refusing to adjust to a rapidly changing world, they found themselves on the wrong side of history.

In 1939, the world was entering six years of brutal warfare. But openminded and sophisticated observers could already see that the totalitarian threat had prompted both a revival of the American creed and an international disequilibrium that would soon push the world toward decolonization and democratic renewal. Despite an air of confidence and natural superiority, DAR leaders were slow to grasp what was happening. The organization would not acknowledge its mistakes for several decades, and by then it was too late to undo the damage or expunge the record. During the 1950s, the exigencies of the Cold War gave old ways new life, but the revival was only temporary. By the mid-1960s, patriotism had reconnected with its democratic roots, relegating elitist organizations such as the DAR to the margins of American life. Even in the South and the Southwest, where a new law-and-order conservatism was on the rise, the old exclusionist hierarchies no longer held sway. Old ways die hard, however, and the DAR would make a series of ill-advised attacks on everything from modern feminism to the United Nations before a more moderate generation of leaders came to the fore.[26]

The first gesture of racial reconciliation came in 1953, when the DAR quietly desegregated Constitution Hall. But the next breakthroughs did not come until 1966, when the DAR published the pamphlet *Statement re Constitution Hall*, and 1973, when President General Eleanor Spicer issued a lengthy statement on the Anderson affair. Spicer's explanation of the DAR's racial history was essentially a rehash of past excuses, but her willingness to discuss the organization's most embarrassing moment was a promising sign.

Unfortunately, few DAR members were able to get beyond the myth-laden rationales of earlier decades. After conducting an extensive series of interviews in the early 1970s, investigative journalist Peggy Anderson concluded that the Daughters were still "extremely defensive about 1939." She advised, "Talk to a daughter long enough and she is sure to mention that she wishes everyone would just forget about Marian Anderson. Then she is likely to attempt to justify the DAR's decision, arguing that it was the only one possible . . . The Daughters badly want to believe that the women involved in the decision to refuse Marian Anderson were only law-abiding citizens trapped by the temper of the times and the strictures involved in being headquartered in a Southern city, and that the organization has thus been wrongly accused of prejudice. The facts do not support this view, nor do they support other, similar excuses."

By the 1970s, the DAR had shed its direct associations with white supremacist reactionaries, as Spicer and others had begun to talk openly about accepting black members. "We are not making any effort to integrate the Society," she confessed to the journalist Anderson in 1973, "but we are certainly not going to resist it." This was a sign of progress, perhaps, but as Anderson pointed out, it fell far short of what was needed to overcome the sins of the past. Rightly or wrongly, the DAR's refusal to accept responsibility for its past actions fueled suspicions that the organization continued to harbor more than a little disdain for racial and ethnic minorities. As Anderson aptly put it, "There are worse crimes than belonging to an organization in the 1970's that discriminated against blacks in the 1930's. One of them is denying that it did."[27]

A half century after the Constitution Hall debacle, the problem of denial persisted, though official DAR pronouncements on the matter had softened considerably. In 1992, the DAR included Marian Anderson in a list of nine distinguished "Women Worthy of Honor." Each honoree, including First Lady Barbara Bush, received a specially struck "Centennial Medallion," commemorating the organization's hundredth birthday. In announcing Anderson's selection, the DAR magazine made no mention of the 1939 controversy; instead, the editors described her as a "musical genius" who had provided "awe-inspiring performances for the great and the small." The tribute continued, "For more than 40 years Marian Anderson's extraordinary voice and character endeared her to millions of people as she traveled throughout the world giving concert tours and performances."[28]

Anderson, ninety-five years old and in the last year of her life, graciously accepted the medallion. But it was probably fortunate that she did not live long enough to witness the DAR's official response to a traveling Smithsonian exhibit four years later. If people thought that the organization's hypersensitivity to any mention of the Anderson affair was a thing of the past, they were disabused of this notion when President General Dorla Eaton Kemper accused the Smithsonian curators of presenting "a half-truth about the unfortunate incident which occurred over 57 years ago." That the exhibit did nothing more than offer a few words of commentary to accompany a display of Anderson's coats did not stop Kemper from lashing out at the organization's critics. "Why must this incident continue to be cast in an untrue and unfavorable light, while ignoring the contributions made by both Miss Anderson and the DAR?" she asked plaintively. ". . . Why not give her beautiful voice the emphasis it deserves? Why not recognize the number of times during her lifetime she did sing in Constitution Hall? Why must the name of a fine women's organization, DAR, continue to be maligned when we have existed over 100 years with objectives to preserve history, provide education and promote patriotism."

In closing, Kemper pleaded with the American public to "put this incident in the past where it belongs." To her credit, Kemper came closer to acknowledging the organization's complicity than any previous DAR official: "The DAR will not defend the actions of the then management of Constitution Hall in 1939. This unfortunate event happened." Yet she could not resist repeating the time-worn half-truths that "the DAR was unfairly singled out as the only group who refused Marian Anderson's agent" and that "the entire city of Washington was a segregated city in 1939."[29]

The best opportunity for the DAR to make amends came nearly a decade later, in January 2005, when the U.S. Postal Service unveiled a commemorative postage stamp bearing Anderson's likeness. Issued as part of the Postal Service's Black Heritage Series, the stamp utilized a portrait of Anderson produced in Finland in 1934, five years before the Constitution Hall controversy. Heartened by the choice of images, the DAR offered to host the unveiling ceremony. Untroubled by the irony of the situation, Anderson's family agreed to participate in the ceremony, which was held at the DAR's Memorial Continental Hall, just a few yards from Constitution Hall. A number of dignitaries and celebrities were on hand, including Anderson's nephew James DePreist, who was then the musical director of the Oregon Symphony; the black operatic stars Kathleen Battle and Denyce Graves; and the DAR's President General Presley Merritt Wagner. After Postmaster General John E. Potter opened the ceremony with a tribute to a woman whose "powerful voice and quiet determination helped in bringing down the walls of inequality and injustice during a time of challenge for our nation," President General Wagner offered similar sentiments. "The beauty of Marian Anderson's voice," she declared, "amplified by her courage and grace, brought attention to the eloquence of the many voices urging our nation to overcome prejudice and intolerance. The Daughters of the American Revolution are proud to participate with the U.S. Postal Service in celebrating the issuance of the Marian Anderson commemorative stamp."

These were just words, of course, but the Anderson family had waited a long time to hear them. Whether a majority of the Daughters shared Wagner's magnanimous feelings remained to be seen, but in the generous spirit of his late aunt, DePreist and other members of the family seemed willing to give the organization the benefit of the doubt. As fresh-faced students from the Duke Ellington School of the Arts added their voices and instrumental creations to the occasion, who could doubt that the nation's greatest singer had finally established a posthumous connection with the nation's most celebrated patriotic organization?[30]

BY that time Marian Anderson had been dead for more than a decade. But she was not an insignificant player in the long scenario leading up to the DAR's apparent epiphany. Her formal retirement in April 1965 turned out to be something of a false ending. While she rarely sang in public after the farewell concert at Carnegie Hall, her life as a public figure continued both on and off the stage. After forty years of touring, her singing voice was all but gone, but as Hurok explained to reporters at the press conference following the Carnegie Hall concert, "She doesn't have to sing. She can do some readings of Lincoln and Jefferson and then maybe sing a few spirituals. It'll go like a house on fire." To Hurok's surprise, Anderson was open to the idea. Although she was tired of critics reminding her that her once great voice had lost its edge, she was not yet ready to leave the concert stage altogether. Fortunately, she found the perfect vehicle to prolong her career.

In 1942, the great American composer Aaron Copland had written a three-movement piece entitled *A Lincoln Portrait*. With two instrumental movements and a third movement spliced with long quotations from Lincoln's speeches, the thirteen-minute-long piece offered a musical representation of the Great Emancipator's life. Originally commissioned by the conductor André Kostelanetz as one of four musical "biographies" of historic American leaders, *A Lincoln Portrait* had become a stock element of patriotic concerts by the 1960s. Anderson's first performance as the Lincoln narrator took place on July 3, 1965, in New York's Lewisohn Stadium, where she had first sung in 1925. Accompanied by the Metropolitan Opera Orchestra under the baton of Arthur Fiedler, she immediately made the piece her own, bringing an intensity of emotion to the narration that no other artist could match. Over the next decade she repeated the moving narration more than thirty times in a variety of settings, from New York's Lincoln Center to the Hollywood Bowl. In April 1969, she appeared at Lincoln Center with her nephew James DePreist, the guest conductor of the Symphony of the New World, and two months later she performed the narration in Philadelphia with Aaron Copland himself conducting. On occasion, she served as a narrator in other programs, but nothing stirred audiences as much as hearing her intone the final lines of the Gettysburg Address. Aware of her historical connection to the Lincoln Memorial, they responded to Anderson's deep-voiced pronouncement "that government of the people, by the people, for the people, shall not perish from the earth" as if Lincoln himself had returned from the grave.[31]

During the long-awaited American bicentennial celebration of 1976, Anderson performed *A Lincoln Portrait* for the last time. Approaching her eightieth birthday, she was finally ready to retire for good. Sol Hurok had died two years earlier, in March 1974, and of the mentors who had guided her during her early years, only Roland Hayes was still alive. When Hayes passed away on New Year's Day 1977, at the age of eighty-nine, she could not help feeling she had outlived her contemporaries. Fortunately, she was neither alone nor forgotten. Her husband, though slowed by a series of strokes, lived on until 1986, and her sister Ethel lived until 1990. Anderson herself suffered from an assortment of ailments, but she was consoled by frequent visits from friends and innumerable awards and special recognitions. In 1977, she received the United Nations Peace Prize, and a year later she was honored with a special congressional medal recognizing her "untiring and unselfish devotion to the promotion of the arts." Perhaps the most moving tribute came in July 1984, when she received the first Eleanor Roosevelt Human Rights Award. Though wheelchairbound, she attended the presentation ceremony, held at New York's City Hall, rising out of her chair long enough to deliver a brief tribute to her old friend. "I have thanked my good Lord for her many times," she told the gathering. "I am only sorry the youngsters of today shall not have seen her in the flesh." When the ceremony closed with a chorus of "He's Got the Whole World in His Hands," she and everyone else in the room fought back the tears.[32]

The Human Rights Award was one of her last public appearances, though she appeared in an hour-long documentary produced by the Washington public television station WETA in 1991. Looking and acting far younger than her ninety-four years, she peered into the camera with an intensity born of uncommon character and hard-earned experience. After a self-deprecating but firm insistence that "music chose me," she recounted her debts to Toscanini, Hayes, and others. Later the narrator assured the American public that this remarkable woman had known "hard times" but had always "stood in dignified opposition to America's stereotypes of blacks." A year after the documentary's release, she moved from Marianna Farms to Portland, Oregon, where she lived with her nephew James DePreist. Less than a year later, on April 8, 1993, one day shy of the fifty-fourth anniversary of the Lincoln Memorial concert, she slipped into a coma and passed away.[33]

As expected, a flood of obituaries hailed Anderson's supreme talent and unfailing dignity, judging her improbable life to be one of the great stories of the twentieth century. Some eulogies stressed her unforgettable voice, others her strength of character. But at some point all returned to the Easter Sunday that had changed America forever. To Allan Kozinn, writing in the *New York Times*, the Lincoln Memorial concert made her "a poignant symbol for the nascent civil rights movement." To the *Washington Post*'s Bart Barnes, Anderson's 1939 recital was "a tour de force that stirred and sensitized the national psyche to the reality of racial discrimination, even as it symbolized bedrock American values." Todd Duncan, who had been at the Lincoln Memorial concert and who had gone on to break racial barriers on his own, recalled the transcendent power of Anderson's accomplishment: "My feelings were so deep that I have never forgotten it, and until I leave this earth, I don't think I ever will forget it. I have never been so proud to be an American . . . I have never been so proud to be an American Negro." Writing in the *New Yorker*, Anthony Heilbut insisted, "Marian Anderson represented an old style of American gentility," an ennobling restraint that served her well on many occasions. To him, the Lincoln Memorial concert was "that rare defining moment when art and ethics coincide," but he also noted the sixteen-year gap between the Lincoln Memorial concert and her Metropolitan Opera debut. "What she might have achieved if that chance had come earlier remains a question," he mused. "In its answer lies one reason that America remembers her with such a hopeless tangle of pride and shame."

It is this tangle that draws us to her still, that leaves us with an enigmatic and fascinating figure worthy of continued exploration. The only certainty is that the accomplishments and limitations of her public life defy easy categorization. Reaching beyond the realms of politics and protest, her achievements and peculiarities cannot be fully understood within the normal dichotomies of Washington and Du Bois, accommodation and dissent, or interracial cooperation and Black Power. Searching for the deepest meaning of the seminal event that changed her life and ours takes us to the crossroads of culture and race, a dark and mysterious place that we are only now beginning to understand. Beyond the contingency of personal heroics was the distinctive and sometimes controlling context of cultural crisis, hard times, and a worldwide totalitarian threat. But the heart of the story resides in a series of individual acts of courage and conviction. Anderson did not act alone and could not have done what she did without the guidance and timely intervention of Eleanor Roosevelt, Walter White, Charles Houston, Sol Hurok, Harold Ickes, and a host of others. She was, however, the one indispensable element—the proverbial right person at the right place at the right time.

While this book chronicles how she became that woman, the exact sources of her strength remain somewhat murky, concealed by her unshakable sense of privacy and discretion. We may never unlock all the secrets of this diffident and self-effacing hero. Fortunately, James DePreist, the beloved nephew who knew her as well as anyone, provided us with a speculative key when he maintained that the combination of a nurturing family of faith and a life of struggle created an individual "grounded enough to fly without fear." In the end, it was not just the voice, as beautiful as it was.

"Even in silence," DePreist assured those who had never had the pleasure of getting close to his famous aunt, "she was a powerful presence, charismatic, simple, radiating grace and compassion." That it took such an extraordinary figure to pierce the consciousness of a nation in denial is a sobering truth, disturbing enough to haunt anyone listening carefully to the voices and echoes of the past.[34]

Acknowledgments

During the past two years, I have often felt that I was living a double life, coexisting in the present world and in the historic moment of April 9, 1939. Almost seventy years separate these two worlds, yet the parallels and historical connections between them underscore the continuing legacy and relevance of Marian Anderson's distinctive contributions to the struggle for civil rights. Writing a book about Marian Anderson and the Lincoln Memorial concert against the backdrop of the Obama campaign and a failing economy has been an eye-opening, sometimes surreal experience, suggesting that the challenges and dilemmas of race and democracy may always lie at the heart of the American experience. While Anderson's voice and mystique are no longer part of American popular culture, except perhaps in the fading memories of a few, the events of 1939 involved challenges and dilemmas that still vex our nation. For a civil rights historian who knew relatively little about Marian Anderson before undertaking this project, it has been a rare privilege to revisit and reconstruct the meaning of what happened on that Easter Sunday during the last year of world peace and economic depression before World War II. As I have figuratively journeyed back and forth in time, I have learned a great deal about Marian Anderson and the evolution of civil rights as a national issue. But I have not traveled or studied alone. At every stage of the journey, I have relied heavily on the expertise and generosity of numerous individuals, all of whom deserve acknowledgment and thanks.

All scholars stand on the shoulders of those who preceded them, and for anyone undertaking a study of Marian Anderson the broadest shoulders are those of Allan Keiler. A distinguished professor of music at Brandeis University, Keiler is the author of an insightful, exhaustive, and authoritative biography of Anderson, published in 2000. As Anderson's first and only biographer, he prepared the ground for me or anyone else hoping to understand the life and career of this remarkable woman. I want to acknowledge his careful research and considered judgment and thank him for pointing the way into the formidable mass of Anderson materials. I would also like to acknowledge the pioneering work of Allida Black on Eleanor Roosevelt, Scott A. Sandage on the political and cultural meaning of the Lincoln Memorial, and Harlow Robinson on Sol Hurok. I am indebted to all three of these talented scholars—especially Allida Black, who offered support and encouragement at an early stage of my research.

Most of the research for this book was conducted at two indispensable sites: the Walter H. and Leonore Annenberg Rare Book and Manuscript Library at the University of Pennsylvania; and the Moorland-Spingarn Research Center at Howard University in Washington, D.C. The Annenberg Library holds the Marian Anderson Papers, a massive archival collection that documents virtually every aspect of Anderson's personal and professional life. Without the help and expertise of the Annenberg Library staff—especially Nancy Shawcross, the curator of manuscripts—I would have been unable to make my way through this amazing resource. I would like to offer special thanks to John Pollack, Amey Hutchins, and Marissa Hendriks, who arranged for photographic reproductions from the library's extensive collection of Anderson photographs. At the Moorland-Spingarn Research Center, the Marian Anderson-DAR Controversy Collection offers a treasure trove of correspondence and other materials related to the Marian Anderson Citizens Committee, the organization that spearheaded the effort to find an appropriate Washington-area concert venue for Anderson in 1939. It is always a delight to work at the Moorland-Spingarn Center, and I want to thank the center's staff for its professionalism and expert guidance.

I am also indebted to the librarians and archivists at the Franklin Delano Roosevelt Library in Hyde Park, New York; the Daughters of the American Revolution Archives in Washington, D.C.; and the Nelson Poynter Memorial Library at the University of South Florida, St. Petersburg. Christina Lehman, the archivist at the DAR library, was unfailingly helpful, as were Dean Kathy Arsenault and Special Collections librarian Jim Schnur of the Poynter Library.

Blanche Burton-Lyles and Phyllis Sims of the Marian Anderson Historical Society, the devoted stewards of Marian Anderson's legacy, deserve special mention and thanks. Without their tireless commitment to maintaining the Marian Anderson House and to organizing commemorative events celebrating Anderson's life, her continuing legacy would not be what it is. I want to thank them for their gracious cooperation and support.

I would also like to thank several staff members at the Department of the Interior and the National Park Service: David McKinney, Erin McKeen, Bill Line, and Lance Hatten. The staff of the Department of the Interior Museum was especially helpful in tracking down photographs of the Marian Anderson mural.

My colleagues and students at the University of South Florida have also been a major source of strength and support during the research and writing of this book. Most obviously, I have relied on the hard work and diligence of several talented research assistants, all graduate students in the interdisciplinary Florida Studies Program. Cathy Salustri was a great help during the early stages of research, Nano Riley and Margaret Brown provided timely assistance later on, and as the manuscript moved toward completion, Peyton Jones served as my indispensable right-hand man. Peyton deserves special praise for his many efforts above and beyond the call of duty. I would also like to thank the Snell House gang—Sudsy Tschiderer, Marti Enright, Mickey Arsenault, Thomas Smith, and Gary Mormino—for their many courtesies and willingness to do whatever they could to encourage and support me. I also want to acknowledge the support of Dean Frank Biafora of the College of Arts and Sciences, Vice-Chancellor for Academic Affairs Mark Durand, and Chancellor Karen White, all of whom have gone out of their way to facilitate a nurturing environment conducive to serious scholarship.

As always, I have drawn upon the friendship and goodwill of a number of close friends, some for food and shelter during research trips, and others for random acts of kindness and encouragement. Special thanks to Sheldon and Lucy Hackney, and to Randall and Linda Miller, for giving me a comfortable place to stay and stimulating conversation during my visits to Philadelphia. I am also deeply indebted to Randall for sharing his immense knowledge of the history and historiography of Philadelphia, not to mention his unmatched expertise in exploring the city's restaurants. Thanks to Sheldon and Lucy for sharing a memorable evening listening to the Philadelphia Orchestra at Kimmel Hall, an experience that deepened my understanding of the city's rich musical heritage. And thanks to Ted and Nan Hammett, not only for patiently listening to my thoughts on Anderson, but also for sharing the joy of the seventh game of the October 2007 American League Championship Series at Fenway Park. Thanks also to Pat Sullivan, for reminding me about Judge Robert Carter's experience at the Lincoln Memorial concert, and to Richard King and Julian Bond, for leading me to Richard Powers's inspiring novel *The Time of Our Singing*, which captures the essence of the concert better than any other work.

Other friends who have provided me with helpful suggestions include John Hope Franklin, David Hackett Fischer, John Demos, Elliott Gorn, Jim Grossman, Blanche Wiesen Cook, Steve Whitfield, Lee Whitfield, Jim Horton, Lois Horton, Paul Taylor, David Blight, Marsha Andrews, John Belohlavek, Susan Turner, Lynne Mormino, Earl Whitlock, Joyce Haines, Jack Davis, David Gould, Mitchell Snay, David Oshinsky, David Moltke-Hansen, David Starr, Jennifer Gallop, Steven Hahn, Chaz Joyner, Susan Betzer, Meeghan Kane, Monica Kile, Jim Bledsoe, Peter Golenbock, Rip Patton, Bob Bickel, Bob Devin Jones, Ray Sanderlin, Burton and Ellen Hersh, Jeanne and Peter Meinke, CeCe Keeton, Rich and Mimi Rice, Dave and Margaret Radens, and Ann Sackett. A memorable interview with John Hope over breakfast in Durham helped propel me into the research, and the Whitfields once again served as my intellectual and emotional lifeline at several key points. Special thanks to the Hortons and David Blight for enriching my understanding of the Lincoln legacy.

I am also grateful to Annie Miller for interviewing her mother, who attended the 1939 Lincoln Memorial concert, and for discussing the intergenerational meaning of the concert within her family. Annie also deserves thanks for willing the Rays into the 2008 World Series, an unexpected experience that buoyed my spirits during the final weeks of writing and editing. Thanks also for the same reason to Daniel Tyson, Jim Schnur, Peter Golenbock, and the cowbell gang in Tropicana Field, Section 300.

This book could not have been written without the guidance of Peter Ginna, an accomplished editor who has also become a dear friend. As an editor at Oxford University Press, Peter oversaw the publication of my last book, *Freedom Riders: 1961 and the Struggle for Racial Justice*, and I have come to rely on his uncommon judgment, literary skill, and historical sensibility. Now at Bloomsbury USA, he has exhibited the same qualities during the preparation of *The Sound of Freedom*. No one else could have kept me to such a tight schedule and such exacting standards. I owe him a great debt of gratitude, part of which I hope will be repaid in the form of a book that makes us both proud. I would also like to acknowledge the tireless efforts of assistant editor Pete Beatty and the guiding hand of managing editor Greg Villepique.

I also want to express my gratitude to Wendy Strothman, the world's greatest agent. After years as a leading editor, she has adapted her skills to the fine art of guiding historians and other writers through the deep thickets of the publishing world. Already a Marian Anderson fan when I met her, Wendy took an active role in conceptualizing and crafting this book. She deserves more than a little credit for whatever strengths the book possesses. Thanks also to her cheerful and efficient assistant Lauren McLeod.

As in the past, my wife, Kathy, and my daughters, Amelia and Anne, were always there when I needed them. Despite busy schedules of their own—Kathy as a university library dean, Amelia as a Ph.D. candidate in global media and public diplomacy, and Anne as a law student—they provided the words and deeds that kept me going. Without their love and support, this book would still be an unrealized dream. Special thanks to Amelia for being my unofficial research assistant on the West Coast, and to both Anne and Amelia for the continuing effort to bring their "techno-peasant" father into the world of twenty-first-century technology.

This book is dedicated to the memory of my father, Oscar W. Arsenault, who passed away on June 1, 2007, at the age of eighty-five. We were unusually close, and he always took a deep interest in my research and writing. Although he did not live to see this book's completion, the story of Marian Anderson intrigued him, prompting fascinating recollections of his "musical experiences" in New York as a young sailor assigned to a training facility at the Brooklyn Navy Yard during World War II. Dedicating this book to him seems especially fitting. Like Marian Anderson, he had a kind heart, a generous spirit, and an uncommon dignity. He, too, was blessed with unusual talent—in his case artful photography, which became his passion and profession. And he loved classical music.

Notes

ABBREVIATIONS USED IN NOTES

DIP Department of Interior Papers, Record Group 48, National Archives, Washington, D.C.

ER Anna Eleanor Roosevelt Papers, Franklin Delano Roosevelt Library, Hyde Park, New York

FDRL Franklin Delano Roosevelt Library, Hyde Park, New York

MA-DARCC Marian Anderson–Daughters of the American Revolution Controversy Collection, Moorland-Spingarn Research Center, Howard University, Washington, D.C.

MAP Marian Anderson Papers, Annenberg Rare Book and Manuscript Library, University of Pennsylvania, Philadelphia, Pennsylvania

NAACPP National Association for the Advancement of Colored People Papers, Library of Congress, Washington, D.C.

PROLOGUE: OCTOBER 1964

1. On Lyndon Johnson, the Great Society, and the 1964 Civil Rights Act, see Nick Kotz, *Judgment Days: Lyndon Baines Johnson, Martin Luther King Jr., and the Laws That Changed America* (Boston: Houghton Mifflin, 2005); Robert Dallek, *Flawed Giant: Lyndon B. Johnson, 1960–1973* (New York: Oxford University Press, 1998); Joseph A. Califano Jr., *The Triumph and Tragedy of Lyndon Johnson: The White House Years* (New York: Simon and Schuster, 1991); Doris Kearns

Goodwin, *Lyndon Johnson and the American Dream* (New York: St. Martin's, 1991); and John A. Andrew III, *Lyndon Johnson and the Great Society* (Chicago: Ivan R. Dee, 1998).

2. Allan Keiler, *Marian Anderson: A Singer's Journey* (New York: Simon and Schuster, 2000), 316–17; and *Washington Post*, October 25, 1964. In 1958, for example, Marian Anderson ranked eighth in the annual Gallup Poll listing the world's most admired living women. Eleanor Roosevelt led the top ten, followed by Queen Elizabeth II, Clare Boothe Luce, Mamie Eisenhower, Helen Keller, Madame Chiang Kai-shek, Princess Grace of Monaco, Anderson, Princess Margaret of Great Britain, and Dinah Shore. *Miami Herald*, December 28, 1958.

CHAPTER 1: FREEDOM'S CHILD

1. These are the final words of Lincoln's Gettysburg Address, delivered on November 19, 1863. See Garry Wills, *Lincoln at Gettysburg: The Words That Remade America* (New York: Touchstone Books, 1993); Gabor Boritt, *The Gettysburg Gospel: The Lincoln Speech That Nobody Knows* (New York: Simon and Schuster, 2006); Kent Graham, *November: Lincoln's Elegy at Gettysburg* (Bloomington: Indiana University Press, 2001); and Philip B. Kunhardt Jr., *A New Birth of Freedom: Lincoln at Gettysburg* (Boston: Little, Brown, 1983).

2. See Charlene Miers, *Independence Hall in American Memory* (Philadelphia: University of Pennsylvania Press, 2002); Constance M. Grieff and Charles B. Hosmer Jr., *Independence: The Creation of a National Park* (Philadelphia: University of Pennsylvania Press, 1987); Richard S. Newman, *Freedom's Prophet: Bishop Richard Allen, the AME Church, and the Black Founding Fathers* (New York: New York University Press, 2008); Richard S. Newman, *The Transformation of American Abolitionism: Fighting Slavery in the Early Republic* (Chapel Hill: University of North Carolina Press, 2001); Jean R. Soderlund, *Quakers and Slavery: A Divided Spirit* (Princeton: Princeton University Press, 1988); and Arthur Zilversmit, *The First Emancipation: The Abolition of Slavery in the North* (Chicago: University of Chicago Press, 1968).

3. Richard Kluger, *Simple Justice* (New York: Random House, 1975), 51–83; Michael J. Klarman, *From Jim Crow to Civil Rights: The Supreme Court and the Struggle for Racial Equality* (New York: Oxford University Press, 2004), 8–97; and C. Vann Woodward, *The Strange Career of Jim Crow*, commemorative edition (New York: Oxford University Press, 2002).

4. Allan Keiler, *Marian Anderson: A Singer's Journey* (New York: Simon and Schuster, 2000), 15–17 (quotation), 18; and Marian Anderson, *My Lord, What a Morning: An Autobiography* (New York: Viking Press, 1956), 3–4.

5. Anderson, *My Lord*, 4–5 (quotation); and Keiler, *Marian Anderson*, 17–19.

6. W. E. B. Du Bois, *The Philadelphia Negro: A Social Study* (New York: Schocken Books, 1967), ix–xix (quotation), xx–xlii (from the introduction by E. Digby Baltzell); and David Levering Lewis, *W. E. B. Du Bois: Biography of a Race, 1868–1919* (New York: Henry Holt, 1993), 179–92, 201–10.

7. Du Bois, *Philadelphia Negro*, xxxvii (first quotation), 58–355, 328 (second quotation); Lewis, *Du Bois*, 201–10; and St. Clair Drake and Horace Cayton, *Black Metropolis: A Study of Negro Life in a Northern City* (New York: Harper and Row, 1962), 787–88.

8. Du Bois, *Philadelphia Negro*, 323 (first quotation), 397 (second quotation).

9. W. E. B. Du Bois, "The Talented Tenth," in *The Negro Problem: A Series of Articles by Representative American Negroes of Today* (New York: James Potter and Co., 1903), 33–75; Lewis, *Du Bois*, 73, 206, 288–91; and Du Bois, *Philadelphia Negro*, 392 (quotation).

10. Du Bois, *Philadelphia Negro*, 203 (first quotation), 207 (second quotation).

11. Keiler, *Marian Anderson*, 17, 24–25; and Anderson, *My Lord*, 16. On Crowdy (1847–1908), see Beersheba Crowdy Walker, *The Life and Works of William Saunders Crowdy* (Philadelphia: Elfreth Walker, 1955); and Elly M. Wynia, *The Church of God and Saints of Christ: The Rise of Black Jews* (New York: Garland, 1994). On Tindley (1851–1933), see Ralph H. Jones, *Charles Albert Tindley: Prince of Preachers* (Nashville: Abingdon Press, 1982); Eileen Southern, *The Music of Black Americans: A History* (New York: W. W. Norton, 1971), 403; Robert Darden, *People Get Ready! A New History of Black Gospel Music* (New York: Continuum International, 2004); and Jon Michael Spencer, *Black Hymnology: A Hymnological History of the African-American Church* (Knoxville: University of Tennessee Press, 1992).

12. Keiler, *Marian Anderson*, 20–22; Anderson, *My Lord*, 7–8, 13; Du Bois, *Philadelphia Negro*, 197–214.

13. Keiler, *Marian Anderson*, 20–21 (first quotation), 22; Anderson, *My Lord*, 7–13, 8 (second quotation).

14. Anderson, *My Lord*, 13–14 (quotation), 23–27, 31–34; and Keiler, *Marian Anderson*, 22.

15. Keiler, *Marian Anderson*, 22 (quotation); and Anderson, *My Lord*, 33. Arthur Hill, the director of the People's Chorus, also worked closely with Anderson. On Hackley, see M. Marguerite Davenport, *Azalia: The Life of Madame E. Azalia Hackley* (Boston: Chapman and Grimes, 1947), esp. 111–20.

16. Anderson, *My Lord*, 3 (quotation), 38–39; Keiler, *Marian Anderson*, 20, 390n20. Prior to attending Stanton, Anderson had four years of primary schooling. After researching school board records, biographer Allan Keiler was unable to determine whether Anderson attended the all-black Pollock School, the primary school closest to her home, or the integrated Chester A. Arthur School. Anderson does not mention either school in her autobiography.

17. Anderson, *My Lord*, 9, 14–19, 16 (quotation); and Keiler, *Marian Anderson*, 22–26.

18. Anderson, *My Lord*, 9, 23–30, 28–29 (quotation); and Keiler, *Marian Anderson*, 26–28, 32, 35–36.

19. On Hayes (1887–1977), see Keiler, *Marian Anderson*, 35–36; Robert C. Hayden, *Singing for All People: Roland Hayes, a Biography* (Boston: Select Publications, 1989); MacKinley Helm, *Angel Mo' and Her Son, Roland Hayes* (Boston: Little, Brown 1942), 93 (quotation); and Southern, *Music of Black Americans*, 418–22.

20. *Philadelphia Tribune*, April 4, 1914 (quotation); Anderson, *My Lord*, 29, 34; and Keiler, *Marian Anderson*, 28–30.

21. Anderson, *My Lord*, 37–38 (quotation); Marian Anderson–Howard Taubman Tapes (1955–56), no. 20, MAP; Emily Kimbrough, "My Life in a White World," *Ladies' Home Journal* 77 (1960): 54, 173–74, 176; and Keiler, *Marian Anderson*, 30–31, 391–93n5. In a lengthy and informative note, Keiler speculates about the identity of the music school. Anderson does not identify the school in any of her reminiscences, but most available evidence points to the Philadelphia Music Academy.

22. E. Digby Baltzell, introduction to Du Bois, *Philadelphia Negro*, xx–xxi, xxix, xxxiv (first and second quotations), xxxix (third quotation); Sadie Tanner Mossell, "The Standard of Living Among One Hundred Negro Migrant Families in Philadelphia," *Annals of the American Academy of Social and Political Science* 98 (1921): 9; and *Population of Philadelphia Sections and Wards: 1860–1960* (Philadelphia: Philadelphia City Planning Commission, 1963).

23. Dennis B. Downey and Raymond M. Hyser, *No Crooked Death: Coatesville, Pennsylvania, and the Lynching of Zachariah Walker* (Urbana: University of Illinois Press, 1991); *New York Times*, August 15, 17–18, 1911; and Kluger, *Simple Justice*, 99 (quotation).

24. Murray Dubin, *South Philadelphia: Mummers, Memories, and the Melrose Diner* (Philadelphia: Temple University Press, 1996), 16–17, 29, 32–33, 59–68; Mossell, "Standard of Living," 9; Du Bois, *Philadelphia Negro*, xxxiii–xxxiv; and *Philadelphia Record*, July 27–30, 1918. For the character of race relations and interracial violence in Philadelphia during the late-nineteenth and early-twentieth centuries, see Du Bois, *Philadelphia Negro*, 25–45, 235–68, 322–67; Roger Lane, *William Dorsey's Philadelphia and Ours: On the Past and Future of the Black City in America* (New York: Oxford University Press, 1991); and Roger Lane, *Roots of Violence in Black Philadelphia, 1860–1900* (Cambridge: Harvard University Press, 1986). See also Gary Nash, *Forging Freedom: The Formation of Philadelphia's Black Community, 1720–1840* (Cambridge: Harvard University Press, 1980); James Oliver Horton and Lois E. Horton, *In Hope of Liberty: Culture, Community, and Protest Among Northern Free Blacks, 1700–1860* (New York: Oxford University Press, 1997), 4, 14–15, 160; and Allen B. Ballard, *One More Day's Journey: The Story of a Family and a People* (New York: McGraw-Hill, 1984).

25. *Philadelphia Tribune,* May 29, 1915 (first quotation); Anderson, *My Lord,* 21 (third quotation), 28, 34–36, 46–47 (second quotation), 48, 62–64; and Keiler, *Marian Anderson,* 29–35, 58.

26. Keiler, *Marian Anderson,* 36–37 (first quotation); and Anderson, *My Lord,* 21, 29 (second quotation).

27. See Arthur E. Barbeau and Florette Henri, *The Unknown Soldiers: Black American Troops in World War I* (Philadelphia: Temple University Press, 1974).

28. Anderson, *My Lord,* 40 (quotations); and Keiler, *Marian Anderson,* 37–38.

29. Anderson, *My Lord,* 40 (quotation)–41. On Wright, see Charles J. Elmore, *Richard R. Wright, Sr. at GSIC, 1891–1921: A Protean Force for the Social Uplift and Higher Education of Black Americans* (Savannah: privately printed, 1996); Clyde W. Hall, *One Hundred Years of Education at Savannah State College, 1890–1990* (East Peoria: IL: Versa Press, 1991); and June O. Patton, "'And the Truth Shall Make You Free': Richard Robert Wright, Sr., Black Intellectual and Iconoclast, 1877–1897," *Journal of Negro History* 81 (1996), 17–30. Wright's granddaughter, Ruth Wright Hayre, earned a Ph.D. at the University of Pennsylvania, worked for several decades as a teacher and administrator in the Philadelphia public schools, and eventually became the first female president of the Philadelphia Board of Education.

30. *Savannah Press,* December 29, 1917 (first quotation); *Savannah Morning News,* December 29, 1917 (second quotation); *Savannah Tribune,* January 5, 1918; and Keiler, *Marian Anderson,* 38.

31. Anderson, *My Lord,* 41 (quotation).

32. Keiler, *Marian Anderson,* 39–40; *New York Age,* April 27, 1918 (quotation); and *Philadelphia Tribune,* April 27, May 4, 1918.

33. Keiler, *Marian Anderson,* 40–41; Anderson, *My Lord,* 41, 64–67. On Fisk and the Jubilee Singers, see Andrew Ward, *Dark Midnight When I Rise: The Story of the Jubilee Singers Who Introduced the World to the Music of Black America* (New York: Farrar, Straus and Giroux, 2000); and Joe M. Richardson, *A History of Fisk University, 1865–1946* (Tuscaloosa, AL: University of Alabama Press, 1980). See also John Lovell Jr., *Black Song: The Forge and the Flame: The Story of How the African-American Spiritual Was Hammered Out* (New York: Macmillan, 1972).

34. Anderson, *My Lord,* 41–42.

35. Ibid., 42.

36. Keiler, *Marian Anderson,* 41–45; Anderson, *My Lord,* 60–61; *Chicago Defender,* August 9, 1919 (quotations). On the Chicago race riot of 1919, see William Tuttle, *Race Riot: Chicago in the Red Summer of 1919* (New York: Atheneum, 1970). Curiously, Anderson does not mention the riot in her autobiography.

37. On the social disruptions and political hysteria of the immediate post–World War I era, see Robert K. Murray, *The Red Scare: A Study in National Hysteria, 1919–1920* (New York: McGraw-Hill, 1964); Burl Noggle, *Into the Twenties: The*

United States from Armistice to Normalcy (Urbana: University of Illinois Press, 1974); and Robert Zieger, *America's Great War: World War I and the American Experience* (Lanham, MD: Rowman and Littlefield, 2000), 187–225. On the repression of black veterans, see Theodore Kornweibel Jr., *"Seeing Red": Federal Campaigns against Black Militancy, 1919–1925* (Bloomington: Indiana University Press, 1998); and Barbeau and Henri, *Unknown Soldiers.*

38. Sol Hurok with Ruth Goode, *Impresario: A Memoir* (New York: Random House, 1946), 251 (first quotation); Anderson, *My Lord*, 48–61, 49 (second quotation); and Keiler, *Marian Anderson*, 45–48. See also *Philadelphia Record*, December 25, 1938; and Helen Traubel, *St. Louis Woman* (New York: Duell, Sloan and Pearce, 1959), 75ff. From the 1920s on, magazine and newspaper reporters, as well as music critics, often referred to Anderson as the "dark contralto." See, for example, "Dark Contralto," *New Yorker* (January 18, 1936), clipping in box 407, MAP.

CHAPTER 2: SINGING IN THE DARK

1. *The Hymnbook* (Atlanta: Presbyterian Church in the United States, 1955), 64. This is the first stanza of the classic hymn composed by Henry F. Lyte in 1820 and adapted by William H. Monk in 1861.
2. Allan Keiler, *Marian Anderson: A Singer's Journey* (New York: Simon and Schuster, 2000), 36, 58. On the emergence of popular black musicians and other black celebrities during the 1920s, see Carole Marks and Diana Edkins, *The Power of Pride: Stylemakers and Rulebreakers of the Harlem Renaissance* (New York: Crown, 1999); Ann Douglas, *Terrible Honesty: Mongrel Manhattan in the 1920s* (New York: Farrar, Straus and Giroux, 1995); Nathan Huggins, *Harlem Renaissance* (New York: Oxford University Press, 1971); Samuel A. Floyd Jr., *Black Music in the Harlem Renaissance: A Collection of Essays* (Knoxville: University of Tennessee Press, 1990); Jervis Anderson, *This Was Harlem: A Cultural Portrait, 1900–1950* (New York: Farrar, Straus and Giroux, 1981); and David Levering Lewis, *When Harlem Was in Vogue* (New York: Alfred A. Knopf, 1981). On Josephine Baker, see Jean-Claude Baker and Chris Case, *Josephine: The Hungry Heart* (New York: Random House, 1993); and Phyllis Rose, *Jazz Cleopatra: Josephine Baker in Her Time* (New York: Doubleday, 1989).
3. Marian Anderson, *My Lord, What a Morning* (New York: Viking Press, 1956), 41–42, 43–44 (quotation), 67; and Keiler, *Marian Anderson*, 54.
4. Anderson, *My Lord*, 66–69, 84–85; and Keiler, *Marian Anderson*, 54–55 (quotation), 56–57.
5. *Philadelphia Tribune*, December 22, 1923 (quotation); and Keiler, *Marian Anderson*, 56–57.
6. Anderson, *My Lord*, 44–45, 66–67, 72; and Keiler, *Marian Anderson*, 57–58.

7. Anderson, *My Lord*, 72–74 (quotations), 75–76, 80–83; and Keiler, *Marian Anderson*, 50–52, 58–61.

8. Kenneth Robert Janken, *Walter White: Mr. NAACP* (Chapel Hill: University of North Carolina Press, 2006), 89–103, 102 (third quotation); Walter White, *A Man Called White: The Autobiography of Walter White* (New York: Viking Press, 1948), 180–81 (quotations); Anderson, *My Lord*, 72; and Keiler, *Marian Anderson*, 61. On James Weldon Johnson, see Eugene Levy, *James Weldon Johnson: Black Leader, Black Voice* (Chicago: University of Chicago Press, 1973); and Johnson's *Along This Way: The Autobiography of James Weldon Johnson* (New York: Viking Press, 1933).

9. On the popularity and geographical distribution of the Ku Klux Klan in the mid-1920s, see David Chalmers, *Hooded Americanism: The History of the Ku Klux Klan* (Chicago: Quadrangle, 1965); Nancy MacLean, *Behind the Mask of Chivalry: The Making of the Ku Klux Klan in a Georgia Town* (New York: Oxford University Press, 1994); Kenneth Jackson, *The Ku Klux Klan in the City, 1915–1930* (New York: Oxford University Press, 1967); and Charles C. Alexander, *The Ku Klux Klan in the Southwest* (Lexington: University of Kentucky Press, 1966). On the power of Southern demagogues during these years, see Raymond Arsenault, "The Folklore of Southern Demagoguery," in Charles Eagles, ed., *Is There a Southern Political Tradition?* (Jackson: University Press of Mississippi, 1996), 82–84, 95–121; and Allan Michie and Frank Rhylick, *Dixie Demagogues* (New York: Vanguard Press, 1939). On the general spirit of intolerance prevalent during the 1920s, see William E. Leuchtenberg, *The Perils of Prosperity, 1914–1932* (Chicago: University of Chicago Press, 1958), 204–24. *New York Herald Tribune*, August 27, 1925 (quotation); Keiler, *Marian Anderson*, 61–63; and Anderson, *My Lord*, 100–106.

10. Anderson, *My Lord*, 107 (quotation).

11. Keiler, *Marian Anderson*, 64; Anderson, *My Lord*, 249–50; Russell Freedman, *The Voice That Challenged a Nation: Marian Anderson and the Struggle for Equal Rights* (New York: Clarion, 2004), 80–82.

12. Anderson, *My Lord*, 108–9 (quotation); and Keiler, *Marian Anderson*, 65–66.

13. Anderson, *My Lord*, 71–72, 87–89, 107; Keiler, *Marian Anderson*, 63–65. On the "tribal twenties," see Leuchtenberg, *Perils of Prosperity*, 204–24; and Frederick Lewis Allen, *Only Yesterday: An Informal History of the 1920s* (New York: Harper and Brothers, 1931).

14. Anderson, *My Lord*, 58, 87, 118 (quotation); and Keiler, *Marian Anderson*, 66.

15. Anderson, *My Lord*, 58, 112, 118–19; and Keiler, *Marian Anderson*, 66. For an insightful analysis of the complex relationship between European culture and American classical music, see Joseph Horowitz, *Classical Music in America: A History* (New York: W. W. Norton, 2005).

16. Keiler, *Marian Anderson*, 68–74; Anderson, *My Lord*, 58, 119–28; and Martin

Bauml Duberman, *Paul Robeson: A Biography* (New York: Ballantine, 1989), 109–20. On Noble Sissle, see Douglas, *Terrible Honesty*, 16, 19, 79, 254, 298, 359, 383–85; and Robert Kimble and William Bolcom, *Reminiscing with Sissle and Blake* (New York: Viking Press, 1973). On Waters, Hunter, and Mills, see Marks and Edkins, *Power of Pride*, 90–103, 128–33, 156–69.

17. Anderson, *My Lord*, 127–30; and Keiler, *Marian Anderson*, 75–81.

18. Anderson, *My Lord*, 108–11; and Keiler, *Marian Anderson*, 81–84.

19. *Philadelphia Tribune*, October 12, 1928; *New York Times*, December 31, 1928; *New York Herald Tribune*, December 31, 1928; and Keiler, *Marian Anderson*, 85–87.

20. Keiler, *Marian Anderson*, 87–89; Anderson, *My Lord*, 112; and *Seattle Daily Times*, June 10, August 5, 12, 1929.

21. Keiler, *Marian Anderson*, 89–90.

22. On Julius Rosenwald and the Rosenwald Fund, see Peter Max Ascoli, *Julius Rosenwald: The Man Who Built Sears, Roebuck and Advanced the Cause of Black Education in the American South* (Bloomington: Indiana University Press, 2006); and Edwin R. Embree, *Julius Rosenwald Fund, 1917–1936* (Chicago: Brousson, 2007) (first quotation). Anderson, *My Lord*, 131–32; and Keiler, *Marian Anderson*, 90–92 (second quotation). See also the complete correspondence between Anderson and the Rosenwald Fund in the Rosenwald Fund Papers, Special Collections, Aurelia and John Hope Franklin Library, Fisk University, Nashville, Tennessee.

23. Anderson, *My Lord*, 132–40; and Keiler, *Marian Anderson*, 92–98 (quotation).

24. Anderson, *My Lord*, 140–41; and Keiler, *Marian Anderson*, 97–103.

25. Kosti Vehanen, *Marian Anderson: A Portrait* (New York: McGraw-Hill, 1941), 21–56; Anderson, *My Lord*, 141–42 (first quotation), 143–44 (second quotation); and Keiler, *Marian Anderson*, 103–5.

26. Anderson, *My Lord*, 145 (quotation), 146.

27. Keiler, *Marian Anderson*, 105–7; and Anderson, *My Lord*, 146.

28. Anderson, *My Lord*, 146; Keiler, *Marian Anderson*, 107–9 (first quotation), 110–13; and Vehanen, *Marian Anderson*, 29, 30–31 (second quotation).

29. Vehanen, *Marian Anderson*, 25–38; Anderson, *My Lord*, 148–49 (quotation); and Keiler, *Marian Anderson*, 112–14. On Jean Sibelius, see Andrew Barnett, *Sibelius* (New Haven: Yale University Press, 2007).

30. Anderson, *My Lord*, 112–17, 146–47; Keiler, *Marian Anderson*, 115–22; and Harlow Robinson, *The Last Impresario: The Life, Times, and Legacy of Sol Hurok* (New York: Viking, 1994), 198–99.

31. Anderson, *My Lord*, 147 (first quotation), 148 (second quotation), 150 (third quotation); Vehanen, *Marian Anderson*, 161–69, 164 (fourth quotation); and Keiler, *Marian Anderson*, 122–32.

32. Keiler, *Marian Anderson*, 132–35, 133 (quotation); Anderson, *My Lord*, 95, 151–55; Vehanen, *Marian Anderson*, 117–18.

33. Anderson, *My Lord*, 153–54 (first and second quotations) incorrectly identifies the year as 1935. Keiler, *Marian Anderson*, 135–37 (third quotation), 138 (fourth quotation); and Robinson, *Last Impresario*, 199–201. For another version of the first meeting between Hurok and Anderson, see Arthur Rubinstein, *My Many Years* (New York: Alfred A. Knopf, 1980), 406. See the *New York Herald Tribune*, January 7, 1951, for an inventive reminiscence by Hurok. See also Sol Hurok with Ruth Goode, *Impresario: A Memoir* (New York: Random House, 1946), 237–38.

34. Robinson, *Last Impresario*, 3–211; Hurok, *Impresario*, 240–41; Keiler, *Marian Anderson*, 138, 159–61; and Anderson, *My Lord*, 155.

35. Anderson, *My Lord*, 174–76 (quotation), Keiler, *Marian Anderson*, 139–48; and Vehanen, *Marian Anderson*, 69–85.

36. Vehanen, *Marian Anderson*, 90–115; Anderson, *My Lord*, 176–83, 179 (first quotation), 157–58 (second quotation); and Keiler, *Marian Anderson*, 148–57. On the Salzburg Festival during the 1920s and 1930s, see Stephen Gallup, *A History of the Salzburg Festival* (Topsfield, MA: Salem House, 1987), 17–103. On Arturo Toscanini see H. Howard Taubman, *The Maestro: The Life of Arturo Toscanini* (Westport, CN: Greenwood, 1977); and Filippo Sacchi, *The Magic Baton: Toscanini's Life for Music* (Whitefish, MT: Kessinger, 2007). Madame Charles Cahier (1870–1951), aka Sarah-Jane Layton Walker and Mrs. Morris Black, was an important figure in the Vienna opera scene during the early twentieth century.

37. Robinson, *Last Impresario*, 200–01; Anderson, *My Lord*, 159; see the numerous clippings from 1936 in box 407, MAP. See especially Irvine Kolodin, "An Anderson Fairy Tale," *Brooklyn Eagle*, January 19, 1936 (quotations).

CHAPTER 3: DEEP RIVERS

1. Harry T. Burleigh, *The Spirituals of Harry T. Burleigh* (Emeryville, CA: Alfred Publishing, 1985). See also Howard Thurman, *Deep River and the Negro Spiritual Speaks of Life and Death* (Richmond, IN: Friends United Press, 1975). Burleigh's arrangement of "Deep River" was first published in 1917. Harry T. Burleigh, *Negro Spirituals, Arranged for Solo Voice* (London: G. Ricordi and Co., 1917).

2. Allan Keiler, *Marian Anderson: A Singer's Journey* (New York: Simon and Schuster, 2000), 157, 161; Marian Anderson, *My Lord, What a Morning: An Autobiography* (New York: Viking Press, 1956), 159–63; Harlow Robinson, *The Last Impresario: The Life, Time, and Legacy of Sol Hurok* (New York: Viking, 1994), 201; and *Palmyra (NJ) News*, January 3, 1936, clipping in box 407, MAP.

3. Robert S. McElvaine, *The Great Depression: America, 1929–1941* (New York: Times Books, 1984), 72–249; William E. Leuchtenberg, *Franklin D. Roosevelt and the New Deal, 1932–1940* (New York: Harper and Row, 1963), 1–142; Jona-

than Alter, *The Defining Moment: FDR's Hundred Days and the Triumph of Hope* (New York: Simon and Schuster, 2006); Anthony J. Badger, *FDR: The First Hundred Days* (New York: Hill and Wang, 2008); Alan Brinkley, *Voices of Protest: Huey Long, Father Coughlin, and the Great Depression* (New York: Alfred A. Knopf, 1982); George Wolfskill, *The Revolt of the Conservatives: A History of the American Liberty League, 1934–1940* (Boston: Houghton Mifflin, 1962); Arthur M. Schlesinger Jr., *The Politics of Upheaval* (Boston: Houghton Mifflin, 1960), 1–207; Greg Mitchell, *The Campaign of the Century: Upton Sinclair's Race for Governor of California and the Birth of Media Politics* (New York: Random House, 1992); and T. Harry Williams, *Huey Long: A Biography* (New York: Alfred A. Knopf, 1970), 676–876.

4. Leuchtenberg, *Franklin D. Roosevelt*, 143–66; McElvaine, *Great Depression*, 250–75; and Schlesinger, *Politics of Upheaval*, 211–523. On the 1935 Labor Day hurricane, see Les Standiford, *Last Train to Paradise: Henry Flagler and the Spectacular Rise and Fall of the Railroad That Crossed an Ocean* (New York: Crown, 2002), 225–59; Jay Barnes, *Florida's Hurricane History* (Chapel Hill: University of North Carolina Press, 1998), 144–59; and Ernest Hemingway, "Who Killed the Vets?" *New Masses*, September 17, 1935, 9–10. On the Dust Bowl, see Donald Worster, *Dust Bowl: The Southern Plains in the 1930s* (New York: Oxford University Press, 1979); and Timothy Egan, *The Worst Hard Time: The Untold Story of Those Who Survived the Great American Dust Bowl* (Boston: Houghton Mifflin, 2006).

5. Charles S. Johnson, *The Economic Status of Negroes* (Nashville: Fisk University Press, 1933); McElvaine, *Great Depression*, 187–95; Harvard Sitkoff, *A New Deal for Blacks: The Emergence of Civil Rights as a National Issue: The Depression Decade* (New York: Oxford University Press, 1978), 29–57; Nancy Weiss, *Farewell to the Party of Lincoln: Black Politics in the Age of FDR* (Princeton: Princeton University Press, 1983), 45–49; and James O. Horton and Lois E. Horton, *Hard Road to Freedom: The Story of African America* (New Brunswick, NJ: Rutgers University Press, 2001), 249–59. For a detailed case study of black poverty during the 1930s, see Arthur F. Raper, *Preface to Peasantry: A Tale of Two Black Belt Counties* (Chapel Hill: University of North Carolina Press, 1936). See also Gunnar Myrdal, *An American Dilemma: The Negro Problem and American Democracy* (New York: Harper and Brothers, 1944), pt. 4.

6. See Weiss, *Farewell to the Party of Lincoln*; Sitkoff, *New Deal for Blacks*; John B. Kirby, *Black Americans in the Roosevelt Era* (Knoxville: University of Tennessee Press, 1980); Patricia Sullivan, *Days of Hope: Race and Democracy in the New Deal Era* (Chapel Hill: University of North Carolina Press, 1996), 1–132; John Egerton, *Speak Now Against the Day: The Generation Before the Civil Rights Movement in the South* (New York: Alfred A. Knopf, 1994), 15–197; Blanche Wiesen Cook, *Eleanor Roosevelt, 1933–1938*, vol. 2 (New York: Viking, 1999), 57–58, 129–89, 270, 278, 301–3;

Jeanne Nienaber Clarke, *Roosevelt's Warrior: Harold L. Ickes and the New Deal* (Baltimore: Johns Hopkins University Press, 1996); T. H. Watkins, *Righteous Pilgrim: The Life and Times of Harold Ickes, 1874–1952* (New York: Henry Holt, 1990); Graham White and John Maze, *Harold Ickes of the New Deal: His Private Life and Public Career* (Cambridge: Harvard University Press, 1985); Kenneth Robert Janken, *Walter White: Mr. NAACP* (Chapel Hill: University of North Carolina Press, 2003); Walter White, *A Man Called White: The Autobiography of Walter White* (New York: Viking, 1948); Joyce A. Hanson, *Mary McLeod Bethune and Black Women's Political Activism* (Columbia: University of Missouri Press, 2003); and Rackham Holt, *Mary McLeod Bethune: A Biography* (Garden City, NY: Doubleday, 1964).

7. Blanche Wiesen Cook, *Eleanor Roosevelt, 1884–1933*, vol. 1 (New York: Viking, 1992), 134–38, 203–5. On Daniels, see Joseph Morrison, *Josephus Daniels: The Small-D Democrat* (Chapel Hill: University of North Carolina Press, 1966); Josephus Daniels, *The Wilson Era: Years of Peace, 1910–1917* (Chapel Hill: University of North Carolina Press, 1944); and Jonathan Daniels, *The End of Innocence* (New York: Da Capo, 1972). On Ellen Wilson, see Carl Sferrazza Anthony, *First Ladies* (New York: William Morrow, 1990), 344–50; and Edith Elmer Wood, "Four Washington Alleys," *Survey* 31, December 6, 1913, 250–52. The granddaughter of the famed nineteenth-century orator Edward Everett, Hopkins headed the women's department of the National Civic Federation in 1914. *New York Times*, September 8, 1935.

8. Cook, *Eleanor Roosevelt, 1933–1938*, 155 (quotation)–56, 159–60; David M. Oshinsky, *Polio: An American Story* (New York: Oxford University Press, 2005), 65–67; and Hanson, *Mary McLeod Bethune*, 1–125. On the evolution of Eleanor Roosevelt's civil rights activism, see Joanna Zangrando and Robert L. Zangrando, "Eleanor Roosevelt and Black Civil Rights," in Joan Hoff-Wilson and Mary Lightman, eds., *Without Precedent: The Life and Career of Eleanor Roosevelt* (Bloomington: Indiana University Press, 1984), 88–107; Allida Black, "Civil Rights," in Maurine H. Beasley, Holly C. Shulman, and Henry R. Beasley, eds., *The Eleanor Roosevelt Encyclopedia* (Westport, CN: Greenwood, 2001), 89–96; Kirby, *Black Americans in the Roosevelt Era*, 76–96; Tamara K. Hareven, *Eleanor Roosevelt: An American Conscience* (Chicago: Quadrangle, 1968), 112–29; Stella K. Hershan, *A Woman of Quality* (New York: Crown, 1970), 155–67; James R. Kearney, *Anna Eleanor Roosevelt: The Evolution of a Reformer* (Boston: Houghton Mifflin, 1968), 57–94; Joseph P. Lash, *Eleanor and Franklin: The Story of Their Relationship, Based on Eleanor Roosevelt's Private Papers* (New York: W. W. Norton, 1971), 512–35; and Allida Black, *Casting Her Own Shadow: Eleanor Roosevelt and the Shaping of Postwar Liberalism* (New York: Columbia University Press, 1996), 85–129.

9. Cook, *Eleanor Roosevelt, 1933–1938*, 156–58, 187–89, 348–49.

10. Ibid., 129–52 (quotation); Clarence Pickett, *For More Than Bread* (Boston: Little,

Brown, 1953), 19–40; and Thomas Coode and Dennis Fabbri, "The New Deal's Arthurdale Project in West Virginia," *West Virginia History* 36 (July 1975): 291–308.

11. Cook, *Eleanor Roosevelt, 1933–1938*, 153; and Pickett, *For More Than Bread*, 49. The presidents of Atlanta University, Howard University, and Tuskegee Institute were respectively John Hope, Mordecai Johnson, and Robert Russa Moton.

12. Cook, *Eleanor Roosevelt, 1933–1938*, 156 (first quotation), 158 (second quotation), 159–61; Hanson, *Mary McLeod Bethune*, 120–63; Mary McLeod Bethune, "My Secret Talks with FDR," reprinted in Bernard Sternsher, ed., *The Negro in Depression and War: Prelude to Revolution, 1930–1945* (Chicago: Quadrangle Books, 1969), 53–65; Weiss, *Farewell to the Party of Lincoln*, 136–55; Kirby, *Black Americans in the Roosevelt Era*, 106–51; John Salmond, *A Southern Rebel: The Life and Times of Aubrey Williams, 1890–1959* (Chapel Hill: University of North Carolina Press, 1983), 122–78; Betty Lindley and Ernest K. Lindley, *A New Deal for Youth: The Story of the National Youth Administration* (New York: Da Capo Press, 1972); and Walter G. Daniel and Carroll L. Miller, "The Participation of the Negro in the National Youth Administration," *Journal of Negro Education* 7 (July 1938): 357–65.

13. White, *A Man Called White*, 3–59, 120–24, 140, 167–68, 169–70 (quotation), 203, 269; Sitkoff, *New Deal for Blacks*, 268–97; Weiss, *Farewell to the Party of Lincoln*, 96–119; Janken, *Walter White*, 1–63, 199–231; Schlesinger, *Politics of Upheaval*, 436–38. See also Walter White, *Rope and Faggot: A Biography of Judge Lynch* (New York: Alfred A. Knopf, 1929); and Robert L. Zangrando, *The NAACP Crusade Against Lynching, 1909–1950* (Philadelphia: Temple University Press, 1980). On the 1906 Atlanta race riot, see Gregory Mixon, *The Atlanta Riot: Race, Class, and Violence in a New South City* (Gainesville: University Press of Florida, 2005).

14. Sitkoff, *New Deal for Blacks*, 58–83, 59 (quotation); Weiss, *Farewell to the Party of Lincoln*, 34–61, 119, 147–79, 296–97; Janken, *Walter White*, 222–31; Kirby, *Black Americans in the Roosevelt Era*, 181–84. See also Kevin J. McMahon, *Reconsidering Roosevelt on Race: How the Presidency Paved the Road to Brown* (Chicago: University of Chicago Press, 2004), for a recent reevaluation of the New Deal's contributions to the struggle for civil rights.

15. Clarke, *Roosevelt's Warrior*, 11–12, 43–45, 96–98, 177, 180–83, 206, 316; White and Maze, *Harold Ickes*, 21–25, 52, 55–57, 65, 91–92, 105–6, 117–18, 140, 203; Watkins, *Righteous Pilgrim*, 199–201; Sitkoff, *New Deal for Blacks*, 47, 66–69, 74, 77–78, 100, 107, 114–15, 331; Weiss, *Farewell to the Party of Lincoln*, 36–37, 51–53, 158–59, 256–57, 266; Kirby, *Black Americans in the Roosevelt Era*, 16 (first quotation), 20, 21 (second quotation), 22–35, 91, 94, 135, 181–82; Sullivan, *Days of Hope*, 24–56; Schlesinger, *Politics of Upheaval*, 432–36; and Egerton, *Speak Now Against the Day*, 92–95.

16. Chris Mead, *Champion: Joe Louis, Black Hero in White America* (New York: Charles Scribner's Sons, 1985), 47–50. On the origins and persistence of traditional assumptions of black inferiority, see Myrdal, *American Dilemma*, xli–153, 573–604; and Daryl Michael Scott, *Contempt and Pity: Social Policy and the Image of the Damaged Black Psyche, 1880–1996* (Chapel Hill: University of North Carolina Press, 1997).

17. Arthur R. Ashe Jr., *A Hard Road to Glory: A History of the African-American Athlete, 1919–1945*, vol. 2 (New York: Amistad, 1988), xiii–xv, 3–24, 59–69, 73–99, 107–10, 345, 359, 440, 470–72, 486–88; John Hoberman, *Darwin's Athletes: How Sport Has Damaged Black America and Preserved the Myth of Race* (Boston: Houghton Mifflin, 1997), xxi (quotation); William J. Baker, *Jesse Owens: An American Life* (New York: Free Press, 1986), 29, 33–72; and William C. Rhoden, *Forty Million Dollar Slaves: The Rise, Fall, and Redemption of the Black Athlete* (New York: Crown, 2006), 35–78. See also Patrick B. Miller and David K. Wiggins, eds., *Sport and the Color Line: Black Athletes and Race Relations in Twentieth-Century America* (New York: Routledge, 2004), pts. 1 and 2; and David K. Wiggins and Patrick B. Miller, eds., *The Unlevel Playing Field: A Documentary History of the African American Experience in Sport* (Urbana: University of Illinois Press, 2003), chaps. 3 and 4.

18. Ashe, *Hard Road to Glory*, vol. 2, 25–41, 44–52, 106–10, 486; Robert W. Peterson, *Cages to Jump Shots: Pro Basketball's Early Years* (New York: Oxford University Press, 1990), 11, 95–101, 130–31; Ron Thomas, *They Cleared the Lane: The NBA's Black Pioneers* (Lincoln: University of Nebraska Press, 2002), xv, 1–16; Robert Peterson, *Only the Ball Was White: A History of Legendary Black Players and All-Black Professional Teams* (New York: McGraw-Hill, 1970); Jules Tygiel, *Baseball's Great Experiment: Jackie Robinson and His Legacy* (New York: Random House, 1983), 10–29; Donn Rogosin, *Invisible Men: Life in Baseball's Negro Leagues* (New York: Atheneum, 1983); Neil Lanctot, *Negro League Baseball: The Rise and Ruin of a Black Institution* (Philadelphia: University of Pennsylvania Press, 2004); Lawrence D. Hogan, *Shades of Glory: The Negro Leagues and the Story of African-American Baseball* (Washington: National Geographic, 2006); Adrian Burgos Jr., *Playing America's Game: Baseball, Latinos, and the Color Line* (Berkeley: University of California Press, 2007), 17–176; William Price Fox, *Satchel Paige's America* (Tuscaloosa: University of Alabama Press, 2005); Steve Jacobson, *Carrying Jackie's Torch: The Players Who Integrated Baseball—and America* (Chicago: Lawrence Hill Books, 2007), 1–12; Hoberman, *Darwin's Athletes*, 28–51; and Rhoden, *Forty Million Dollar Slaves*, 97–125.

19. Ashe, *Hard Road to Glory*, vol. 2, 7–24, 345–58; Mead, *Champion*, 19–75; Rhoden, *Forty Million Dollar Slaves*, 92–96; Hoberman, *Darwin's Athletes*, 11–14, 52–56, 77–82; Randy Roberts, *Papa Jack: Jack Johnson and the Era of White Hopes* (New York: Free Press, 1983); Geoffrey C. Ward, *Unforgivable Blackness: The Rise and*

Fall of Jack Johnson (New York: Alfred A. Knopf, 2004); Lewis Erenberg, *The Greatest Fight of Our Generation: Louis vs. Schmeling* (New York: Oxford University Press, 2006), 7–70; and David Margolick, *Beyond Glory: Joe Louis vs. Max Schmeling, and a World on the Brink* (New York: Alfred A. Knopf, 2005), 34–145.

20. Myrdal, *American Dilemma*, 304–32, 654–55, 734–35, 986–94. On De Preist, Mitchell, and black politics in Chicago, see William J. Grimshaw, *Bitter Fruit: Black Politics and the Chicago Machine, 1931–1991* (Chicago: University of Chicago Press, 1995); Harold F. Gosnell, *Negro Politicians: The Rise of Negro Politics in Chicago* (Chicago: University of Chicago Press, 1966); and St. Clair Drake and Horace R. Cayton, *Black Metropolis: A Study of Negro Life in a Northern City* (Chicago: University of Chicago Press, 1993).

21. Juliet E. K. Walker, *The History of Black Business in America: Capitalism, Race, Entrepreneurship* (New York: Macmillan, 1998). On the accomplishments and obscurity of black artists, see Samella Lewis, *African American Art and Artists* (Berkeley: University of California Press, 2003); Romare Bearden and Harry Henderson, *A History of African-American Art: From 1792 to the Present* (New York: Pantheon, 1993); Sharon F. Patton, *African-American Art* (New York: Oxford University Press, 1998); Richard J. Powell, *Black Art: A Cultural History* (London: Thames and Hudson, 2002); Nell Irvin Painter, *Creating Black Americans: African-American History and Its Meanings, 1619 to the Present* (New York: Oxford University Press, 2005), 172–217; Lisa Gail Collins and Lisa Mintz Messinger, *African-American Artists, 1929–1945: Prints, Drawings, and Paintings in the Metropolitan Museum of Art* (New York: Metropolitan Museum of Art, 2003); and Gwen Everett, *African-American Masters: Highlights from the Smithsonian American Art Museum* (Washington: Smithsonian Institution, 2003). On Carver and other black academics, see Linda O. McMurry, *George Washington Carver: Scientist and Symbol* (New York: Oxford University Press, 1982); Jonathan Scott Holloway, *Confronting the Veil: Abram Harris Jr., E. Franklin Frazier, and Ralph Bunche, 1919–1941* (Chapel Hill: University of North Carolina Press, 2001); Brian Urquhart, *Ralph Bunche: An American Odyssey* (New York: Norton, 1993); Charles Henry, *Ralph Bunche: Model Negro or American Other?* (New York: New York University Press, 1999); Kenneth Robert Janken, *Rayford Logan and the Dilemma of the African American Intellectual* (Amherst: University of Massachusetts Press, 1993; and Benjamin E. Mays, *Born to Rebel: An Autobiography* (Athens: University of Georgia Press, 1987), 125–212.

22. Nathan I. Huggins, *Harlem Renaissance* (New York: Oxford University Press, 1971); David Levering Lewis, *When Harlem Was in Vogue* (New York: Oxford University Press, 1982); Victor Kramer, *The Harlem Renaissance Re-Examined* (New York: AMS Press, 1987); Steven Watson, *The Harlem Renaissance: Hub of African-American Culture, 1920–1930* (New York: Pantheon, 1995); Arna Bontemps, *The Harlem Renaissance Remembered* (New York: Dodd, Mead, 1972);

Ann Douglas, *Terrible Honesty: Mongrel Manhattan in the 1920s* (New York: Noonday Press, 1995); Sterling Brown, *The Negro in American Fiction* (New York: Atheneum, 1969); Arnold Rampersad, *The Life of Langston Hughes*, vol. 1, *I, Too, Sing America, 1902–1941* (New York: Oxford University Press, 1986); Valerie Boyd, *Wrapped in Rainbows: The Life of Zora Neale Hurston* (New York: Scribner, 2003), 13–294; Robert E. Hemenway, *Zora Neale Hurston: A Literary Biography* (Urbana: University of Illinois Press, 1977); Willard Thorp, *A Southern Reader* (New York: Alfred A. Knopf, 1955); and Arnold Rampersad, *Ralph Ellison: A Biography* (New York: Alfred A. Knopf, 2007), 258–92. *Invisible Man* won the National Book Award in 1953, beating out Ernest Hemingway's *Old Man and the Sea* and John Steinbeck's *East of Eden*.

23. Langston Hughes and Milton Meltzer, *Black Magic: A Pictorial History of the Negro in American Entertainment* (Englewood Cliffs, NJ: Prentice-Hall, 1967); Mel Watkins, *On the Real Side: Laughing, Lying, and Signifying: The Underground Tradition of African-American Humor That Transformed American Culture, from Slavery to Richard Pryor* (New York: Simon and Schuster, 1994), 266–99, 279 (quotation); J. Fred MacDonald, *Don't Touch That Dial! Radio Programming in American Life, 1920–1960* (Chicago: Nelson-Hall, 1979); Barbara Dianne Savage, *Broadcasting Freedom: Radio, War, and the Politics of Race, 1938–1948* (Chapel Hill: University of North Carolina Press, 1999), 5–14; Melvin Patrick Ely, *The Adventures of Amos 'n' Andy: A Social History of an American Phenomenon* (New York: Free Press, 1991); Arthur Frank Werthheim, *Radio Comedy* (New York: Oxford University Press, 1979); Michele Hilmes, *Radio Voices: American Broadcasting, 1922–1952* (Minneapolis: University of Minnesota Press, 1997), 85–90; and Sitkoff, *New Deal for Blacks*, 29.

24. Thomas Cripps, *Slow Fade to Black: The Negro in American Film, 1900–1942* (New York: Oxford University Press, 1977), 203–308; Thomas Cripps, *Making Movies Black: The Hollywood Message Movie from World War II to the Civil Rights Era* (New York: Oxford University Press, 1993), 3–15; Donald Bogle, *Toms, Coons, Mulattoes, Mammies, and Bucks: An Interpretive History of Blacks in American Films* (New York: Viking, 1973), 35–94, 36 (quotation); Watkins, *On the Real Side*, 200–265; Carlton Jackson, *Hattie: The Life of Hattie McDaniel* (Lanham, MD: Madison Books, 1990), xi–32; Clarence Muse, *The Dilemma of the Negro Actor* (n.p.: c. 1934); "Louise Beavers," in Cary D. Wintz, ed., *Encyclopedia of the Harlem Renaissance* (New York: Routledge, 2004), 108; Michael H. Price, *Mantan the Funnyman: The Life and Times of Mantan Moreland* (Baltimore: Midnight Marquee Press, 2006); Jim Haskins and N. R. Mitgang, *Mr. Bojangles: The Biography of Bill Robinson* (New York: William Morrow, 1988); Mel Watkins, *Stepin Fetchit: The Life and Times of Lincoln Perry* (New York: Pantheon, 2005); and Champ Clark, *Shuffling to Ignominy: The Tragedy of Stepin Fetchit* (iUniverse, 2005).

25. Bogle, *Toms, Coons,* 57–62, 60 (quotation); Cripps, *Slow Fade to Black,* 299–302; and Watkins, *On the Real Side,* 240.

26. Bogle, *Toms, Coons,* 25, 31, 33, 35, 60, 70, 94–100; Cripps, *Slow Fade to Black,* 95, 170–235, 267, 293–94, 310, 315–22, 349–89; Martin Bauml Duberman, *Paul Robeson: A Biography* (New York: Ballantine, 1989), 77, 101, 120, 156–90, 194–97, 202–10, 222, 228–39, 259–62, 180 (quotations).

27. Duberman, *Paul Robeson,* 44–58, 71, 83, 103–55, 194–97, 203–4, 223–28, 237–38, 259–62; Bogle, *Toms, Coons,* 95–100; Cripps, *Slow Fade to Black,* 112–13, 257; and Watkins, *On the Real Side,* 104–80, 207–13, 225–26, 228, 363–99. See also Loften Mitchell, *Black Drama: The Story of the American Negro in the Theatre* (New York: Hawthorne Books, 1967). On racial stereotypes and minstrelsy, see Robert Toll, *Blacking Up: The Minstrel Show in Nineteenth-Century America* (New York: Oxford University Press, 1974); Joseph Boskin, *Sambo: The Rise and Demise of an American Jester* (New York: Oxford University Press, 1986); William J. Mahar, *Behind the Burnt Cork Mask: Early Blackface Minstrelsy and Antebellum American Popular Culture* (Urbana: University of Illinois Press, 1998); John Strausbaugh, *Black Like You: Blackface, Insult and Imitation in American Popular Culture* (New York: Tarcher, 2006); Henry T. Sampson, *Blacks in Blackface: A Sourcebook on Early Black Musical Shows* (Metuchen, NJ: Scarecrow Press, 1980); Ann Charters, *Nobody: The Story of Bert Williams* (New York: Macmillan, 1969); Louis Chude-Sokei, *The Last "Darky": Bert Williams, Black-on-Black Minstrelsy, and the African Diaspora* (Durham, NC: Duke University Press, 2005); Camille F. Forbes, *Introducing Bert Williams: Burnt Cork, Broadway, and the Story of America's First Black Star* (New York: Basic Civitas Books, 2008); and Lynn Abbott and Doug Seroff, *Ragged but Right: Black Traveling Shows, Coon Songs, and the Dark Pathway to Blues and Jazz* (University: University of Mississippi Press, 2007).

28. See Eileen Southern, *The Music of Black Americans: A History* (New York: Norton, 1971), 278–446; Andrew Ward, *Dark Midnight When I Rise: The Story of the Jubilee Singers Who Introduced the World to the Music of Black America* (New York: Farrar, Straus and Giroux, 2000); Lynn Abbott and Doug Seroff, *Out of Sight: The Rise of African-American Popular Music, 1889–1895* (Jackson: University of Mississippi, 2003); Rudi Blesh, *They All Played Ragtime* (New York: Music Sales Corp., 1974); Warren Forma, *They Were Ragtime* (New York: Grosset and Dunlap, 1976); David A. Jasen and Jay Tichenor, *Rags and Ragtime: A Musical History* (New York: Seabury Press, 1978); Lewis A. Erenberg, *Steppin' Out: New York Nightlife and the Transformation of American Culture, 1890–1930* (Westport, CN: Greenwood Press, 1981); Jim Haskins, *The Cotton Club* (New York: Random House, 1977); W. C. Handy, *Father of the Blues: An Autobiography* (New York: Da Capo Press, 1961); LeRoi Jones, *Blues People: Negro Music in White America* (New York: William Morrow, 1963); Giles Oakley, *The Devil's Music: A History of the Blues* (New York: Da Capo, 1997); Jeff Todd Titon, *Early Downhome Blues* (Urbana:

University of Illinois Press, 1977); Margaret McKee and Fred Chisenhall, *Beale Black and Blue: Life and Music on America's Main Street* (Baton Rouge: Louisiana State University Press, 1981); Marshall Stearns, *The Story of Jazz* (New York: Oxford University Press, 1970); and Carole Marks and Diana Edkins, *The Power of Pride: Stylemakers and Rulebreakers of the Harlem Renaissance* (New York: Crown, 1999). On individual black musicians, see Martin T. Williams, *King Oliver* (London: A. S. Barnes, 1961); Alan Lomax, *Mister Jelly Roll: The Fortunes of Jelly Roll Morton* (Berkeley: University of California Press, 2001); Carman Moore, *Somebody's Angel Child: The Story of Bessie Smith* (New York: Thomas Crowell, 1969); Chris Albertson, *Bessie* (New Haven: Yale University Press, 2005); Ethel Waters with Charles Samuels, *His Eye Is on the Sparrow: An Autobiography* (New York: Pyramid Books, 1972); Louis Armstrong, *Satchmo: My Life in New Orleans* (New York: Da Capo Press, 1986); James Collier, *Louis Armstrong: An American Genius* (New York: Oxford University Press, 1983); Gary Giddins, *Satchmo: The Genius of Louis Armstrong* (New York: Da Capo, 2001); Stanley Dance and Earl Hines, *The World of Earl Hines* (New York: Da Capo, 1983); Ed Kirkeby, *Ain't Misbehavin': The Story of Fats Waller* (New York: Da Capo, 1988); Charles Fox, *Fats Waller* (London: A. S. Barnes, 1961); Joel Vance, *Fats Waller: His Life and Times* (New York: Berkley Medallion Books, 1979); Frank C. Taylor, *Alberta Hunter: A Celebration in Blues* (New York: McGraw-Hill, 1988); Benetta Jules Rosette, *Josephine Baker in Art and Life: The Icon and the Image* (Urbana: University of Illinois Press, 2007); Phyllis Rose, *Jazz Cleopatra: Josephine Baker in Her Time* (New York: Doubleday, 1989); Count Basie with Albert Murray, *Good Morning Blues: The Autobiography of Count Basie* (New York: Random House, 1985); Peter Gammond, ed., *Duke Ellington: His Life and Music* (New York: Da Capo, 1977); Cab Calloway and Bryant Rollins, *Of Minnie the Moocher and Me* (New York: Thomas Crowell, 1976); Lionel Hampton with James Haskins, *Hamp: An Autobiography* (New York: Warner Books, 1990); Stuart Nicholson, *Ella Fitzgerald: A Biography of the First Lady of Jazz* (New York: Routledge, 2004); Ron Fritts, *Ella Fitzgerald: The Chick Webb Years and Beyond, 1935–1948* (Metuchen, NJ: Scarecrow Press, 2003); and Billie Holiday with William Dufty, *Lady Sings the Blues* (New York: Harlem Moon, 2006). On African-American performers in France, see Tyler Stovall, *Paris Noir: African-Americans in the City of Light* (Boston: Houghton Mifflin, 1996); and Jody Blake, *Le Tumulte Noir: Modernist Art and Popular Entertainment in Jazz-Age Paris, 1900–1930* (University Park: Pennsylvania State University Press, 1999).

29. Joseph Horowitz, *Classical Music in America: A History* (New York: W. W. Norton, 2007), 6–10, 65–66, 195, 224, 227–29, 231, 460–72; and Southern, *Music of Black Americans*, 105–48, 255–77.

30. Southern, *Music of Black Americans*, 142, 252–57, 272; and Ken Wlaschin, *Encyclopedia of American Opera* (Jefferson, NC: McFarland, 2006), 8.

31. Southern, *Music of Black Americans*, 295–99, 316, 323, 345, 348–49, 353, 368–69, 386, 391, 432–33, 448; and Horowitz, *Classical Music in America*, 223–31, 247–48, 227 (quotation). On Dvorak, see John Tibbets, ed., *Dvorak in America* (Portland, OR: Amadeus Press, 1993); and Michael Beckerman, *New Worlds of Dvorak: Searching in America for the Composer's Inner Life* (New York: W. W. Norton, 2003).

32. Southern, *Music of Black Americans*, 291–93, 323, 330, 353, 386, 399, 407–9, 424, 436, 438, 440, 444, 448–52, 464, 509, 451 (quotation).

33. Ibid., 449, 474.

34. Ibid., 454 (quotation)–462, 477.

35. Reyann King, *Ignatius Sancho: African Man of Letters* (London: National Portrait Gallery, 2008); Walter E. Smith, *The Black Mozart: Le Chevalier de Saint Georges* (Bloomington, IN: AuthorHouse, 2004); Cleofe Person de Mattos, *José Mauricio Nunes Garcia: Biografia* (Rio de Janeiro: Ministerio da Cultura, Fundacao Biblioteca Nacional, 1997); John Gray, *Blacks in Classical Music: A Bibliographical Guide to Composers, Performers, and Ensembles* (Westport, CT: Greenwood, 1988), 47, 130; Aaron Horne, *Keyboard Music of Black Composers: A Bibliography* (Westport, CT: Greenwood, 1992), 235, 237; Robin D. Moore, *Music and Revolution: Cultural Change in Socialist Cuba* (Berkeley: University of California Press, 2006), 35; Peter Manuel, Kenneth Bilby, and Michael Largey, *Caribbean Currents: Caribbean Music from Rumba to Reggae* (Philadelphia: Temple University Press, 2006), 40, 158; and Gage Averill, *A Day for the Hunter, a Day for the Prey: Popular Music and Power in Haiti* (Chicago: University of Chicago Press, 1997), 35. See also John Storm Roberts, *The Latin Tinge: The Impact of Latin American Music on the United States* (New York: Oxford University Press, 1999); Ed Morales, *The Latin Beat: The Rhythm and Roots of Latin Music, from Bossa Nova to Salsa and Beyond* (New York: Da Capo, 2003); Raul A. Fernandez, *From Afro-Cuban Rhythm to Latin Jazz* (Berkeley: University of California Press, 2006); and Ned Sublette, *Cuba and Its Music: From the First Drums to the Mambo* (Chicago: Chicago Review Press, 2007).

36. Wlaschlin, *Encyclopedia of American Opera*, 8; Southern, *Music of Black Americans*, 345, 418–27, 439, 442, 500–501; Anderson, *My Lord*, 293–305; Keiler, *Marian Anderson*, 77–78, 166, 269–76. See also the video *Aida's Brothers and Sisters: Black Voices in Opera* (PBS Great Performances, 2000), directed by Jan Schmidt-Garre and Marieke Schroeder.

37. On the period between May 1954 and December 1956, see Numan V. Bartley, *The Rise of Massive Resistance: Race and Politics in the South During the 1950s* (Baton Rouge: Louisiana State University Press, 1969), 65–125; Richard Kluger, *Simple Justice* (New York: Vintage, 1975), 748–50; and John Egerton, *Speak Now Against the Day: The Generation Before the Civil Rights Movement in the South* (New York: Alfred A. Knopf), 613–27. On the situation in Germany, both be-

fore and after the Nazi rise to power, see Anton Gill, *A Dance Between Flames: Berlin Between the Wars* (London: Abacus, 1993).

38. Anderson, *My Lord*, 141–59 (quotation); Keiler, *Marian Anderson*, 155–59.

39. On Hayes's frustrations related to race and his career, see MacKinley Helm, *Angel 'Mo and Her Son, Roland Hayes* (Boston: Little, Brown, 1942), 93, 98–99, 107, 124, 188, 193, 200–206, 276–89; and Robert C. Hayden, *Singing for All People: Roland Hayes, a Biography* (Boston: Select Publications, 1989).

40. Keiler, *Marian Anderson*, 162–68; Anderson, *My Lord*, 169–73; and *New York Age*, December 14, 1935 (quotation), copy in box 407, MAP.

41. *New York Times*, December 31, 1935 (quotation); *Pittsburgh Courier*, January 11, 1936; Keiler, *Marian Anderson*, 58–63, 157–62; Anderson, *My Lord*, 72–74, 86, 161–68; Robinson, *Last Impresario*, 201; Howard Taubman, *The Pleasure of Their Company: A Reminiscence* (Portland, OR: Amadeus Press, 1994), 311–15.

42. *New York Post*, December 31, 1935 (first quotation), box 407, MAP; *New York Daily Eagle*, December 31, 1935 (second quotation), box 407, MAP; and *New York Sun*, December 31, 1935 (third quotation), box 407, MAP. See also reviews in *New York World-Telegram*, December 31, 1935; *New York Journal*, December 31, 1935; *New York Musical Courier*, January 11, 1936; *New York News*, January 4, 1936; *New York News-Week*, January 11, 1936; *Ellwood City Messenger*, January 11, 1936; and *Washington Tribune*, January 14, 1936, clippings in box 407, MAP. The *Washington Tribune* article observed that Kosti Vehanen's "interpretation of Negro music revealed no racial handicap whatever." Anderson, *My Lord*, 167–69; Keiler, *Marian Anderson*, 161–62, 168–69; Robinson, *Last Impresario*, 202.

43. Anderson, *My Lord*, 164–65 (quotation); Hurok, *Impresario*, 254; and Robinson, *Last Impresario*, 202. On segregation and civil rights in New York City during the pre–World War II era, see Martha Biondi, *To Stand and Fight: The Struggle for Civil Rights in Postwar New York City* (Cambridge: Harvard University Press, 2006), 1–16.

44. "Colored Contralto," *Time* 35 (January 13, 1936): 35–36 (first quotation); and "Dark Contralto," *New Yorker*, January 18, 1936, 7 (second quotation), clippings in box 407, MAP.

45. *Philadelphia Record*, January 17, 1936 (quotation); *Philadelphia Bulletin*, January 14, 17, 1936; *Philadelphia Evening Ledger*, January 17, 1936; *Camden Post*, January 3, 11, 1936; and *New York World-Telegram*, January 2, 1936, clippings in box 407, MAP. *Pittsburgh Courier*, January 25, 1936; *Philadelphia Tribune*, January 17, 23, 1936; Keiler, *Marian Anderson*, 162–63; and Anderson, *My Lord*, 163, 168.

46. *Philadelphia Record*, January 19, 1936 (first quotation); *Brooklyn Eagle*, January 19, 1936; *New York Herald Tribune*, January 21, 1936 (second quotation); *New York Age*, December 14, 1935; *Chicago Tribune*, January 28, 1936; "Dark Contralto," *New Yorker*; Martin Chapman, "Gracious Lady," *Tops* 1, no. 2, (1936): 2–4; and

Ollie Stewart, "The Girl Who Wouldn't Quit," *Commentator*, 1936, 113–15, clippings in box 407, MAP. Robinson, *Last Impresario*, 201.

47. Anderson, *My Lord*, 169–70; Keiler, *Marian Anderson*, 162–64; Robinson, *Last Impresario*, 203; *New York Times*, January 21, 1936; *New York Herald Tribune*, January 21, 1936; *Washington Tribune*, January 28, 1936; and "Marian Anderson, American Concert" handbill, clippings in box 407, MAP. On the history of Carnegie Hall, see Richard Schickel and Michael Walsh, *Carnegie Hall: The First One Hundred Years* (New York: Abrams, 1987).

48. Keiler, *Marian Anderson*, 164–65. See the voluminous clippings on the 1936 tour in box 407, MAP. See especially *Pittsburgh Courier*, February 6, 1936; *New York Musical Courier*, February 8, 1936; *Washington Tribune*, February 4, 1936; *Atlanta Constitution*, February 9, 1936; *Atlanta Journal*, February 15, 1936; *Utica Dispatch*, February 1, 10 (first quotation), 11, 1936; *Utica Press*, February 8, 11, 1936; *Chicago Examiner*, January 27, 1936 (second quotation); *Chicago Times*, February 2, 1936; *Chicago American*, January 27, 1936 (third quotation); and *Chicago Defender*, February 1, 1936 (fourth and fifth quotations).

49. *Washington Star*, February 9, 1936, in box 407, MAP. *Philadelphia Daily News*, February 18, 1936 (first quotation); and *Philadelphia Independent*, February 20, 1936 (second quotation), both in box 205, MAP.

50. Constance McLaughlin Green, *The Secret City: A History of Race Relations in the Nation's Capital* (Princeton: Princeton University Press, 1967), 3–12, 184–289; William H. Jones, *Recreations and Amusement Among Negroes in Washington, D.C.: A Sociological Analysis of the Negro in an Urban Environment* (Washington: Howard University Press, 1927); Keiler, *Marian Anderson*, 165; and Anson Phelps Stokes, *Art and the Color Line* (Washington: Phelps Stokes Fund, 1939), 1–8. *Washington Daily News*, January 11, 1936; *Washington Tribune*, January 14, 28, February 4, 21, 28, 1936; and *Washington Star*, February 9, 1936, clippings in box 407, MAP. On Howard University's historical connections to Washington's black community, see Rayford W. Logan, *The Howard University: The First Hundred Years, 1867–1967* (New York: New York University Press, 2004); and Walter Dyson, *Howard University, The Capstone of Negro Education, a History: 1867–1940* (Washington: Howard University Graduate School, 1941).

51. Myrdal, *American Dilemma*, 528, 631–32, 1127; Green, *Secret City*, 8 (first quotation), passim; Victor R. Daly, "Washington's Minority Problem," *Crisis* 46 (1939): 170–71; Peggy Anderson, *The Daughters: An Unconventional Look at America's Fan Club—the DAR* (New York: St. Martin's, 1974), 138–39 (Brown quotations), 140; George E. Haynes and Sterling A. Brown, *Negro Newcomers in Detroit* (New York: Arno Press, 1969); William H. Jones, *The Housing of Negroes in Washington, D.C.: A Study in Human Ecology* (Washington: Howard University Press, 1929); and David Brinkley, *Washington Goes to War* (New York:

Alfred A. Knopf, 1988), 15–19. On the black middle class, see the classic study by Howard University professor E. Franklin Frazier, *Black Bourgeoisie* (Glencoe, IL: Free Press, 1957). For a revealing case study of black street life in Washington, see Elliott Liebow, *Talley's Corner: A Study of Negro Streetcorner Men* (Boston: Little, Brown, 1967). See also Washington League of Women Voters, *Washington, D.C.: A Tale of Two Cities* (Washington: League of Women Voters, 1962); and *Segregation in Washington* (Chicago: National Committee on Segregation in Washington, 1948).

52. Keiler, *Marian Anderson*, 165. On Cohen and the evolution of the Howard University Lyceum concert series, see the voluminous correspondence in folders 26–29, box 1–1, MA-DARCC.

53. Anderson, *Daughters*, 125–30; Keiler, *Marian Anderson*, 181–89; and Stokes, *Art and the Color Line*, 8–12. On Washington's lack of a municipal auditorium, see Senator Arthur Capper to John Lovell Jr., March 13, 1939, folder 14; and Corinne K. Robinson to *Washington Post*, February 21, 1939, folder 19, both in box 1–1, MA-DARCC; and "The Anderson Episode," editorial in the *Washington Post*, February 21, 1939. On the origins of Constitution Hall, see Edith Scott Magna, "Constitution Hall," *Daughters of the American Revolution Magazine* 63, no. 9 (1929): 517–22. On the DAR, see Anderson, *Daughters*; Margaret Gibbs, *The DAR* (New York: Holt, Rinehart and Winston, 1969); Martha Strayer, *The D.A.R.: An Informal History* (Washington, D.C.: Public Affairs Press, 1958); and Ann Arnold Hunter, *A Century of Service: The Story of the D.A.R.* (Washington, D.C.: National Society of the Daughters of the American Revolution, 1991).

54. Patrick Hayes, "White Artists Only," *Washingtonian*, April 1989, 96–97 (quotations); Helm, *Angel Mo' and Her Son*, 201–2; Anderson, *Daughters*, 109, 125–32; Keiler, *Marian Anderson*, 186–87; Stokes, *Art and the Color Line*, 8.

55. *Washington Daily News*, c. March 22, 1931, quoted in Anderson, *Daughters*, 126–27. Anderson, pp. 125–27, provides a detailed account of the controversy surrounding the 1931 Hampton Choir concert at Constitution Hall.

56. Anderson, *Daughters*, 112; and Keiler, *Marian Anderson*, 165. *Washington Star*, February 9 (first quotation), 19 (third quotation), 1936; *Washington Tribune*, February 4, 21 (second quotation), 1936; *Washington News*, February 1, 1936; and *Washington Post*, February 9, 1936, clippings in box 407, MAP.

57. Kosti Vehanen, *Marian Anderson: A Portrait* (New York: McGraw-Hill, 1941), 220–24; Keiler, *Marian Anderson*, 165–66; and Elise Kirk, *Musical Highlights from the White House* (Malabar, FL: Krieger, 1992), 111–14.

58. *Philadelphia Independent*, February 27, 1936 (first quotation); *Philadelphia Daily News*, February 26, 1936; *New York News*, February 29, 1936 (second quotation), clippings in box 407, MAP. Keiler, *Marian Anderson*, 166–67; Vehanen, *Marian Anderson*, 220, 223 (quotations); Marian Anderson, *My Lord*, 194–96.

CHAPTER 4: THE HEART OF A NATION

1. At the age of six, Anderson made her "first public appearance," singing the hymn "Dear to the Heart of the Shepherd" during a Sunday service at Union Baptist Church. She sang as part of a duo with Viola Johnson. Mary B. Wingate wrote the words to the hymn in 1899, and William J. Kilpatrick of Philadelphia (1838–1921) wrote the music. Marian Anderson, *My Lord, What a Morning* (New York: Viking Press, 1956), 8; Willam J. Kilpatrick, *Sunday-School Praises* (Cincinnati: Jennings and Pye, 1900); and William J. Kilpatrick and Howard Doane, *Glorious Praises* (Louisville: Baptist Book Concern, 1904).

2. *Akron Press*, February 21, 1936 (quotation), in box 407, MAP.

3. *Boston Globe*, February 29, 1936 (first and second quotations); *Boston Herald*, February 23, March 7, 1936 (third quotation); *Boston Transcript*, February 21, March 2, 1936; *Boston Traveler*, February 29, 1936; *Washington Tribune*, February 21, 1936; *Philadelphia News*, February 28, 1936; *Chicago Defender*, March 7, 1936; and *New York Post*, March 14, 1936, all in box 407, MAP. *Philadelphia Independent*, February 20, 1936; and *Philadelphia Gazette*, February 20, 1936, both in box 405, MAP.

4. Allan Keiler, *Marian Anderson: A Singer's Journey* (New York: Simon and Schuster, 2000), 167–69; Anderson, *My Lord*, 169–71, 170 (quotation); Harlow Robinson, *The Last Impresario: The Life, Times, and Legacy of Sol Hurok* (New York: Viking Press, 1994), 227–28; Sol Hurok with Ruth Goode, *Impresario: A Memoir by Sol Hurok* (New York: Random House, 1946), 244; and Peggy Anderson, *The Daughters: An Unconventional Look at America's Fan Club—the DAR* (New York: St. Martin's, 1974), 111. See also Isaac Fisher, "Marian Anderson: Ambassador of Beauty from Her Race," *Southern Workman* 65 (March 1936): 72–80.

5. *Boston Herald*, February 23, 1936 (quotation).

6. *Chicago Defender*, March 7, 1936 (quotation), in box 407, MAP; and Keiler, *Marian Anderson*, 169.

7. Keiler, *Marian Anderson*, 170; and Anderson, *My Lord*, 174. On Mussolini and the fascist occupation of Ethiopia, see R. J. B. Bosworth, *Mussolini's Italy: Life Under the Fascist Dictatorship, 1915–1945* (New York: Penguin, 2006), 367–95; and Alberto Scacchi, *Legacy of Bitterness: Ethiopia and Fascist Italy, 1935–1941* (Trenton, NJ: Red Sea Press, 1997).

8. Kosti Vehanen, *Marian Anderson: A Portrait* (New York: McGraw-Hill, 1941), 177 (quotation)–82; Keiler, *Marian Anderson*, 170–71; and Anderson, *My Lord*, 174–83. On the disruptions in Spain just prior to the Spanish Civil War, see Hugh Thomas, *The Spanish Civil War* (New York: Penguin, 2003), 1–186; and Anthony Beevor, *The Battle for Spain: The Spanish Civil War, 1936–1939* (New York: Penguin, 2006), 9–96.

9. Keiler, *Marian Anderson*, 171–73; Bruno Walter, *Themes and Variations: An Auto-*

biography, trans. James A. Galston (New York: Alfred A. Knopf, 1946), 320; *New York Times*, July 19, 1936 (quotations); and Stephen Gallup, *A History of the Salzburg Festival* (Topsfield, MA: Salem House, 1987), 57–102. Gallup makes no mention of Anderson but offers extensive commentary on the Salzburg Festival's difficulties with Nazi interference. On Walter (1876–1962), see Erik Ryding and Rebecca Pechefsky, *Bruno Walter: A World Elsewhere* (Lincoln: University of Nebraska Press, 2006). On Austria and Nazism, see Evan Burr Bukey, *Hitler's Austria: Popular Sentiment in the Nazi Era, 1938–1945* (Chapel Hill: University of North Carolina Press, 2000); and Thomas Weyr, *The Setting of the Pearl: Vienna under Hitler* (New York: Oxford University Press, 2005).

10. Keiler, *Marian Anderson*, 94–114, 171, 174; Anderson, *My Lord*, 130–41, 174; Vehanen, *Marian Anderson*, 15–18; Martin Duberman, *Paul Robeson: A Biography* (New York: Ballantine, 1989), 184–85; William J. Baker, *Jesse Owens: An American Life* (New York: Free Press, 1986), 73–128; Lewis Erenberg, *The Greatest Fight of Our Generation: Louis vs. Schmeling* (New York: Oxford University Press, 2006); David Margolick, *Beyond Glory: Joe Louis vs. Max Schmeling, and a World on the Brink* (New York: Alfred A. Knopf, 2005); and Chris Mead, *Champion: Joe Louis, Black Hero in White America* (New York: Penguin, 1986), 75–159.

11. Keiler, *Marian Anderson*, 174–75; Anderson, *My Lord*, 174; and Hurok, *Impresario*, 244. For commentary on the leading "classical" black musicians of 1936, see Shirley Graham, "Spirituals to Symphonies," *Étude* 54 (November 1936): 681–92, 723; and "Singers: Roland Hayes, Jules Bledsoe, Marian Anderson, and Others," in Benjamin Bradley, *The Negro Genius* (New York: Dodd, Mead, 1937), 313–14, 366.

12. See the 1937 tour clippings in box 406, MAP. *San Francisco News*, February 25, 1937 (first quotation); and *Toronto Globe and Mail*, c. March 1937 (second quotation), both in box 406, MAP; Keiler, *Marian Anderson*, 175. According to the *Norfolk Journal and Guide*, April 15, 1939, Anderson's 1937 tour yielded a gross income of $150,000, from which she netted $30,000.

13. *New York Herald Tribune*, quoted in *Pittsburgh Courier*, March 18, 1937 (first quotation); *New York Amsterdam News*, March 13, 1937 (second quotation); and *Harlem New York News*, c. March 1937 (third quotation), all in box 406, MAP.

14. *New York Evening Journal*, c. May 1937 (first quotation); *Chicago Daily News*, April 28, 1937 (second quotation), May 3, 1937 (third quotation); *San Francisco Chronicle*, February 25, 1937 (fourth quotation); *San Francisco Examiner*, March 6, 1937 (fifth quotation); and *Houston Chronicle*, c. February 1937 (sixth quotation), all in box 406, MAP.

15. Anderson, *My Lord*, 239–52; and Vehanen, *Marian Anderson*, 227–36. *New York Age*, March 27, 1937, in box 406, MAP. On Houston's racial history, see Howard Beeth and Cary D. Wintz, eds., *Black Dixie: Afro-Texan History and Culture in Houston* (College Station: Texas A&M University Press, 1992). On the special character of race relations in Oklahoma, see Jimmie Lee Franklin,

Journey Toward Hope: A History of Blacks in Oklahoma (Norman: University of Oklahoma Press, 1982); Buck Colbert Franklin, *My Life and an Era: The Autobiography of Buck Colbert Franklin* (Baton Rouge: Louisiana State University Press, 2000); Tim Madigan, *Burning: Massacre, Destruction, and the Tulsa Race Riot of 1921* (New York: St. Martin's, 2001); and Scott Ellsworth, *Death in a Promised Land: The Tulsa Race Riot of 1921* (Baton Rouge: Louisiana State University Press, 1992). On Einstein and Anderson, see Walter Isaacson, *Einstein: His Life and Universe* (New York: Simon and Schuster, 2007), 445; James W. Leowen, *Sundown Towns: A Hidden Dimension of American Racism* (New York: Simon and Schuster, 2005), 196, 247; and Anderson, *My Lord*, 266–67.

16. Anderson, *My Lord*, 239 (quotation)–52; and Vehanen, *Marian Anderson*, 227–36. On two occasions in 1938, once in Los Angeles and once in Kalamazoo, Michigan, Anderson was forced to use freight elevators because the hotel management did not want to challenge the racial sensibilities of white guests. Anderson, *Daughters*, 148–49; and *Kalamazoo Gazette*, October 14, 1975. On the vagaries of segregation during the 1930s and 1940s, see Gunnar Myrdal, *An American Dilemma: The Negro Problem and American Democracy* (New York: Harper and Brothers, 1944), 573–663; Leowen, *Sundown Towns*; Stetson Kennedy, *Jim Crow Guide: The Way It Was* (Boca Raton: Florida Atlantic University Press, 1990); and Thomas J. Sugrue, *Sweet Land of Liberty: The Forgotten Struggle for Civil Rights in the North* (New York: Random House, 2008), 130–35.

17. Robinson, *Last Impresario*, 197–98, 228–29; Keiler, *Marian Anderson*, 177–78; Anderson, *My Lord*, 174–83; Vehanen, *Marian Anderson*, 69–115; and *New York World-Telegram*, January 2, 1936 (quotation). In his published memoir, Hurok gives the distinct impression that Anderson was less passionate and assertive on matters of racial and social justice than he was. Hurok, *Impresario*, 251–54.

18. Anderson, *My Lord*, 240–44 (quotations); Vehanen, *Marian Anderson*, 227–36; Robinson, *Last Impresario*, 229; and Hurok, *Impresario*, 251–54, 260. On the conflicting philosophies of Washington and Du Bois, see August Meier, *Negro Thought in America, 1880–1915: Racial Ideologies in the Age of Booker T. Washington* (Ann Arbor: University of Michigan Press, 1963); and David Levering Lewis, *W. E. B. Du Bois: Biography of a Race, 1868–1919* (New York: Henry Holt, 1993), 229–45, 258–64, 273–77, 286–88, 296, 303–4, 311–13, 341–42, 365, 385, 501–3.

19. Robinson, *Last Impresario*, 229 (first quotation); Hurok, *Impresario*, 251, 260; Vehanen, *Marian Anderson*, 210–12; and "A Great New Singer Tours America," *Life* 1 (February 27, 1937): 20 (second quotation), in box 406, MAP.

20. Keiler, *Marian Anderson*, 176–77.

21. Vehanen, *Marian Anderson*, 183–204; and *New York Times*, October 23, 1938. "Marian Anderson," *Stage*, December 1938; and *Harlem Bulletin*, November 26, 1938, both in box 408, MAP. For an enlightening discussion of race, color, and the distinctive social relations that have influenced the histories of the United States

and Brazil, see Carl Degler, *Neither Black Nor White: Slavery and Race Relations in Brazil and the United States* (New York: Macmillan, 1971). See also Frank Tannenbaum, *Slave and Citizen: The Negro in the Americas* (New York: Alfred A. Knopf, 1946); and Stuart B. Schwartz, "Patterns of Slaveholding in the Americas," *American Historical Review* 87 (February 1982): 55–86.

22. Keiler, *Marian Anderson*, 175–79; and Robinson, *Last Impresario*, 229. *Camden Courier-Post*, February 17, 1939, in box 408, MAP.

23. *New York Amsterdam News*, April 9, 1938 (first quotation); *San Francisco News*, February 14, 1938 (second quotation); *Dallas Times*, March 16, 1938 (third quotation); *Daily Worker*, May 1, 1938 (fourth quotation); and Glenn Dillard Gunn, "Random Notes on Music and Celebrities," unidentified clipping, 1938 (fifth quotation), all in box 407, MAP.

24. *San Francisco Chronicle*, February 14, 1938 (first quotation); unidentified New York newspaper clipping, March 2, 1938 (second quotation); and *Houston Post*, March 18, 1938 (third quotation), all in box 407, MAP.

25. *St. Louis Globe*, March 14, 1938 (first quotation); *St. Louis Dispatch*, March 14, 1938 (second quotation); and Damon Kerby, "Noted Singer's Spiritual Depth," *St. Louis Dispatch*, March 22, 1938 (third quotation), all in box 407, MAP.

26. Vehanen, *Marian Anderson*, 153–55; Keiler, *Marian Anderson*, 179–80; *Philadelphia News*, February 28, 1936, May 27, 1938; *Pittsburgh Sun-Telegraph*, January 11, 1938; *San Francisco Examiner*, February 14, 1938; *Richmond Leader*, March 20, 1938; *Pawtucket Times*, November 15, 1938; and *San Francisco News*, February 21, 1938 (quotation), all in box 407, MAP.

27. Vehanen, *Marian Anderson*, 142–45, 161–76. Marsha Davenport, "Music Will Out," *Collier's* 102 (December 3, 1938): 17, 40 (quotation); and "Marian Anderson," *Stage*, December 1938, both in box 408, MAP. *San Francisco Examiner*, February 25, 1937; and *New York Sun*, March 30, 1938, both in box 406, MAP. *New York Amsterdam News*, April 1938; and "Brown Nightingale," unidentified New York newspaper clipping, March 1938, both in box 407, MAP. *Pittsburgh Courier*, January 7, 1939; "Ex-Choir Singer," *Newsweek* 12 (December 19, 1938): 24–25; and Hurok, *Impresario*, 251. On Anderson's strong connections to her mother and Philadelphia's church-centered black community, see Marian Anderson, "My Mother's Gift—Grace Before Greatness," in Norman Vincent Peale, *Guideposts: Faith Made Them Champions* (New York: Prentice-Hall, 1954), 65–68.

28. Keiler, *Marian Anderson*, 176–78, 180; and Hurok, *Impresario*, 241–42. *New York Sun*, March 30, 1938, in box 407, MAP.

29. "Extract from Stenographic Record, District of Columbia Board of Education Meeting, March 1, 1939," folder 21, box 1-1, MA-DARCC; Keiler, *Marian Anderson*, 189; Anderson, *Daughters*, 112; Allida M. Black, "Championing a Champion: Eleanor Roosevelt and the Marian Anderson 'Freedom Concert,'" *Presidential Studies Quarterly* 20, no. 4 (1990): 721.

30. Keiler, *Marian Anderson*, 189–90; Robinson, *Last Impresario*, 229–30; Hurok, *Impresario*, 255; Black, "Championing a Champion," 722; and Todd Duncan interview in *Marian Anderson*, video produced by Greater Washington Educational Communications, WETA Public Television, 1991.

31. V. D. Johnston to *Washington Times-Herald*, January 12, 1939; and Gerald Goode, memo for Sol Hurok, "The D. A. R. versus Marian Anderson," c. March 1, 1939, both in box 412, MAP. *Washington Times-Herald*, January 12 (first quotation), 15 (second quotation), 1939; Keiler, *Marian Anderson*, 190, 192; Anderson, *Daughters*, 112–13; Hurok, *Impresario*, 255; and Black, "Championing a Champion," 722.

32. Keiler, *Marian Anderson*, 194; Kenneth Robert Janken, *Walter White: Mr. NAACP* (Chapel Hill: University of North Carolina Press, 2006), 247.

33. Blanche Wiesen Cook, *Eleanor Roosevelt: 1933–1938* (New York: Viking, 1999), 563–65; Patricia Sullivan, *Days of Hope: Race and Democracy in the New Deal Era* (Chapel Hill: University of North Carolina Press, 1996), 99–100; and John Egerton, *Speak Now Against the Day: The Generation Before the Civil Rights Movement in the South* (New York: Alfred A. Knopf, 1994), 191–94. On the Southern Conference for Human Welfare, see Linda Reed, *Simple Decency and Common Sense: The Southern Conference Movement, 1938–1963* (Bloomington: Indiana University Press, 1991); and Glenda Elizabeth Gilmore, *Defying Dixie: The Radical Roots of Civil Rights, 1919–1950* (New York: W. W. Norton, 2007), 269–72. On the trend toward a bipartisan conservative coalition during the 1930s, see James T. Patterson, *Congressional Conservatives and the New Deal: The Growth of the Conservative Coalition in Congress, 1933–1939* (Lexington: University of Kentucky Press, 1967); and William E. Leuchtenberg, *Franklin Roosevelt and the New Deal, 1932–1940* (New York: Harper and Row, 1963), 252–74.

34. Walter White to Eleanor Roosevelt, January 16, 1939, in Misc. Correspondence 1939, ER; Walter White to Marian Anderson, telegram, January 17, 1939, in box 412, MAP. Walter White to Marian Anderson, January 21, 1939 (third quotation); and *Philadelphia Christian Review*, January 26, 1939 (first and second quotations), both in box 408, MAP. Keiler, *Marian Anderson*, 180, 194–95, 204; Black, "Championing a Champion," 723; and Janken, *Walter White*, 247. On Anderson's many awards, honors, and honorary degrees, see Janet L. Sims, *Marian Anderson: An Annotated Bibliography and Discography* (Westport, CT: Greenwood, 1981), 193–218; and boxes 482–87, MAP.

35. Charles C. Cohen to Sol Hurok, January 19, 1939; Sol Hurok to Fred Hand, January 23, 1939 (first and second quotations); Fred Hand to Sol Hurok, January 25, 1939 (third quotation); Sol Hurok to Charles C. Cohen, January 25, 1939, all in box 412, MAP. Keiler, *Marian Anderson*, 192–93; Robinson, *Last Impresario*, 228–30, 232; Hurok, *Impresario*, 256; Anderson, *Daughters*, 113, 120; Margaret Gibbs, *The DAR* (New York: Holt, Rinehart and Winston, 1969), 161; and

Carleton Smith, "Roulades and Cadenzas," *Esquire*, 12 (July 1939): 79, 167–68. See also the DAR's version of the escalating controversy of January and February 1939 in *Statement re Constitution Hall* (Washington, D.C.: Daughters of the American Revolution, 1966), 2.

36. Sol Hurok to Mrs. H. M. Robert Jr., January 27, 1939 (first quotation), in box 412, MAP; *Philadelphia Independent*, February 5, 1939, in box 408, MAP; Walter White to the Board of Management, DAR, January 31, 1939, Group II, Marian Anderson General 1938–1939, box L2, NAACPP (second quotation); Keiler, *Marian Anderson*, 195–96; Anderson, *Daughters*, 113–14, 119; and Janken, *Walter White*, 247.

37. Harold Ickes to Mrs. H. M. Robert Jr., January 30, 1939 (quotation), Record Group 48, I-280, Racial Discrimination, DIP; Anderson, *Daughters*, 113–14; Keiler, *Marian Anderson*, 195; and *New York Times*, March 3, 1939.

38. Keiler, *Marian Anderson*, 182–84; Anderson, *Daughters*, 8–10, 115, 123–24; Gibbs, *DAR*, 5, 160; Anne S. Musgrave, "Sarah Corbin Robert: President General, 1938–1941," *Daughters of the American Revolution Magazine* 106 (October 1972): 772–73, 828; and *Who Was Who in America*, vol. 5, 1969–73 (Chicago: Marquis, 1973), 610. Robert was born on August 26, 1886, and died at her home in Annapolis, Maryland, on May 3, 1972. On the career of the noted military engineer and parliamentarian, Brigadier General Henry Martyn Robert Sr. (1837–1923), see Don H. Doyle, "Henry Martyn Robert and the Popularization of American Parliamentary Law," *American Quarterly* 32 (Spring 1980): 3–18. Born in Robertville, South Carolina, General Robert was a son of the Baptist minister and abolitionist Joseph Thomas Robert, the first president of Augusta Institute, a school for freed slaves that evolved into Morehouse College in Atlanta.

39. Anderson, *Daughters*, 115 (first quotation), 120–21, 132; Keiler, *Marian Anderson*, 196–97; Hurok, *Impresario*, 256 (second quotation); Mrs. Henry M. Robert Jr. to Sol Hurok, February 3, 1939, in box 412, MAP; Smith, "Roulades and Cadenzas," 79, 167.

40. Sol Hurok to Charles C. Cohen, February 7, 1939; and Sol Hurok to Mrs. Frank L. Nason, Registrar-General, DAR, February 28, 1939, both in box 412, MAP. Keiler, *Marian Anderson*, 198; Anderson, *Daughters*, 115, 119–20; Robinson, *Last Impresario*, 230; Patrick Hayes, "White Artists Only," *Washingtonian*, April 1989, 98; and Hurok, *Impresario*, 256–57.

41. Keiler, *Marian Anderson*, 190, 199; Anderson, *Daughters*, 138; Cohen to Hurok, January 19, 1939; "The D. A. R. versus Marian Anderson," 3; and Hurok, *Impresario*, 257.

42. "Extract from Stenographic Record . . . Board of Education Meeting, March 1, 1939"; Frank W. Ballou, "Statement on the Application for the Use of Central High School Auditorium for a Recital by Miss Marian Anderson," February 28, 1939, transcript in folder 38, box 1-2, MA-DARCC (quotation); Keiler, *Marian*

Anderson, 197–99; Anderson, *Daughters*, 116; Green, *Secret City*, 211, 246–48; and Hurok, *Impresario*, 257.

43. Elizabeth Peeples to Charles C. Cohen, February 3, 1939, folder 27, box 1-1, MA-DARCC (quotation); and Keiler, *Marian Anderson*, 191–92, 199–200.

44. Charles C. Cohen, Gustav Ausenne, Dorothy Cline, Glenn Dillard Gunn, and Doxey A. Wilkerson to District of Columbia Board of Education, memorandum, February 15, 1939, folder 21, box 1-1, MA-DARCC; "Chronology: Marian Anderson Concert Case," March 26, 1939, folder 33, box 1-2, MA-DARCC; and Keiler, *Marian Anderson*, 200.

45. Sol Hurok to Charles C. Cohen, February 7, 1939, in box 412, MAP; Charles C. Cohen to Fred Hand, February 8, 1939, folder 27; Fred Hand to Charles C. Cohen, February 10, 1939 (first quotation), folder 27; and memorandum from Mrs. Henry M. Robert Jr., February 13, 1939, folder 25, all in box 1-1, MA-DARCC. Robinson, *Last Impresario*, 230 (second quotation); Hayes, "White Artists Only," 98; Keiler, *Marian Anderson*, 197–98 (third quotation); Anderson, *Daughters*, 116, 123; Gibbs, *DAR*, 161–63, 165; and Martha Strayer, *The D. A. R.: An Informal History* (Washington: Public Affairs Press, 1958), 83.

46. Charles C. Cohen et al. to Board of Education, memorandum, February 15, 1939 (quotations); Keiler, *Marian Anderson*, 200; Robinson, *Last Impresario*, 233; Hayes, "White Artists Only," 99–100 (quotation); NAACP press release, typescript, February 17, 1939, in folder 44, box 1-2, MA-DARCC (White quotation).

47. Washington Agency, North Carolina Mutual Life Insurance Company to Frank Ballou, February 17, 1939 (first quotation), in folder 20; and John Lovell to West Hamilton, February 19, 1939 (second and third quotations), in folder 13, both in Box 1-1, MA-DARCC. "To the Board of Education of the District of Columbia," February 18, 1939, typescript of resolution (fourth quotation), in folder 35; "Resolution of censure against John H. Wilson," in folder 40; and "Chronology," in folder 33, all in Box 1-2, MA-DARCC. Keiler, *Marian Anderson*, 200; Black, "Championing a Champion," 723–24; Smith, "Roulades and Cadenzas," 167.

48. Keiler, *Marian Anderson*, 191–92, 200–201. Houston served on the District of Columbia School Board from 1933 to 1935, following in the footsteps of his father, William Houston, who was a member of the board from 1921 to 1924. Genna Rae McNeil, *Groundwork: Charles Hamilton Houston and the Struggle for Civil Rights* (Philadelphia University of Pennsylvania Press, 1983), 123–25. On Houston's role as chair of the MACC, see the correspondence in folders 4–11, box 1-1, MA-DARCC. The correspondence related to John Lovell's role as secretary is in folders 13 and 14, box 1-1, MA-DARCC. See also Abram L. Harris, "Open Letter to the Post," February 23, 1939, folder 19, box 1-1, MA-DARCC; Hayes, "White Artists Only," 100; and *Washington Post*, February 26, 1939.

49. On the press coverage of the Anderson controversy in February and March 1939, see the various typescripts "Expressions Through the Press," in folder 44, box 1-2, MA-DARCC. See also the voluminous clippings organized by V. D. Johnston, available on microfilm on rolls A, B, and C, box 1-3, MA-DARCC. See especially *Washington Post*, February 21, 1939; *Philadelphia Record*, February 21, 1939; *Washington Daily News*, February 16, 1939; *Central Bulletin* (Central High School), March 3, 1939; and the NAACP press release, February 17, 1939, all in folder 44. John Lovell Jr. to *Washington Post*, February 21, 1939 (quotations), in folder 14, box 1-1, MA-DARCC; Keiler, *Marian Anderson*, 194–95; and Black, "Championing a Champion," 723.

50. Keiler, *Marian Anderson*, 201; Anderson, *Daughters*, 116; DEFEND OUR DEMOCRATIC RIGHT . . . , February 26, 1939, broadside (first quotation), folder 45, box 1-2, MA-DARCC; and *Washington Daily News*, February 28, 1939. *Philadelphia Evening Bulletin*, February 21, 1939 (second, third, and fourth quotations), box 408, MAP. On the Heifetz incident, see "Heifetz Ashamed" typescript, "Expressions Through the Press," folder 44, box 1-2, MA-DARCC; *Washington Post*, February 20, 1939; *Daily Worker*, February 21, 1939 (fifth quotation), box 408, MAP; and Hurok, *Impresario*, 257. On the organizational endorsements and petition efforts of the MACC in late February, see folders 13 and 14, box 1-1, and folders 40–43, box 1-2, MA-DARCC. See also Black, "Championing the Champion," 724; Keiler, *Marian Anderson*, 201–2; Janken, *Walter White*, 246–47; Eleanor Roosevelt to V. D. Johnston, February 9, 1939; and John Lovell Jr. to Eleanor Roosevelt, February 25, 1939, both in box 1505–07, ER. "Chronology," folder 33, box 1-2, MA-DARCC.

51. *Pittsburgh Courier*, February 4, 1939; *New York Times*, February 23, 1939; Anderson, *Daughters*, 114, 120; Keiler, *Marian Anderson*, 196; and "Expressions Through the Press," folder 44, box 1-2, MA-DARCC. On the local focus of the MACC's early activities, see the correspondence of Houston and Lovell in folders 4–11, and 13–14, box 1-1, MA-DARCC.

52. Hurok, *Impresario*, 258; Robinson, *Last Impresario*, 236 (quotation); Keiler, *Marian Anderson*, 207; *Washington Post*, February 18, 1939; *Washington Afro-American*, February 25, 1939.

53. Black, "Championing the Champion," 724; Keiler, *Marian Anderson*, 201–2; and Janken, *Walter White*, 246–47. Eleanor Roosevelt to V. D. Johnston, February 9, 1939; and John Lovell Jr. to Eleanor Roosevelt, February 25, 1939, both in box 1505–07, ER.

54. Eleanor Roosevelt to John Lovell Jr., February 26, 1939 (first quotation), folder 14, box 1-1, MA-DARCC; Eleanor Roosevelt to Mrs. Henry M. Robert Jr., February 26, 1939, box 1521–22, series 100, 1939, ER; *My Day* column, February 27, 1939 (second quotation), box 3145, ER; *New York Times*, February 28, 1939; *New York World-Telegram*, February 27, 1939; *New York Herald Tribune*, February 28, 1939;

Black, "Championing the Champion," 724–26; Keiler, *Marian Anderson*, 202; Hurok, *Impresario*, 257–58; and Anderson, *Daughters*, 117.

55. Maurine Beasley, *The White House Press Conferences of Eleanor Roosevelt* (New York: Garland, 1983), 92–93 (first and second quotations); *New York Times*, February 28, 1939; Eleanor Roosevelt to Mrs. Henry M. Robert Jr., February 26, 1939 (third quotation); Mrs. Henry Robert Jr. to Eleanor Roosevelt, c. March 1, 1939 (fourth quotation), box 1521-22, series 100, 1939, ER; Keiler, *Marian Anderson*, 202; and Robinson, *Last Impresario*, 233–34.

56. *New York Times*, March 16, April 17–18, 21, 1933, April 17, 21, 1934; Anderson, *Daughters*, 117 (quotation); Black, "Championing a Champion," 719, 724; *Washington Post*, February 28, 1939; and Gibbs, *DAR*, 166.

57. Gibbs, *DAR*, 163, 165; Anderson, *Daughters*, 117, 119, 143; and Keiler, *Marian Anderson*, 202. *New York Times*, February 28, March 1, 1939; *Washington Post*, February 28, 1939; Hurok, *Impresario*, 257–58; *Philadelphia Tribune*, March 2 (third quotation), 10 (first quotation), 1939; *Pittsburgh Courier*, March 4 (second quotation), 18, 1939; *New York World-Telegram*, February 27–28, 1939; *New York Sun*, February 27, 1939; *New York Post*, February 28, 1939; *Philadelphia Record*, February 28, 1939; and *Philadelphia Evening Bulletin*, February 28, 1939, all in box 408, MAP. See also Arthur Huff Fauset, *For Freedom* (Philadelphia: Franklin Publishing and Supply Co., 1927), 129–35; and Elmer A. Carter, "The Ladies of the D. A. R.," *Opportunity* 17 (March 1939): 67.

58. Smith, "Roulades and Cadenzas" (quotation); Anderson, *Daughters*, 117; and Black, "Championing a Champion," 726. On the national press response to the resignation, see "Expressions from the Press," six typescripts in folder 44, box 1-2, MA-DARCC.

59. *New York Times*, March 1, 1939 (quotation); Anderson, *Daughters*, 117, 119; Hurok, *Impresario*, 258; and Keiler, *Marian Anderson*, 202.

60. *New York World-Telegram*, February 29, 1939 (quotation); *Philadelphia Record*, March 1, 1939; and *Washington News*, March 1, 1939, all in box 408, MAP. On Broun, see John O'Connor, *Heywood Broun, A Biography: The Life and Career of the Most Famous and Controversial Journalist of His Time* (New York: G. P. Putnam's, 1975).

61. *Newark Evening News*, March 1, 1939 (first and second quotations), folder 44, box 1-2, MA-DARCC; *Philadelphia Record*, February 28, 1939 (third quotation), box 408, MAP.

62. *Cleveland Plain Dealer*, March 1, 1939 (first quotation); and *New Yorker*, March 4, 1939 (third quotation), both in "Expressions Through the Press," folder 44, box 1-2, MA-DARCC. *Washington Post*, March 7, 1939 (second quotation); *New York Daily News*, March 3, 1939; and *Philadelphia Afro-American*, March 4, 1939, all in box 408, MAP. Anderson, *Daughters*, 119; and Janken, *Walter White*, 246.

63. *Boston Evening Transcript*, February 28, 1939 (quotations), in "Expressions Through the Press," folder 44, box 1-2, MA-DARCC.

64. *Springfield Daily Republican*, February 28, 1939 (quotation), in "Expressions Through the Press," folder 44, box 1-2, MA-DARCC. Despite its name, the *Springfield Daily Republican* did not support the Republican Party in 1939.

65. *Ocala Banner*, March 8, 1939 (first quotation); *Montgomery Advertiser*, February 28, 1939 (second quotation); and *Greenville Delta Democrat-Times*, March 11, 1939 (third quotation), all in "Expressions Through the Press," folder 44, box 1-2, MA-DARCC. The *Montgomery Advertiser* editorial was written by Grover C. Hall Sr., who won a Pulitzer Prize in 1928 for his coverage of the Ku Klux Klan. See Daniel Webster Hollis, *An Alabama Newspaper Tradition: Grover C. Hall and the Hall Family* (University: University of Alabama Press, 1983. The editorial in the *Greenville Delta Democrat-Times* was written by Hodding Carter, one of the South's most prominent "liberal" journalists. See Hodding Carter, *Southern Legacy* (Baton Rouge: Louisiana State University Press, 1950); Hodding Carter, *Where Main Street Meets the River* (New York: Rinehart, 1953); and Ann Waldron, *Hodding Carter: The Reconstruction of a Racist* (Chapel Hill: Algonquin Books, 1993). On Hall, Carter, and other moderate and liberal Southern journalists of the 1920s and 1930s, see John T. Kneebone, *Southern Liberal Journalists and the Issue of Race, 1920–1944* (Chapel Hill: University of North Carolina Press, 1985); and Egerton, *Speak Now Against the Day*, 248–64.

66. *Richmond Times-Dispatch*, March 1, 1939 (quotation), in "Expressions Through the Press," folder 44, box 1-2, MA-DARCC. During the 1930s, Dabney was considered the "dean" of liberal Southern journalists. See Virginius Dabney, *Liberalism in the South* (Chapel Hill: University of North Carolina Press, 1932); Virginius Dabney, *Below the Potomac: A Book about the New South* (New York: D. Appleton-Century, 1942); and Egerton, *Speak Now Against the Day*, 137–39.

67. *Charleston News and Courier*, March 1, 1939 (quotation), in "Expressions Through the Press," folder 44, box 1-2, MA-DARCC. *Dallas Daily Texan*, March 23, 1939; and *New York Post*, March 2, 1939, both in box 408, MAP.

68. *New York Times*, March 2 (third quotation), 17 (first and second quotations), 27 (fourth quotation), 1939. William Borah to Charles Houston, March 3, 1939 (fifth quotation), folder 4; and Fiorello La Guardia to John Lovell Jr., February 27, 1939, folder 13, both in box 1-1, MA-DARCC. *New York Herald Tribune*, March 2, 1939; and *Philadelphia Independent*, March 2, 1939, both in box 408, MAP. Hurok, *Impresario*, 258. On the correspondence between the MACC and liberal Northern politicians, see folder 1, box 1-1, MA-DARCC. One exception to the silence among conservative Southern politicians was Senator Allen J. Ellender of Louisiana, who objected to Secretary Harold Ickes's decision to permit the Anderson concert organizers to use the Lincoln Memorial. *New York Times*, April 8, 1939.

69. *Philadelphia Tribune,* March 16, 1939, box 408, MAP. Joseph A. Gavagan to Charles Houston, telegram, March 25, 1939 (first quotation), folder 5; Charles Houston to Adolph A. Berle, March 4 and 5, 1939, folder 4; Charles Houston to Robert M. La Follette, February 23, 25, and March 7, 1939, folder 7; Robert M. La Follette to Charles Houston, February 24, 1939, folder 7, all in box 1-1, MA-DARCC. *New York Times,* March 20, 1939 (second and third quotations). *Washington Times-Herald,* March 29, 1939; and *Washington Daily News,* March 1, 1939, both in box 408, MAP. Hayes, "White Artists Only," 99. On Cutting, see Richard Lowitt, *Bronson M. Cutting: A Progressive Politician* (Albuquerque: University of New Mexico Press, 1992).

70. Henry Cabot Lodge Jr. to Mrs. Butler R. Wilson, March 1, 1939, folder 19, box 1-1, MA-DARCC; *Washington Post,* March 19, 1939; *New York Times,* March 19, 1939 (quotations); Keiler, *Marian Anderson,* 202–3; Robinson, *Last Impresario,* 235; and Anderson, *Daughters,* 118.

71. Hurok, *Impresario,* 256–57; Robinson, *Last Impresario,* 230–35, 234 (first quotation); Keiler, *Marian Anderson,* 193 (second quotation); and Anderson, *Daughters,* 144–46.

72. Hurok, *Impresario,* 260; Keiler, *Marian Anderson,* 203 (first quotation)–4; *New York Times,* February 28, 1939 (second quotation); Anderson, *Daughters,* 147; Vehanen, *Marian Anderson,* 224–26; and Anderson, *My Lord,* 185 (third quotation). *New York Herald Tribune,* March 1, 1939; and *Philadelphia Afro-American,* March 18, 1939, both in box 408, MAP.

73. Anderson, *Daughters,* 46–47, 121–24; Strayer, *D. A. R.,* 83; and Hurok, *Impresario,* 258. *Philadelphia Inquirer,* March 4, 1939; *New York Daily News,* March 23, 1939; *Philadelphia Tribune,* March 10, 1939; *Pittsburgh Courier,* March 18, 1939 (first quotation); *New York Daily Mirror,* March 2, 1939; *Philadelphia Afro-American,* March 18, 1939 (second quotation), all in box 408, MAP. Carolyn Punderson to Sol Hurok, February 25, 1939, box 412, MAP; and *New York Times,* March 2, 20, 1939.

74. *New York World-Telegram,* March 8, 1939; and *Washington Times-Herald,* March 30, 1939 (first quotation), both in box 408, MAP. "Protests on Marian Anderson, the D. A. R. and Democracy," *News from the Rand School of Social Science,* March 10, 1939 (second quotation), box 412, MAP; *Washington Post,* April 23, 1939; Anderson, *Daughters,* 121–25; Robinson, *Last Impresario,* 258; and Hurok, *Impresario,* 258.

75. Keiler, *Marian Anderson,* 205; "Extract from Stenographic Record . . . Meeting of Board of Education held March 1, 1939" (quotations). See folder 42, box 1-2, MA-DARCC, for material on the petitions presented to the board on March 1, 1939. The Central High School PTA sanctioned the School Board's ban. *Washington Daily News,* February 3, 1939.

76. Ballou, "Statement on the Application for the Use of Central High School . . . ," February 28, 1939; "Report of Committee of the Board of Education on the Community Use of Buildings, March 3, 1939" (first and second quotations),

folder 33, box 1-1; and Elizabeth Peeples to Charles Cohen, March 6, 1939, folder 27, box 1-1, MA-DARCC. *Washington Star*, May 4, 1939; *Washington Post*, March 2–4, 1939; *New York Times*, March 4, 1939; *New York Daily News*, March 4, 1939; *Pittsburgh Courier*, March 11, 1939; Charles Houston to Walter White and Hubert Delany, March 4, 1939, memorandum (third and fourth quotations), Group II, Marian Anderson, Central High School Conflict 1939, box L1, NAACPP; Keiler, *Marian Anderson*, 205–6; Anderson, *Daughters*, 118; Robinson, *Last Impresario*, 233.

77. *Washington Star*, March 12, 1939. Anson Phelps Stokes to Frank Ballou, March 10, 1939; and Anson Phelps Stokes to Charles Houston, March 25, 1939, both in folder 10, box 1-1, MA-DARCC. Walter White to Charles Houston, March 6, 1939 (quotation); Charles Houston to Board of Education, March 9, 1939, folder 4, box 1-1, MA-DARCC; Walter White to Charles Houston and V. D. Johnston, March 21, 1939, Group 1, General Correspondence, March 17–23, 1939, box C-59, NAACPP; Keiler, *Marian Anderson*, 206–7; and Anderson, *Daughters*, 117–18, 142.

78. Walter White to Sol Hurok, March 13, 1939; and Walter White to Charles Houston, March 13, 1939, both in folder 11. Lulu Childers, Madeline Coleman, and Charles Cohen to the Board of Education of the District of Columbia, March 9, 1939, folder 29, all in box 1-1, MA-DARCC; Frank Ballou to Charles Cohen, March 17, 1939 (first quotation), box 412, MAP; *New York Times*, March 21, 1939 (second quotation); "Concert Plans Not Dead," MACC press release draft, March 18, 1939 (third quotation), folder 34, box 1-2, MA-DARCC; *New York Herald Tribune*, March 19, 1939; *Pittsburgh Courier*, March 25, April 1, 1939; *Washington Post*, March 27, 1939; and Keiler, *Marian Anderson*, 206–8.

CHAPTER 5: SWEET LAND OF LIBERTY

1. Scott A. Sandage, "A Marble House Divided: The Lincoln Memorial, the Civil Rights Movement, and the Politics of Memory, 1939–1963," *Journal of American History* 80 (June 1993): 135–36, noted the change in the third line from *I* to *we* after listening to the radio broadcast of the April 9, 1939, Lincoln Memorial concert. Sandage argues that "the change made the national hymn subtly political," but he offers no conclusions regarding Anderson's motivation. Neither Anderson nor any of her contemporaries commented on the change in 1939. Why she substituted the word *we* remains a mystery. The broadcast is available at the Division of Recorded Sound, Library of Congress. See "Marian Anderson Concert at the Lincoln Memorial," April 9, 1939, tape RWA-2850, NBC Radio Collection. On the historical significance of the song "America," see Robert James Branham and Stephen J. Hartnett, *Sweet Freedom's Song: "My Country 'Tis of Thee" and Democracy in America* (New York: Oxford University Press, 2002).

Samuel Francis Smith wrote the lyrics, and the music is based on the traditional British anthem "God Save the King."

2. *Houston Post*, March 24, 1939; *Houston Chronicle*, March 24, 1939; and *Pittsburgh Courier*, March 25, 1939, all in box 408, MAP. Walter White, NAACP memorandum, March 22, 1939, quoted in Allan Keiler, *Marian Anderson: A Singer's Journey* (New York: Simon and Schuster, 2000), 208; and Peggy Anderson, *The Daughters: An Unconventional Look at America's Fan Club—the DAR* (New York: St. Martin's, 1974), 138, 147–48.

3. *Philadelphia Record*, February 28, 1939, box 408, MAP; Anderson, *Daughters*, 116; Keiler, *Marian Anderson*, 207; Sol Hurok with Ruth Goode, *Impresario: A Memoir* (New York: Random House, 1946), 258; Walter White to Charles Houston, March 21, 1939 (quotation), Group II, General Correspondence, box C-59, NAACPP.

4. Walter White to Houston, March 21, 1939; "Compromise in Ban on Marian Anderson," *Crisis* 46 (April 1939): 117; minutes, NAACP Board of Directors meeting, March 13, 1939, Group II, box L2, NAACPP; *New York Times*, March 21, 1939; *Washington Star*, March 30, 1939; Keiler, *Marian Anderson*, 206–8; Anderson, *Daughters*, 146; Harlow Robinson, *The Last Impresario: The Life, Times, and Legacy of Sol Hurok* (New York: Viking Penguin, 1994), 236–37; Kenneth Robert Janken, *Walter White: Mr. NAACP* (Chapel Hill: University of North Carolina Press, 2006), 247–48; T. H. Watkins, *Righteous Pilgrim: The Life and Times of Harold L. Ickes, 1874–1952* (New York: Henry Holt, 1990), 650–51; Allida M. Black, "Championing a Champion, Eleanor Roosevelt and the Marian Anderson 'Freedom Concert,'" *Presidential Studies Quarterly* 20, no. 4 (1990): 726; and Sandage, "Marble House Divided," 144. For an insightful history of the Lincoln Memorial as the site of public memory and protest from 1939 to 1963, see Sandage, "Marble House Divided," 135–67.

5. Walter White to Sol Hurok, March 13, 1939 (quotation), Group II, box L1, Marian Anderson Central High School Conflict 1939, NAACPP; and Keiler, *Marian Anderson*, 208.

6. *New York Times*, March 21, 1939 (first quotation); Walter White, *A Man Called White: The Autobiography of Walter White* (New York: Viking, 1948), 181 (second quotation); Black, "Championing a Champion," 726; Anderson, *Daughters*, 144; Sandage, "Marble House Divided," 136–43 (third quotation); Merrill D. Peterson, *Lincoln in American Memory* (New York: Oxford University Press, 1994), 195–255; and Roy P. Basler, *The Lincoln Legend: A Study in Changing Conceptions* (Boston: Houghton Mifflin, 1935).

7. Sandage, "Marble House Divided," 141 (quotations); Peterson, *Lincoln in American Memory*, 214–17; *Washington Post*, May 31, 1922; *New York Times*, May 31, 1922; and *Chicago Defender*, June 10, 1922. On French (1850-1931), see Michael Richman, Daniel Chester French, and the Metropolitan Museum of Art, *Dan-*

iel Chester French: An American Sculptor (Washington, DC: Preservation Books, 1983); and Margaret French Cresson, *The Life of Daniel Chester French: Journey into Fame* (Cambridge: Harvard University Press, 1947). On Moton (1867-1940), see William Hardin Hughes and Frederick D. Peterson, *Robert Russa Moton of Hampton and Tuskegee* (Chapel Hill: University of North Carolina Press, 1956); Robert Russa Moton, *What the Negro Thinks* (New York: Doubleday, 1929); and Robert Russa Moton, *Finding a Way Out: An Autobiography* (Garden City, NY: Doubleday, Page, 1921).

8. "Lincoln, Harding, James Crow, and Taft," *Crisis* 24 (July 1922): 122; *Chicago Defender*, June 10, 1922; Sandage, "Marble House Divided," 141–42; and Peterson, *Lincoln in American Memory*, 255–310. See also Richard N. Current, *Speaking of Abraham Lincoln: The Man and His Meaning for Our Times* (Urbana: University of Illinois Press, 1983). On the dramatic upsurge in Franklin Roosevelt's black electoral support in 1936, see Nancy J. Weiss, *Farewell to the Party of Lincoln: Black Politics in the Age of FDR* (Princeton: Princeton University Press, 1983), 180–235.

9. "Protest Meeting," March 26, 1939, broadside, folder 45, box 1-2, MA-DARCC. Robert F. Wagner to Oscar Chapman, March 24, 1939, folder 22; and V. D. Johnston to Oscar Chapman, March 31, 1939, folder 28, both in box 1-1, MA-DARCC. Walter White to Marian Anderson, April 4, 1939 (first quotation), box 97, MAP; Keiler, *Marian Anderson*, 208; Watkins, *Righteous Pilgrim*, 651 (second quotation); Jeanne Nienaber Clarke, *Roosevelt's Warrior: Harold L. Ickes and the New Deal* (Baltimore: Johns Hopkins University Press, 1996), 312; Joseph P. Lash, *Eleanor and Franklin* (New York: W. W. Norton, 1971), 527; Sandage, "Marble House Divided," 135, 144; Robinson, *Last Impresario*, 236–37; Hurok, *Impresario*, 258–59; White, *A Man Called White*, 181–82; and Anderson, *Daughters*, 116–17.

10. Clarke, *Roosevelt's Warrior*, 312–13 (first quotation); Watkins, *Righteous Pilgrim*, 651; Black, "Championing the Champion," 726; White, *A Man Called White*, 182 (second quotation); Keiler, *Marian Anderson*, 208–9; Harold L. Ickes, *The Secret Diary of Harold L. Ickes*, vol. 2, *The Inside Struggle, 1936–1939* (New York: Simon and Schuster, 1954), 612–13; Patrick Hayes, "White Artists Only," *Washingtonian*, April 1989, 101; and Sandage, "Marble House Divided," 144 (third quotation).

11. *New York Times*, March 31, 1939; *New York Herald Tribune*, March 31, 1939; Keiler, *Marian Anderson*, 209; and Anderson, *Daughters*, 118.

12. Keiler, *Marian Anderson*, 209; White, *A Man Called White*, 182 (quotations); Janken, *Walter White*, 248; Anderson, *Daughters*, 117, 145, 148; Hurok, *Impresario*, 259; Black, "Championing a Champion," 727; Hayes, "White Artists Only," 101; and Robinson, *Last Impresario*, 238. Charles Houston to Walter White, April 26, 1939, folder 11, box 1-1, MA-DARCC, notes Hurok's claim that he had lost $2,500 sponsoring the Lincoln Memorial concert.

13. White, *A Man Called White*, 182 (first quotation); Keiler, *Marian Anderson*, 209; Black, "Championing the Champion," 727; and Ickes, *Secret Diary*, 2: 613. See the sponsorship telegrams (second quotation) in folder 24, box 1-1, MA-DARCC.

14. Telegrams, folder 24, box 1-1, MA-DARCC; Lincoln Memorial concert program, April 9, 1939, folder 47, box 1-2, MA-DARCC. The program is also available in box 412, MAP. The sponsors are listed on the program. *New York Times*, April 5, 1939; *Washington Daily News*, April 3, 1939; Robinson, *Last Impresario*, 238; Keiler, *Marian Anderson*, 209; and Watkins, *Righteous Pilgrim*, 651. On the high-profile senators who agreed to serve as sponsors, see Steve Suitts, *Hugo Black of Alabama: How His Roots and Early Career Shaped the Great Champion of the Constitution* (Montgomery: NewSouth Books, 2005); Patrick J. Maney, *Young Bob: A Biography of Robert M. La Follette, Jr.* (Madison: University of Wisconsin Press, 2002); Richart Lowitt, *George W. Norris: The Persistence of a Progressive, 1913–1933* (Urbana: University of Illinois Press, 1971); Norman L. Zucker, *George W. Norris: Gentle Knight of American Democracy* (Urbana: University of Illinois Press, 1966); and Homer E. Socolofsky, *Arthur Capper: Publisher, Politician, and Philanthropist* (Lawrence: University of Kansas Press, 1962).

15. Ickes, *Secret Diary*, 2: 613 (quotation), 616–17, 654; White, *A Man Called White*, 183; Clarke, *Roosevelt's Warrior*, 313–14; Robinson, *Last Impresario*, 239; Lash, *Eleanor and Franklin*, 528; Watkins, *Righteous Pilgrim*, 651; and Drew Pearson and Robert S. Allen, "Washington Daily Merry Go-Round," *Washington Times Herald*, April 10, 1939. Vice President Garner was considered to be a leading candidate for the 1940 Democratic presidential nomination. Ickes and President Roosevelt, both strongly opposed to Garner's nomination, privately rejoiced when Garner, a staunch segregationist, was caught off guard by the Anderson affair. On Garner, see Bascom M. Timmons, *Garner of Texas: A Personal History* (New York: Harper and Brothers, 1948); Marquis James, *Mr. Garner of Texas* (Indianapolis: Bobbs-Merrill, 1939); and O. C. Fisher, *Cactus Jack: A Biography of John Nance Garner* (Waco: Texian Press, 1982).

16. Lincoln Memorial concert program, folder 47, box 1-2, MA-DARCC; and White, *A Man Called White*, 183 (quotation).

17. Lincoln Memorial concert program (quotations); Keiler, *Marian Anderson*, 210; Sandage, "Marble House Divided," 144–45; and Robinson, *Last Impresario*, 238.

18. Gerald Goode to Walter White, March 31, 1939, folder 5; and Walter White to Charles Houston and V. D. Johnston, March 31, 1939 (quotation), folder 11, both in box 1-1, MA-DARCC. Keiler, *Marian Anderson*, 210; Sandage, "Marble House Divided," 144–45.

19. Kosti Vehanen, *Marian Anderson: A Portrait* (New York: McGraw-Hill, 1941), 237–38; and Marian Anderson, *My Lord, What a Morning: An Autobiography* (New York: Viking Press, 1956), 189.

20. Anderson, *My Lord*, 188–90 (quotations).

21. *Washington Daily News*, April 4, 1939; White to Houston and V. D. Johnston, March 31, 1939 (quotation); Keiler, *Marian Anderson*, 209–10; Hurok, *Impresario*, 259; Black, "Championing the Champion," 727; Robinson, *Last Impresario*, 238; and Clarke, *Roosevelt's Warrior*, 320.

22. Vehanen, *Marian Anderson*, 241–42 Robert L. Carter, *A Matter of Law: A Memoir of Struggle in the Cause of Civil Rights* (New York: New Press, 2005), 27–28 (first quotation); Raymond Sanderlin, interview by author, November 17, 2008; Willis was later a Tuskegee airman and Harvard professor, Ray a prominent Washington teacher, and Jim an NAACP attorney and Florida state judge. Ickes, *Secret Diary*, 2: 615 (second quotation); and Anderson, *My Lord*, 185–87 (quotation). On Rupp, see Anderson, *My Lord*, 228–38, 245; and Keiler, *Marian Anderson*, 225–27.

23. Anderson, *My Lord*, 187 (quotation), 190; Vehanen, *Marian Anderson*, 241–42; Hurok, *Impresario*, 260; Keiler, *Marian Anderson*, 210–11; and Clarke, *Roosevelt's Warrior*, 314. On Gifford Pinchot (1865-1946), see Char Miller, *Gifford Pinchot and the Making of Modern Environmentalism* (Washington, DC: Island Press, 2001); and Gifford Pinchot, *Breaking New Ground* (Washington, DC: Island Press, 1998).

24. White, *A Man Called White*, 183 (first quotation); Anderson, *My Lord*, 190 (second and third quotations); *New York Times*, April 10, 1939; *Washington Post*, April 10, 1939; *Washington Star*, April 10, 1939; *Washington Daily News*, April 10, 1939; *New York Amsterdam News*, April 15, 1939; Hurok, *Impresario*, 260; Robinson, *Last Impresario*, 239; Vehanen, *Marian Anderson*, 242–44; Keiler, *Marian Anderson*, 211–12; Ickes, *Secret Diary*, 2: 614–15 (fourth quotation); Harold Ickes's speech, April 9, 1939, typescript (fifth quotation), box 412, MAP; Clarke, *Roosevelt's Warrior*, 315–16; and Graham White and John Maze, *Harold Ickes of the New Deal: His Private Life and Public Career* (Cambridge: Harvard University Press, 1985), 1–2. See also Harold Ickes to Sol Hurok, April 17, 1939, box 412, MAP; and Charles Houston to Harold Ickes, April 11, 1939, folder 6, box 1-1, MA-DARCC.

25. Vehanen, *Marian Anderson*, 244–45 (first quotation); Anderson, *My Lord*, 190–91 (second quotation); Keiler, *Marian Anderson*, 212; Hurok, *Impresario*, 261 (third quotation); and Barbara Klaw, "'A Voice One Hears Once in a Hundred Years': An Interview with Marian Anderson," *American Heritage* 28, no. 2 (1977): 56–57.

26. Sandage, "Marble House Divided," 135–36; and Keiler, *Marian Anderson*, 213.

27. Anderson, *My Lord*, 191–92 (quotation); Keiler, *Marian Anderson*, 56, 213; Robinson, *Last Impresario*, 239–40; and Anson Phelps Stokes, *Art and the Color Line* (Washington, D.C.: Phelps Stokes Foundation, 1939), 3–4.

28. White, *A Man Called White*, 184–85 (quotation); Anderson, *My Lord*, 191; Janken, *Walter White*, 248; and Keiler, *Marian Anderson*, 213.

29. Anderson, *My Lord*, 192 (first and second quotations); and *New York Times*,

April 10, 1939 (third quotation). Following the concert, Anderson and her mother were dinner guests at the Pennsylvania Avenue home of Dr. Milton and Beatrice Francis. Beatrice Francis to Marian Anderson, April 16, 1939, box 412, MAP.

30. Constance McLaughlin Green, *The Secret City: A History of Race Relations in the Nation's Capital* (Princeton: Princeton University Press, 1967), 249 (first quotation); Vehanen, *Marian Anderson*, 246; Robinson, *Last Impresario*, 240; Howard Taubman, *The Pleasure of Their Company: A Reminiscence* (Portland, OR: Amadeus, 1994), 307; Sandage, "Marble House Divided," 145–47; and Mary McLeod Bethune to Charles Houston, April 10, 1939 (second quotation), folder 4, box 1-1, MA-DARCC. For some examples of personal reactions to the concert, see J. Bernard McDowell to Marian Anderson, April 5, 1939; Lowell D. Hoxsey and family to Marian Anderson, April 10, 1939; Mabel Thomas Topping to Marian Anderson, c. April 15, 1939; and Ralph William Nixon, *The Lincoln Memorial: A Tribute in Verse* (Boston: Acorn, 1939) in Nixon to Marian Anderson, September 29, 1939, all in box 412, MAP.

31. *New York Times*, April 10, 1939; Robinson, *Last Impresario*, 238, 240; Hayes, "White Artists Only," 103; Black, "Championing the Champion," 728; and John Hope Franklin, interview by author, March 1, 2007 (first quotation). On Franklin, see *Mirror to America: The Autobiography of John Hope Franklin* (New York: Farrar, Straus and Giroux, 2005). Charles Houston, "To the Washington Public," memorandum, April 8, 1939 (second quotation), folder 35, box 1-2, MA-DARCC.

32. Anderson, *My Lord*, 194; Sandage, "Marble House Divided," 145, 148; Robinson, *Last Impresario*, 238; Janken, *Walter White*, 247; Hayes, "White Artists Only," 103; Gibbs, *DAR*, 166; Lash, *Eleanor and Franklin*, 527; Clarke, *Roosevelt's Warrior*, 315; Watkins, *Righteous Pilgrim*, 652 (White quotation); Mollie D. Somerville, *Eleanor Roosevelt as I Knew Her* (Charlottesville, VA: Howell Press, 1996), 148; James R. Kearney, *Anna Eleanor Roosevelt: The Evolution of a Reformer* (Boston: Houghton Mifflin, 1968), 91–94; Allida Black, conversation with author, March 28, 2008. For Eleanor Roosevelt's comings and goings in March and April 1939, see the "My Day" columns, March 6–April 24, 1939, in "My Day, by Eleanor Roosevelt: An Electronic Archive," available online at http://www.gwu.edu/~erpapers/my day. "Welcome to Marian Anderson," press release, c. April 15, 1939, box 412, MAP; Stokes, *Art and the Color Line*, 12–13; *Pittsburgh Courier*, April 15, 1939; *New York Age*, April 15, 1939; *Norfolk Journal and Guide*, April 15, 1939; *New York Amsterdam News*, April 8, 15, 1939; "Anderson Affair," *Time* 33 (April 17, 1939): 23; Anderson, *Daughters*, 144–45; Black, "Championing the Champion," 728; and *Chicago Daily News*, April 18, 1939 (O'Brien quotations), box 412, MAP. "Easter 1939, May Inspire Historians," *Washington Star*, April 6, 11, 1939 (quotation); and "Thank the DAR," *Washington Daily*

News, April 10, 1939 (quotation), both in folder 44, box 1-2, MA-DARCC. See also the voluminous newspaper clippings collected by V. D. Johnston in roll D, box 1-3, MA-DARCC. David Brinkley, *Washington Goes to War* (New York: Alfred A. Knopf, 1988), 19 (quotation). The New Negro Alliance won an important employment discrimination case in 1938. See *New Negro Alliance v. Sanitary Grocery Co.*, 303 U.S. 552 (1938).

33. *New York Times*, April 13, 17 (quotation), 24, May 26, 1939; and Keiler, *Marian Anderson*, 214–15.

34. *New York Times*, April 19, 1939, October 15, 1940. "Announcement of the Marian Anderson Mural Fund," press release, c. April 18, 1939 (quotation); and Walter White to Marian Anderson, April 29, 1939, both in box 412, MAP. Charles Houston to Edward Bruce, January 15, 1943, folder 4, box 1-1, MA-DARCC; Keiler, *Marian Anderson*, 214–15; and Janken, *Walter White*, 248.

35. Charles Houston and John Lovell Jr. to Mrs. Henry M. Robert Jr., April 13, 1939 (quotation), box 412, MAP. Charles Houston to Oscar Chapman, April 11, 1939, folder 4; Charles Houston to D.C. Board of Commissioners, April 20, 1939, folder 4; Charles Houston and John Lovell Jr. to DAR, April 17, 1939, folder 5; Walter White to Charles Houston, April 14, 1939, folder 11; G. M. Thornett to Charles Houston, April 28, 1939, folder 10, all in box 1-1, MA-DARCC. *New York Times*, April 17, 20, 1939; *Newark Ledger*, April 17, 1939; *Washington Star*, April 1, 1939; Victor R. Daly, "Washington's Minority Problem," *Crisis* 46 (June 1939): 170–71; and Keiler, *Marian Anderson*, 214.

36. Eleanor Roosevelt to Walter White, April 12, 1939 (first quotation), folder 11; John Lovell Jr. to Dear Friend, April 13, 1939 (second quotation), folder 18; Walter White to Charles Houston, April 14, 1939, folder 11; Eugene Davidson, Chair of MACC Picketing Committee, to Dear Friend, April 4, 1939, folder 18; Mary Church Terrell to Mr. Scott, April 12, 1939, folder 17; T. L. Hungate to MACC, April 18, 1939, folder 2; Henry Morgenthau Jr. to Bertha Blair, April 17, 1939, folder 2; Caroline O'Day to Bertha Blair, April 21, 1939, folder 2, all in box 1-1, MA-DARCC. MACC Executive Committee minutes, April 26, 1939, folder 33, box 1-2, MA-DARCC; *New York Times*, April 22, 1939; Lash, *Eleanor and Franklin*, 527; Janken, *Walter White*, 248–49; and Black, "Championing the Champion," 729–30.

37. See the protest letters in folders 1, 2, and 25, box 1-1, MA-DARCC. See especially Joseph Gavagan to Mrs. Henry M. Robert Jr., April 17, 1939; MACC to Mary Howe, April 18, 1939; and Carl Murphy to Mrs. Henry M. Robert Jr., April 25, 1939, all in folder 1. Walter White to DAR, telegram, April 17, 1939; Sol Hurok to Mrs. Henry M. Robert Jr., April 19, 1939, both in box 412, MAP. *New York Times*, April 17, 23, 1939; Anderson, *Daughters*, 120–22; and Clark and Mairi Foreman to Mrs. Henry M. Robert Jr., April 15, 1939 (quotation), folder

25, box 1-1, MA-DARCC. On Clark Foreman's family background, see Patricia Sullivan, *Days of Hope: Race and Democracy in the New Deal Era* (Chapel Hill: University of North Carolina Press, 1996), 25–26.

38. Charles Houston to Elwood H. Seal, April 20, 1939; and Charles Houston to Emmeline Street, April 20, 1939, both in folder 10, box 1-1, MA-DARCC. Anderson, *Daughters*, 110.

39. *Forty-Second Report of the National Society of the Daughters of the American Revolution, April 1, 1938, to April 1, 1939* (Washington: Government Printing Office, 1940), 23–24 (quotations); *New York Times*, April 19, 1939; Anderson, *Daughters*, 120–21, 129; and Margaret Gibbs, *The DAR* (New York: Holt, Rinehart and Winston, 1969), 165.

40. Anderson, *Daughters*, 121 (first quotation); and *Forty-Second Report of the National Society*, 24 (second quotation).

41. *Forty-Second Report of the National Society*, 25 (quotations); Anderson, *Daughters*, 110–11, 121–23; and Roy Wilkins, "The Real D. A. R.," *Crisis* 46 (May 1939): 145.

42. Keiler, *Marian Anderson*, 214. See Stokes, *Art and the Color Line*, for a comprehensive summary of the MACC's negotiations with the DAR in April and May 1939. See also Anson Phelps Stokes to Mrs. Henry M. Robert Jr., March 11, 1939, folder 25; Anson Phelps Stokes to John Lovell Jr., April 15, 1939, folder 14; Anson Phelps Stokes to Charles Houston, April 16, 1939 (quotation), folder 10; Charles Houston to Mrs. Henry M. Robert Jr., April 20, 1939, folder 9; Charles Houston and John Lovell Jr. to Mrs. Henry M. Robert Jr., April 19, 1939, folder 9; Mrs. Henry M. Robert Jr. to Charles Houston, May 20, 1939, folder 9; Doxey Wilkerson to Mrs. Henry M. Robert Jr., April 17, 1939, folder 25; and Anson Phelps Stokes to V. D. Johnston, December 4, 1939, folder 28, all in box 1-1, MA-DARCC.

43. Charles Houston to Marian Wade Doyle, April 6, 1939; Charles Houston to Mrs. Henry Grattan Doyle, April 17, 1939, both in folder 5; Vincent Nicholson to Frank W. Ballou, April 8, 1939, folder 8; and Charles Cohen to Sol Hurok, April 26, 1939, folder 27, all in box 1-1, MA-DARCC. *Washington Post*, March 27, 1939 (quotation); Green, *Secret City*, 250–312.

44. Stokes, *Art and the Color Line*, 4–12, 20–26; Mrs. Henry M. Robert Jr. to Charles Houston, May 20, 1939 (first quotation); Charles Houston to Mrs. Henry M. Robert Jr., May 28, 1939 (second quotation), both in folder 9; John Lovell Jr. to Charles Houston, June 1, 1939 (third quotation), folder 7; Charles Houston to John Lovell Jr., May 22, 1939, folder 7; John Lovell Jr. to Charles Houston, June 22, 1939, folder 7; and John Lovell Jr. to Mrs. Henry M. Robert Jr., May 27, 1939, folder 14, all in box 1-1, MA-DARCC. "Who's Who of the MACC Delegation," folder 31, box 1-2, MA-DARCC. See also the various letters written between August 14 to November 4, 1939, folder 10, box 1-1, MA-DARCC.

45. *New York Times*, May 28, 29, 31, June 4, 1939; *Philadelphia Afro-American*, March 25, 1939, box 408, MAP; Keiler, *Marian Anderson*, 215. Sandage, "Marble House Divided," 147–48, notes the irony that in 1940 Eleanor Roosevelt crossed a picket line to attend the premiere of the film *Abe Lincoln in Illinois*. The premiere was held at a segregated movie theater in Washington, but she chose to attend anyway. According to Raymond Massey, the star of the film, Mrs. Roosevelt ignored the protest because "the picketing organization was not approved by the NAACP." Raymond Massey, *A Hundred Different Lives: An Autobiography* (Boston: Little, Brown, 1970), 257.

46. Anderson, *My Lord*, 194 (quotation)–95; Vehanen, *Marian Anderson*, 220, 224–26; Hurok, *Impresario*, 245; Ickes, *Secret Diary*, 3: 644–47, 654; Eleanor Roosevelt, *This I Remember* (New York: Harper and Brothers, 1949), 187, 191; *New York Times*, June 9, 11, 1939; *Washington Tribune*, June 17, 1939; Maurine Beasley, *The White House Press Conferences of Eleanor Roosevelt* (New York: Garland, 1983), 105, 108; Mollie D. Sommerville, *Eleanor Roosevelt as I Knew Her* (Charlottesville, VA: Howell Press, 1996), 99–100; Lash, *Eleanor and Franklin*, 580; and Keiler, *Marian Anderson*, 215–16. The invitation was first announced in mid-March. *Pittsburgh Courier*, March 18, 1939; and *Philadelphia Afro-American*, March 18, 1939, both in box 408, MAP.

47. *New York Times*, July 3, 1939 (quotations); Walter White to Eleanor Roosevelt, June 13, 1939, ER; Walter White to Eleanor Roosevelt, June 20, 1939, Group 1, Annual Conference, 1939, NAACPP; Walter White to Franklin Delano Roosevelt, September 15, 1939, folder 19, box 1-1, MA-DARCC; NAACP 30th Annual Conference Program, Spingarn Medal, July 2, 1939, box 256, MAP; Black, "Championing a Champion," 730–31; Allida M. Black, *Casting Her Own Shadow: Eleanor Roosevelt and the Shaping of Postwar Liberalism* (New York: Columbia University Press, 1996), 43; Keiler, *Marian Anderson*, 216; and James R. Kearney, *Anna Eleanor Roosevelt: The Evolution of a Reformer* (Boston: Houghton Mifflin, 1968), 91–92.

48. *New York Times*, February 14, October 21, December 29, 1940 (quotation), June 25, 1941, January 6, December 10, 13, 1943; Hurok, *Impresario*, 246; and Keiler, *Marian Anderson*, 229. See also boxes 252 and 254, MAP.

49. *New York Times*, March 18 (quotations), 19, December 12, 1941; Anderson, *My Lord*, 275; Keiler, *Marian Anderson*, 229; Bok Award, March 17, 1941, box 256, MAP; Hurok, *Impresario*, 246; Howard Taubman, "Voice of a Race," *New York Times Magazine*, April 6, 1941, 9ff.

50. Hurok, *Impresario*, 287; *New York Times*, October 30, December 10, 1939, January 13, April 7, 14, May 27, July 19, 21, September 29, December 2, 1940; and Keiler, *Marian Anderson*, 224–25.

51. Keiler, *Marian Anderson*, 224; Anderson, *Daughters*, 143; Black, "Championing

a Champion," 731–32; Ickes, *Secret Diary*, 3: 362; and Arthur Krock, "The Fine and Very Liberal Arts Go Political," *New York Times*, November 5, 1940.

52. Thomas Cripps, *Making Movies Black: The Hollywood Message Movie from World War II to the Civil Rights Era* (New York: Oxford University Press, 1993), 35–125; Thomas Cripps and David Culbert, "The Negro Soldier (1944): Film Propaganda in Black and White," in Peter C. Rollins, ed., *Hollywood as Historian: American Film in a Cultural Context* (Lexington: University of Kentucky Press, 1983), 109–33; Chris Mead, *Champion: Joe Louis, Black Hero in White America* (New York: Charles Scribner's Sons, 1985), 203–36; Anderson, *My Lord*, 271 (quotation), 273; *New York Times*, December 14, 16, 1941, January 12, May 31, September 21, 1942, April 18, 1943, December 8, 13, 19, 1944, May 21, 1945; and Keiler, *Marian Anderson*, 233–34.

53. *New York Times*, September 30, 1942; *Washington Post*, September 30, 1942; and *Washington Star*, October 6, 1942. Walter White to Sol Hurok, telegram, October 1, 1942 (first quotation), and Walter White to Marian Anderson, telegram, October 1, 1942, both in part 15, reel 2, NAACPP (microfilm). Sol Hurok to Fred Hand, October 3, 1942 (second quotation), MAP, quoted in Keiler, *Marian Anderson*, 235; Anderson, *Daughters*, 133–34; and Gibbs, *DAR*, 166.

54. Keiler, *Marian Anderson*, 235–36 (first quotation); and Gerald Goode to Walter White, telegram, November 9, 1942 (second quotation), part 15, reel 2, NAACPP (microfilm).

55. *New York Times*, November 5 (first and second quotations), 7 (third quotation), 1942; *Washington Post*, November 5, December 17, 1942; Keiler, *Marian Anderson*, 237; and Anderson, *Daughters*, 133–34.

56. On the creation of the Marian Anderson mural, see folders 48 and 49, box 1-2, MA-DARCC; Marian Anderson mural program, January 6, 1943 (quotations), folder 48, box 1-2, MA-DARCC; *New York Times*, December 30, 1942; and Keiler, *Marian Anderson*, 238.

57. Anderson, *My Lord*, 193–94; Hurok, *Impresario*, 261; Keiler, *Marian Anderson*, 238; and Remarks, "delivered at the ceremony marking formal presentation to the Federal Government of the Marian Anderson Lincoln Memorial Concert mural painting," January 6, 1943, typescript, folder 49, box 1-2, MA-DARCC (quotations). Folder 48 includes the program, a photograph of the mural, and a list of donors to the "Marian Anderson Mural Gift."

58. Remarks, January 6, 1943 (quotations); Charles Houston to Helene Morse, January 15, 1943, folder 8, box 1-1; "Roster of the Double-Quartet of Negro Seamen, Great Lakes Naval Training Station," folder 48, box 1-2, all in MA-DARCC; *New York Times*, December 10, 30, 1942, January 4, 1943; Anderson, *Daughters*, 133–34; *Washington Star*, January 7, 1943; and *Washington Post*, January 7, 1943. The winning artist, Mitchell Jamieson, was an ensign in the U.S. navy at the

time of the ceremony. "Presentation of the Marian Anderson Mural Commemorating the Easter Sunday Concert of 1939," program, January 6, 1943,
folder 48, box 1-2, MA-DARCC.

59. Remarks, January 6, 1943 (quotations); Charles Houston to Edward Bruce,
January 15, 1939, folder 4, box 1-1, MA-DARCC; *Washington Star*, January 7,
1943; *Washington Post*, January 7, 10, 1943; and Sandage, "Marble House Divided," 151.

60. Remarks, January 6, 1943 (quotation); *New York Times*, January 4–6, 1943; Hurok, *Impresario*, 261; and Anderson, *My Lord*, 193.

61. Anderson, *My Lord*, 192–93 (first quotation); *New York Times*, January 8, 1943
(second quotation); *Washington Post*, January 8, 1943; Keiler, *Marian Anderson*,
238–39; Anderson, *Daughters*, 134; and Martha Strayer, *The D. A. R.: An Informal History* (Washington, DC: Public Affairs Press, 1958), 83. On Carver's
death, see Linda O. McMurry, *George Washington Carver: Scientist and Symbol*
(New York: Oxford University Press, 1981), 302–3.

62. "My Day," January 9, 1943 in http://www.gwu.edu/~erpapers/myday.

EPILOGUE: AN AMERICAN ICON, 1943–93

1. Marian Anderson, *My Lord, What a Morning* (New York: Viking, 1956), 309.

2. Ibid., 184–88, 192–93; and Howard Taubman, *The Pleasure of Their Company: A
Reminiscence* (Portland, OR: Amadeus Press, 1994), 307–13. Allan Keiler, *Marian
Anderson: A Singer's Journey* (New York: Simon and Schuster, 2000), 280, notes that
Anderson reacted negatively to the first draft of her autobiography, *My Lord, What
a Morning*, a manuscript based on interviews conducted by Howard Taubman.
Among other concerns, Anderson "wanted all mention of the Lincoln Memorial
concert removed." After consulting with her friend Rex Stout, who agreed to read
the manuscript, she relented. But she was never entirely comfortable with the tone
and content of the autobiography that was published under her name in 1956. The
original Taubman tapes, transcripts, and drafts are available in Ms. Coll. 201,
boxes 1–10, MAP. See also the draft with Anderson's corrections in box 140,
MAP. Emily Kimbrough, "My Life in a White World," *Ladies' Home Journal* 77
(1960): 54, 173–74, 176, copy in box 138, MAP; Barbara Klaw, "'A Voice One Hears
Once in a Hundred Years': An Interview with Marian Anderson," *American Heritage* 28, no. 2 (1977): 50–57; and Israel Shenker, "Marian Anderson," transcribed
interview and draft of Klaw article in *American Heritage*, box 139, MAP.

3. Alan Pomerance, *Repeal of the Blues: How Black Entertainers Influenced Civil
Rights* (New York: Citadel Press, 1991). On Belafonte's civil rights activism, see
Raymond Arsenault, *Freedom Riders: 1961 and the Struggle for Racial Justice*
(New York: Oxford University Press, 2006), 76, 265, 330, 396, 446, 450.

4. Keiler, *Marian Anderson*, 218–32, 239–319; and Taubman, *Pleasure of Their Company*, 311. On Anderson's evolving financial situation, see boxes 162–72, MAP.

5. From the 1940s on, Anderson often appeared on lists of successful and admired women. For an early example, see "Women of Achievement," *Coronet* 25 (1948): 58, box 233, MAP. See also George H. Gallup, *The Gallup Poll: Public Opinion, 1935–1971* (New York: Random House, 1971).

6. *New York Times*, January 10, 1951, January 25, 1952; *Washington Star*, January 25, 1952; and "Marian Anderson Sings to Mixed Florida Audience," *Jet* 1 (February 7, 1952): 5. Mae Frohman to Walter White, January 12, 1951; and Walter White to Mary McLeod Bethune, January 26, 1951, both in part 15, series B, reel 2, NAACPP (microfilm); Keiler, *Marian Anderson*, 255–56, 257–58 (quotation), 259, 265. See also "Diary 1951," box 148; and the newspaper clippings from 1950 to 1953, box 218, both in MAP.

7. *Washington Post*, April 5, 21, 1952; *Washington Star*, April 21, 1952; *Washington Times Herald*, April 21, 1952; T. H. Watkins, *Righteous Pilgrim: The Life and Times of Harold L. Ickes, 1874–1952* (New York: Henry Holt, 1990), 858–59; Graham White and John Maze, *Harold Ickes of the New Deal: His Private Life and Public Career* (Cambridge: Harvard University Press, 1985), 1–2; and Keiler, *Marian Anderson*, 259, 266.

8. Richard Kluger, *Simple Justice* (New York: Random House, 1975), 239–581; James T. Patterson, *Brown v. Board of Education: A Civil Rights Milestone and Its Troubled Legacy* (New York: Oxford University Press, 2001), 1–117; Michael J. Klarman, *From Jim Crow to Civil Rights* (New York: Oxford University Press, 2004), 289–442; and Richard M. Dalfiume, *Desegregation of the U.S. Armed Forces: Fighting on Two Fronts, 1939–1953* (Columbia: University of Missouri Press, 1969). On the racial climate in the South during the 1950s, see Numan V. Bartley, *The Rise of Massive Resistance: Race and Politics in the South During the 1950s* (Baton Rouge: Louisiana State University Press, 1969); Clive Webb, *Massive Resistance: Southern Opposition to the Second Reconstruction* (New York: Oxford University Press, 2005); and Pete Daniel, *Lost Revolutions: The South in the 1950s* (Chapel Hill: University of North Carolina Press, 2000).

9. Margaret Gibbs, *The DAR* (New York: Holt, Rinehart and Winston, 1969), 167–76, 168 (quotations); Martha Strayer, *The D. A. R.: An Informal History* (Washington: Public Affairs Press, 1958), 83–89; Peggy Anderson, *The Daughters: An Unconventional Look at America's Fan Club—the DAR* (New York: St. Martin's, 1974), 134–35; and Keiler, *Marian Anderson*, 259.

10. *New York Times*, March 4, 1953; *Washington Post*, March 15, 1953; *Washington Times Herald*, March 8, 15, 1953; "Constitution Hall," *Variety* 190 (March 18, 1953): 56; Anderson, *Daughters*, 135; Keiler, *Marian Anderson*, 259–60; Constance McLaughlin Green, *The Secret City: A History of Race Relations in the Nation's Capital* (Princeton: Princeton University Press, 1967), 329–37; and Paul V.

Cooke, "Racial Integration in Education in the District of Columbia," *Journal of Negro Education* 25, no. 3 (Summer 1956): 237–45.

11. Anderson, *My Lord*, 176–77 (first quotation), 293–96 (second and third quotations); Kosti Vehanen, *Marian Anderson: A Portrait* (New York: McGraw-Hill, 1941), 81, 153–54; and Keiler, *Marian Anderson*, 147–48, 245, 267, 269, 271.

12. Anderson, *My Lord*, 297 (first quotation)–99. See the critical reviews of Anderson's declining voice published in *Jet* (April 22, 1954) (second quotation). *Washington Star*, March 31, 1954; *New York Times*, October 8, 9, 17, 1954; *Washington Post*, October 8, 24, 1954; "No One Is Speechless," *Time* 64 (October 18, 1954): 87; "Opera's Gain," *Newsweek* 44 (October 18, 1954): 96; "A Barrier Is Broken," *Musical America* 74 (November 1, 1954): 4; Keiler, *Marian Anderson*, 267–70 (third quotation), 271–73; Taubman, *Pleasure of Their Company*, 313–15; and Harlow Robinson, *The Last Impresario: The Life, Times, and Legacy of Sol Hurok* (New York: Viking Press, 1994), 380. See also Allan Morrison, "Who Will Be the First to Crack Met Opera?" *Negro Digest* 8 (September 1950): 52–56.

13. Keiler, *Marian Anderson*, 269–71; and *New York Times*, October 8, 1954.

14. *New York Times*, October 17, December 25, 1954, January 8, 9, 13, 1955; "Anderson 'Ball' Hottest Ticket," *Variety* 197 (December 29, 1954): 52; *Pittsburgh Courier*, January 8, 1955; *Washington Daily News*, January 8, 1955; *Washington Post*, January 7, 8, 1955; *Washington Star*, January 8, 1955; "Debut," *Time* 65 (January 17, 1955): 68; "Stranger at the Met," *Newsweek* 45 (January 17, 1955): 50; Ronald Eyer, "Anderson Debut in *Masked Ball* Makes Metropolitan History," *Musical America* 75 (January 15, 1955): 3, 12; Irving Kolodin, "Miss Anderson Makes History," *Saturday Review* 38 (January 22, 1955): 46; Keiler, *Marian Anderson*, 272–75; Anderson, *My Lord*, 299–302, 304 (quotations); and Wallace McLain Cheatham, "Black Male Singers at the Metropolitan Opera," *Black Perspective in Music* 16 (Spring 1988): 3–20. On Anderson's preparation for the role of Ulrica, see notebook on "Coaching," box 148, MAP. See also the script of the *See It Now* television interview of Anderson by Edward R. Murrow, October 29, 1954, reel 41, Edward R. Murrow Papers (microfilm).

15. Kenneth Janken, *Walter White: Mr. NAACP* (Chapel Hill: University of North Carolina Press, 2006), 361–72; Stephen J. Whitfield, *A Death in the Delta: The Story of Emmett Till* (Baltimore: Johns Hopkins University Press, 1991); and Taylor Branch, *Parting the Waters: America in the King Years, 1954–63* (New York: Simon and Schuster, 1988), 1–205.

16. Taubman, *Pleasure of Their Company*, 307, 313; Keiler, *Marion Anderson*, 281–84 (quotations); and *New York Times*, August 27, November 17, December 29, 1957. For the details of Anderson's 1957 trip to the Far East, see "We Remember Asia," typescript, box 135; diary, 1957, box 149; notebook (Korea), box 427; and scrapbooks, Far Eastern Tour, box 427, all in MAP. On the filming of and reactions to "The Lady from Philadelphia," see the script and other materials on reel 41, Ed-

ward R. Murrow Papers (microfilm). On the Little Rock crisis, see Elizabeth Jacoway, *Turn Away Thy Son: Little Rock, the Crisis That Shocked the Nation* (New York: Free Press, 2007); John A. Kirk, *Beyond Little Rock: The Origins and Legacies of the Central High Crisis* (Fayetteville: University of Arkansas Press, 2007); John A. Kirk, *Redefining the Color Line: Black Activism in Little Rock, Arkansas, 1940–1970* (Gainesville: University Press of Florida, 2002); and Mary L. Dudziak, *Cold War Civil Rights: Race and the Image of American Democracy* (Princeton: Princeton University Press, 2000), 115–51.

17. *New York Times*, September 19–20, 26, October 16, November 26, 30, 1957; *Pittsburgh Courier*, September 28, 1957; David Margolick, "The Day Louis Armstrong Made Noise," *New York Times*, September 23, 2007; Penny M. Von Eschen, *Satchmo Blows Up the World: Jazz Ambassadors Play the Cold War* (Cambridge: Harvard University Press, 2004), 58–64, 63 (quotations); and Dudziak, *Cold War Civil Rights*, 66–67.

18. Keiler, *Marian Anderson*, 287–89; Dudziak, *Cold War Civil Rights*, 145; Howard Taubman, "Cold War on the Cultural Front," *New York Times Magazine*, April 13, 1958, 12–13, 107–8; Harold Schonberg, "The Other Voice of Marian Anderson," *New York Times Magazine*, August 10, 1958, 17, 38–39, copy in box 238, MAP; and Charles E. Potter, "Marian Anderson: Ambassador Extraordinaire," March 25, 1958, box 139, MAP. See the correspondence related to "The Lady from Philadelphia," in boxes 127–28, 136–37, MAP.

19. Vehanen, *Marian Anderson*, 185–91; *New York Times*, September 18, 1958 (quotations); and Keiler, *Marian Anderson*, 291.

20. Keiler, *Marian Anderson*, 291–92; and *New York Times*, November 26 (quotation), 27, 1958. Speech for United Nations reception, October 20, 1958; statement to the UN General Assembly, November 4, 1958; statement on the UN Trusteeship Council report, November 5, 1958, all in box 135, MAP. "A New Kind of Ambassador," *Presbyterian Life*, February 1959, 18–21, 42, copy in box 239, MAP; Padmin S. Sandgupta, "The Message of a Singer," 1958 typescript, box 139, MAP; Abram E. Nepomnyashchiy, interview with Marian Anderson, October 31, 1958, transcript, box 139, MAP; notebook 1958 (United Nations), box 149, MAP; Victor T. LeVine, *The Cameroons: From Mandate to Independence* (Berkeley: University of California Press, 1964); and Keesing's Research Report, *Africa Independent: A Study of Political Developments* (New York: Charles Scribner's Sons, 1972), 209–12. See also Emil L. Sady, *The United Nations and Dependent Peoples* (Westport, CN: Greenwood Press, 1974); and John N. Murray Jr., *The United Nations Trusteeship System* (Urbana: University of Illinois Press, 1957).

21. On Anderson's honors, awards, and philanthropic activities see boxes 248–57, MAP. On the Black Sea conference, see box 150, MAP; and Norman Cousins,

"Dialogue with the Russians," *Saturday Review* 44 (1961): 8–10, 46. Keiler, *Marian Anderson*, 297–99, 302–3; *New York Times*, June 1, November 23, 1961; Marc Crawford, "Should Marian Anderson Retire?" *Ebony* 15 (June 1960): 77–81; and "A Voice of Splendor," *Life* 49 (December 26, 1960): 67–68.

22. Keiler, *Marian Anderson*, 304–7, 315; and *New York Times*, November 8, 1962, September 6, October 8, 1963, February 27, March 7, 1964.

23. Keiler, *Marian Anderson*, 308–11; "Marian Anderson Texas Dates All Unsegregated," *Variety* 228 (September 26, 1962): 1; *Houston Post*, February 24, 1963; *New York Times*, July 29, 1963; Walter White to Marian Anderson, August 21, 1963, telegram, box 96, MAP; Branch, *Parting the Waters*, 881; Thomas Gentile, *March on Washington, August 28, 1963* (Washington, DC: New Day Publications, 1983), 216–17; and Patrik Henry Bass, *Like a Mighty Stream* (Philadelphia: Running Press, 2003).

24. Keiler, *Marian Anderson*, 310–12; and *New York Times*, December 7, 13 (quotations) 1963, January 10, 1964. On the Presidential Medal of Freedom, see box 257, MAP.

25. On the farewell tour, see 1964–66 clippings, box 222; farewell tour interview of Anderson by Francis Robinson (Metropolitan Opera), 1965, box 135; and interview of Anderson by Bruce Gee (Winnipeg), November 27, 1964, box 138, all in MAP. Keiler, *Marian Anderson*, 316 (second and third quotations)–18; *New York Times*, January 15, 1963, April 18–19, 1965; *New York Herald Tribune*, April 19, 1965; William Hawkins, "Marian Anderson Says Farewell," *Musical America* 84 (September 1964): 8–11, box 138, MAP; Gustl Breuer, "Farewell to a Great Lady," *RCA Victor International Post* 2 (January 1, 1965), box 138, MAP; and Dan T. Carter, *The Politics of Rage: George Wallace, the Origins of the New Conservatism, and the Transformation of American Politics* (New York: Simon and Schuster, 1995), 9–11 (first quotation), 110–55. On the RCA–Constitution Hall controversy, see Roger G. Hall to Harold Maynard, October 15, 1964, box 56, MAP.

26. Anderson, *Daughters*, 1–17, 154–85, 271–342; Strayer, *D. A. R.*, 57–205; Gibbs, *DAR*, 177–215; and Sara R. Jones, "United Nations Resolutions, D. A. R. Endorsements to Repudiation, 1946–63," *Daughters of the American Revolution Magazine* 98 (March 1964): 266–68.

27. Anderson, *Daughters*, 12 (first and second quotations), 119, 135, 137, 151–54 (fourth quotation), 160 (third quotation)–69. See also Daughters of the American Revolution, *Statement re Constitution Hall* (Washington: Daughters of the American Revolution, 1966).

28. "Women Worthy of Honor," *Daughters of the American Revolution Magazine* 126 (May 1992): 393–95 (quotation), 408.

29. "The President General's Response: Smithsonian Traveling Exhibition Refer-

encing Marian Anderson, DAR and Constitution Hall," *Daughters of the American Revolution Magazine* 130 (July 1996): 410 (quotations).

30. "Legendary Singer Returns to Constitution Hall on U.S. Postage Stamp," U.S. Postal Service press release, January 4, 2005, www.usps.com (first quotation); "DAR President General Presley Merritt Wagoner, Welcome Remarks, Marian Anderson Commemorative Stamp Dedication Ceremony, January 27, 2005," DAR press release, January 28, 2005, www.dar.org (second quotation); and *Washington Post*, January 28, 2005.

31. On the closing years of Anderson's career, see the clippings in box 223, MAP. Keiler, *Marian Anderson*, 319–23, 425n108; *New York Times*, April 19 (quotation), July 5, 1965, April 28, 1969; Merrill D. Peterson, *Lincoln in American Memory* (New York: Oxford University Press, 1994), 325, 347; Aaron Copland and Vivian Perlis, *Copland: 1900 Through 1942* (New York: St. Martin's Press, 1984), 342–45; Copland and Perlis, *Copland: Since 1943* (New York: St. Martin's Press, 1989), 287, 385; and Elizabeth B. Crist, *Music for the Common Man: Aaron Copland during Depression and War* (New York: Oxford University Press, 2005), 148–65. Other notable narrators of *A Lincoln Portrait* include Will Geer, Adlai Stevenson, Gregory Peck, and Coretta Scott King, who performed the narration at a memorial concert honoring her slain husband in May 1968. See ibid., 163; and *New York Times*, February 2, 1966, August 15, 1976.

32. Keiler, *Marian Anderson*, 323–29, 332; *New York Times*, March 6, 1974 (Hurok obituary), January 2, 1977 (Hayes obituary), February 28, 1977 (first quotation), July 26, 1984 (second quotation); and Robinson, *Last Impresario*, 458–63. Anderson delivered the eulogy at Hurok's funeral, praising his "wise and understanding heart" and comparing him to his namesake King Solomon. See ibid., 160. On the congressional medal, see box 349, MAP.

33. WETA Television, *Marian Anderson* (Washington, DC: Greater Washington Educational Communications, 1990) (quotations); Keiler, *Marian Anderson*, 331–34; and Walter Goodman, "Marian Anderson's Life of Unfailing Dignity," *New York Times*, May 8, 1991.

34. *New York Times*, April 9, 1993 (first quotation); *Washington Post*, April 9, 1993 (second quotation); Joseph McLellan, "The Voice That Tumbled Walls," *Washington Post*, undated clipping, c. April 10, 1993 (third quotation); Anthony Heilbut, "Marian Anderson," *New Yorker*, April 26, 1993, 82 (fourth quotation); and James DePreist, "Grounded in Faith, Free to Fly," *New York Times*, April 18, 1993 (fifth and sixth quotations), all in Marian Anderson file, FDRL. See also "Marian Anderson," editorial, *Washington Post*, April 10, 1993; "A Voice for Easter," editorial, *Poughkeepsie Journal*, April 10, 1993; Ellen Goodman, "Singer of the Century," *Washington Post*, April 10, 1993; Tim Page, "Marian Anderson's Undying Voice," *Washington Post*, March 1, 1997; and David Mermelstein, "Two Marian Andersons, Both Real," *New York Times*, February 23, 1997, all in Mar-

ian Anderson file, FDRL. Keiler, *Marian Anderson*, 334–35. For additional obituaries, see box 138, MAP. A memorial service for Anderson, featuring fourteen recordings and eulogies by Isaac Stern and James DePreist, was held at Carnegie Hall on June 7, 1993. Taubman, *Pleasure of Their Company*, 307, 311, 315–16; and *New York Times*, June 1, 8, 1993.

Bibliography

MANUSCRIPT AND ARCHIVAL COLLECTIONS

Franklin Delano Roosevelt Library, Hyde Park, New York
    Anna Eleanor Roosevelt Papers
    Marian Anderson File

Howard University, Moorland-Spingarn Research Center, Washington, D.C.
    Marian Anderson–Daughters of the American Revolution Controversy
    Collection

Library of Congress, Washington, D.C.
    Harold L. Ickes Papers
    National Association for the Advancement of Colored People Papers
    National Urban League Papers

National Archives, Washington, D.C.
    Records of the Department of the Interior

University of Pennsylvania, Annenberg Rare Book and Manuscript Library,
Philadelphia, Pennsylvania
    Marian Anderson Papers

University of South Florida Libraries, Tampa and St. Petersburg, Florida
    Edward R. Murrow Papers (microfilm)
    National Association for the Advancement of Colored People Papers
    (microfilm)
    Tuskegee Institute Race Relations Clipping File (microfilm)

NEWSPAPERS

Atlanta Constitution
Atlanta Journal
Baltimore Afro-American
Boston Evening Transcript
Boston Globe
Boston Herald
Boston Traveler
Brooklyn Eagle
Camden Post
Charleston News and Courier
Chicago American
Chicago Daily News
Chicago Defender
Chicago Examiner
Chicago Tribune
Cleveland Plain Dealer
Daily Worker
Dallas Daily Texan
Ellwood City Messenger
Greenville Delta Democrat-Times
Harlem Bulletin
Houston Chronicle
Houston Post
Miami Herald
Montgomery Advertiser
Newark Evening News
Newark Ledger
New York Age
New York Amsterdam News
New York Daily Eagle
New York Daily Mirror
New York Evening Journal
New York Herald Tribune
New York Journal
New York Musical Courier

New York News
New York News-Week
New York Post
New York Sun
New York Times
New York World-Telegram
Norfolk Journal and Guide
Ocala Banner
Pawtucket Times
Philadelphia Afro-American
Philadelphia Bulletin
Philadelphia Daily News
Philadelphia Evening Bulletin
Philadelphia Evening Ledger
Philadelphia Gazette
Philadelphia Independent
Philadelphia Inquirer
Philadelphia News
Philadelphia Record
Philadelphia Tribune
Pittsburgh Courier
Pittsburgh Sun-Telegraph
Poughkeepsie Journal
Richmond Leader
Richmond Times-Dispatch
San Francisco Chronicle
San Francisco Examiner
San Francisco News
Savannah Morning News
Savannah Tribune
Springfield Daily Republican
St. Louis Dispatch
St. Louis Globe
Toronto Globe and Mail
Utica Press
Washington Afro-American
Washington Daily News
Washington Post
Washington Star
Washington Times-Herald
Washington Tribune

AUTOBIOGRAPHIES, MEMOIRS, AND INTERVIEWS

Anderson, Marian. *My Lord, What a Morning: An Autobiography.* New York: Viking, 1956.

———. "My Mother's Gift—Grace Before Greatness." In Norman Vincent Peale, *Guideposts: Faith Made Them Champions,* 65–68. New York: Prentice-Hall, 1954.

Armstrong, Louis. *Satchmo: My Life in New Orleans.* New York: Da Capo Press, 1986.

Basie, Count, with Albert Murray. *Good Morning Blues: The Autobiography of Count Basie.* New York: Random House, 1985.

Carter, Robert L. *A Matter of Law: A Memoir of Struggle in the Cause of Equal Rights.* New York: New Press, 2005.

Copland, Aaron, and Vivian Perlis. *Copland: 1900 Through 1942.* New York: St. Martin's Press, 1984.

———. *Copland: Since 1943.* New York: St. Martin's Press, 1989.

Franklin, Buck Colbert. *My Life and an Era: The Autobiography of Buck Colbert Franklin.* Baton Rouge: Louisiana State University Press, 2000.

Franklin, John Hope. *Mirror to America: The Autobiography of John Hope Franklin.* New York: Farrar, Straus and Giroux, 2005.

———. Interview by author, March 1, 2007.

Hampton, Lionel, with James Haskins. *Hamp: An Autobiography.* New York: Warner Books, 1990.

Handy, W. C. *Father of the Blues: An Autobiography.* New York: Da Capo Press, 1961.

Holiday, Billie, with William Duffy. *Lady Sings the Blues.* New York: Harlem Moon, 2006.

Hurok, Sol, with Ruth Goode. *Impresario: A Memoir.* New York: Random House, 1946.

Ickes, Harold L. *The Secret Diary of Harold L. Ickes.* 3 vols. New York: Simon and Schuster, 1954.

Johnson, James Weldon. *Along This Way: The Autobiography of James Weldon Johnson.* New York: Viking Press, 1933.

Klaw, Barbara. "'A Voice One Hears Once in a Hundred Years': An Interview with Marian Anderson." *American Heritage* 28, no. 2 (1977): 50–57.

Massey, Raymond. *A Hundred Different Lives: An Autobiography.* Boston: Little, Brown, 1970.

Mays, Benjamin E. *Born to Rebel: An Autobiography.* Athens: University of Georgia Press, 1987.

Moton, Robert Russa. *Finding a Way Out: An Autobiography.* Garden City, New York: Doubleday, Page, 1921.

Roosevelt, Eleanor. *The Autobiography of Eleanor Roosevelt.* New York: Harper and Brothers, 1961.

_____. *This I Remember.* New York: Harper and Brothers, 1949.

Rubinstein, Arthur. *My Many Years.* New York: Alfred A. Knopf, 1980.

Sanderlin, Raymond. Interview by author, November 17, 2008.

Somerville, Mollie D. *Eleanor Roosevelt as I Knew Her.* Charlottesville, VA: Howell Press, 1996.

Taubman, Howard. *The Pleasure of Their Company: A Reminiscence.* Portland, OR: Amadeus, 1994.

Vehanen, Kosti. *Marian Anderson: A Portrait.* New York: McGraw-Hill, 1941.

Walter, Bruno. *Themes and Variations: An Autobiography.* New York: Alfred A. Knopf, 1946.

Waters, Ethel, with Charles Samuels. *His Eye Is on the Sparrow: An Autobiography.* New York: Pyramid Books, 1972.

White, Walter Francis. *A Man Called White: The Autobiography of Walter White.* Athens: University of Georgia Press, 1948.

BOOKS AND PAMPHLETS

Abbott, Lynn, and Doug Seroff. *Out of Sight: The Rise of African American Popular Music, 1889–1895.* Jackson: University of Mississippi Press, 2003.

_____, eds. *Ragged but Right: Black Traveling Shows, Coon Songs, and the Dark Pathway to the Blues and Jazz.* Jackson: University of Mississippi Press, 2007.

Albertson, Chris. *Bessie.* New Haven: Yale University Press, 2005.

Albus, Harry James. *The "Deep River" Girl: The Life of Marian Anderson.* Grand Rapids, MI: W. B. Eerdmans, 1949.

Alexander, Charles C. *The Ku Klux Klan in the Southwest.* Lexington: University of Kentucky Press, 1966.

Allen, Frederick Lewis. *Only Yesterday: An Informal History of the 1920s.* New York: Harper and Brothers, 1931.

Alter, Jonathan: *The Defining Moment: FDR's Hundred Days And the Triumph of Hope.* New York: Simon and Schuster, 2006.

Anderson, Jervis. *This Was Harlem: A Cultural Portrait, 1900–1950.* New York: Farrar, Straus and Giroux, 1981.

Anderson, Peggy. *The Daughters: An Unconventional Look at America's Fan Club— the DAR.* New York: St. Martin's Press, 1974.

Andrew, John A., III. *Lyndon Johnson and the Great Society.* Chicago: Ivan R. Dee, 1998.

Anthony, Carl Sferrazza. *First Ladies.* New York: William Morrow, 1990.

Arsenault, Raymond. *Freedom Riders: 1961 and the Struggle for Racial Justice.* New York: Oxford University Press, 2006.

Ascoli, Peter Max. *Julius Rosenwald: The Man Who Built Sears, Roebuck and Advanced the Cause of Black Education in the American South*. Bloomington: Indiana University Press, 2006.

Ashe, Arthur R., Jr. *A Hard Road to Glory: A History of the African-American Athlete, 1919–1945*. New York: Amistad, 1988.

Averill, Gage. *A Day for the Hunter, a Day for the Prey: Popular Music and Power in Haiti*. Chicago: University of Chicago Press, 1997.

Badger, Anthony J. *FDR: The First Hundred Days*. New York: Hill and Wang, 2008.

Baker, Jean Claude, and Chris Case. *Josephine Baker: The Hungry Heart*. New York: Random House, 1993.

Baker, William J. *Jesse Owens: An American Life*. New York: Free Press, 1986.

Ballard, Allan B. *One More Day's Journey: The Story of a Family and a People*. New York: McGraw-Hill, 1984.

Barbeau, Arthur E., and Florette Henri. *The Unknown Soldiers: Black American Troops in World War I*. Philadelphia: Temple University Press, 1974.

Bardolph, Richard. *The Negro Vanguard*. New York: Rinehart and Company, 1959.

Barnes, Jay. *Florida's Hurricane History*. Chapel Hill: University of North Carolina Press, 1998.

Barnett, Andrew. *Sibelius*. New Haven: Yale University Press, 2007.

Bartley, Numan V. *The Rise of Massive Resistance: Race and Politics in the South During the 1950s*. Baton Rouge: Louisiana State University Press, 1969.

Basler, Roy P. *The Lincoln Legend: A Study in Changing Conceptions*. Boston: Houghton Mifflin, 1935.

Bass, Patrik Henry. *Like a Mighty Stream*. Philadelphia: Running Press, 2003.

Bearden, Romare, and Harry Henderson. *A History of African-American Art: From 1972 to the Present*. New York: Pantheon, 1993.

Beasley, Maurine. *The White House Press Conferences of Eleanor Roosevelt*. New York: Garland, 1983.

Beasley, Maurine, Holly C. Schulman, and Henry R. Beasley, eds. *The Eleanor Roosevelt Encyclopedia*. Westport, CT: Greenwood, 2001.

Beckerman, Michael. *New Worlds of Dvorak: Searching in America for the Composer's Inner Life*. New York: W. W. Norton, 2003.

Beeth, Howard, and Cary D. Wintz, eds. *Black Dixie: Afro-Texan History and Culture in Houston*. College Station: Texas A&M University Press, 1992.

Beevor, Anthony. *The Battle for Spain: The Spanish Civil War, 1936–1939*. New York: Penguin, 2006.

Berger, Arthur. *Aaron Copland*. New York: Oxford University Press, 1953.

Biondi, Martha. *To Stand and Fight: The Struggle for Civil Rights in Postwar New York City*. Cambridge: Harvard University Press, 2006.

Black, Allida M. *Casting Her Own Shadow: Eleanor Roosevelt and the Shaping of Postwar Liberalism.* New York: Columbia University Press, 1996.

_____, ed. *Courage in a Dangerous World: The Political Writings of Eleanor Roosevelt.* New York: Columbia University Press, 1999.

Blake, Jody. *Le Tumulte Noir: Modernist Art and Popular Entertainment in Jazz-Age Paris, 1900–1930.* University Park: Pennsylvania State University Press, 1999.

Blesh, Rudi. *They All Played Ragtime.* New York: Music Sales Corp., 1967.

Bogle, Donald. *Toms, Coons, Mulattoes, Mammies, and Bucks: An Interpretive History of Blacks in American Films.* New York: Viking, 1973.

Bontemps, Arna. *The Harlem Renaissance Remembered.* New York: Dodd, Mead, 1972.

Boritt, Gabor. *The Gettysburg Gospel: The Lincoln Speech That Nobody Knows.* New York: Simon and Schuster, 2006.

Boskin, Joseph. *Sambo: The Rise and Demise of an American Jester.* New York: Oxford University Press, 1986.

Bosworth, R. J. B. *Mussolini's Italy: Life Under the Fascist Dictatorship, 1915–1945.* New York: Penguin, 2006.

Boyd, Valerie. *Wrapped in Rainbows: The Life of Zora Neale Hurston.* New York: Scribner, 2003.

Bradley, Benjamin. *The Negro Genius.* New York: Dodd, Mead, 1937.

Branch, Taylor. *Parting the Waters: America in the King Years, 1954–63.* New York: Simon and Schuster, 1988.

Branham, Robert James, and Stephen J. Hartnett. *Sweet Freedom's Song: "My Country 'Tis of Thee" and Democracy in America.* New York: Oxford University Press, 2002.

Brinkley, Alan. *Voices of Protest: Huey Long, Father Coughlin, and the Great Depression.* New York: Alfred A. Knopf, 1982.

Brinkley, David. *Washington Goes to War.* New York: Alfred A. Knopf, 1988.

Brown, Sterling. *The Negro in American Fiction.* New York: Atheneum, 1969.

Bukey, Evan Burr. *Hitler's Austria: Popular Sentiment in the Nazi Era, 1938–1945.* Chapel Hill: University of North Carolina Press, 2000.

Burgos, Adrian, Jr. *Playing America's Game: Baseball, Latinos, and the Color Line.* Berkeley: University of California Press, 2007.

Burleigh, Harry T. *Negro Spirituals, Arranged for Solo Voice.* London: G. Ricordi and Co., 1917.

_____. *The Spirituals of Harry T. Burleigh.* Emeryville, CA: Alfred Publishing, 1985.

Burns, James McGregor. *Roosevelt: The Lion and the Fox.* New York: Harcourt, Brace, 1956.

Butterworth, Neil. *The Music of Aaron Copland.* New York: Toccata Press, 1985.

Califano, Joseph A., Jr. *The Triumph and Tragedy of Lyndon Johnson: The White House Years*. New York: Simon and Schuster, 1991.

Calloway, Cab, and Bryant Rollins. *Of Minnie the Moocher and Me*. New York: Thomas Crowell, 1976.

Carter, Dan T. *The Politics of Rage: George Wallace, the Origins of the New Conservatism, and the Transformation of American Politics*. New York: Simon and Schuster, 1995.

Carter, Hodding. *Southern Legacy*. Baton Rouge: Louisiana State University Press, 1950.

_____. *Where Main Street Meets the River*. New York: Rinehart, 1953.

Chalmers, David. *Hooded Americanism: The History of the Klu Klux Klan*. Chicago: Quadrangle, 1965.

Charters, Ann. *Nobody: The Story of Bert Williams*. New York: Macmillan, 1969.

Chude-Sokei, Louis. *The Last Day "Darky": Bert Williams, Black-on-Black Minstrelsy, and the African Diaspora*. Durham, NC: Duke University Press, 2005.

Clark, Champ. *Shuffling to Ignominy: The Tragedy of Stepin Fetchit*. iUniverse, 2005.

Clarke, Jeanne Nienaber. *Roosevelt's Warrior: Harold L. Ickes and the New Deal*. Baltimore: Johns Hopkins University Press, 1996.

Collier, James. *Louis Armstrong: An American Genius*. New York: Oxford University Press, 1983.

Collins, Lisa Gail, and Lisa Mintz Messinger. *African-American Artists, 1929–1945: Prints, Drawings, and Paintings in the Metropolitan Museum of Art*. New York: Metropolitan Museum of Art, 2003.

Cook, Blanche Wiesen. *Eleanor Roosevelt. Vol. 1, 1884–1933*. New York: Penguin Books, 1992.

_____. *Eleanor Roosevelt. Vol. II, 1933–1938*. New York: Penguin Books, 1999.

Cresson, Margaret French. *The Life of Daniel Chester French: Journey into Fame*. Cambridge: Harvard University Press, 1974.

Cripps, Thomas. *Making Movies Black: The Hollywood Message Movie from World War II to the Civil Rights Era*. New York: Oxford University Press, 1993.

_____. *Slow Fade to Black: The Negro in American Film, 1900–1942*. New York: Oxford University Press, 1977.

Crist, Elizabeth B. *Music for the Common Man: Aaron Copland during Depression and War*. New York: Oxford University Press, 2005.

Current, Richard N. *Speaking of Abraham Lincoln: The Man and His Meaning for Our Times*. Urbana: University of Illinois Press, 1983.

Dabney, Virginius. *Below the Potomac: A Book about the New South*. New York: D. Appleton-Century, 1942.

_____. *Liberalism in the South*. Chapel Hill: University of North Carolina Press, 1932.

Dalfiume, Richard M. *Desegregation of the U.S. Armed Forces: Fighting on Two Fronts, 1939–1953.* Columbia: University of Missouri Press, 1969.

Dallek, Robert. *Flawed Giant: Lyndon B. Johnson, 1960–1973.* New York: Oxford University Press, 1998.

Daniel, Pete. *Lost Revolutions: The South in the 1950s.* Chapel Hill: University of North Carolina Press, 2000.

Daniels, Jonathan. *The End of Innocence.* New York: Da Capo, 1972.

Daniels, Josephus. *The Wilson Era: Years of Peace, 1910–1917.* Chapel Hill: University of North Carolina Press, 1944.

Darden, Robert. *People Get Ready! A New History of Black Gospel Music.* New York: Continuum International, 2004.

Daughters of the American Revolution. *Forty-second Report of the National Society of the Daughters of the American Revolution, April 1, 1938, to April 1, 1939.* Washington, D.C.: Government Printing Office, 1940.

_____. *Statement re Constitution Hall.* Washington, DC: Daughters of the American Revolution, 1966.

Davenport, M. Marguerite. *Azalia: The Life of Madame E. Azalia Hackley.* Boston: Chapman and Grimes, 1947.

Davis, Kenneth S. *FDR: Into the Storm, 1937–1940.* New York: Random House, 1993.

Degler, Carl. *Neither Black Nor White: Slavery and Race Relations in Brazil and the United States.* New York: Macmillan, 1971.

Douglas, Ann. *Terrible Honesty: Mongrel Manhattan in the 1920s.* New York: Farrar, Straus and Giroux, 1995.

Downey, Dennis B., and Raymond M. Hyers. *No Crooked Death: Coatesville, Pennsylvania, and the Lynching of Zachariah Walker.* Urbana: University of Illinois Press, 1991.

Drake, St. Clair, and Horace Cayton. *Black Metropolis: A Study of Negro Life in a Northern City.* Chicago: University of Chicago Press, 1993.

Duberman, Martin Bauml. *Paul Robeson: A Biography.* New York: Ballantine Books, 1989.

Dubin, Murray. *South Philadelphia: Mummers, Memories, and the Melrose Diner.* Philadelphia: Temple University Press, 1996.

Du Bois, W. E. B. *The Philadelphia Negro: A Social Study.* Philadelphia: University of Pennsylvania, 1899.

Dudziak, Mary L. *Cold War Civil Rights: Race and the Image of American Democracy.* Princeton: Princeton University Press, 2000.

Egan, Timothy. *The Worst Hard Time: The Untold Story of Those Who Survived the Great American Dust Bowl.* Boston: Houghton Mifflin, 2006.

Egerton, John. *Speak Now Against the Day: The Generation Before the Civil Rights Movement in the South.* New York: Alfred A. Knopf, 1994.

Ellsworth, Scott. *Death in a Promised Land: The Tulsa Race Riot of 1921.* Baton Rouge: Louisiana State University Press, 1992.

Elmore, Charles J. *Richard R. Wright Sr. at GSIC, 1891–1921: A Protean Force for the Social Uplift and Higher Education of Black Americans.* Savannah, GA: privately printed, 1996.

Ely, Melvin Patrick. *The Adventures of Amos 'N' Andy: A Social History of an American Phenomenon.* New York: Free Press, 1991.

Embree, Edwin R. *Julius Rosenwald Fund, 1917–1936.* Chicago: Brousson, 2007.

Erenberg, Lewis. *Steppin' Out: New York Nightlife and the Transformation of American Culture, 1890–1930.* Westport, CT: Greenwood Press, 1981.

———. *The Greatest Fight of Our Generation: Louis vs. Schmeling.* New York: Oxford University Press, 2006.

Everet, Gwen. *African-American Masters: Highlights from the Smithsonian American Art Museum.* Washington: Smithsonian Institution, 2003.

Fauset, Arthur Huff. *For Freedom.* Philadelphia: Franklin Publishing and Supply Co., 1937.

Fernandez, Raul A. *From Afro-Cuban Rhythm to Latin Jazz.* Berkeley: University of California Press, 2006.

Fisher, O. C. *Cactus Jack: A Biography of John Nance Garner.* Waco: Texian Press, 1982.

Floyd, Samuel, Jr. *Black Music in the Harlem Renaissance: A Collection of Essays.* Knoxville: University of Tennessee Press, 1990.

Forbes, Camille F. *Introducing Bert Williams: Burnt Cork, Broadway, and the Story of America's First Black Star.* New York: Basic Civitas Books, 2008.

Forma, Warren. *They Were Ragtime.* New York: Grosset and Dunlap, 1967.

Fox, Charles. *Fats Waller.* London: A. S. Barnes, 1961.

Fox, William Price. *Satchel Paige's America.* Tuscaloosa: University of Alabama Press, 2005.

Franklin, Jimmie Lee. *Journey Toward Hope: A History of Blacks in Oklahoma.* Norman: University of Oklahoma Press, 1982.

Franklin, Vincent P. *The Education of Black Philadelphia: The Social and Educational History of a Minority Community, 1900–1950.* Philadelphia: University of Pennsylvania Press, 1979.

Frazier, E. Franklin. *Black Bourgeosie.* Glencoe, IL: Free Press, 1957.

Freedman, Russell. *The Voice That Challenged a Nation: Marian Anderson and the Struggle for Equal Rights.* New York: Clarion, 2004.

Fritts, Ron. *Ella Fitzgerald: The Chick Webb Years and Beyond, 1935–1948.* Metuchen, NJ: Scarecrow Press, 2003.

Gallup, George H. *The Gallup Poll: Public Opinion, 1935–1971.* New York: Random House, 1971.

Gallup, Stephen. *History of the Salzburg Festival.* London: Weidenfeld and Nicolson, 1987.

Gammond, Peter, ed. *Duke Ellington: His Life and Music.* New York: Da Capo, 1977.

Gentile, Thomas. *March on Washington, August 28, 1963.* Washington, DC: New Day Publications, 1983.

Gerson, Robert A. *Music in Philadelphia.* Westport, CT: Greenwood Press, 1940.

Gibbs, Margaret. *The DAR.* New York: Holt, Rinehart and Winston, 1969.

Giddins, Gary. *Satchmo: The Genius of Louis Armstrong.* New York: Da Capo, 2001.

Gill, Anton. *A Dance Between Flames: Berlin Between the Wars.* London: Abacus, 1993.

Gilmore, Glenda Elizabeth. *Defying Dixie: The Radical Roots of Civil Rights, 1919–1950.* New York: W. W. Norton, 2007.

Goodwin, Doris Kearns. *Lyndon Johnson and the American Dream.* New York: St. Martin's, 1991.

Gosnell, Harold F. *Negro Politicians: The Rise of Negro Politics in Chicago.* Chicago: University of Chicago Press, 1966.

Graham, Kent. *November: Lincoln's Elegy at Gettysburg.* Bloomington: Indiana University Press, 2001.

Gray, John. *Blacks in Classical Music: A Bibliographical Guide to Composers, Performers, and Ensembles.* Westport, CT: Greenwood, 1988.

Green, Constance McLaughlin. *The Secret City: A History of Race Relations in the Nation's Capital.* Princeton: Princeton University Press, 1967.

Grieff, Constance M., and Charles B. Hosmer Jr. *Independence: The Creation of a National Park.* Philadelphia: University of Pennsylvania Press, 1987.

Grimshaw, William J. *Bitter Fruit: Black Politics and the Chicago Machine, 1931–1991.* Chicago: University of Chicago Press, 1995.

Hall, Clyde W. *One Hundred Years of Education at Savannah State College, 1890–1990.* East Peoria, IL: Versa Press, 1991.

Hanson, Joyce A. *Mary McLeod Bethune and Black Women's Political Activism.* Columbia: University of Missouri Press, 2003.

Hareven, Tamara K. *Eleanor Roosevelt: An American Conscience.* Chicago: Quadrangle, 1961.

Haskins, Jim. *The Cotton Club.* New York: Random House, 1977.

Haskins, Jim, and N. R. Mitgang. *Mr. Bojangles: The Biography of Bill Robinson.* New York: William Morrow, 1988.

Hayden, Robert C. *Singing for All People: Roland Hayes, a Biography.* Boston: Select Publications, 1989.

Haynes, George E., and Sterling A. Brown. *Negro Newcomers in Detroit.* New York: Arno Press, 1969.

Helm, MacKinley. *Angel Mo' and Her Son, Roland Hayes.* Boston: Little, Brown, 1942.

Hemenway, Robert E. *Zora Neale Hurston: A Literary Biography.* Urbana: University of Illinois Press, 1977.

Henry, Charles. *Ralph Bunche: Model Negro or American Other?* New York: New York University Press, 1991.

Hershan, Stella K. *A Woman of Quality.* New York: Crown, 1970.

Hilmes, Michele. *Radio Voices: American Broadcasting, 1922–1952.* Minneapolis: University of Minnesota Press, 1997.

Hoberman, John. *Darwin's Athletes: How Sport Has Damaged Black America and Preserved the Myth of Race.* Boston: Houghton Mifflin, 1997.

Hogan, Lawrence D. *Shades of Glory: The Negro Leagues and the Story of African-American Baseball.* Washington: National Geographic, 2006.

Hollis, Daniel Webster. *An Alabama Newspaper Tradition: Grover C. Hall and the Hall Family.* Tuscaloosa: University of Alabama Press, 1983.

Holloway, Jonathon Scott. *Confronting the Veil: Abram Harris Jr., E. Franklin Frazier, and Ralph Bunche, 1919–1941.* Chapel Hill: University of North Carolina Press, 2001.

Holt, Rackham. *Mary McLeod Bethune: A Biography.* Garden City, NJ: Doubleday, 1964.

Horne, Aaron. *Keyboard Music of Black Composers: A Bibliography.* Westport, CT: Greenwood, 1992.

Horowitz, Joseph. *Classical Music in America: A History.* New York: W. W. Norton, 2005.

Horton, James O., and Lois E. Horton. *Hard Road to Freedom: The Story of African America.* New Brunswick, NJ: Rutgers University Press, 2001.

Huggins, Nathan. *Harlem Renaissance.* New York: Oxford University Press, 1971.

Hughes, Langston, and Milton Meltzer. *Black Magic: A Pictorial History of the Negro in American Entertainment.* Englewood Cliffs, NJ: Prentice-Hall, 1967.

Hughes, William Hardin, and Frederick D. Peterson. *Robert Russa Moton of Hampton and Tuskegee.* Chapel Hill: University of North Carolina Press, 1965.

Hunter, Ann Arnold. *A Century of Service: The Story of the D.A.R.* Washington, D.C.: National Society of the Daughters of the American Revolution, 1991.

Isaacson, Walter. *Einstein: His Life and Universe.* New York: Simon and Schuster, 2007.

Jackson, Carlton. *Hattie: The Life of Hattie McDaniel.* Lanham, MD: Madison Books, 1990.

Jackson, Kenneth. *The Ku Klux Klan in the City, 1915–1930.* New York: Oxford University Press, 1967.

Jacobson, Steve. *Carrying Jackie's Torch: The Players Who Integrated Baseball—and America.* Chicago: Lawrence Hill Books, 2007.

Jacoway, Elizabeth. *Turn Away Thy Son: Little Rock, the Crisis That Shocked the Nation.* New York: Free Press, 2007.

James, Marquis. *Mr. Garner of Texas.* Indianapolis: Bobbs-Merrill, 1939.

Janken, Kenneth Robert. *Rayford Logan and the Dilemma of the African American Intellectual.* Amherst: University of Massachusetts Press, 1993.

————. *Walter White: Mr. NAACP.* Chapel Hill: University of North Carolina Press, 2006.

Jasen, David A., and Jay Tichenor. *Rags and Ragtime: A Musical History.* New York: Seabury Press, 1978.

Johnson, Charles S. *The Economic Status of Negroes.* Nashville: Fisk University Press, 1933.

Jonas, Gilbert. *Freedom's Sword: The NAACP and the Struggle Against Racism in America, 1909–1969.* New York: Routledge, 2005.

Jones, LeRoi. *Blues People: Negro Music in White America.* New York: William Morrow, 1963.

Jones, William H. *Recreation and Amusement Among Negroes in Washington, D.C.: A Sociological Analysis of the Negro in an Urban Environment.* Washington, DC: Howard University Press, 1927.

————. *The Housing of Negroes in Washington, D.C.: A Study in Human Ecology.* Washington, DC: Howard University Press, 1929.

Kaplan, Howard S. *Marian Anderson.* San Francisco: Pomegranate, 2007.

Kearney, James R. *Anna Eleanor Roosevelt: The Evolution of a Reformer.* Boston: Houghton Mifflin, 1968.

Keesing's Research Report. *Africa Independent: A Study of Political Developments.* New York: Scribner's Sons, 1972.

Keiler, Allan. *Marian Anderson: A Singer's Journey.* New York: Simon and Schuster, 2000.

Kennedy, Stetson. *Jim Crow: The Way It Was.* Boca Raton: Florida Atlantic University Press, 1990.

Kimbal, Robert, and William Bolcom. *Reminiscing with Sissel and Blake.* New York: Viking Press, 1973.

King, Reyann. *Ignatius Sancho: African Man of Letters.* London: National Portrait Gallery, 2008.

Kirby, John B. *Black Americans in the Roosevelt Era: Liberalism and Race.* Knoxville: University of Tennessee Press, 1980.

Kirk, Elsie K. *Musical Highlights from the White House.* Malabar, FL: Krieger Publishing Company, 1992.

Kirk, John A. *Beyond Little Rock: The Origins and Legacies of the Central High Crisis.* Fayetteville: University of Arkansas Press, 2007.

————. *Redefining the Color Line: Black Activism in Little Rock, Arkansas, 1940–1970.* Gainesville: University Press of Florida, 2002.

Kirkeby, Ed. *Ain't Misbehavin': The Story of Fats Waller.* New York: Da Capo, 1988.

Klarman, Michael J. *From Jim Crow to Civil Rights: The Supreme Court and the Struggle for Racial Equality*. New York: Oxford University Press, 2004.

Kluger, Richard. *Simple Justice*. New York: Random House, 1975.

Kneebone, John T. *Southern Liberal Journalists and the Issue of Race, 1920–1944*. Chapel Hill: University of North Carolina Press, 1985.

Kornweibel, Theodore Jr. *Seeing Red: Federal Campaigns against Black Militancy, 1919–1925*. Bloomington: Indiana University Press, 1998.

Kotz, Nick. *Judgment Days: Lyndon Baines Johnson, Martin Luther King Jr., and the Laws That Changed America*. Boston: Houghton Mifflin, 2005.

Kramer, Victor. *The Harlem Renaissance Re-Examined*. New York: AMS Press, 1987.

Kunhardt, Phillip B., Jr. *A New Birth of Freedom: Lincoln at Gettysburg*. Boston: Brown, 1983.

Lanctot, Neil. *Negro League Baseball: The Rise and Ruin of a Black Institution*. Philadelphia: University of Pennsylvania Press, 2004.

Lane, Roger. *Roots of Violence in Black Philadelphia, 1900–1960*. Cambridge: Harvard University Press, 1986.

_____. *William Dorsey's Philadelphia and Ours: On the Past and Future of the Black City in America*. New York: Oxford University Press, 1991.

Lash, Joseph P. *Eleanor and Franklin: The Story of Their Relationship Based on Eleanor Roosevelt's Private Papers*. New York: W. W. Norton, 1971.

Leowen, James W. *Sundown Towns: A Hidden Dimension of American Racism*. New York: Simon and Schuster, 2005.

Leuchtenberg, William E. *Franklin D. Roosevelt and the New Deal, 1932–1940*. New York: Harper and Row, 1963.

_____. *The Perils of Prosperity, 1914–1932*. Chicago: University of Chicago Press, 1958.

LeVine, Victor T. *The Cameroons, from Mandate to Independence*. Berkeley: University of California Press, 1964.

Levy, Eugene. *James Weldon Johnson: Black Leader, Black Voice*. Chicago: University of Chicago Press, 1958.

Lewis, David Levering. *W. E. B. Du Bois: Biography of a Race, 1868–1919*. New York: Henry Holt, 1993.

_____. *When Harlem Was in Vogue*. New York: Alfred A. Knopf, 1981.

Lewis, Samella. *African American Art and Artists*. Berkeley: University of California Press, 2003.

Liebow, Elliot. *Talley's Corner: A Study of Negro Streetcorner Men*. Boston: Little, Brown, 1967.

Lindley, Betty, and Ernest K. Lindley. *A New Deal for Youth: The Story of the National Youth Administration*. New York: Da Capo Press, 1972.

Logan, Rayford. *The Howard University: The First Hundred Years, 1867–1940*. Washington, D.C.: Howard University Graduate School, 1941.

Lomax, Alan. *Mister Jelly Roll: The Fortunes of Jelly Roll Morton.* Berkeley: University of California Press, 2001.

Lovell, John, Jr. *Black Song: The Forge and the Flame: The Story of How the African-American Spiritual Was Hammered Out.* New York: Macmillan, 1972.

Lowitt, Richard. *Bronson M. Cutting: A Progressive Politician.* Albuquerque: University of New Mexico Press, 1992.

_____. *George W. Norris: The Persistence of a Progressive, 1913–1933.* Urbana: University of Illinois Press, 1971.

MacDonald, J. Fred. *Don't Touch That Dial! Radio Programming in American Life, 1920–1960.* Chicago: Nelson-Hall, 1979.

Maclean, Nancy. *Behind the Mask of Chivalry: The Making of the Ku Klux Klan in a Georgia Town.* New York: Oxford University Press, 1994.

Madigan, Tim. *Burning, Massacre, Destruction, and the Tulsa Race Riot of 1921.* New York: St. Martin's Press, 2001.

Mahar, William J. *Behind the Burnt Cork Mask: Early Blackface Minstrelsy and Antebellum American Popular Culture.* Urbana: University of Illinois Press, 1998.

Maney, Patrick J. *Young Bob: A Biography of Robert M. La Follette, Jr.* Madison: University of Wisconsin Press, 2002.

Manuel, Peter, Kenneth Bilby, and Michael Largey. *Caribbean Currents: Caribbean Music from Rumba to Reggae.* Philadelphia: Temple University Press, 2006.

Margolick, David. *Beyond Glory: Joe Louis vs. Max Schmeling, and a World on the Brink.* New York: Alfred A. Knopf, 2005.

Marks, Charles, and Diana Edkins. *The Power of Pride: Stylemakers and Rulebreakers of the Harlem Renaissance.* New York: Crown, 1999.

Mattos, Cleofe Person de. *Jose Mauricio Nunes Garcia: Biografia.* Rio de Janeiro: Ministerio de Cultura, Fundacao Biblioteca Nacional, 1997.

McElvaine, Robert S. *The Great Depression: America, 1929–1941.* New York: Times Books, 1984.

McKee, Margaret, and Fred Chisenhall. *Beale Black and Blue: Life and Music on America's Main Street.* Baton Rouge: Louisiana State University Press, 1981.

McMahon, Kevin J. *Reconsidering Roosevelt on Race: How the Presidency Paved the Road to* Brown. Chicago: University of Chicago Press, 2004.

McMurry, Linda O. *George Washington Carver: Scientist and Symbol.* New York: Oxford University Press, 1982.

McNeil, Genna Rae. *Groundwork: Charles Hamilton Houston and the Struggle for Civil Rights.* Philadelphia: University of Pennsylvania Press, 1983.

Mead, Chris. *Champion: Joe Louis, Black Hero in White America.* New York: Charles Scribner's Sons, 1985.

Meier, August. *Negro Thought in America, 1880–1915: Racial Ideologies in the Age of Booker T. Washington.* Ann Arbor: University of Michigan Press, 1963.

Michie, Allan, and Frank Rhylick. *Dixie Demagogues.* New York: Vanguard Press, 1939.

Miers, Charlene. *Independence Hall in American Memory.* Philadelphia: University of Pennsylvania Press, 2002.

Miller, Char. *Gifford Pinchot and the Making of Modern Environmentalism.* Washington, D.C.: Island Press, 2001.

Miller, Nathan. *FDR: An Intimate History.* Garden City, NY: Doubleday, 1983.

Miller, Patrick B., and David K. Wiggins, eds. *Sport and the Color Line: Black Athletes and Race Relations in Twentieth Century America.* New York: Routledge, 2004.

Mitchell, Greg. *The Campaign of the Century: Upton Sinclair's Race for Governor of California and the Birth of Media Politics.* New York: Random House, 1992.

Mitchell, Loften. *Black Drama: The Story of the American Negro in the Theatre.* New York: Hawthorne Books, 1967.

Mixon, Gregory. *The Atlanta Riot: Race, Class, and Violence in a New South City.* Gainesville: University Press of Florida, 2005.

Moore, Carman. *Somebody's Angel Child: The Story of Bessie Smith.* New York: Thomas Crowell, 1969.

Moore, Robin D. *Music and Revolution: Cultural Change in Socialist Cuba.* Berkeley: University of California Press, 2006.

Morales, Ed. *The Latin Beat: The Rhythm and Roots of Latin Music, from Bossa Nova to Salsa and Beyond.* New York: Da Capo, 2003.

Morrison, Joseph. *Josephus Daniels: The Small-D Democrat.* Chapel Hill: University of North Carolina Press, 1966.

Moton, Robert Russa. *What the Negro Thinks.* New York: Doubleday, 1929.

Murray, John N., Jr. *The United Nations Trusteeship System.* Urbana: University of Illinois Press, 1957.

Murray, Robert K. *The Red Scare: A Study in National Hysteria, 1919–1920.* New York: McGraw-Hill, 1964.

Muse, Clarence. *The Dilemma of the Negro Actor.* N.p., 1934.

Myrdal, Gunnar. *An American Dilemma: The Negro Problem in American Democracy.* New York: Harper and Brothers, 1944.

Nash, Gary. *Forging Freedom: The Formation of Philadelphia's Black Community, 1720–1840.* Cambridge: Harvard University Press, 1997.

Newman, Richard S. *Freedom's Prophet: Bishop Richard Allen, the AME Church, and the Black Founding Fathers.* New York: New York University Press, 2008.

———. *The Transformation of American Abolitionism: Fighting Slavery in the Early Republic.* Chapel Hill: University of North Carolina Press, 2001.

Newman, Shirlee P. *Marian Anderson: Lady from Philadelphia.* Philadelphia: Westminster, 1965.

Nicholson, Stuart. *Ella Fitzgerald: A Biography of the First Lady of Jazz.* New York: Routledge, 2004.

Nixon, Ralph William. *The Lincoln Memorial: A Tribute in Verse.* Boston: Acorn, 1993.

Noggle, Burl. *Into the Twenties: The United States from Armistice to Normalcy.* Urbana: University of Illinois Press, 1974.

Oakley, Giles. *The Devil's Music: A History of the Blues.* New York: Da Capo, 1997.

O'Connor, John. *Heywood Broun, a Biography: The Life and Career of the Most Famous and Controversial Journalist of His Time.* New York: G. P. Putnam's, 1975.

Olson, Lynne. *Freedom's Daughters: The Unsung Heroines of the Civil Rights Movement from 1830 to 1970.* New York: Scribner, 2001.

Oshinsky, David M. *Polio: An American Story.* New York: Oxford University Press, 2005.

Painter, Nell Irvin. *Creating Black Americans: African-American History and Its Meanings, 1619 to the Present.* New York: Oxford University Press, 2005.

Patterson, James T. *Brown v. Board of Education: A Civil Rights Milestone and Its Troubled Legacy.* New York: Oxford University Press, 2001.

———. *Congressional Conservatives and the New Deal: The Growth of the Conservative Coalition in Congress, 1933–1939.* Lexington: University of Kentucky Press, 1967.

Patton, Sharon F. *African-American Art.* New York: Oxford University Press, 1998.

Peterson, Merrill D. *Lincoln in American Memory.* New York: Oxford University Press, 1994.

Peterson, Robert W. *Cages to Jump Shots: Pro Basketball's Early Years.* New York: Oxford University Press, 1990.

———. *Only the Ball Was White: A History of Legendary Black Players and All-Black Professional Teams.* New York: McGraw-Hill, 1970.

Pickett, Clarence. *For More Than Bread.* Boston: Little, Brown, 1953.

Pinchot, Gifford. *Breaking New Ground.* Washington, D.C.: Island Press, 1998.

Pollack, Howard. *Aaron Copland: The Life and Work of an Uncommon Man.* New York: Henry Holt, 1999.

Pomerance, Alan. *Repeal of the Blues: How Black Entertainers Influenced Civil Rights.* New York: Citadel Press, 1991.

Powell, Richard J. *Black Art: A Cultural History.* London: Thames and Hudson, 2002.

Powers, Richard. *The Time of Our Singing.* New York: Farrar, Straus and Giroux, 2003.

Price, Michael H. *Mantan the Funnyman: The Life and Times of Mantan Moreland.* Baltimore: Midnight Marquee Press, 2006.

Rampersad, Arnold. *The Life of Langston Hughes, Volume 1: 1902–1941: I, Too, Sing America*. New York: Oxford University Press, 1986.

_____. *Ralph Ellison: A Biography*. New York: Alfred A. Knopf, 2007.

Raper, Arthur F. *Preface to Peasantry: A Tale of Two Black Belt Counties*. Chapel Hill: University of North Carolina Press, 1936.

Reed, Linda. *Simple Decency and Common Sense: The Southern Conference Movement, 1938–1963*. Bloomington: Indiana University Press, 1991.

Rhoden, William C. *Forty Million Dollar Slaves: The Rise, Fall, and Redemption of the Black Athlete*. New York: Crown, 2006.

Richardson, Joe M. *A History of Fisk University, 1865–1946*. Tuscaloosa: University of Alabama Press, 1980.

Richman, Michael, Daniel Chester French, and the Metropolitan Museum of Art. *Daniel French: An American Sculptor*. Washington, D.C.: Preservation Books, 1983.

Roberts, John Storm. *The Latin Tinge: The Impact of Latin American Music on the United States*. New York: Oxford University Press, 1999.

Roberts, Randy. *Papa Jack: Jack Johnson and the Era of White Hopes*. New York: Free Press, 1983.

Robinson, Harlow. *The Last Impresario: The Life, Times, and Legacy of Sol Hurok*. New York: Viking Press, 1994.

Rogosin, Donn. *Invisible Men: Life in Baseball's Negro Leagues*. New York: Atheneum, 1983.

Roosevelt, Felicia W. *Doers and Dowagers*. New York: Doubleday, 1975.

Rose, Phyllis. *Jazz Cleopatra: Josephine Baker in Her Time*. New York: Doubleday, 1989.

Rosette, Benetta Jules. *Josephine Baker in Art and Life: The Icon and the Image*. Urbana: University of Illinois Press, 2007.

Ryding, Erik, and Rebecca Pechefsky. *Bruno Walter: A World Elsewhere*. Lincoln: University of Nebraska Press, 2006.

Sacchi, Filippo. *The Magic Baton: Toscanini's Life for Music*. Whitefish, MT: Kessinger, 2007.

Sady, Emil L. *The United Nations and Dependent Peoples*. Westport, CT: Greenwood Press, 1974.

Salmond, John. *A Southern Rebel: The Life and Times of Aubrey Williams, 1890–1959*. Chapel Hill: University of North Carolina Press, 1983.

Sampson, Henry T. *Blacks in Blackface: A Sourcebook on Early Black Musical Shows*. Metuchen, NJ: Scarecrow Press, 1980.

Savage, Barbara Dianne. *Broadcasting Freedom: Radio, War, and the Politics of Race, 1938–1948*. Chapel Hill: University of North Carolina Press, 1999.

Scacchi, Alberto. *Legacy of Bitterness: Ethiopia and Fascist Italy, 1935–1941*. Trenton, NJ: Red Sea Press, 1997.

Schickel, Richard, and Michael Walsh. *Carnegie Hall: The First One Hundred Years.* New York: Abrams, 1987.

Schlesinger, Arthur M., Jr. *The Politics of Upheaval.* Boston: Houghton Mifflin, 1960.

Scott, Daryl Michael. *Contempt and Pity: Social Policy and the Image of the Damaged Black Psyche, 1880–1996.* Chapel Hill: University of North Carolina Press, 1997.

Sheann, Vincent. *Between the Thunder and the Sun.* New York: Random House, 1943.

Sims, Janet L. *Marian Anderson: An Annotated Bibliography and Discography.* Westport, CT: Greenwood Press, 1981.

Sitkoff, Harvard. *A New Deal for Blacks: The Emergence of Civil Rights as a National Issue.* New York: Oxford University Press, 1978.

Smith, Walter E. *The Black Mozart: Le Chevalier de Saint Georges.* Bloomington, IN: AuthorHouse, 2004.

Socolofsky, Homer E. *Arthur Capper: Publisher, Politician, and Philanthropist.* Lawrence: University of Kansas Press, 1962.

Soderlund, Jean R. *Quakers and Slavery: A Divided Spirit.* Princeton: Princeton University Press, 1988.

Sommerville, Mollie D. *Eleanor Roosevelt as I Knew Her.* Charlottesville, VA: Howell Press, 1996.

Southern Eileen. *The Music of Black Americans: A History.* 2nd ed. New York: W. W. Norton, 1983.

Spencer, Jon Michael. *Black Hymnology: A Hymnological History of the African-American Church.* Knoxville: University of Tennessee Press, 1992.

Standiford, Les. *The Last Train to Paradise: Henry Flagler and the Spectacular Rise and Fall of the Railroad That Crossed an Ocean.* New York: Crown, 2002.

Stearns, Marshall. *The Story of Jazz.* New York: Oxford University Press, 1970.

Stevenson, Janet. *Marian Anderson: Singing to the World.* New York: Encyclopedia Britannica Press, 1963.

Stokes, Anson Phelps. *Art and the Color Line.* Washington, D.C.: Phelps Stokes Fund, 1939.

Story, Rosalyn M. *And So I Sing: African-American Divas of Opera and Concert.* New York: Warner Books, 1990.

Stovall, Tyler. *Paris Noir: African Americans in the City of Light.* Boston: Houghton Mifflin, 1996.

Strausbaugh, John. *Black Like You: Blackface, Whiteface, Insult and Imitation in American Popular Culture.* New York: Tarcher, 2006.

Strayer, Martha. *The D.A.R: An Informal History.* Washington, D.C.: Public Affairs Press, 1958.

Sublette, Ned. *Cuba and Its Music: From the First Drums to the Mambo.* Chicago: Chicago Review Press, 2007.

Sugrue, Thomas J. *Sweet Land of Liberty: The Forgotten Struggle for Civil Rights in the North.* New York: Random House, 2008.

Suits, Steve. *Hugo Black of Alabama: How His Roots and Early Career Shaped the Great Champion of the Constitution.* Montgomery, AL: New South Books, 2005.

Sullivan, Patricia. *Days of Hope: Race and Democracy in the New Deal Era.* Chapel Hill: University of North Carolina Press, 1996.

Tannenbaum, Frank. *Slave and Citizen: The Negro in the Americas.* New York: Alfred A. Knopf, 1946.

Taubman, H. Howard. *The Maestro: The Life of Arturo Toscanini.* Westport, CT: Greenwood, 1977.

Taylor, Frank C. *Alberta Hunter: A Celebration in Blues.* New York: McGraw-Hill, 1988.

Thomas, Hugh. *The Spanish Civil War.* New York: Penguin, 2003.

Thomas, Ron. *They Cleared the Lane: The NBA's Black Pioneers.* Lincoln: University of Nebraska Press, 2002.

Thorp, Willard. *A Southern Reader.* New York: Alfred A. Knopf, 1955.

Thurman, Howard. *Deep River and the Negro Spiritual Speaks of Life and Death.* Richmond, IN: Friends United Press, 1975.

Tibbets, John, ed. *Dvorak in America.* Portland, OR: Amadeus Press, 1993.

Timmons, Bascom M. *Garner of Texas: A Personal History.* New York: Harper Brothers, 1948.

Titon, Jeff Todd. *Early Downhome Blues.* Urbana: University of Illinois Press, 1977.

Toll, Robert. *Blacking Up: The Minstrel Show in Nineteenth-Century America.* New York: Oxford University Press, 1974.

Traubel, Helen. *St. Louis Woman.* New York: Duell, Sloan and Pearce, 1959.

Tuttle, William M., Jr. *Race Riot: Chicago in the Red Summer of 1919.* New York: Atheneum, 1970.

Tygiel, Jules. *Baseball's Great Experiment: Jackie Robinson and His Legacy.* New York: Random House, 1983.

Urquhart, Brian. *Ralph Bunche: An American Odyssey.* New York: Norton, 1993.

Vance, Joel. *Fats Waller: His Life and Times.* New York: Berkley Medallion Books, 1979.

Von Eschen, Penny M. *Satchmo Blows Up the World: Jazz Ambassadors Play the Cold War.* Cambridge: Harvard University Press, 2004.

Waldron, Ann. *Hodding Carter: The Reconstruction of a Racist.* Chapel Hill: Algonquin Books, 1993.

Walker, Beersheba Crowdy. *The Life and Works of William Saunders Crowdy.* Philadelphia: Elfreth Walker, 1955.

Walker, Juliet E. K. *The History of Black Business in America: Capitalism, Race, Entrepreneurship.* New York: Macmillan, 1998.

Ward, Andrew. *Midnight, When I Rise: The Story of the Jubilee Singers Who Introduced the World to the Music of Black America*. New York: Farrar, Straus and Giroux, 2000.

Ward, Geoffrey C. *Unforgivable Blackness: The Rise and Fall of Jack Johnson*. New York: Alfred A. Knopf, 2004.

Watkins, Mel. *On the Real Side: Laughing, Lying, and Signifying: The Underground Tradition of African-American Humor That Transformed American Culture, from Slavery to Richard Pryor*. New York: Simon and Schuster, 1994.

———. *Stepin Fetchit: The Life and Times of Lincoln Perry*. New York: Pantheon, 2005.

Watkins, T. H. *Righteous Pilgrim: The Life and Times of Harold L. Ickes, 1874–1952*. New York: Henry Holt, 1990.

Watson, Steven. *The Harlem Renaissance: Hub of African-American Culture, 1920–1930*. New York: Pantheon, 1995.

Webb, Clive. *Massive Resistance: Southern Opposition to the Second Reconstruction*. New York: Oxford University Press, 2005.

Weiss, Nancy J. *Farewell to the Party of Lincoln: Black Politics in the Age of FDR*. Princeton: Princeton University Press, 1983.

Wertheim, Arthur Frank. *Radio Comedy*. New York: Oxford University Press, 1979.

Weyr, Thomas. *The Setting of the Pearl: Vienna Under Hitler*. New York: Oxford University Press, 2005.

White, Graham, and John Maze. *Harold Ickes of the New Deal: His Private Life and Public Career*. Cambridge: Harvard University Press, 1985.

White, Walter. *Rope and Faggot: A Biography of Judge Lynch*. New York: Alfred A. Knopf, 1929.

Whitfield, Stephen J. *A Death in the Delta: The Story of Emmett Till*. Baltimore: Johns Hopkins University Press, 1991.

Wiggins, David K., and Patrick B. Miller, eds. *The Unlevel Playing Field: A Documentary History of the African American Experience in Sport*. Urbana: University of Illinois Press, 2003.

Williams, Martin T. *King Oliver*. London: A. S. Barnes, 1961.

Williams, T. Harry. *Huey Long: A Biography*. New York: Alfred A. Knopf, 1970.

Wills, Gary. *Lincoln at Gettysburg: The Words That Remade America*. New York: Touchstone Books, 1993

Wilson, Joan Hoff, and Marjorie Lightfoot, eds. *Without Precedent: The Life and Career of Eleanor Roosevelt*. Bloomington: Indiana University Press, 1984.

Wlaschin, Ken. *Encyclopedia of American Opera*. Jefferson, NC: McFarland, 2006.

Wolfskill, George. *The Revolt of the Conservatives: A History of the American Liberty League, 1934–1940*. Boston: Houghton Mifflin, 1960.

Woodward, C. Vann. *The Strange Career of Jim Crow*. New York: Oxford University Press, 2002.

Worster, Donald. *Dust Bowl: The Southern Plains in the 1930s.* New York: Oxford
     University Press, 1979.
Wynia, Elly. *The Church of God and Saints of Christ: The Rise of Black Jews.* New
     York: Garland, 1994.
Zangrando, Robert L. *The NAACP Crusade Against Lynching, 1909–1950.* Philadel-
     phia: Temple University Press, 1980.
Zeiger, Robert. *America's Great War: World War I and the American Experience.*
     Lanham, MD: Rowman and Littlefield, 2000.
Zilversmit, Arthur. *The First Emancipation: The Abolition of Slavery in the North.*
     Chicago: University of Chicago Press, 1968.
Zucker, Norman L. *George M. Norris: Gentle Knight of American Democracy.*
     Urbana: University of Illinois Press, 1966.

ARTICLES AND CHAPTERS

"Anderson Affair." *Time* 33 (April 17 1939): 23.
"Anderson 'Ball' Hottest Ticket." *Variety* 197 (December 29, 1954): 52.
Arsenault, Raymond. "The Folklore of Southern Demagoguery." In *Is There a
     Southern Political Tradition?* ed. Charles Eagles, 79–132. Jackson: University of
     Mississippi Press, 1996.
"At Home with Marian Anderson." *Ebony* 9 (February 1954): 52–59.
"A Barrier Is Broken." *Musical America* 74 (November 1, 1954): 4.
Bethune, Mary McLeod. "My Secret Talks with FDR." In *The Negro in Depression
     and War: Prelude to Revolution, 1930–1945,* ed. by Bernard Sternsher, 53–65.
     Chicago: Quadrangle Books, 1969.
Black, Allida M. "Championing a Champion: Eleanor Roosevelt and the Marian
     Anderson 'Freedom Concert.'" *Presidential Studies Quarterly* 20, no. 4 (1990):
     719–36.
———. "A Reluctant but Persistent Warrior: Eleanor Roosevelt and the Early
     Civil Rights Movement." In *Women in the Civil Rights Movement: Trailblazers
     and Torchbearers,* ed. Vicki L. Crawford, Jacqueline L. Rouse, and Barbara
     Woods, 233–49. *Black Women in United States History,* vol. 16. Brooklyn:
     Carlson Publishing, 1990.
Bronson, Arthur. "Marian Anderson." *American Mercury* 61 (September 1945): 282–88.
Brosseau, Grace Lincoln Hall. "The Completion of a Great Project." *Daughters of
     the American Revolution Magazine* 64, no. 4 (1930): 197–210.
Carter, Elmer A. "The Ladies of the D. A. R." *Opportunity* 17 (March 1939): 67.
Chapman, Martin. "Gracious Lady." *Tops* 1, no. 2 (1936): 2–4.
Cheatham, Wallace McLain. "Black Male Singers at the Metropolitan Opera."
     Black Perspective in Music 16 (Spring 1988): 3–20.

Cherry, Gwendolyn, Ruby Thomas, and Pauline Willis. "Marian Anderson." In *Portraits in Color: The Lives of Colorful Negro Women*, 63–71, 212–14. New York: Pageant, 1962.

"Colored Contralto," *Time* 35 (January 13, 1936): 35–36.

"Compromise in Ban on Marian Anderson." *Crisis* 46 (April 1939): 117.

"Constitution Hall." *Variety* 190 (March 18, 1953): 56.

Coode, Thomas, and Dennis Fabbri. "The New Deal's Arthurdale Project in West Virginia." *West Virginia History* 36 (July 1975), 291–308.

Cooke, Paul V. "Racial Integration in Education in the District of Columbia." *Journal of Negro Education* 25 (Summer 1956): 237–45.

Cousins, Norman. "Dialogue with the Russians." *Saturday Review* 44 (1961): 8–10, 46.

Crawford, Marc. "Should Marian Anderson Retire?" *Ebony* 15 (June 1960): 77–81.

Cripps, Thomas, and David Culbert. "The Negro Soldier (1944): Film Propaganda in Black and White." In *Hollywood as Historian: American Film in a Cultural Context*, ed. Peter C. Rollins, 109–33. Lexington: University Press of Kentucky, 1983.

Daly, Victor R. "Washington's Minority Problem." *Crisis* 46 (1939): 170–71.

Daniel, Walter G., and Carroll L. Miller. "The Participation of the Negro in the National Youth Administration." *Journal of Negro Education* 7 (July 1938): 357–65.

"Dark Contralto." *New Yorker*, January 18, 1936, 7.

Davenport, Marsha. "Music Will Out." *Collier's* 102 (December 3, 1938): 17, 40.

"A Day at Marian Anderson's Country Hideaway." *Ebony* 2 (April 1947): 9–14.

"Debut." *Time* 65 (January 17, 1955): 68.

Doyle, Don H. "Henry Martyn Robert and the Popularization of American Parliamentary Law." *American Quarterly* 32 (Spring 1980): 3–18.

Du Bois, W. E. B. "The Talented Tenth." In *The Negro Problem: A Series of Articles by Representative American Negroes of Today*. New York: James Potter and Co., 1903.

Embree, Edwin. "Deep River of Song." In Edwin Embree, *13 Against the Odds*, 139–52. New York: Viking Press, 1944.

Ewen, David. "Marian Anderson." In *Men and Women Who Make Music*, 80–89. New York: Merlin Press, 1949.

"Ex-Choir Singer." *Newsweek* 12 (December 12, 1938): 24–26.

Eyer, Ronald. "Anderson Debut in *Masked Ball* Makes Metropolitan History." *Musical America* 75 (January 15, 1955): 46.

Fisher, Isaac. "Marian Anderson: Ambassador of Beauty from Her Race." *Southern Workman* 65 (March 1936): 72–80.

Graham, Shirley. "Spirituals to Symphonies." *Étude* 54 (November 1936): 681–92, 723.

Hawkins, William. "Marian Anderson Says Farewell." *Musical America* 84 (September 1964): 8–11.

"A Great New Singer Tours America." *Life* 1 (February 27, 1937): 20.

Hayes, Patrick. "White Artists Only." *Washingtonian*, April 1989, 95–103.

Hemingway, Ernest. "Who Killed the Vets?" *New Masses*, September 17, 1935, 9–10.

Hughes, Langston. "Marian Anderson: Famous Concert Singer." In *Famous American Negroes*, 25–31. New York: Dodd, Mead, 1954.

_____. "Marian Anderson, Metropolitan Opera Star." In *Famous Negro Music Makers*, 127–31. New York: Dodd, Mead, 1955.

Hunting, Harold B. "Marian Anderson, Singer." In *Rising Above Color*, ed. Philip H. Lotz, 11–17. New York: Fleming H. Revell, 1943.

"In Egypt Land." *Time* 48 (December 30, 1946): 59–60, 62, 64.

Jones, Sara R. "United Nations Resolutions, D.A.R. Endorsements to Repudiation, 1946–63." *Daughters of the American Revolution Magazine* 98 (March 1964): 266–68.

Kimbrough, Emily. "My Life in a White World." *Ladies' Home Journal* 77 (1960): 54, 173–74, 176.

Kolodin, Irving. "Miss Anderson Makes History." *Saturday Review* 38 (January 22, 1955): 46.

Kostman, Samuel. "Marian Anderson." In *Twentieth Century Women of Achievement*, 138–54. New York: Rosen Press, 1976.

Lincoln, Natalie Sumner. "Constitution Hall Consecrated." *Daughters of the American Revolution Magazine* 63, no. 11 (1929): 645–50.

"Lincoln, Harding, James Crow, and Taft." *Crisis* 24 (July 1922): 122.

Locke, Alain. "Negro Music Goes to Par." *Opportunity* 17 (July 1939): 196–200.

Lovell, John Jr. "Washington Fights." *Crisis* 46 (1939): 276–77.

Magna, Edith Scott. "Constitution Hall." *Daughters of the American Revolution Magazine* 63, no. 9 (1929): 517–22.

"Marian Anderson Sings to Mixed Florida Audience." *Jet* 1 (February 7, 1952): 5.

"Marian Anderson's Voice Failing." *Jet* 5 (April 22, 1954): 56–57.

"Marian Anderson Texas Dates All Unsegregated." *Variety* 228 (September 26, 1962): 1.

Morrison, Allan. "Who Will Be the First to Crack Met Opera?" *Negro Digest* 8 (September 1950), 52–56.

Mossell, Sadie Tanner. "The Standard of Living Among One Hundred Negro Migrant Families in Philadelphia." *Annals of the American Academy of Social and Political Science* 98 (1921): 173–218.

Musgrave, Anne S. "Sarah Corbin Robert: President General, 1938–1951." *Daughters of the American Revolution Magazine* 106 (October 1972): 772–73, 828.

"A New Kind of Ambassador." *Presbyterian Life*, February 1959, 18–21, 42.

"No One Is Speechless." *Time* 64 (October 18, 1954): 87.

"Opera's Gain." *Newsweek* 44 (October 18, 1954): 96.

Patton, June O. "And the Truth Shall Make You Free: Richard Wright, Sr., Black Intellectual and Iconoclast, 1877–1897." *Journal of Negro History* 81 (1996): 17–30.

Peterson, Frank L. "Humbleness Before Greatness." In Frank Peterson, *Climbing High Mountains*, 86–95. Washington, D.C.: Review and Herald Publishing Company, 1962.

"The President General's Response: Smithsonian Traveling Exhibition Referencing Marian Anderson, DAR and Constitution Hall." *Daughters of the American Revolution Magazine* 130 (July 1996): 410.

"The Real Marian Anderson." *Our World* 4 (April 1949): 11–15.

Sandage, Scott A. "A Marble House Divided: The Lincoln Memorial, the Civil Rights Movement, and the Politics of Memory, 1939–1963." *Journal of American History* 80 (June 1993): 135–67.

Schonberg, Harold. "The Other Voice of Marian Anderson." *New York Times Magazine*, August 10, 1958, 17, 38–39.

Schwartz, Stuart B. "Patterns of Slaveholding in the Americas." *American Historical Review* 87 (February 1982): 55–86.

Sedwick, Ruth W. "Over Jordan." *Christian Century* 57 (February 21, 1940): 245–47.

"Singer and Citizen." *Newsweek* 33 (April 25, 1949): 84–86.

Smith, Carleton. "Roulades and Cadenzas." *Esquire* 12 (July 1939): 79, 167–69.

Stewart, Ollie. "The Girl Who Wouldn't Quit." *Commentator*, 1936, 113–15.

Stoddard, Hope. "Marian Anderson." In *Famous American Women*, 24–35. New York: Crowell, 1970.

"Stranger at the Met." *Newsweek* 45 (January 17, 1955): 50.

Taubman, Howard. "Cold War on the Cultural Front." *New York Times Magazine*, April 13, 1958, 12–13, 107–8.

————. "Voice of a Race." *New York Times Magazine*, April 6, 1941, 9, 21.

Thomas, Henry, and Dana Lee Thomas. "Marian Anderson." In *50 Great Modern Lives*, 479–88. New York: Hanover House, 1956.

Truman, Margaret. "Triumph of Marian Anderson." *McCall's* 103 (April 1976): 114, 116, 120, 124.

"A Voice of Splendor." *Life* 49 (December 26, 1960): 67–68.

Wald, Richard C. "How to Live with a Famous Wife." *Ebony* 13 (August 1958): 52–54, 56.

Wilkins, Roy. "The Real D.A.R." *Crisis* 46 (May 1939): 145.

Wintz, Cary D. "Louise Beavers." In *Encyclopedia of the Harlem Renaissance*. New York: Routledge, 2004.

"Women of Achievement." *Coronet* 25 (1948): 58.

Wood, Edith Elmer. "Four Washington Alleys." *Survey* 31 (December 6, 1913): 250–52.

Woolf, S. J. "High Priestess of Song." *Negro Digest* 4 (March 1946): 83–86.

———. "Marian Anderson's Recipe for Success." *New York Times Magazine*, December 30, 1945, 53–54.

Zangrando, Joanna S., and Robert L. Zangrando. "Eleanor Roosevelt and Black Civil Rights." In *Without Precedent: The Life and Career of Eleanor Roosevelt*, ed. Joan Hoff-Wilson and Mary Lightman, 88–107. Bloomington: Indiana University Press, 1984.

UNPUBLISHED THESES AND DISSERTATIONS

La Ganke, Lucile Evelyn. "The National Society of the Daughters of the American Revolution: Its History, Policies, and Influence, 1890–1945." Ph.D. thesis, Western Reserve University, 1951.

Vriend, Sharon R. "The Controversy Before the Concert: The Dialogue in the European Press Regarding the Discrimination Against Marian Anderson, 6 January 1939 through 8 April 939." M.A. thesis, Bowling Green State University, 1994.

FILMS, DOCUMENTARIES, SOUND RECORDINGS, AND TELEVISION VIDEOS

Aida's Brothers and Sisters: Black Voices in Opera. New York: WNET, 2000.

Marian Anderson: The Lincoln Memorial Concert. In *Treasures from American Film Archives, 50 Preserved Films*. Program 4, film 11. Los Angeles: National Film Preservation Foundation, 2000. (Eight-minute version, copy at Library of Congress.)

Marian Anderson: The Lincoln Memorial Concert. Los Angeles: National Film Preservation Foundation, 1998. (Thirty-one-minute version, copy at UCLA Film and Television Archive.)

Marian Anderson. Washington: WETA-TV, 1991.

News of the Day 10, no. 259. *Nation's Capital Gets a Lesson in Tolerance*. (Hearst Production footage.) Los Angeles: Metro-Goldwyn-Mayer, 1939. (Copy at UCLA Film and Television Archive.)

The Lady from Philadelphia. (Sound recording.) Camden, NJ: RCA Victor, 1958.

The Lady in the Lincoln Memorial. New York: *New York Times* and Arno Press (a Rediscovery Production), 1970.

The March of Time: Upbeat in Music. New York: ABC-TV, 1951. (Reissue of 1943 film.)

WEB SITES

African Heritage in Classical Music. www.AfriClassical.com

Black in Time. www.izania.com

Marian Anderson Historical Society. www.mariananderson.org

Marian Anderson Papers. www.library.upenn.edu/collections/rbm/mss/anderson/
anderson.html

My Day by Eleanor Roosevelt: Electronic Edition. http://www.gwu.edu/
~erpapers/myday.

National Society, Daughters of the American Revolution. www.dar.org

Philadelphia City Archives. www.PhillyHistory.org

Public Broadcasting System. www.pbs.org

UCLA Film and Television Archive. http://cinema.library.ucla.edu

United States Department of the Interior Museum. http://www.doi.gov/interior-
museum

United States Postal Service. www.usps.com

White House Historical Association. www.whitehousehistory.org

Index

A NOTE ON THE AUTHOR

Raymond Arsenault is the John Hope Franklin Professor of Southern History at the University of South Florida, St. Petersburg. Educated at Princeton and Brandeis universities, he is the author of three prizewinning books, including *Freedom Riders: 1961 and the Struggle for Racial Justice*. Named an Editor's Choice by the *New York Times* and one of the best books of 2006 by the *Washington Post*, *Freedom Riders* won the Southern Historical Association's Frank L. and Harriet C. Owsley Prize as the most important book published in the field of Southern history in 2006.